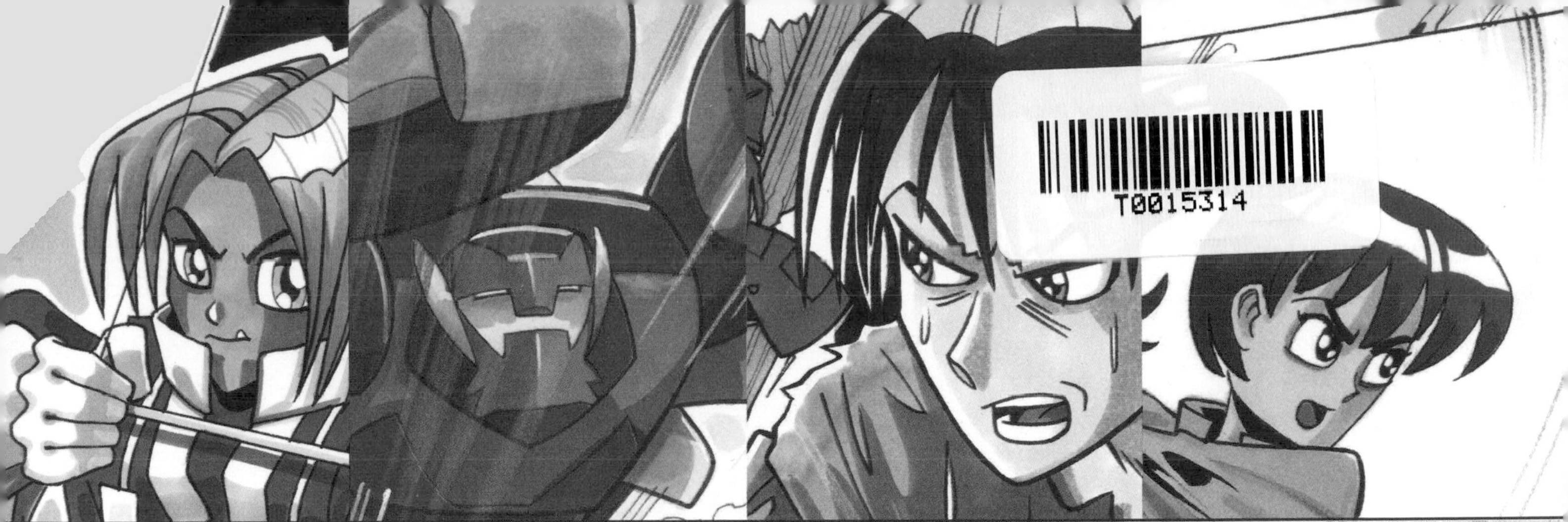

MANGA NOW!

HOW TO DRAW ACTION FIGURES FOR GRAPHIC NOVELS

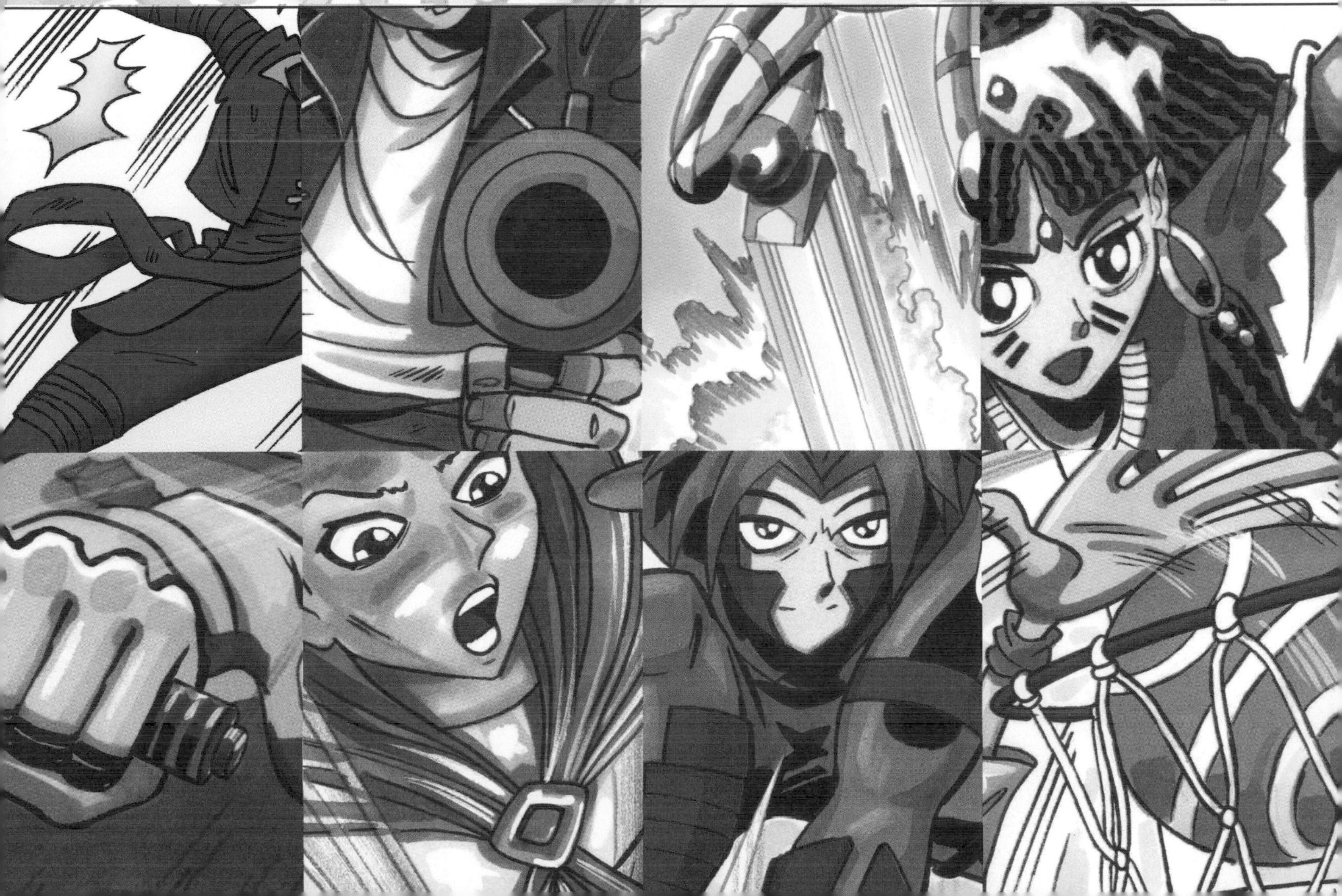

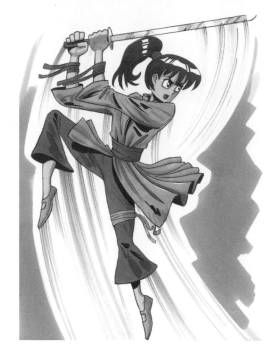

ACKNOWLEDGEMENTS

Thanks to Roz Dace, Juan Hayward, Becky Robbins and Marrianne Miall at Search Press; to my sons Frank and Joe; to my pugs Leo and Maisie; to my local library in Truro for keeping a healthy stock of manga and comics in general to keep me reading; to Stan Lee and Roy Thomas for inspiring me to read, and John Buscema and Katsuhiro Otomo for making me want to draw. To all the amazingly talented and driven artists and writers who produce manga, I would like to say *domo arigato*!

GLOSSARY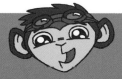

Anime
Japanese animated productions, often based on popular manga series.

Bunkobon
Small-format paperback books that are collections of manga titles.

Cosplay
Costumed role play popular with many manga or anime fans.

Manga
Generic term for comics usually created in Japan, by Japanese artists.

Mangaka
Artist or creator of manga.

Otaku
Term used for devoted fans of manga, anime and related interests.

Shojo
Manga stories usually aimed at young girls.

Shonen
Manga stories usually aimed at young boys.

Shonen Jump
Best-selling manga magazine in Japan.

Tankobon
Generic name for collected manga works published in large volumes.

MANGA NOW!

HOW TO DRAW ACTION FIGURES FOR GRAPHIC NOVELS

Keith Sparrow

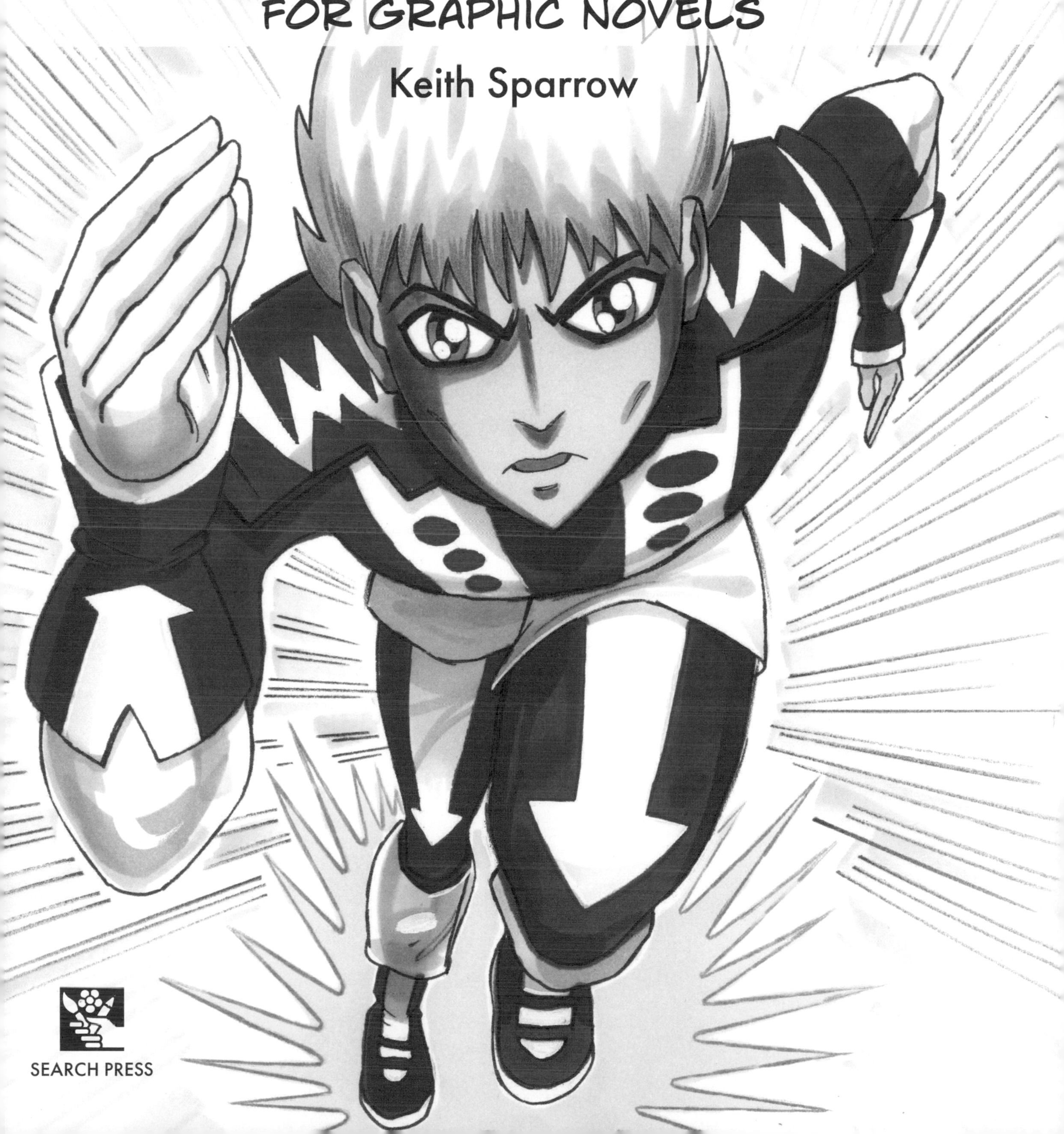

SEARCH PRESS

Previously published in 2014 as
Manga Now! How to Draw Action Figures

This edition published in 2024
Search Press Limited
Wellwood, North Farm Road,
Tunbridge Wells, Kent TN2 3DR

ISBN: 978-1-80092-051-4
ebook ISBN: 978-1-80093-050-6

Suppliers
If you have difficulty in obtaining any of the materials and equipment mentioned in this book, then please visit the Search Press website for details of suppliers: www.searchpress.com

Bookmarked Hub
A bonus project, 'Take Aim', is available to download free from the Bookmarked Hub. Search for this book by title or ISBN: the files can be found under 'Book Extras'. Membership of the Bookmarked online community is free: www.bookmarkedhub.com

You are invited to visit the author's:
Instagram: @sparrowmanga
Facebook: Ato-gami

FSC www.fsc.org
MIX
Paper | Supporting responsible forestry
FSC® C020056

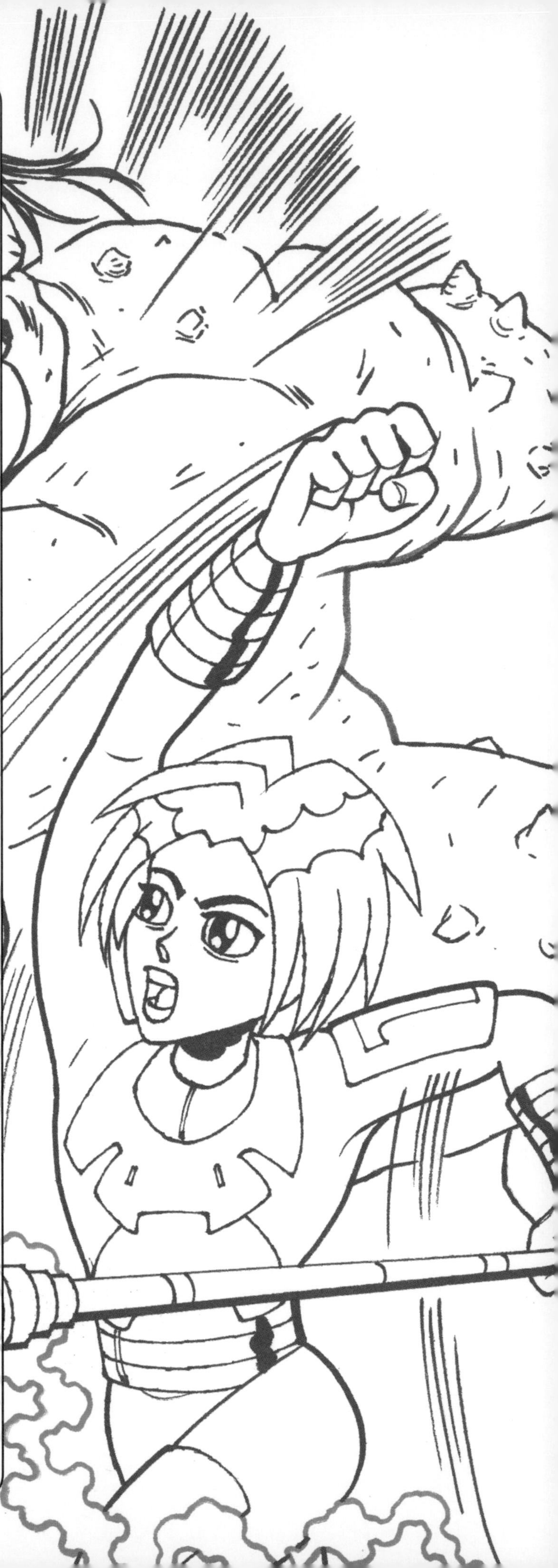

CONTENTS

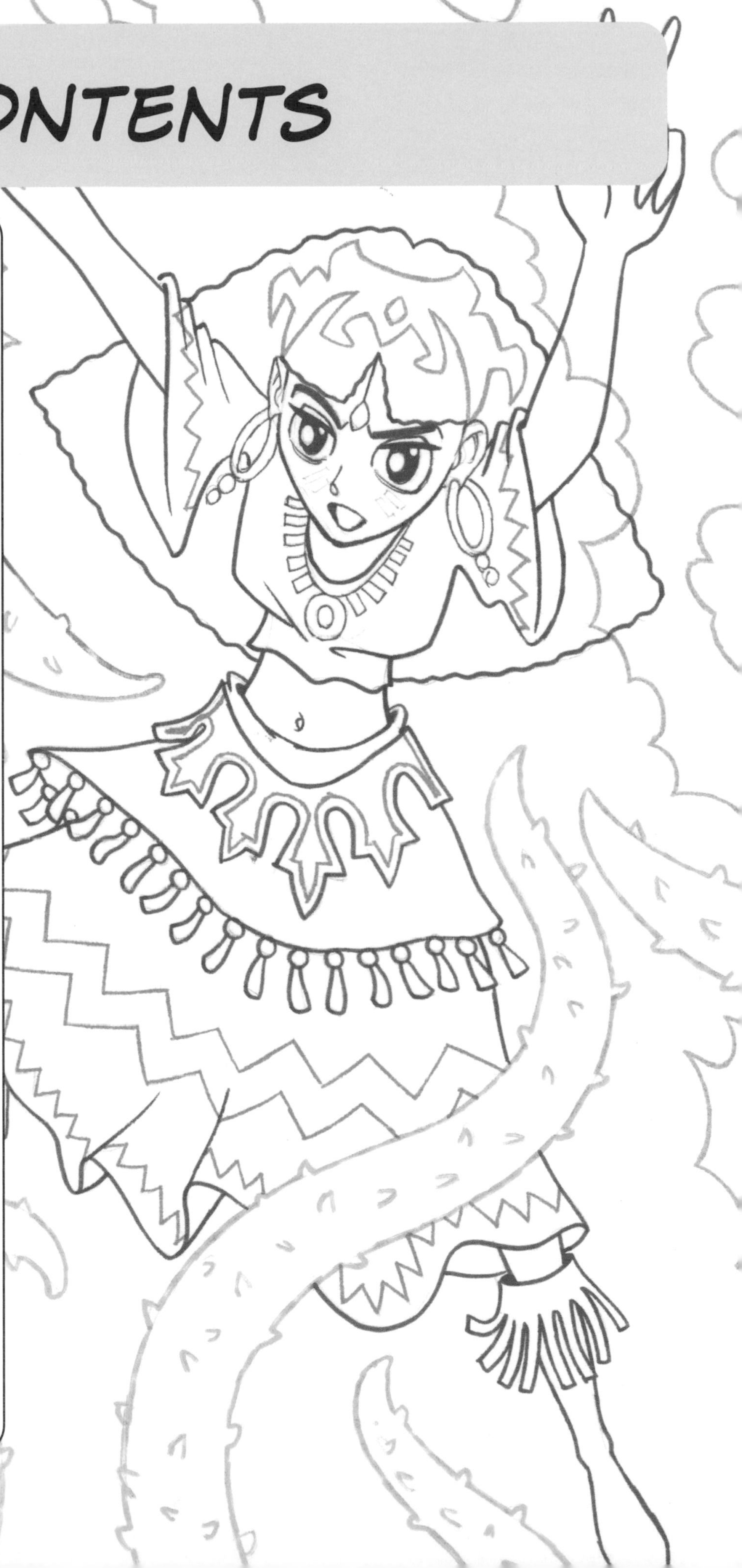

INTRODUCTION

If you've picked up this book because you already like drawing manga, or because you enjoy reading manga and watching anime, and want to start drawing your own pictures, then you may already know all you need about manga! But in case you're a complete beginner, here are a few pointers:

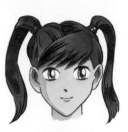

WHAT IS MANGA, AND WHAT MAKES IT UNIQUE?

The simplest explanation is that the word 'manga' is used as a generic term to describe serialized graphic stories created and read in Japan. Of course, today they are also widely read in many other countries, and artists outside Japan create stories in a 'manga' style, or produce books, such as this one, designed to help aspiring manga creators (or *mangaka*).

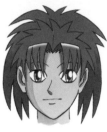

Japanese manga stories have a distinct graphic feel and tempo, very different from those produced in the USA or Europe. They often start as serials in anthology titles such as the hugely popular weekly magazine, *Shonen Jump*. Readers are polled regularly to decide which strips they like most, and the most popular of these go on to be collected in separate volumes – the ultimate seal of approval is adaptation to an animated version, or anime. Manga can be an extremely competitive business, and mangaka are renowned for their devotion to their work. The stories are mostly printed in black and white, with colour pages limited to covers, chapter headings or pin-up pages. The most successful may also have high-quality colour books published with pin-ups and character studies. If you're interested in life as a mangaka, there is an excellent series called *Bakuman*, by Tsugumi Ohba and Takeshi Obata, which explores the life of hard-working manga creators trying to make a successful series in *Shonen Jump*. More recently, Hirohito Araki (creator of the popular *Jojo's Bizarre Adventure*) has written a very useful guide to creating manga, entitled *Manga in Theory and Practice*. Both of these are highly recommended to any aspiring manga creator.

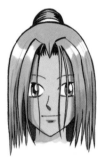

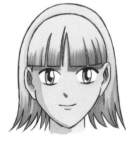

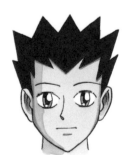

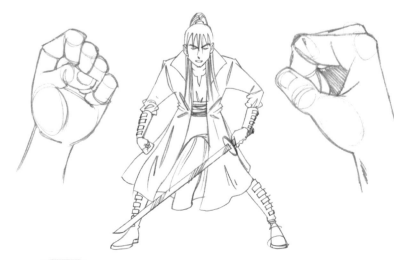

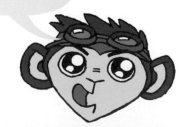

BE A MANGAKA!

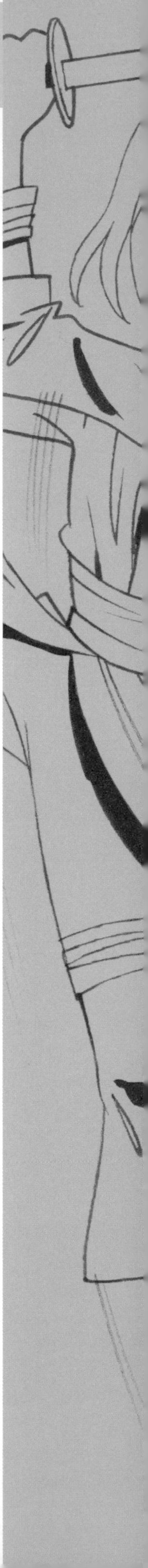

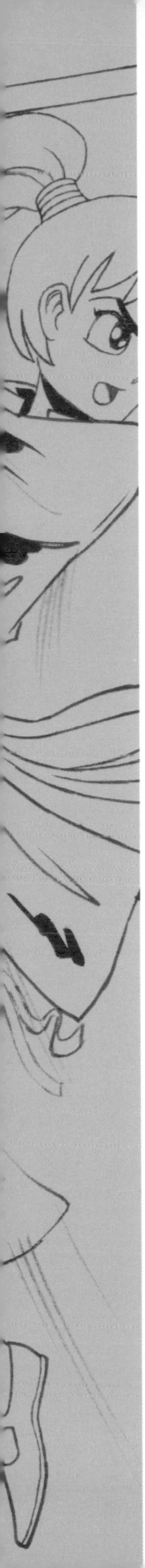

THE HISTORY OF MANGA

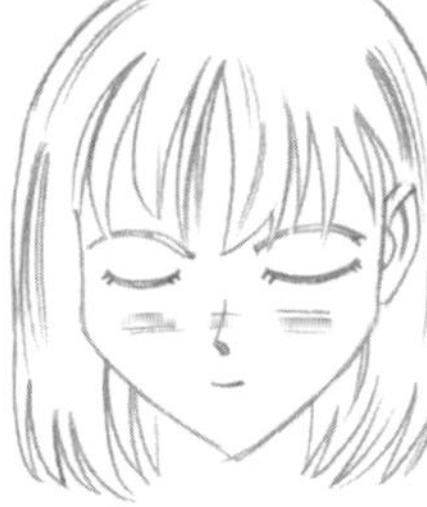

The origins of modern manga can be traced back to post-Second World War Japan, when the first modern manga anthologies began to appear. In the 1950s, the global obsession with science and technology was reflected in manga stories about giant robots and battle-suits, and this trend was exemplified by Osamu Tezuka's tale of a young robot boy, *Tetsuwan Atom* (Astro Boy). *Tetsuwan Atom* became the first animated TV series, or anime, with regular characters to make the jump from the pages of manga, and its visual style set the template for what we now recognize as the action manga look.

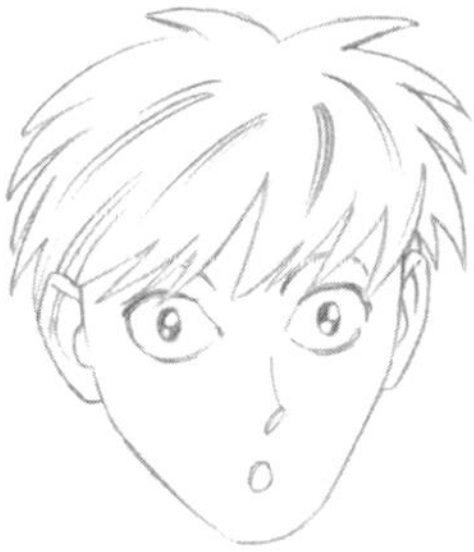

As manga became more and more popular, an ever-increasing number of mangaka experimented with stories about sports, such as boxing and baseball, science fiction robots and mecha-suits, gangster stories, traditional samurai warriors, magical girls, horror, romance and even the difficult subject of the nuclear bombs that were dropped on Hiroshima and Nagasaki at the end of the Second World War. In fact, just about any subject you could think of was given the manga treatment, and sold in huge amounts in thick 200-page digest volumes known as *tankobon*, or the paperback-sized *bunkobon*.

KEY ACTION MANGA

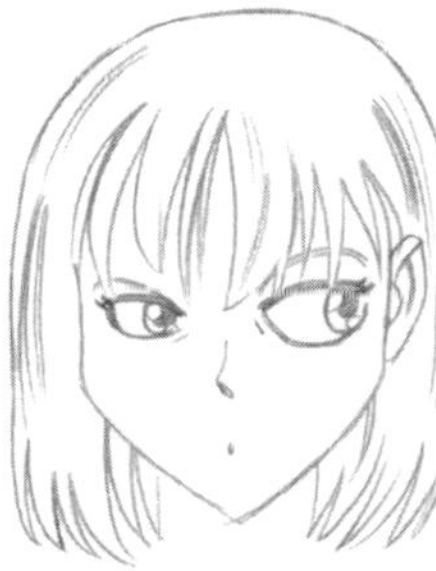

Three of the most popular action-based series of the last few decades are Akira Toriyama's *Dragon Ball*, Masashi Kishimoto's *Naruto*, and Hajime Isayama's *Attack on Titan*. *Dragon Ball* began in 1984, and told the tale of Goku, a boy who trained in the martial arts while searching the globe for the legendary Dragon Balls – mystical orbs with the power to summon a dragon that can grant a wish to the summoner. It established the idea of characters fighting in a series of tournament situations, something that has been used to great success in later series like *Pokémon* and *Yu-Gi-Oh! Dragon Ball* became a global success in manga and anime, and was a big influence on many up-and-coming mangaka.

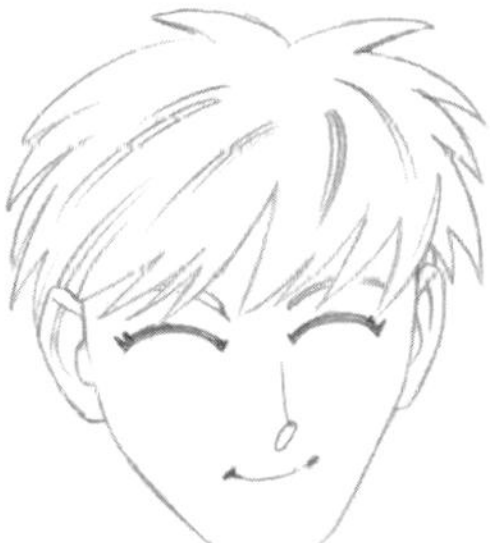

Kishimoto's *Naruto* began serialization in 1999 in *Shonen Jump*. Like *Dragon Ball*, *Naruto* features the title character in a seemingly endless series of battles as a developing ninja warrior; he discovers that he contains the spirit of the evil Nine-Tailed Fox, which was trapped inside his body when he was a baby. Naruto is, like Goku, a fairly comical character. The appeal of the series lies in its deceptive complexity, but also in its incredibly dynamic art style, which at times feels like it's about to burst off the page. As well as being a regular cover mainstay of *Shonen Jump*, *Naruto* has been a long-running anime series since 2002, and has crossed over into film, CDs, video games, trading cards and T-shirts.

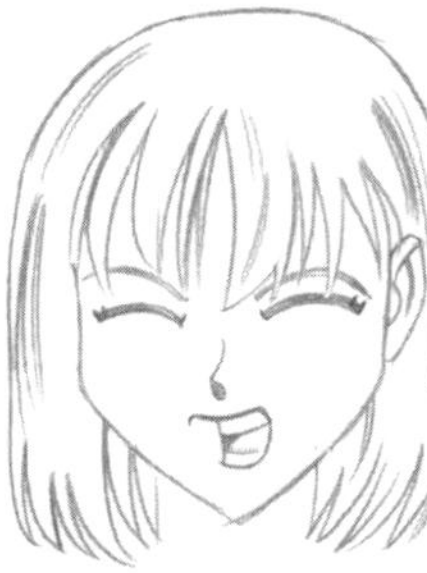

Attack on Titan has been one of the best-selling manga series of all time. Isayama's story takes place in a world where humans live in cities, surrounded by enormous walls to protect them from the attacks of the Titans (giant, flesh-eating humanoids). The action is fast and the art style reflects that with lots of movement lines and dazzling camera angles. The anime is also hugely popular and *Attack...* is a common theme for cosplay (the art of dressing as your favourite characters).

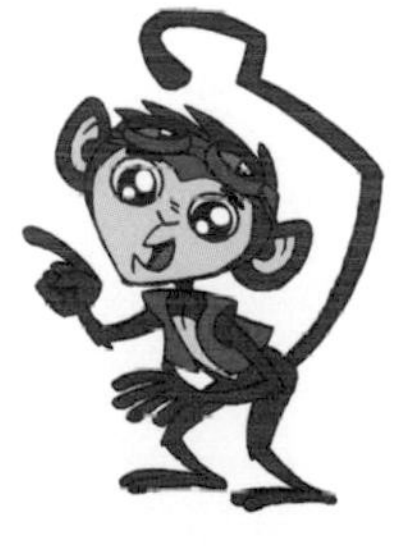

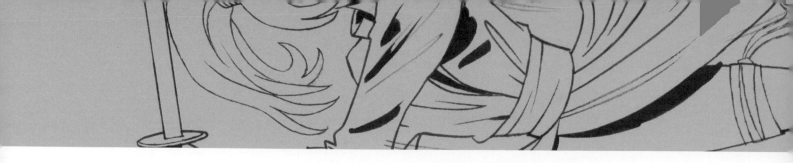

WHAT IS MANGA ART?

There's a short and a long answer to this! The short one is that most people now have a rough notion of a typical manga 'look'. It may involve characters having large eyes and luxuriant hair for example. While that's true of many manga characters, it's also true that there's a huge variation in art styles from title to title. Styles range from the cartoony to the ultra-realistic. A 'chibi' or super-cute style can also be used within a story to comic effect.

So, the correct answer is to say *your* style is manga art. Manga is all about storytelling, and developing your own unique style is crucial.

MY FAVOURITE MANGA ARTISTS

We all have our preferences, and while I love the scratchy, expressive style of a manga like *Chainsaw Man* (Tatsuki Fujimoto), or the relatively crude stylings of *Mob Psycho 100* (One), one of my personal favourites would probably be the wonderful Rumiko Takahashi. Takahashi began her manga career in way back in 1978 with *Urusei Yatsura*, and her current title, *Mao*, shows how a drawing style can evolve and develop with time, losing none of its freshness.

IT'S A MANGA WORLD

In recent years, the manga style of art has become increasingly popular with artists and animators in the West, particularly since the hugely successful *Pokémon* brand. The name 'Pokémon' is derived from the Japanese toy brand, *Poketto Monsutâ* (Pocket Monsters). Originally a video game, *Pokémon* became a phenomenon in the gaming, toy, trading card, manga and anime markets, and introduced many Western readers to the basic principle of combat-style manga, where a multitude of characters with different abilities, skills or powers are pitted against each other in a never-ending struggle.

Another big influence has been the live action series *Mighty Morphin Power Rangers*. Produced in the USA, *Power Rangers* used footage from the Japanese series *Super Sentai*, and is a typical example of the mecha manga genre, with martial arts, giant robot battle-suits and hideous monsters all put together in a mad rush of colour and cartoon violence. Although not a manga, *Power Rangers* went a long way to develop a love of Japanese-style culture around the world. The increasing popularity of manga and anime has led to a noticeable shift in the style of cartoons and comics outside Japan.

Today, a quick glance at popular animated shows on children's TV demonstrates this influence quite clearly. Even the traditional superhero worlds of Marvel and DC Comics have incorporated this style to a large degree, and manga-style versions of popular comics such as *Spider-Man* and *X-Men* have also been created.

SPACE TO WORK

A very important factor in drawing, and one that is often overlooked, is a comfortable working space. If possible, find a table or desk that you can use exclusively so that your things won't get moved about – maybe a desk in your own room, or perhaps part of the family kitchen table that could be designated as your drawing area. Some people prefer a flat desk, some a sloping desk like a draughtsman's table – this is a personal choice. I prefer a flat space, but you can buy small adjustable sloping desktops if that suits you better.

Once you have a space, try to keep it clear, clean and tidy when not in use. Use containers to store your pens, pencils and markers – you could use mugs or old jam jars, for example.

If you leave an unfinished drawing on your desk, cover it with a piece of paper to keep it clean.

YOUR LIGHT SOURCE

While you're drawing, make sure there's a good light source nearby. Drawing can put a strain on the eyes, especially in dim light, so if you're not near a window, or you're working at night, use a desk lamp. Some artists use daylight bulbs, which have a blue tinge and more closely resemble natural light.

WHERE TO SIT

You also need to ensure you have a comfortable seat. Many people have bad posture when they draw, often hunched over a desk for hours on end. This can have a negative impact on your drawing technique, not to mention giving you back pain.

BREAK IT UP

Take regular short breaks and get up and move about, gently stretching your back if you can. Taking a break from drawing is also important for your eyes – staring closely at a drawing for long periods of time can quickly lead to tired eyes, so changing your surroundings now and then is good for them, and will also help to keep your mind fresh.

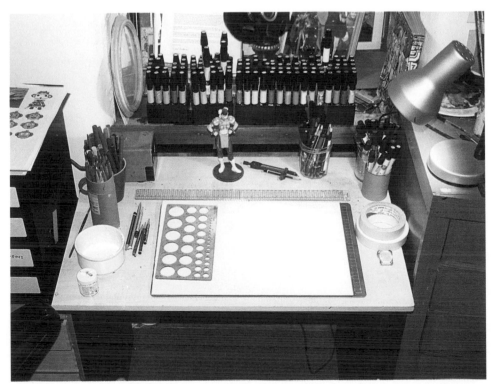

MY CREATIVE ENVIRONMENT

Here's a photo of my drawing space, showing a variety of tools and equipment. Notice the drawers on either side for storing reference materials and other tools.

A MATERIAL WORLD...

As for any other job, to get the best results you need the right tools. Those tools will vary from artist to artist, and what works for you may not work for the next person. So how do you choose? Simple: TRIAL AND ERROR.

PENCILS

A pencil is an essential tool for any artist, so invest in some quality pencils – it's worth paying slightly more for a good-quality pencil. There is a range of pencil grades from hard (H) to soft (B) – the hardest is 9H, through to the softest at 9B. In the middle you have an HB and an F grade (midway between H and HB). A very hard pencil gives a cleaner line but tends to cut into the paper and is not suitable for non-technical drawing such as manga. On the other hand, a very soft pencil can smudge easily and can quickly lead to a very messy sketch! The best place to start is in the middle, with an HB grade. This will give you a reasonably clean line but is soft enough to allow for some flexibility in your drawing. Use a softer grade such as a 2B or 3B to add some shading once you have the basic drawing in place.

Don't be afraid to go to your local art shop and ask for advice on which brands of pencils to try. There are lots to choose from and it's worth trying a selection to find the one you're most comfortable with. You will be constantly sharpening your pencils, and inferior brands often fracture along the lead and become useless. Make sure you have a decent pencil sharpener – if possible, get an electric one; you will be using this a lot, as a sharp point is essential to good drawing.

ERASER

As you work on your drawing, you will sometimes need to erase a line or two. Make life easy for yourself by not pressing too hard when using your pencil – it's a lot easier to clean up a light drawing! Later, when you've inked your drawing, you will also need to erase unwanted pencil marks, especially if you want to colour it.

Erasers are available in all shapes and sizes, but avoid novelty types as they can smear your work and leave lots of bits behind. Plastic and rubber erasers can also be quite messy and can damage your paper surface with heavy use. I usually use putty erasers, which don't tend to leave any mess behind and are quite safe on paper. You can buy them in any high street art shop.

PAPER

Choice of paper is also important. There are lots of styles and colours: smooth, rough, white, off-white – experiment with as many as you can. Local art shops may have some samples you can try – don't be afraid to ask. The paper you use will depend on how you want to finish your drawing and whether or not you want to colour it.

To start with, I would suggest buying a cheap cartridge paper sketchbook to practise in so that you won't be afraid to make mistakes or take chances with your drawing. Cartridge paper is a very comfortable and strong surface and will take coloured pencils well if you wish to try those. If you intend to ink your drawing (using an ink-based pen or brush to finish off your pencil sketch), you should use a smoother, high-grade paper. You will find pads of suitable paper in your art shop, some actually branded as 'manga paper', which are good for clean linework, but any smooth surface paper will do. Marker or layout pads are very good if you intend to colour with marker pens, as many manga artists do.

Another option is to make your pencil drawing on one sheet of paper, then trace over the linework on a separate sheet, leaving you with a clean, pencil-free version to colour in. A desktop lightbox is very useful for this method.

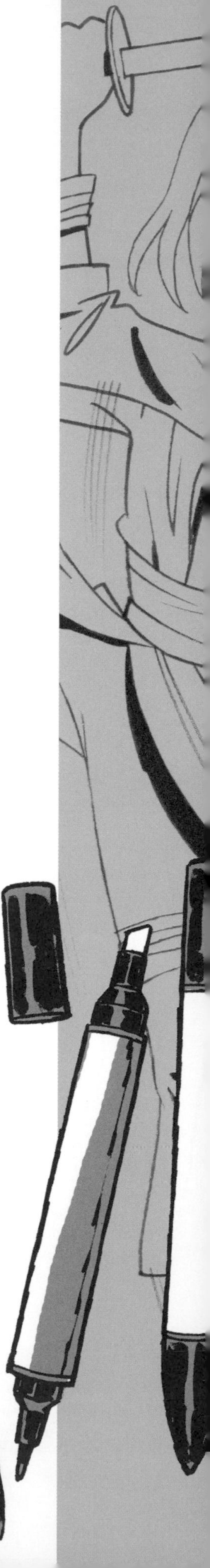

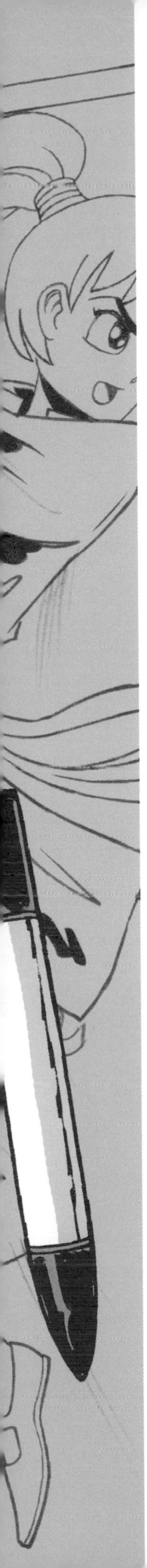

INKING & COLOURING

When you're happy with your pencil drawing, the next stage is to ink and colour it. There is a multitude of ink pens, brushes and inks you can use – it's worth having a look in your local art shop, where you can usually try them out before buying.

Pens come in grades of nib thickness, from 0.1mm up to 0.8mm and above. A good starting point is a medium-size nib, such as 0.5mm. It's also worth thinking about how you will use different pens within your drawings: you might want to use a thicker pen for the outside line of a figure and for objects in the foreground, and a finer pen for smaller details or background objects, as this will give your drawing a sense of depth. As well as regular pens there are brush pens, which can be useful for lines of varying width – from very fine lines to broad brush strokes – or for putting in strong shadows. These are normally cartridge pens with a brush tip instead of a nib.

When you've inked your drawing, let it dry completely before erasing any unwanted pencil marks. You can colour your drawing using a number of different media, such as colour pencils, markers, paint, or on the computer.

Colour pencils

The simplest way to colour your drawing is with colour pencils. These are relatively cheap and come in an excellent range of colours. As with all things, it's well worth paying a little bit more for a quality set, and don't forget to keep a reasonably sharp point on them.

Markers

Probably the most common medium for budding mangaka is coloured markers. They come in a wide range of colours and shades of grey, and can be blended and combined to excellent effect. Most are double-ended, with a broad, wedged tip at one end and a thinner, rounded tip at the other. Some also have a third, fine-line tip. These markers can take a little getting used to but are very versatile. Their downside is that they aren't very practical for small details, as the colour tends to 'bleed' out from the point of contact with the paper surface.

Paint

Some artists like to use paint such as watercolour on their manga art. With a bit of practice this can be a lovely way to give your art a vibrant look. You must ensure you use a waterproof ink to do your linework, which should be drawn onto a smooth watercolour paper – use a desktop lightbox if you need to trace your outline.

White-out paint

Whichever method you use to colour your drawing, it's worth also having a small thin brush on hand with a pot of white bleed-proof paint – this is handy for cleaning up any linework mistakes or tidying up colour that has bled through the linework. Keep a pot of water nearby to wash your brush immediately after use. When paint dries on the brush it can be hard to remove without damaging the bristles.

Computer

If you're familiar with computer programs such as Adobe® Photoshop®, you can achieve some fantastic results by scanning in your linework – or even drawing it straight onto the screen if you use a tablet – and colouring it in digitally. The advantage of this is that you can easily create special effects and gradients, as well as being able to edit and change your drawing. Scan your linework in at high resolution (at least 300dpi), clean it up, then increase your contrast to 100 per cent, adjusting the brightness as needed. Then you can select areas of your drawing to colour. It's a good idea to duplicate your linework layer in case you go wrong, and make sure you save at regular intervals. You don't want to spend hours on a piece of artwork and then lose it if your computer crashes!

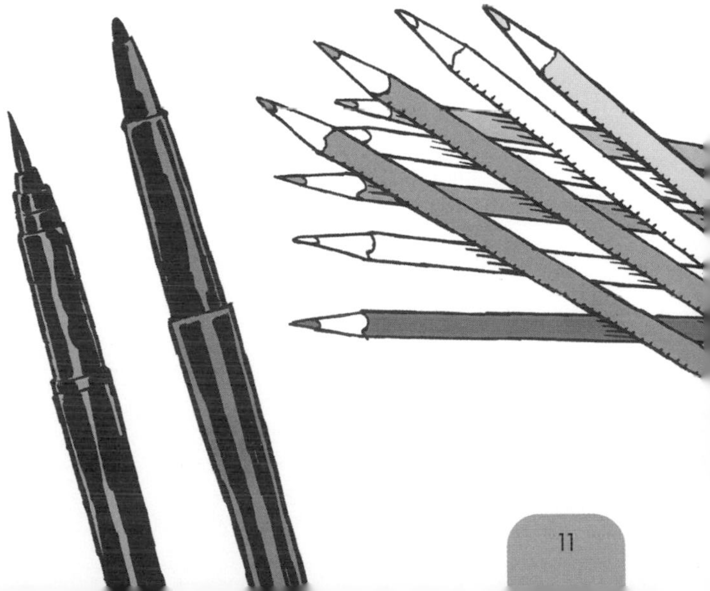

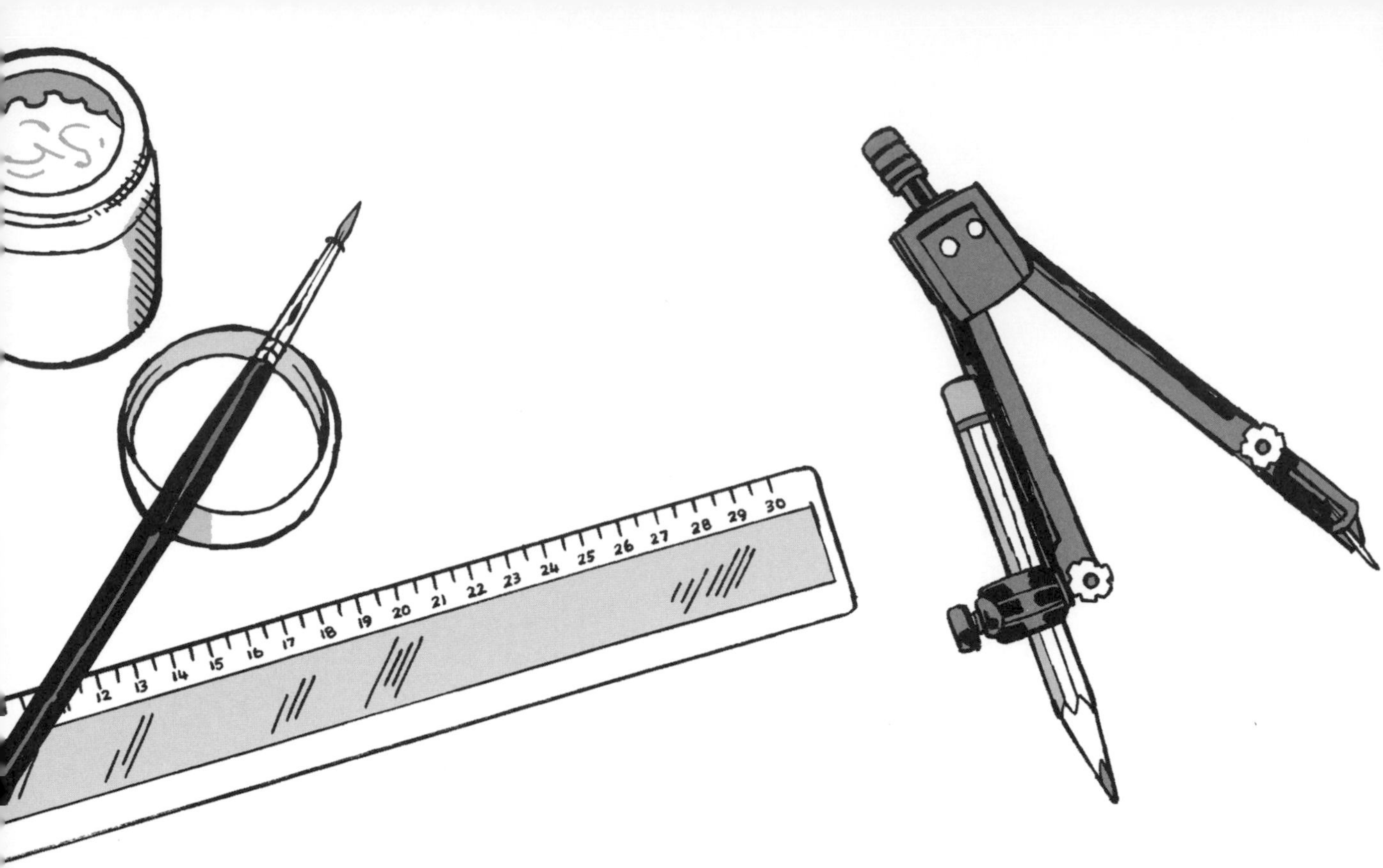

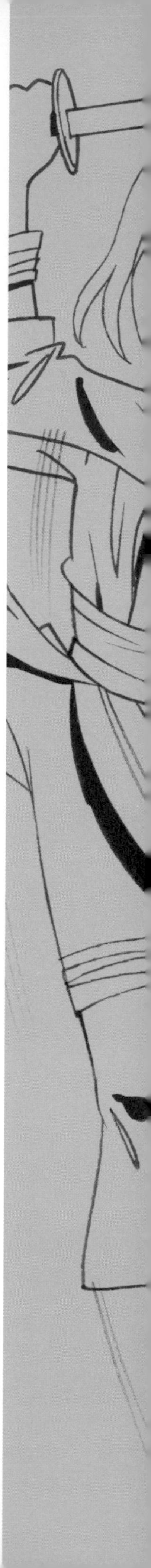

RULERS AND DRAWING AIDS

Sometimes you will need perfectly straight lines or neat curves in your drawing. Manga is renowned for its painstakingly accurate depiction of things such as streets, buildings and cars, so to get your drawing as accurate as possible you should have a clear, sturdy plastic ruler for straight lines, and a circle guide and small pair of compasses for curves and circles. All of these can be bought from stationery or art shops. Think about how big your workspace is and don't buy a ruler that's too long for practical use – if it's too long you'll find yourself always knocking pens off your board when you change angles – very frustrating! I find that a 30cm (12in) ruler is usually sufficient for most straight lines.

Circle guides are plastic templates with a variety of circle sizes cut out, but for larger circles you should use a pair of compasses. Remember not to press too hard into the paper with your point though – gently but firmly is the rule here. I prefer to draw curved lines freehand, but if you're not confident doing this, you can buy plastic curve templates in a variety of shapes, or use flexi-curves, which can be bent to any degree of curve you want.

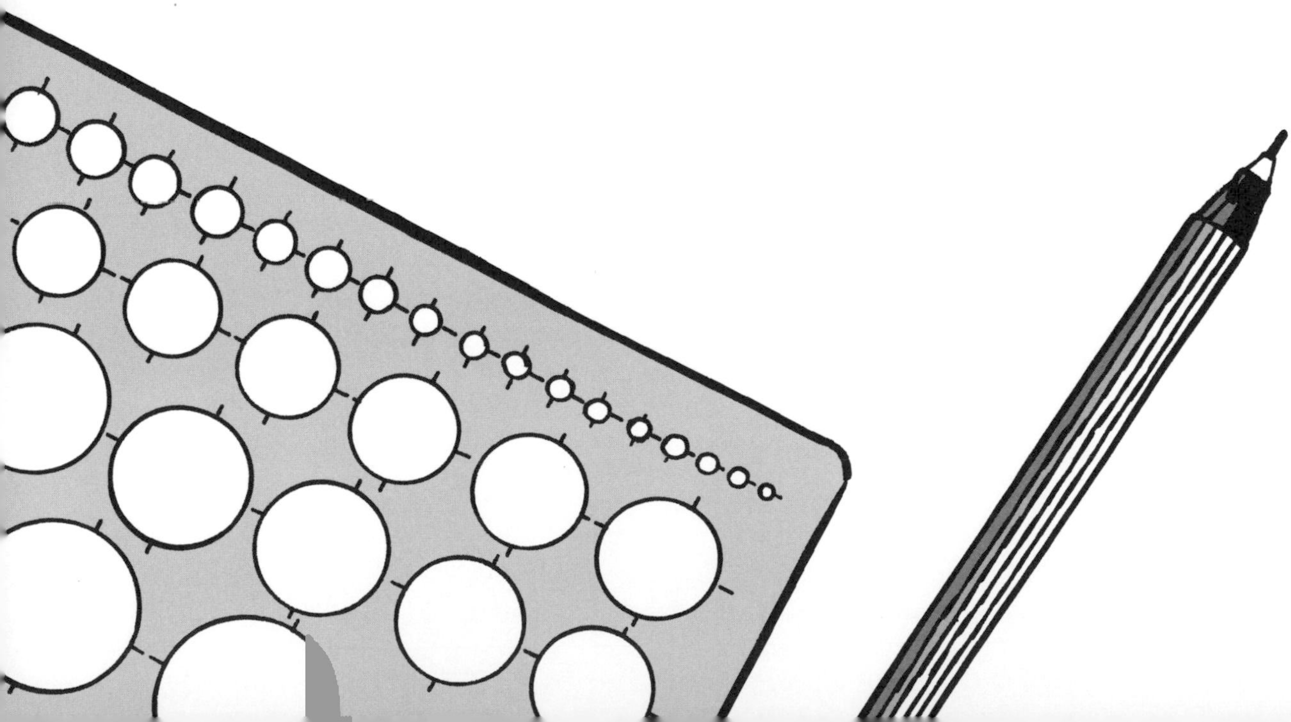

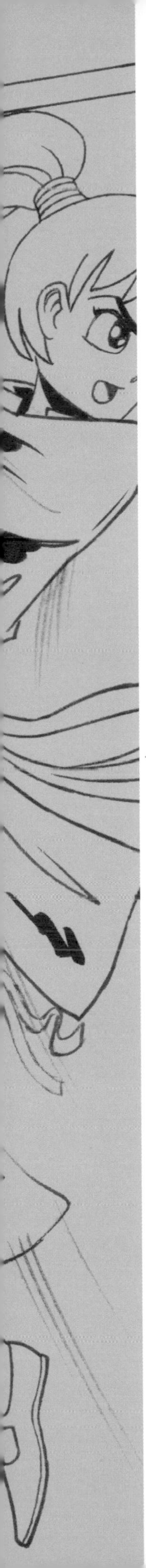

OVERCOMING THE FEAR OF A BLANK PAGE

The best thing about drawing your own manga, or drawing anything for that matter, is that YOU MAKE THE RULES! No one can tell you what you should or shouldn't draw: it's completely up to you.

The trouble is – as any self-respecting superhero will tell you – with great power comes great responsibility. If no one tells you what to draw, how do you know where to start? What I have learnt is that the only way to conquer the fear of a blank space is to begin to FILL IT! Once you break the spell of an empty piece of paper you'll find it gets easier with every stroke of the pencil. Doodling is a very useful way to do this, and with doodling you can let your mind wander while you ponder the possibilities in front of you. Keep well away from the main area of the paper and limit yourself to the margins; all manner of ideas may actually evolve from the tiny marks you make.

Another way to combat the blank space is to draw random lines, shapes and curves in big swathes across the page. Keep it light enough to erase if need be, and once you've made a few marks you can begin to construct your image using those lines as a kind of very rough plan. Treat the blank space as an enemy in combat: treat it with respect and caution, but don't fear it and you won't go wrong.

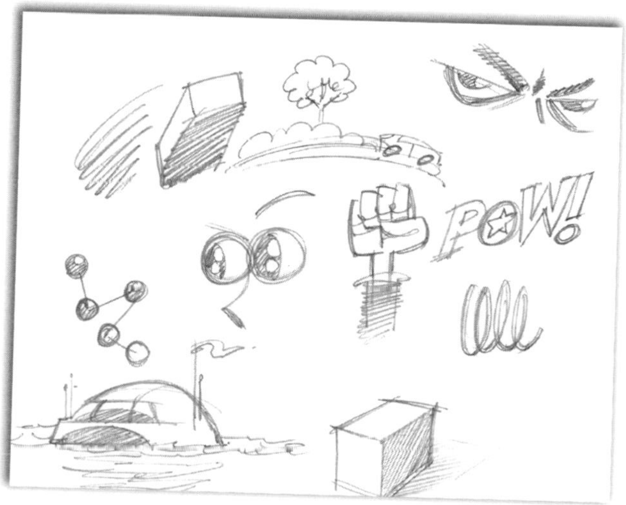
POW!

REFERENCE IT!

Any professional artist will tell you how useful it is to use reference material as part of your drawing technique. Although you can draw what you want, how you want, it's a good idea to do a little research into the real world.

WHAT TO LOOK FOR

If you want to draw an imaginary vehicle, you can make it more believable by looking at how a real one is constructed. Where does the driver sit? How do you steer it? How does it move along – on wheels or through the air? If you look at pictures of real cars or aeroplanes, you can see where the driver or pilot should sit, how the weight is distributed between the wheels or wings, and imagine how it might be powered. If it has an engine, does it need exhaust pipes? Would the engine be visible on the outside of the vehicle, or hidden under a smooth body? It's up to you how it looks but thinking about the answers to these questions lends authenticity to your art.

In the same way, if you draw a weapon such as a sword or a gun, you can make it much more dynamic by looking at references of how a gun or sword is held – how do the hands grip? What does it do to the shape of the arm and how does that work in relation to the body? Would it be held close to the body or at arm's length?

WHERE TO FIND INSPIRATION

These days it's easy to find all the reference material you need on the internet. If you have a printer you can print off useful images and have them by you as you draw. Alternatively, your local library will have lots of books you can take home to study at your leisure. Another good tip is to visit a charity/thrift shop or boot sale for bargain books – you will find all kinds of great reference books, and very cheaply!

Another good way to improve your drawing is to look at your favourite manga and see how the artist works. There's no shame in practising your drawing by copying a good artist whose work you admire. Most artists will admit to copying drawings at some point in their career – the important thing is to move on and develop your own style. And this can only be done by drawing – lots and lots of it!

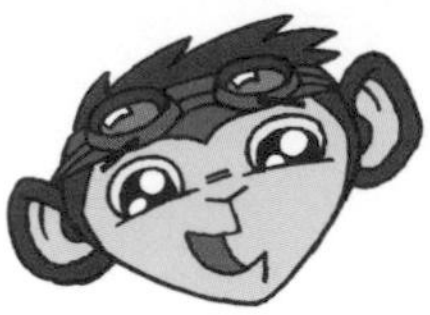
KEEP A SMALL MIRROR BY YOUR DRAWING SPACE – USE IT TO HELP DRAW FACIAL EXPRESSIONS AND HAND SHAPES.

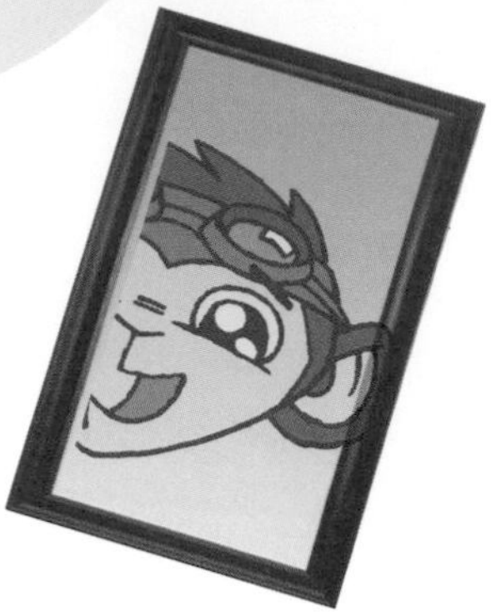

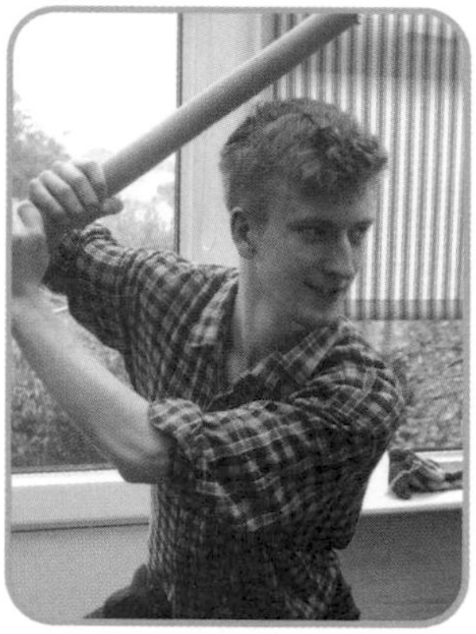

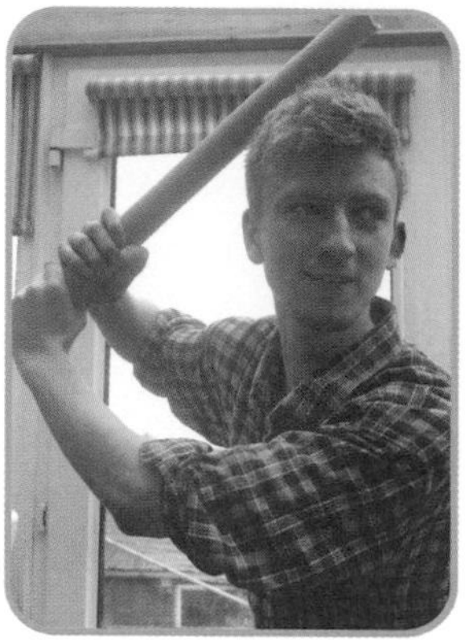

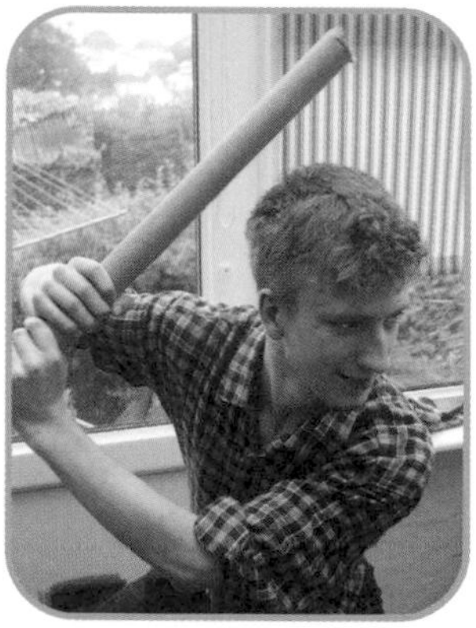

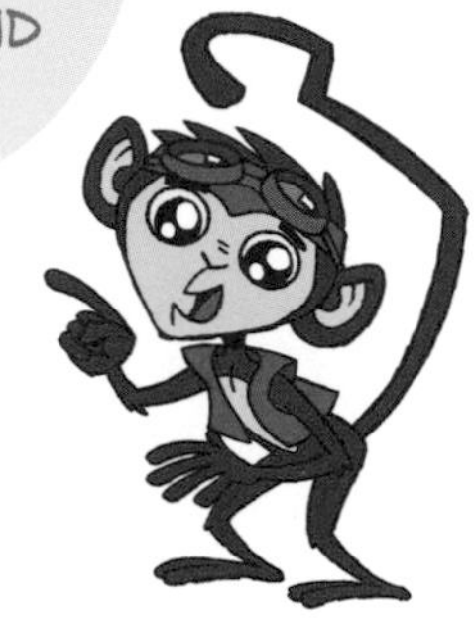
ASK YOUR FRIENDS OR FAMILY TO POSE FOR REFERENCE PHOTOS, WHICH YOU CAN USE AS GUIDES TO POSTURE AND CLOTHING WHILE DRAWING. THEY MAY BE SLIGHTLY EMBARRASSED AT FIRST BUT IT'S A LOT OF FUN AND REALLY USEFUL!

BODY BASICS

OK, let's imagine we have a good set of drawing tools, a clean sheet of paper, and we're sitting in a comfortable position at a tidy, well-lit table. Where shall we begin?

CREATING WIREFRAMES

At their most basic, manga figures can be broken down into a simple series of connected circles and triangles, known as a wireframe. Once you understand how the shapes relate to each other, you can draw figures in any position you like, simply by using this basic construction method. Let's look at a male figure, for example (see opposite, top left).

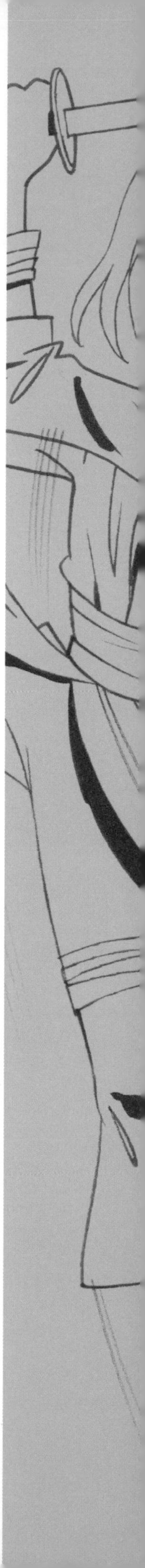

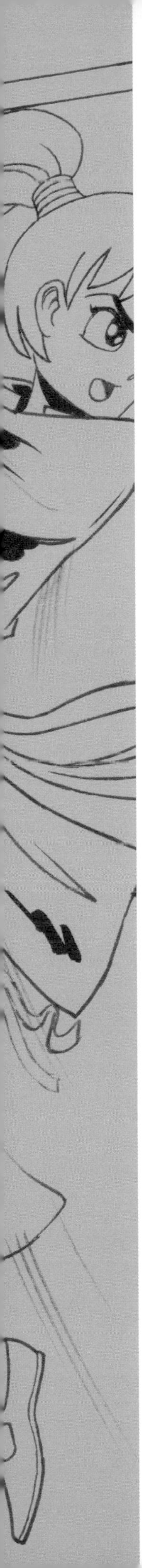

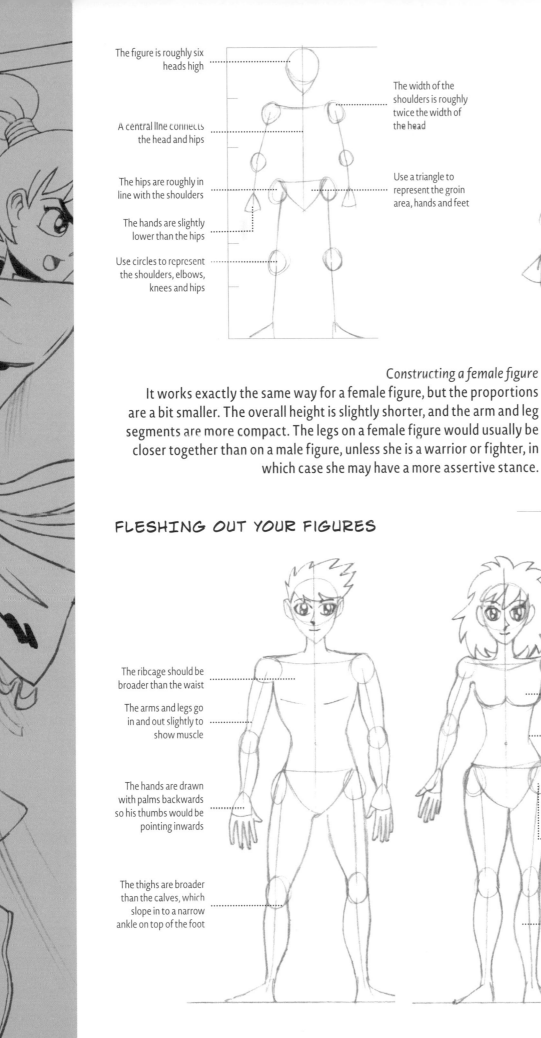

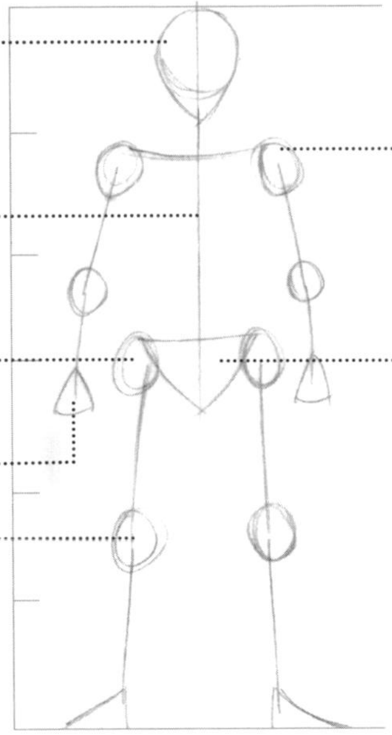
The figure is roughly six heads high
A central line connects the head and hips
The hips are roughly in line with the shoulders
The hands are slightly lower than the hips
Use circles to represent the shoulders, elbows, knees and hips
The width of the shoulders is roughly twice the width of the head
Use a triangle to represent the groin area, hands and feet

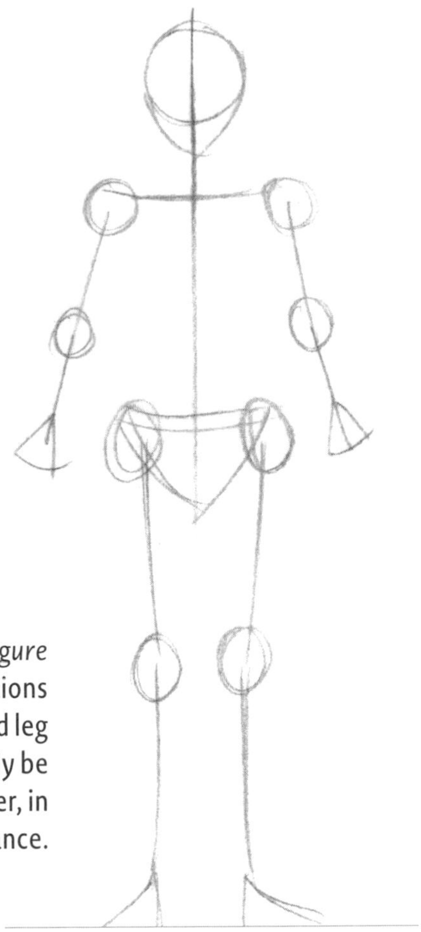

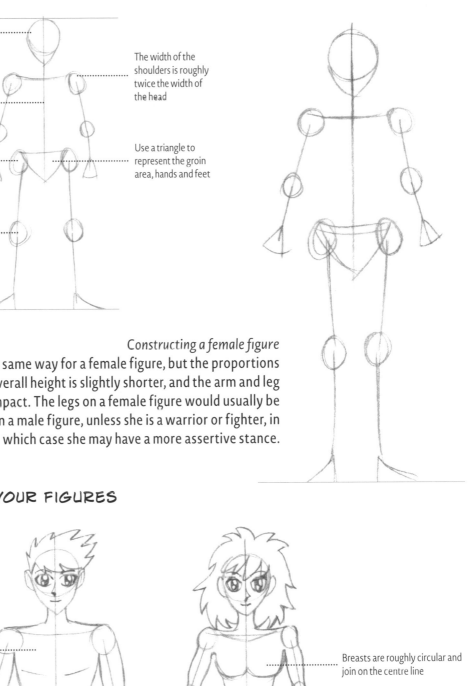

Constructing a female figure

It works exactly the same way for a female figure, but the proportions are a bit smaller. The overall height is slightly shorter, and the arm and leg segments are more compact. The legs on a female figure would usually be closer together than on a male figure, unless she is a warrior or fighter, in which case she may have a more assertive stance.

FLESHING OUT YOUR FIGURES

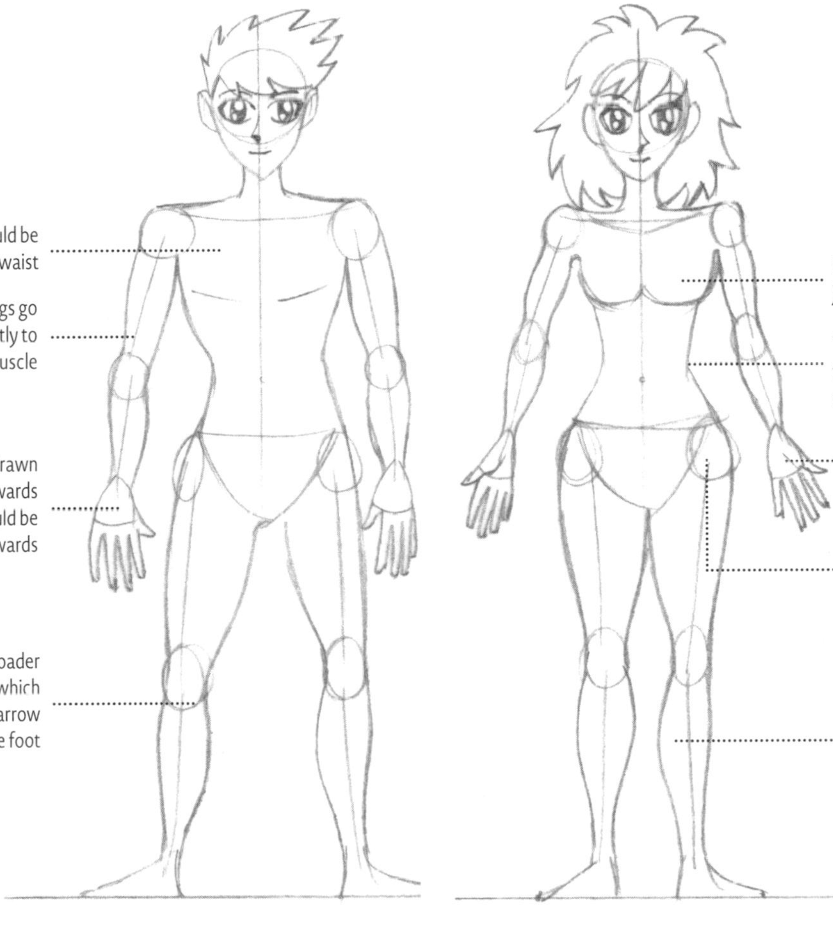
The ribcage should be broader than the waist
The arms and legs go in and out slightly to show muscle
The hands are drawn with palms backwards so his thumbs would be pointing inwards
The thighs are broader than the calves, which slope in to a narrow ankle on top of the foot
Breasts are roughly circular and join on the centre line
The waist goes in further than on the male, to give a more curvy shape to the body
The palms are facing forwards, so the thumbs are pointing away from the body
The hips are wide in relation to the waist
Muscle masses on the arms and legs

A MATTER OF PERSPECTIVE

It's important when you're drawing action manga figures to use interesting viewpoints to keep the viewer engaged. Varying the perspective can add dynamism to your drawing, and it's not as difficult as you might think. If you stand on a chair and look down on someone, you'll see how it works.

THE VIEW FROM ABOVE

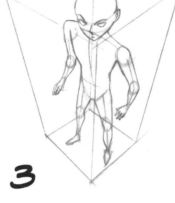

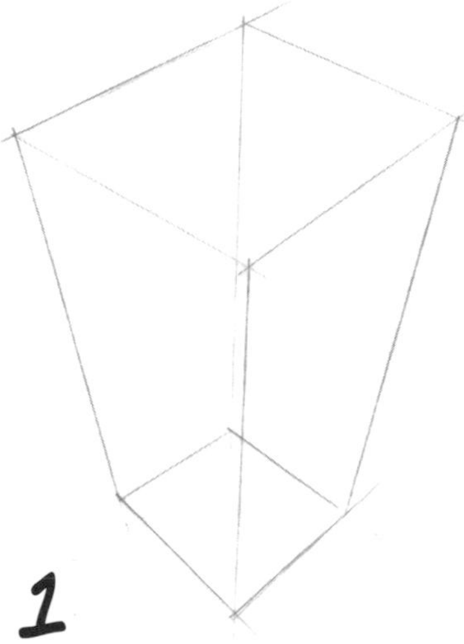

1

I like to start by creating a rectangular three-dimensional box as seen from above. Draw two diamond shapes, one above the other, and connect the corners with straight lines. Notice how much larger the top diamond is than the bottom one: even though they are different sizes, they create the illusion of being the two ends of one shape.

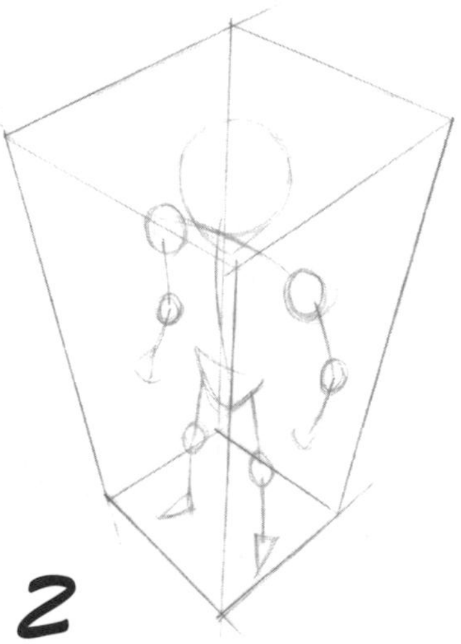

2

Sketch a wireframe figure inside the box – draw in the head at the top and the feet at the bottom first. Bear in mind that you are looking at the figure from above: the head needs to be much larger than the feet. Connect up the rest of the body – the limbs will look much shorter from this angle than they would from straight on.

3

Flesh out the figure. The facial features should be in the lower part of the face, with the neck concealed by the head.

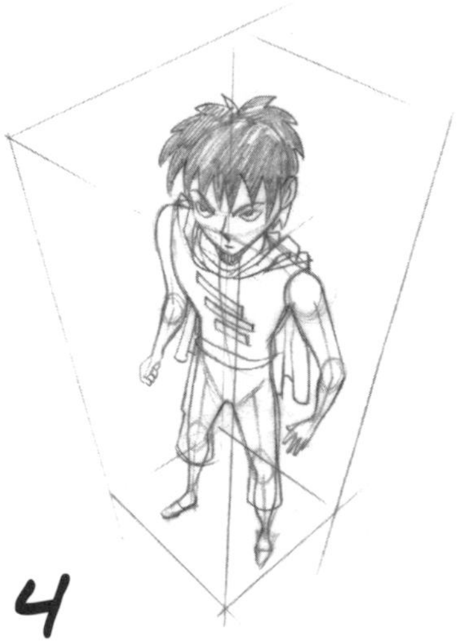

4

Finish off the sketch by adding details such as hair and clothing.

THE VIEW FROM BELOW

It works the same way for a low viewpoint, but in reverse – your figure's feet will be much larger than its head.

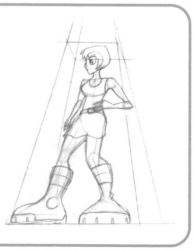

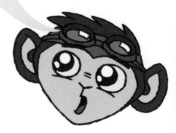

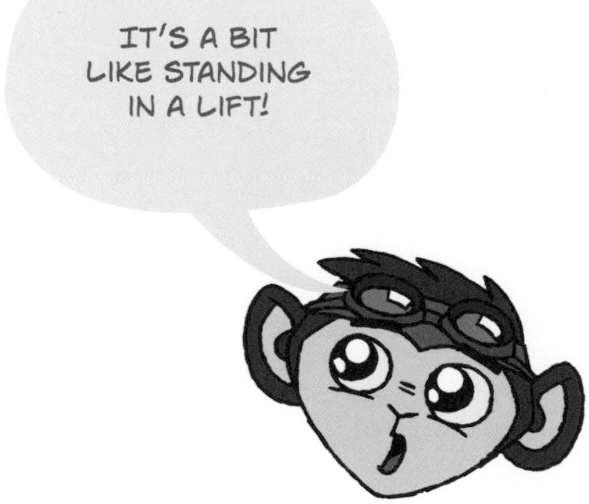

IT'S A BIT LIKE STANDING IN A LIFT!

LET'S FACE IT!

Of course, every face is individual and unique in its own right – that's what makes humans interesting! – but as with everything about drawing manga characters, there are some simple rules you can follow. We'll look at different facial expressions and hair styles later in the book – for now let's focus on getting the proportions right.

CONSTRUCTING A FACE

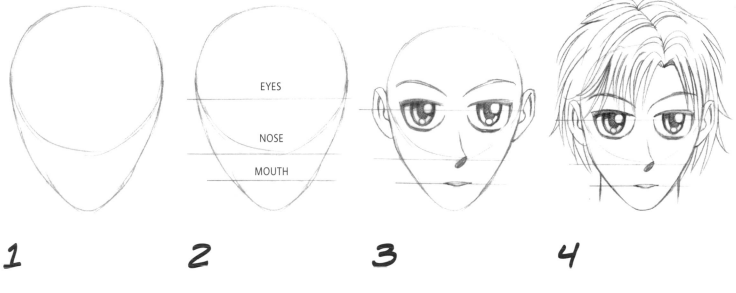

EYES

NOSE

MOUTH

1

The basic shape of the head is a bit like a balloon, or an egg. Start by drawing a circle, then add on an elongated curve underneath: this forms the lower jaw and is where you will put the nose and mouth.

2

Draw a horizontal line across your circle, just over halfway down; use a ruler to keep the line straight and only draw lightly in pencil so that you will be able to rub out the marks later. Bisect the lower half, then do the same with the bottom quarter. These three lines show you where to draw in the eyes, nose and mouth.

3

Sketch in your character's features. The ears should be roughly in line with the eyes. Eyes are often large and expressive in manga, whereas noses and mouths are just the opposite! Female faces are constructed in the same way as male faces but with smaller proportions. The chin is often more pointed, the nose smaller and the eyes wider and deeper.

4

The final stage is to add hair. The style shown here is a loose, floppy style often seen in manga, with lots of individual strands that add detail and interest. There is a parting on one side, and you can see how the hair stems from this line. Remember that the hair grows up out of the head before it falls down onto the face and behind the ears.

Even though manga characters have very exaggerated features, such as larger-than-normal eyes, tiny noses and thin-lipped mouths, you should still check your own expression when you're drawing. Keep a small mirror handy: if you want an angry face, for example, practise grimacing or snarling into the mirror so you can see how it alters your features.

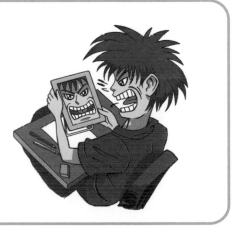

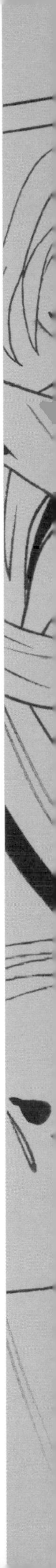

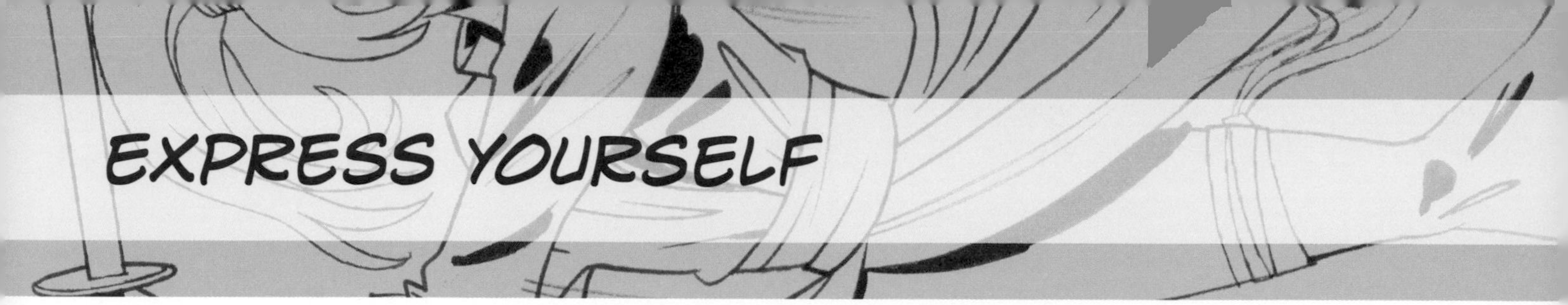

EXPRESS YOURSELF

One of the most effective ways to tell a graphic story is through facial expression – that's how we read each other's emotions; how we know if someone is happy or sad, surprised or angry. Look at this range of emotions: notice how the eyes and mouth change shape in response to the character's emotions.

MALE FACE

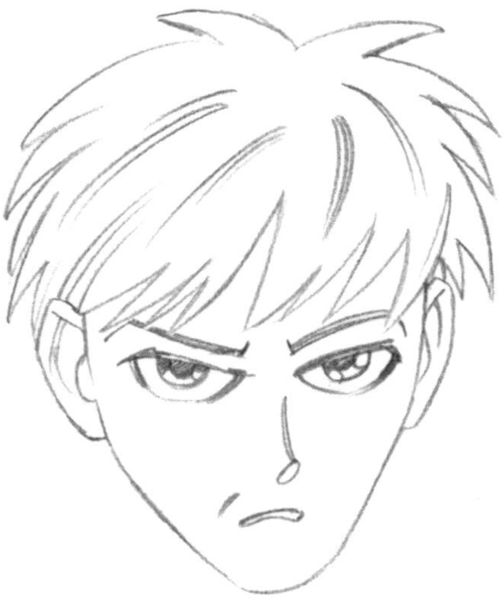

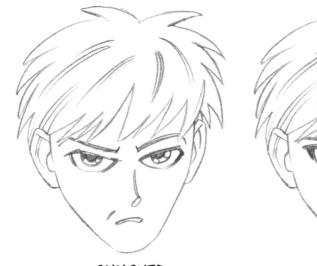

ANNOYED

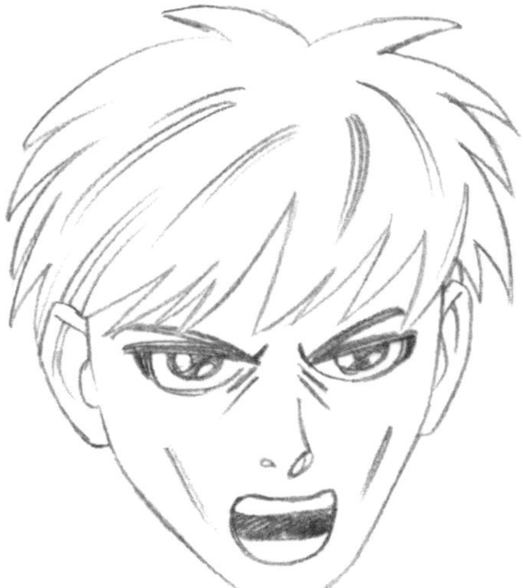

ANGRY

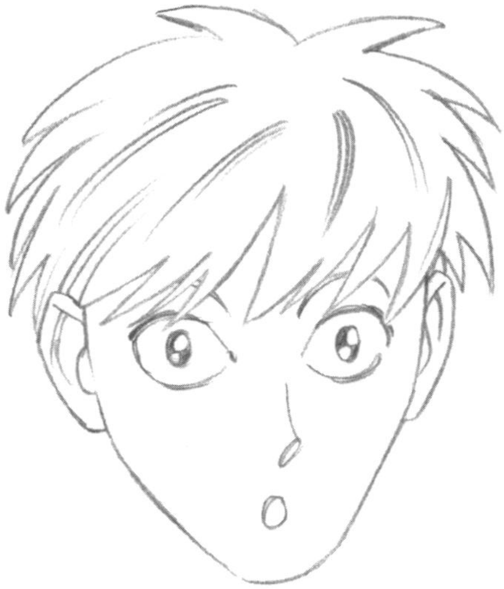

SURPRISED

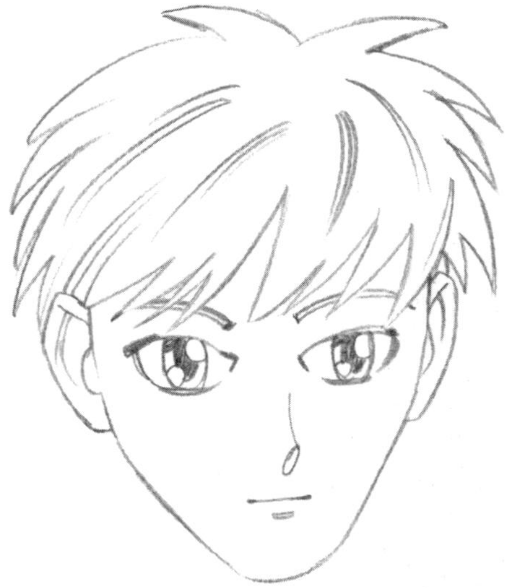

COMPOSED

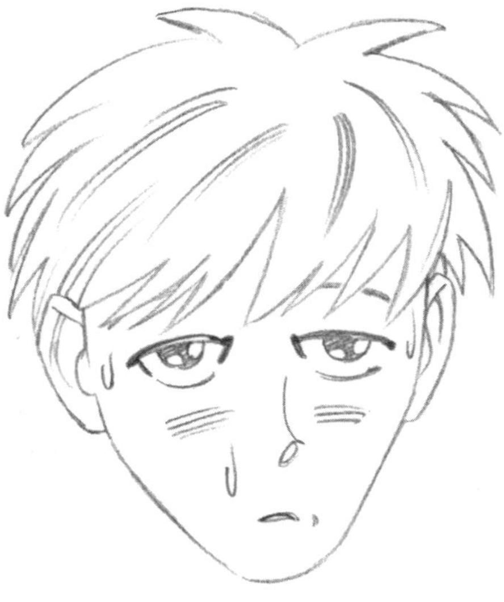

WEARY

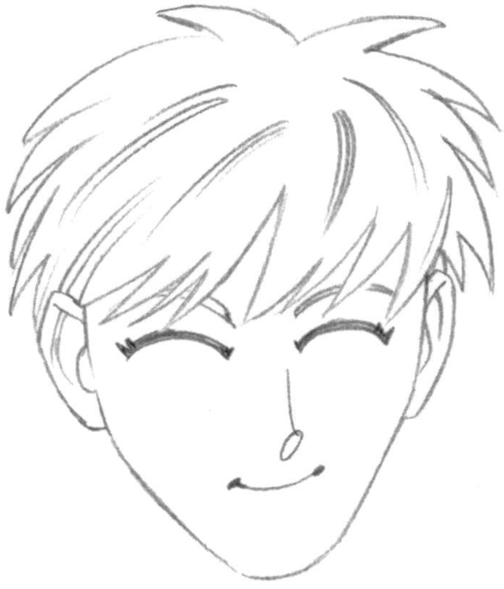

HAPPY

FEMALE FACE

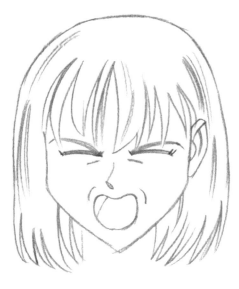

IN PAIN

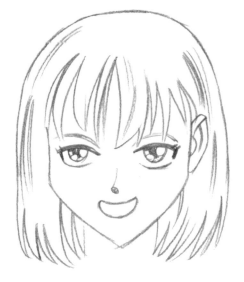

PLEASED

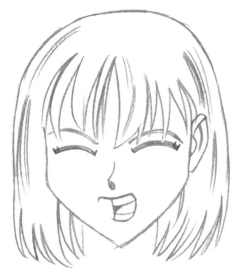

SHOUTING

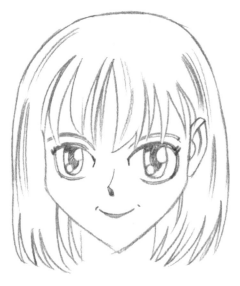

OPTIMISTIC

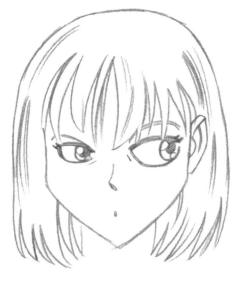

SUSPICIOUS

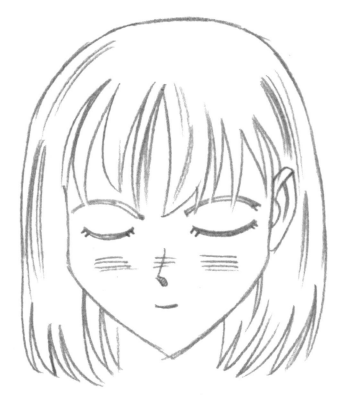

EMBARRASSED/
FLATTERED

HAIR WE GO!

Hair styles are a great way to distinguish one character from another. There's often not a lot of difference between male and female styles, so here are a few ideas to get you started.

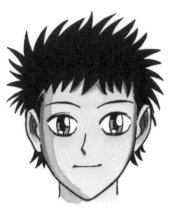
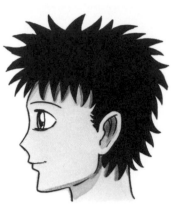

SHORT & SPIKY

Lots of short, soft spikes – this style is ideal for boys or girls.

LONG FRINGE BOWL

Bowl cut with spiky, asymmetric fringe falling down over the eyes. Useful for boys or girls.

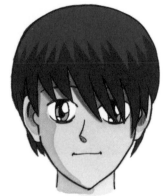
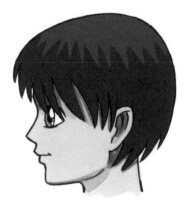

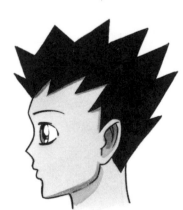

STIFF SPIKES

Angular, bold spikes, typical of a young male action hero.

LONG SHAGGY SPIKES

Short fringe over the eyes, long spikes on top of the head and long at the back. Ideal for boys or girls.

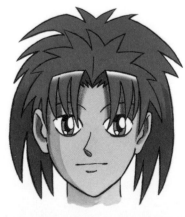
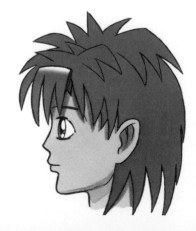

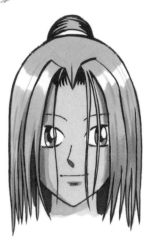
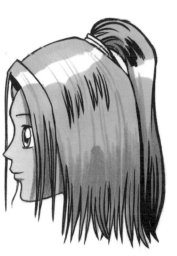

LONG & STRAIGHT WITH TOPKNOT

A long fringe overhanging the face with long straight hair and a topknot. A modern version of a traditional Japanese style. Could be used for boys or girls.

TWIN PONYTAILS

A common style for young female characters in school settings.

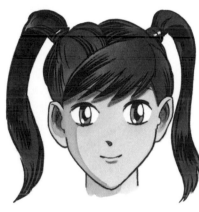

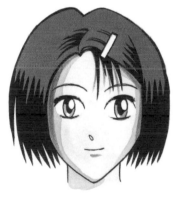
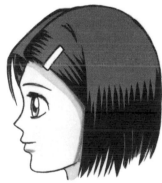

BOB WITH PARTING

Girl's standard short bob cut with a parting and a hair grip.

EYE-LEVEL FRINGE

Shoulder-length straight hair that flicks out at the bottom, and a straight, eye-level fringe.

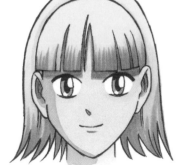
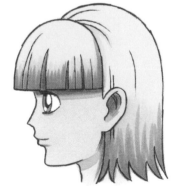

SHOW YOUR HANDS

The hand can be a tricky thing to get right, but once you understand the basic construction it's as easy as A-B-C.

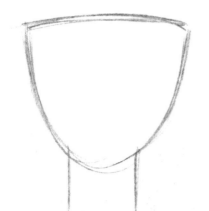

1

For a relaxed hand with the palm facing forwards, draw a shape a bit like a goblet or egg cup, with a thick stem. This will form the palm of your hand and the wrist.

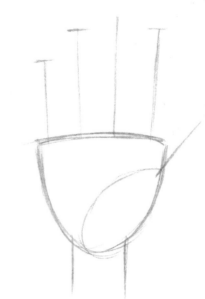

2

Draw four evenly spaced vertical lines to form the fingers. The index and third finger are the same length, the middle finger is longer and the little finger is shorter. Add an oval shape and a line at an angle to indicate the thumb.

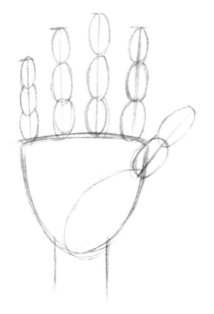

3

The fingers are separated by the knuckles into three roughly even segments. Draw these in as oval shapes. The thumb should have two equal-sized segments, as shown.

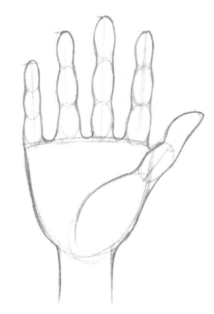

4

Outline your shape. Note how the outline flows in and out around the segments of each finger. The thumb is drawn sideways on, so is smoother on the outer face.

USEFUL ACTION HAND SHAPES

When drawing wireframes for other hand positions, use your own hands as a guide to help you visualize the joints.

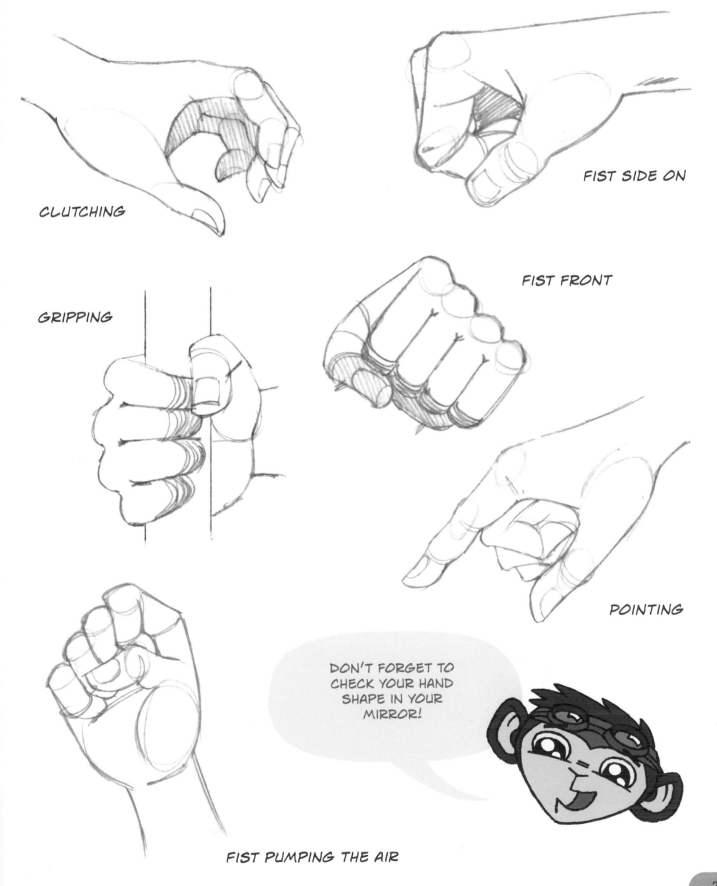

CLUTCHING

FIST SIDE ON

FIST FRONT

GRIPPING

POINTING

FIST PUMPING THE AIR

DON'T FORGET TO CHECK YOUR HAND SHAPE IN YOUR MIRROR!

FABRICATION...

Dynamic folds and ripples in costumes can make your figures come to life! Here are two different examples of how loose fabric works with the body: a sword-carrying prince and a sharp-suited businessman...

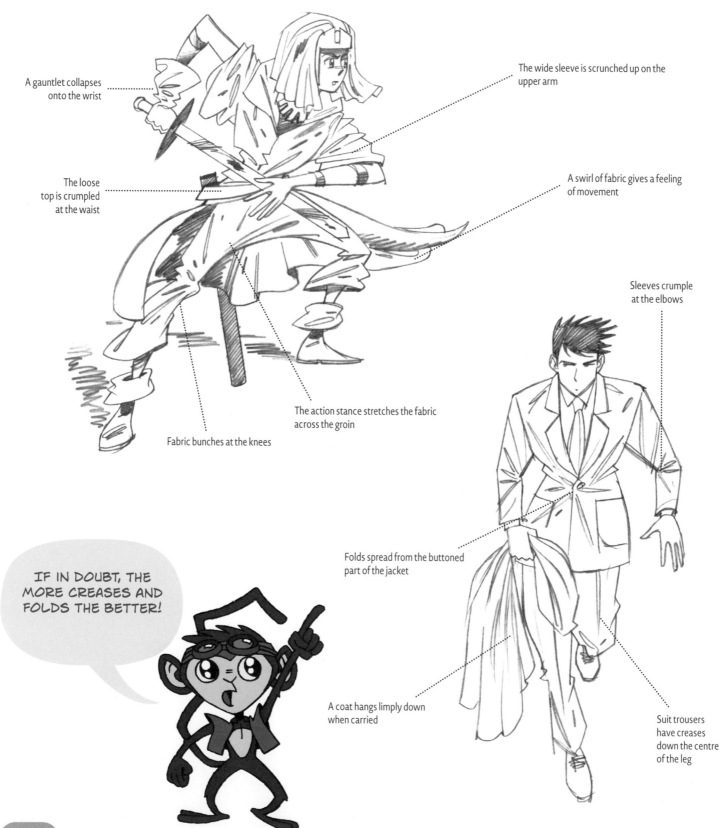

A gauntlet collapses onto the wrist
The wide sleeve is scrunched up on the upper arm
The loose top is crumpled at the waist
A swirl of fabric gives a feeling of movement
The action stance stretches the fabric across the groin
Fabric bunches at the knees

Sleeves crumple at the elbows
Folds spread from the buttoned part of the jacket
A coat hangs limply down when carried
Suit trousers have creases down the centre of the leg

IF IN DOUBT, THE MORE CREASES AND FOLDS THE BETTER!

EVERYDAY ITEMS

Here are some more folded and creased items of clothing. I've drawn them with a brush pen and added some loose grey marker to give some interest and depth. Practise lots of examples in different positions to build up your confidence.

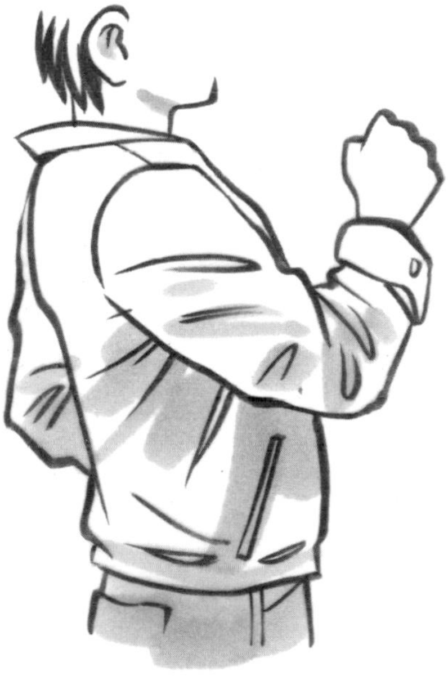

SHORT JACKET

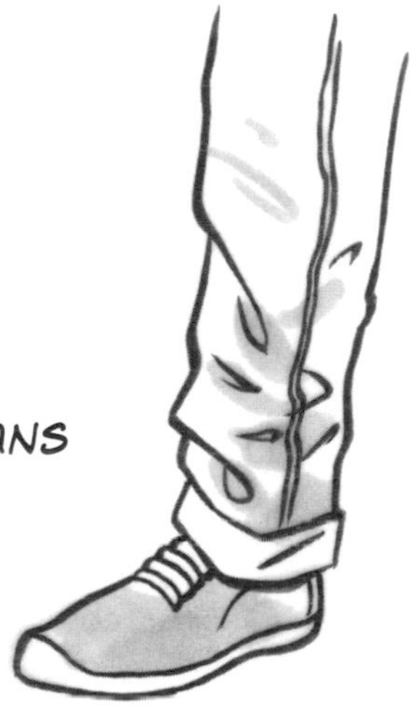

JEANS

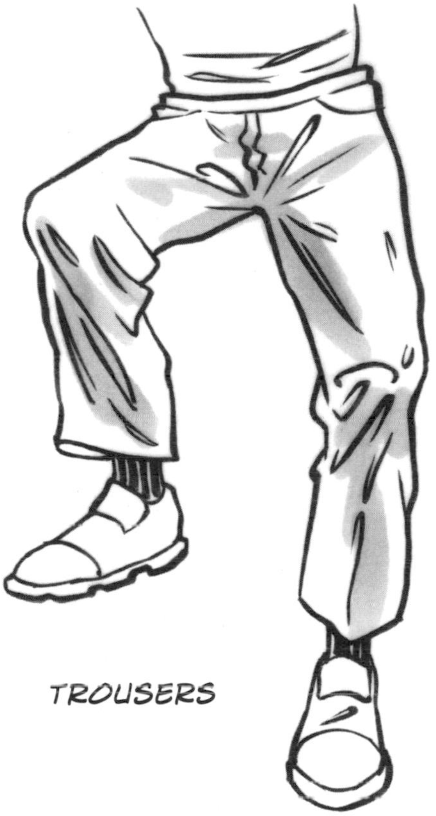

TROUSERS

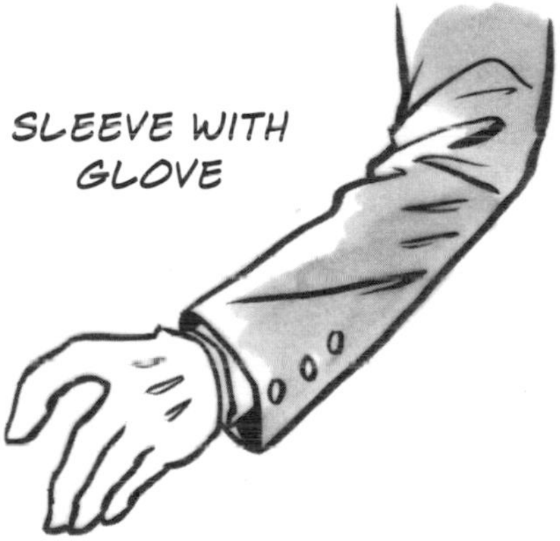

SLEEVE WITH GLOVE

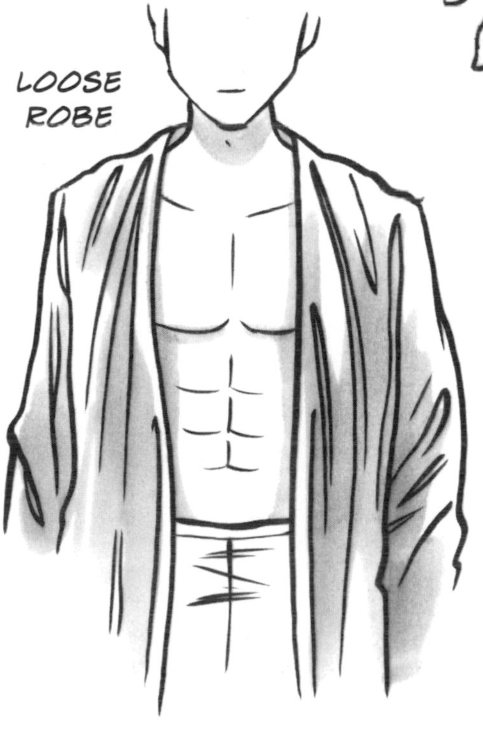

LOOSE ROBE

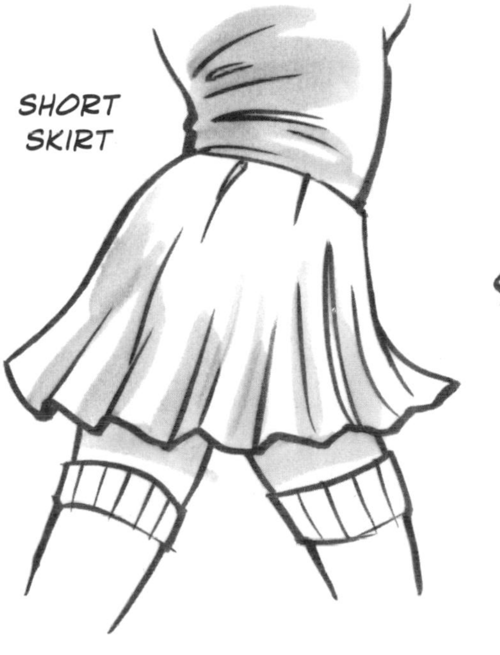

SHORT SKIRT

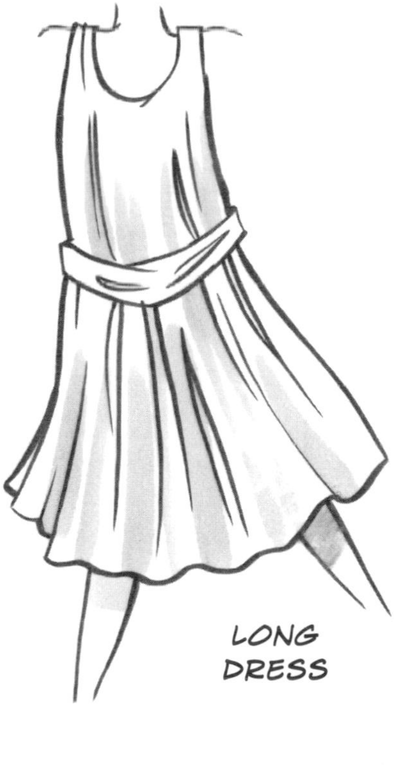

LONG DRESS

ACCESSORIZE!

As well as clothing and hair styles, you can use a whole variety of weird and wonderful accessories to individualize your action characters. These can be based on real objects or could be creations from your imagination. Here are a few examples to get you thinking...

WRISTBAND

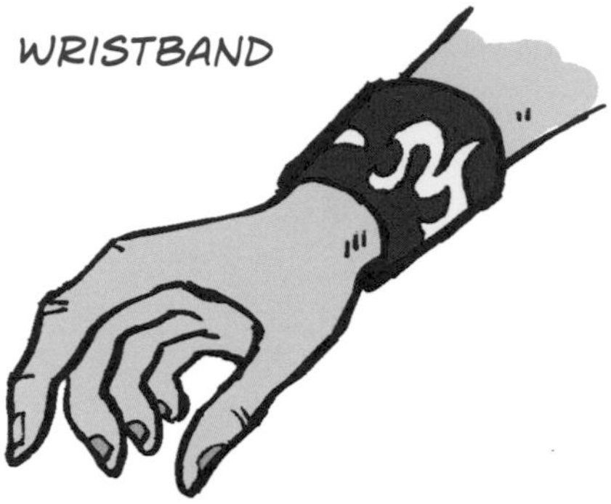

BEANIE HAT

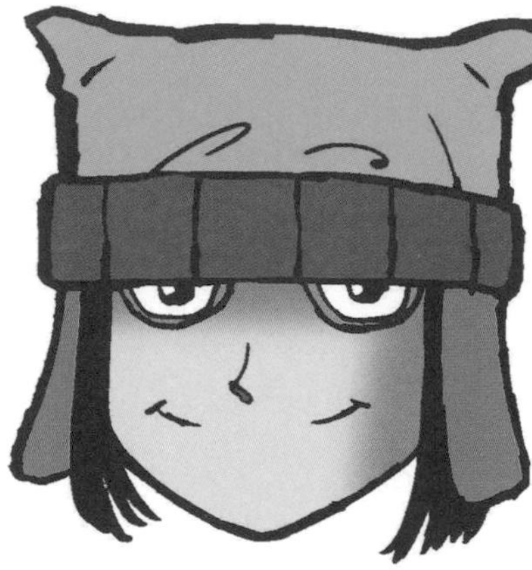

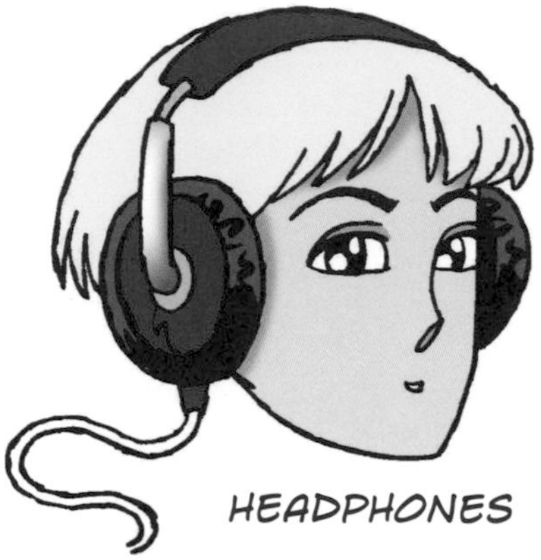

HEADPHONES

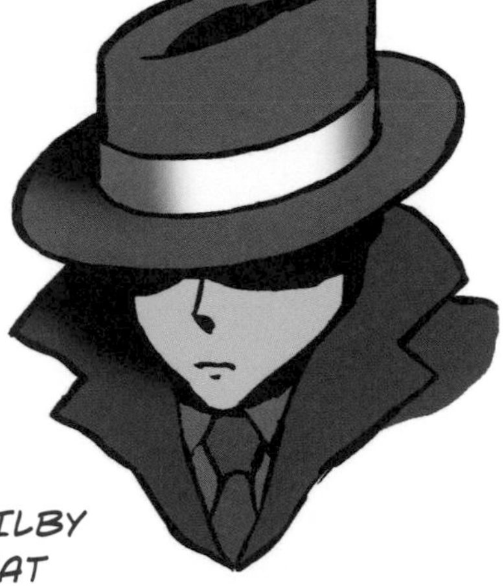

TRILBY HAT

GAUNTLET

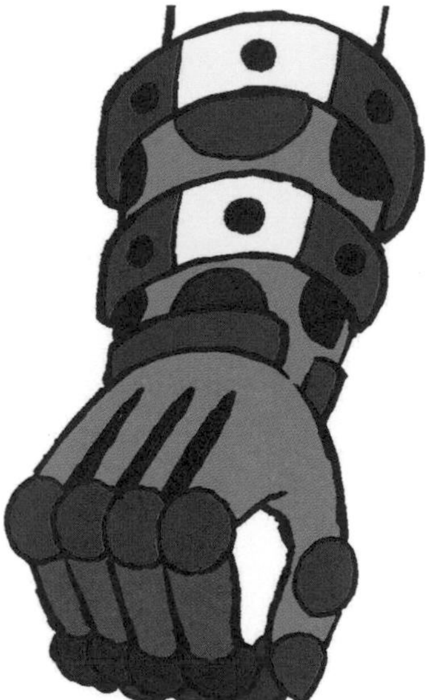

HELMET

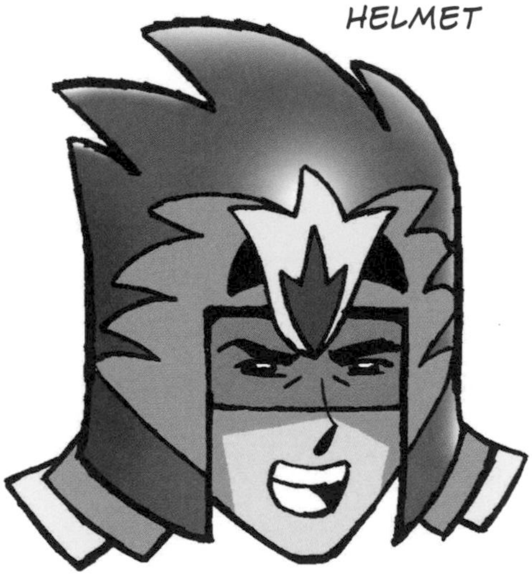

TECH BOOT

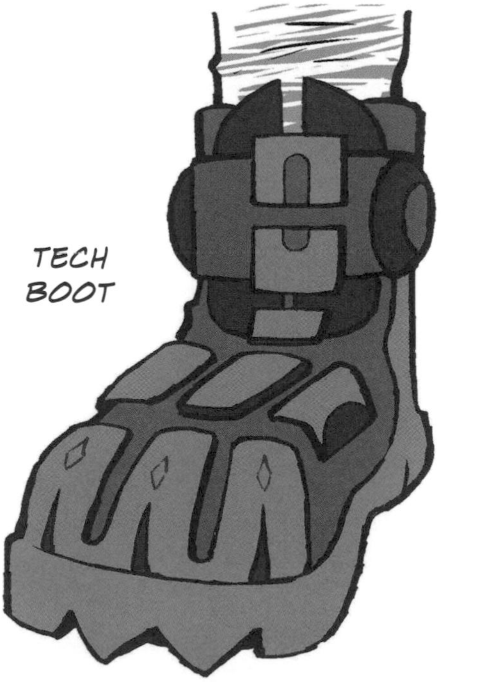

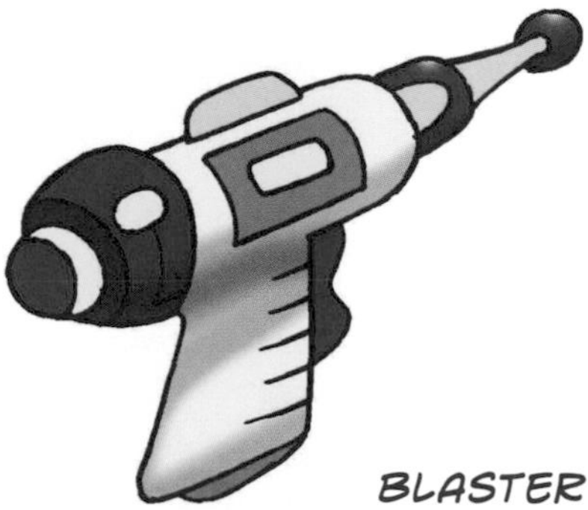

BLASTER

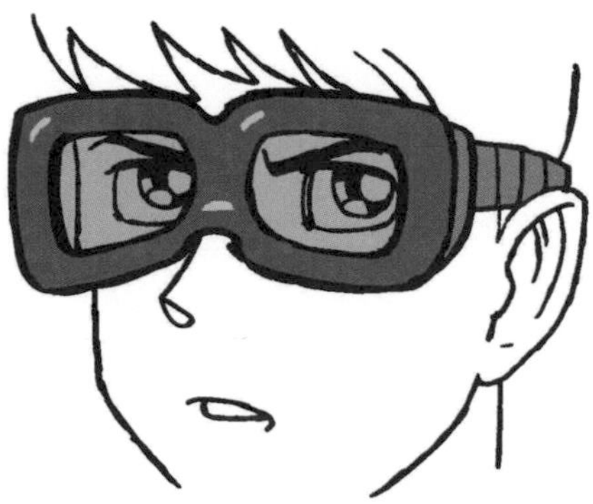

GOGGLES

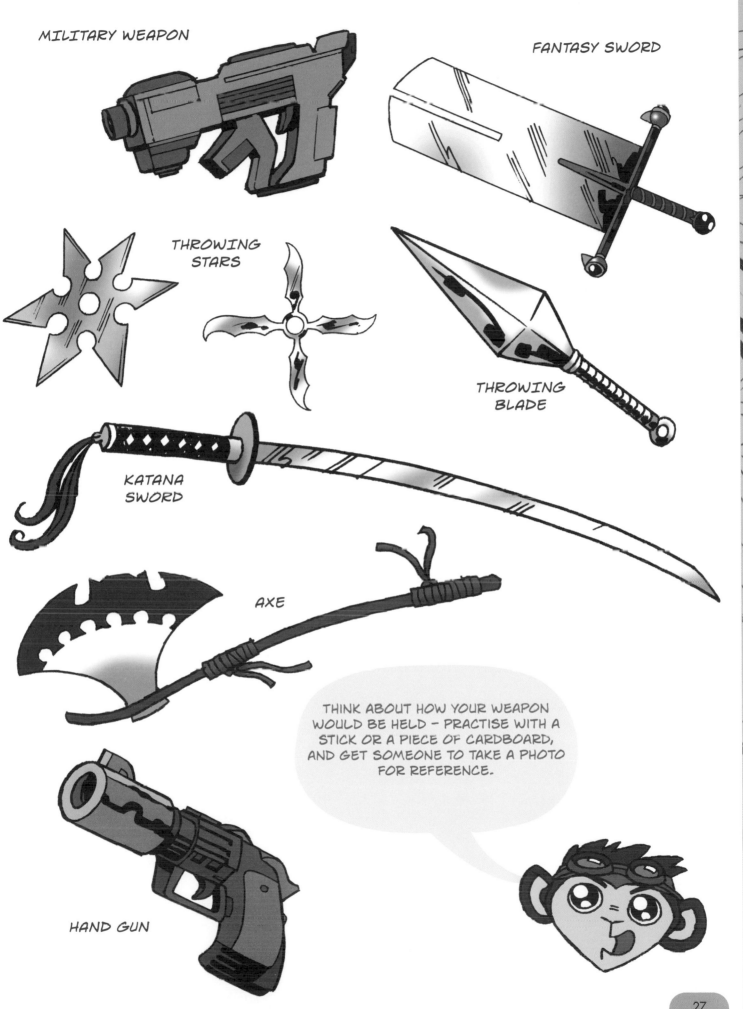

MILITARY WEAPON

FANTASY SWORD

THROWING STARS

THROWING BLADE

KATANA SWORD

AXE

THINK ABOUT HOW YOUR WEAPON WOULD BE HELD – PRACTISE WITH A STICK OR A PIECE OF CARDBOARD, AND GET SOMEONE TO TAKE A PHOTO FOR REFERENCE.

HAND GUN

LIGHT STUFF

Light and shade are vital parts of an action manga drawing, particularly as the vast majority of manga is printed in black and white. It's important to know where your light source is and what effect it has on your figure. Let's look at a basic character, like this swordsman, lit from four different directions.

CHANGING THE LIGHT SOURCE

Strong light from the right puts the left side into shadow

Light source

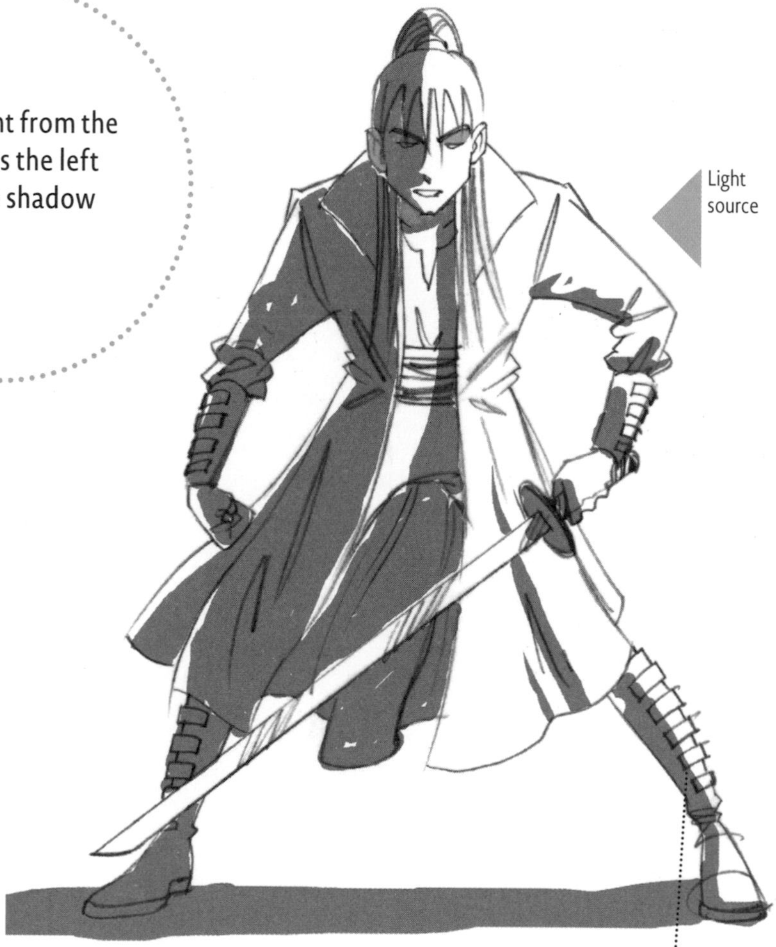

Legs are spread wide in a strong stance

Body is hunched forward, so neck is hidden

Light source

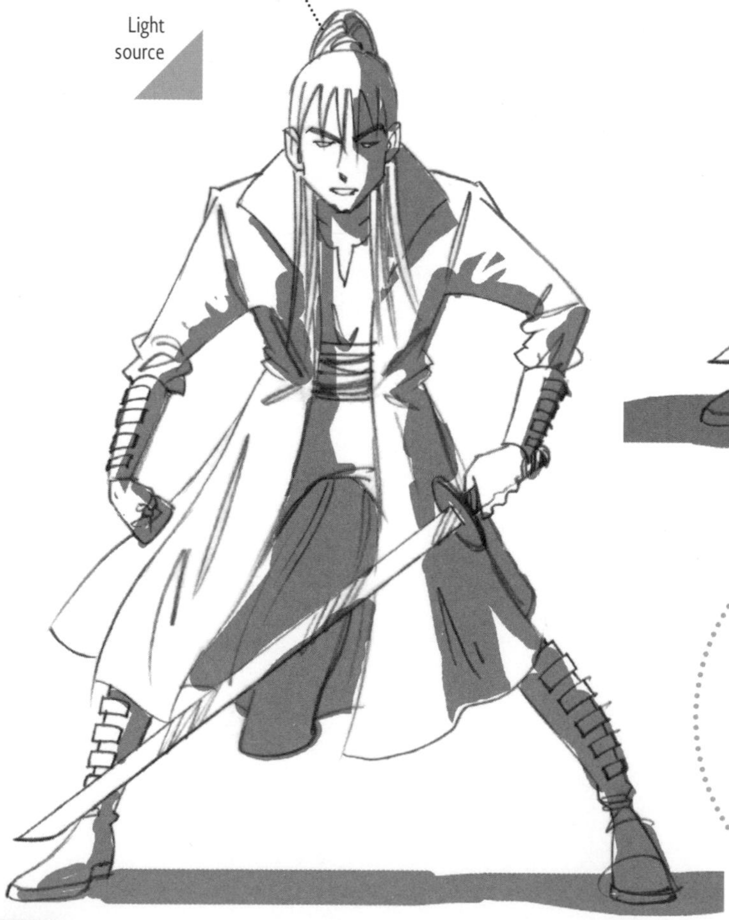

Moderate light from the left puts the right side into shadow

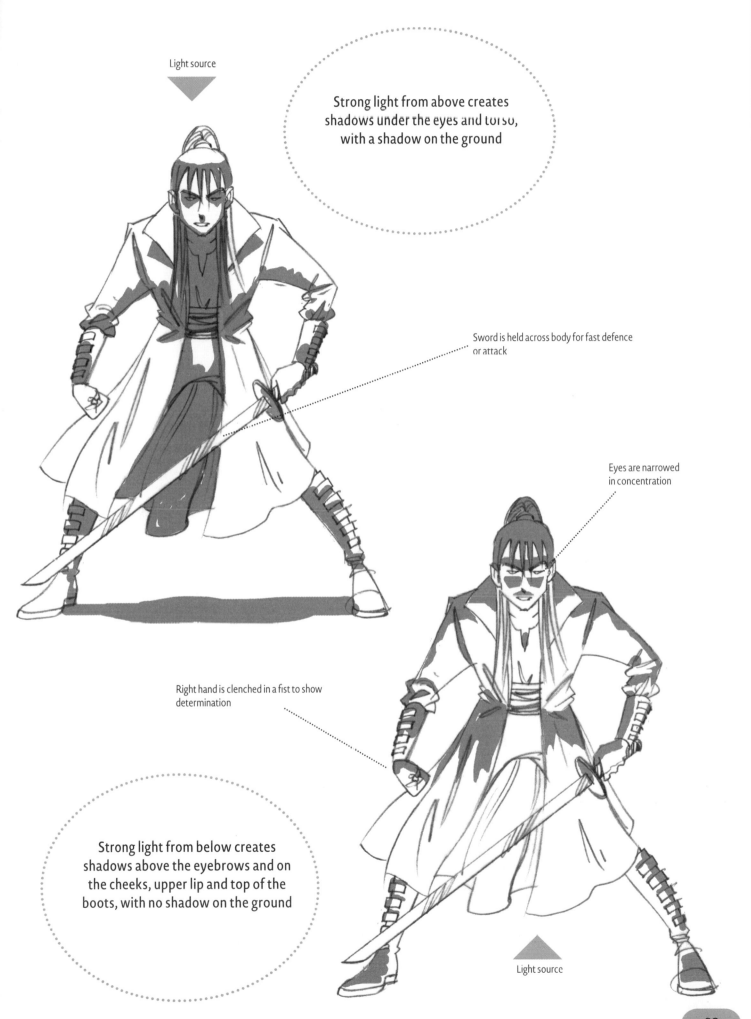

Light source

Strong light from above creates shadows under the eyes and torso, with a shadow on the ground

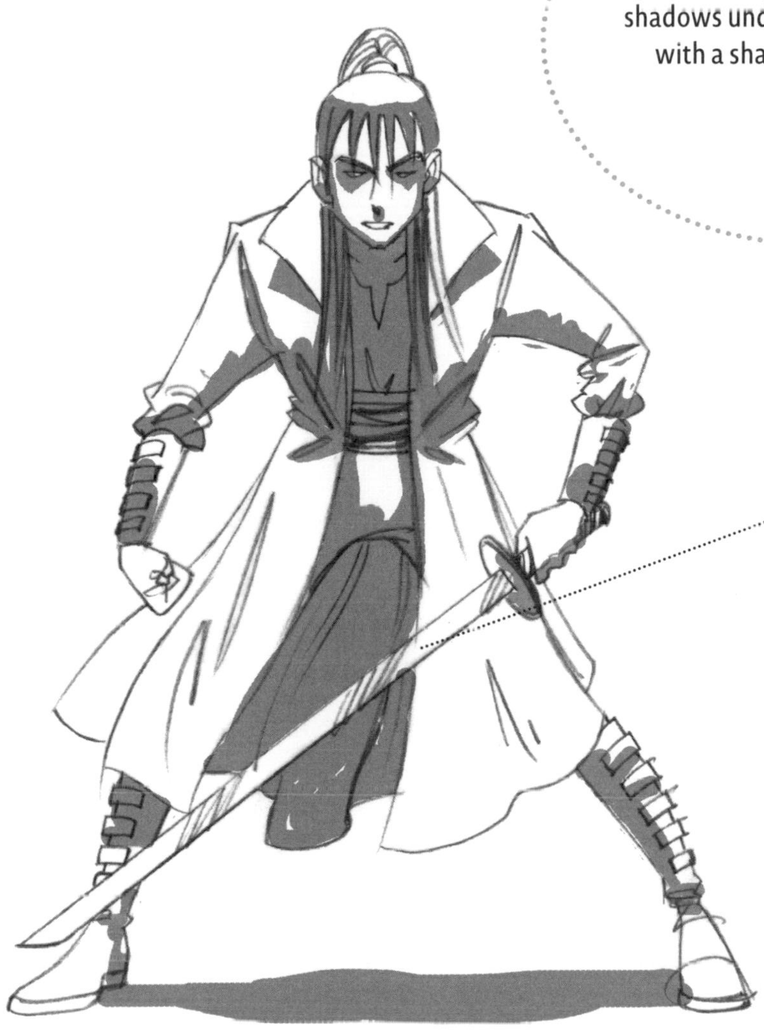

Sword is held across body for fast defence or attack

Eyes are narrowed in concentration

Right hand is clenched in a fist to show determination

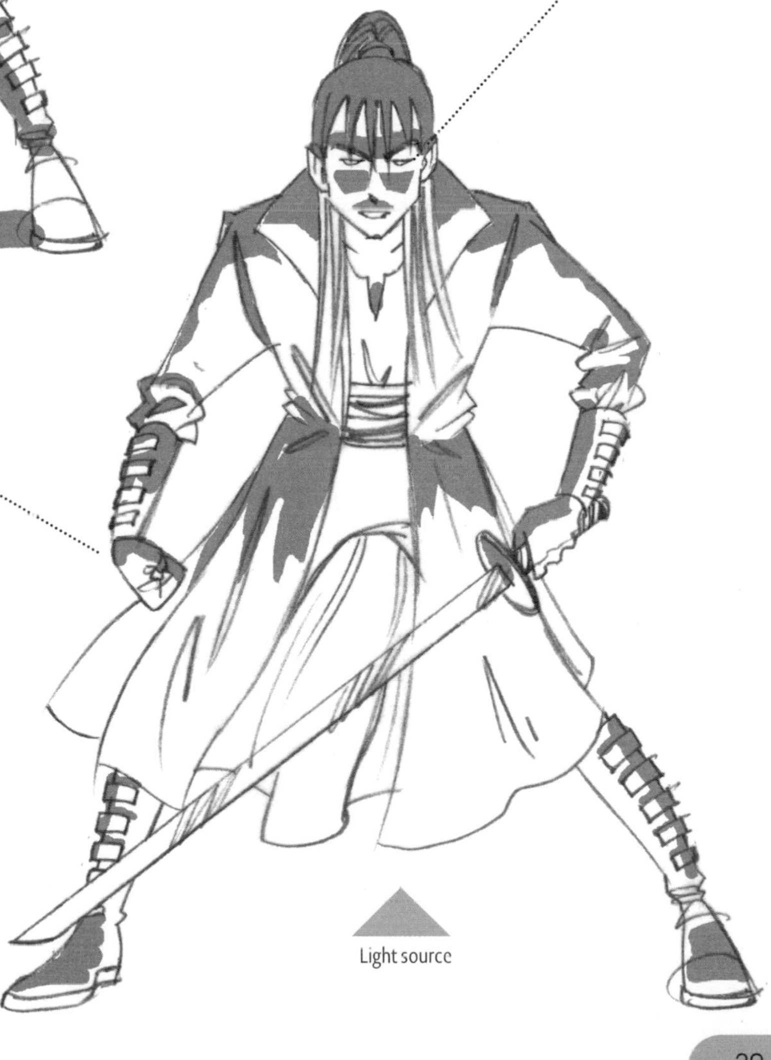

Strong light from below creates shadows above the eyebrows and on the cheeks, upper lip and top of the boots, with no shadow on the ground

Light source

SPECIAL FX...

Manga is full of graphic symbols and techniques that make it unique.
Here are a few of the most common, which you can add to your drawings.
It's a bit like having a special language that all manga readers learn to speak...

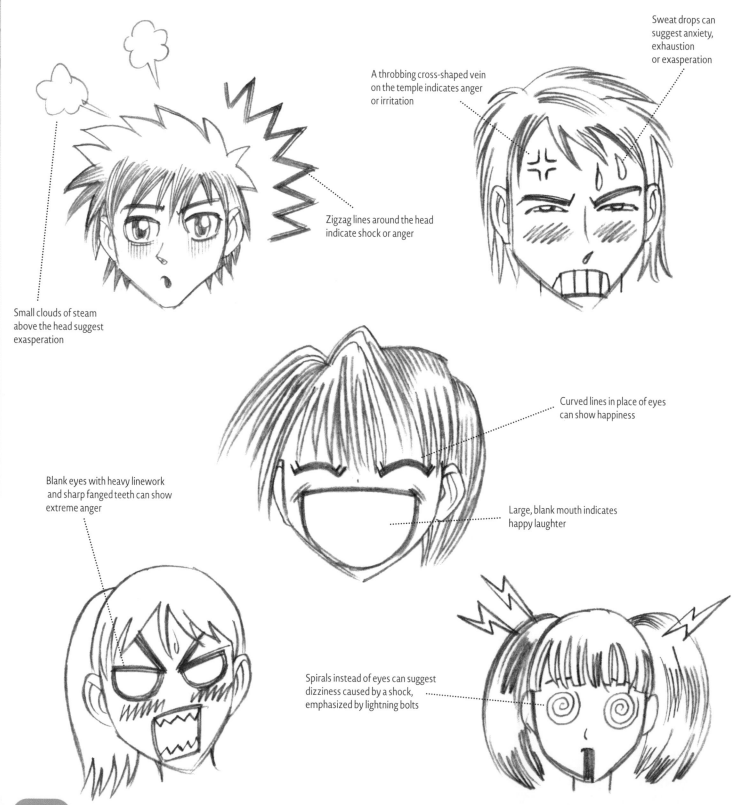

Sweat drops can suggest anxiety, exhaustion or exasperation

A throbbing cross-shaped vein on the temple indicates anger or irritation

Zigzag lines around the head indicate shock or anger

Small clouds of steam above the head suggest exasperation

Curved lines in place of eyes can show happiness

Blank eyes with heavy linework and sharp fanged teeth can show extreme anger

Large, blank mouth indicates happy laughter

Spirals instead of eyes can suggest dizziness caused by a shock, emphasized by lightning bolts

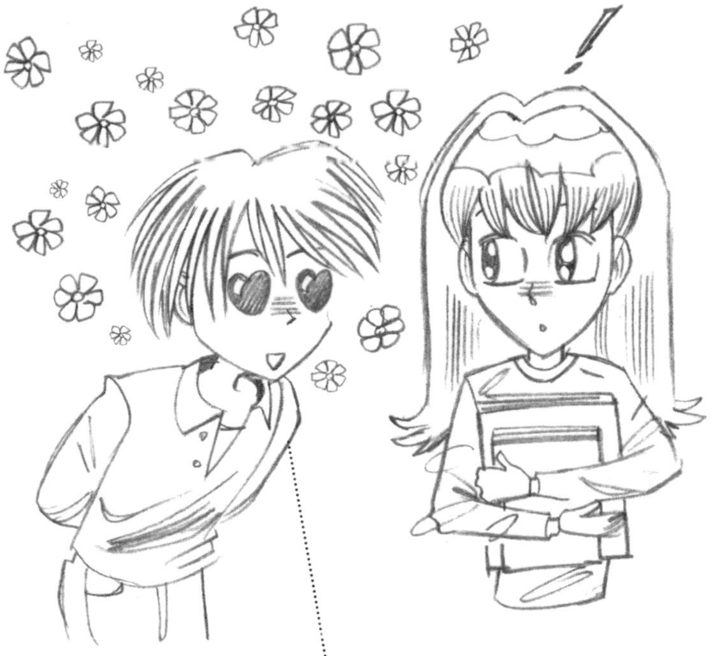
!

When a character is feeling romantic his or her eyes may turn into hearts and small flowers or petals may appear floating around them. In more traditional manga these can turn into full blossoms sprouting on branches

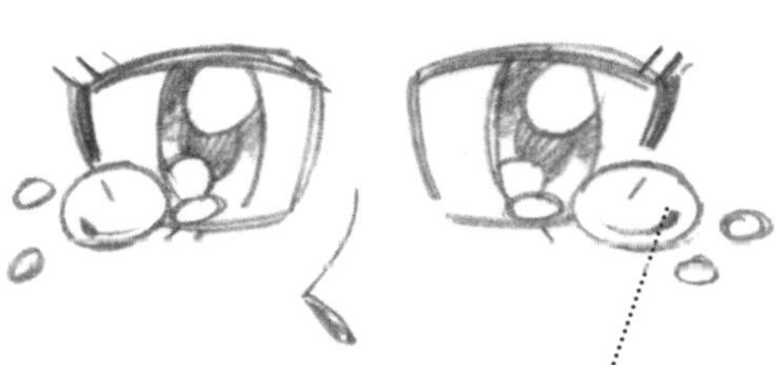

If someone is about to cry you may find these small circles appear in the bottom corners of their eyes

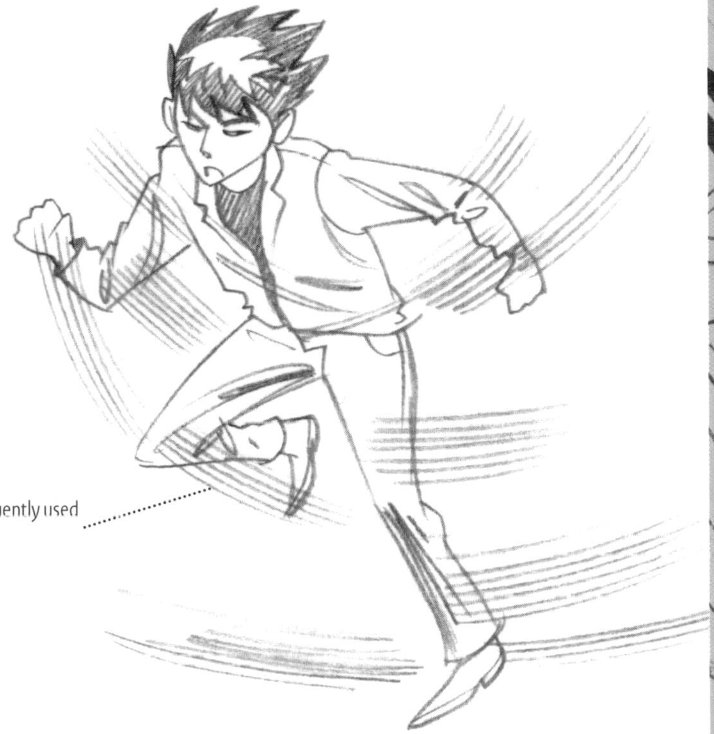

Speed lines are frequently used to show movement

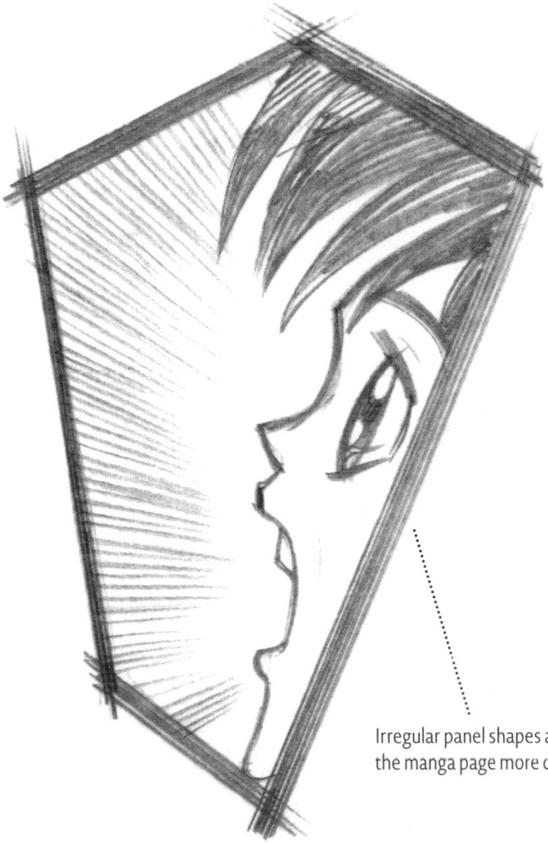

Irregular panel shapes are used to make the manga page more dynamic

A variety of speech and sound bubbles can be used for exclamations, thoughts and sound effects

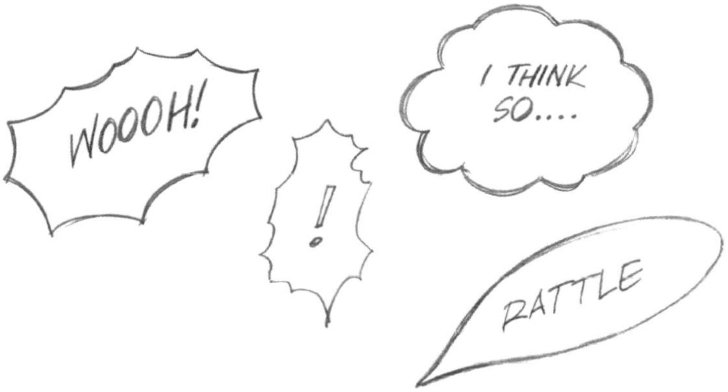
WOOOH!
I THINK SO....
!
RATTLE

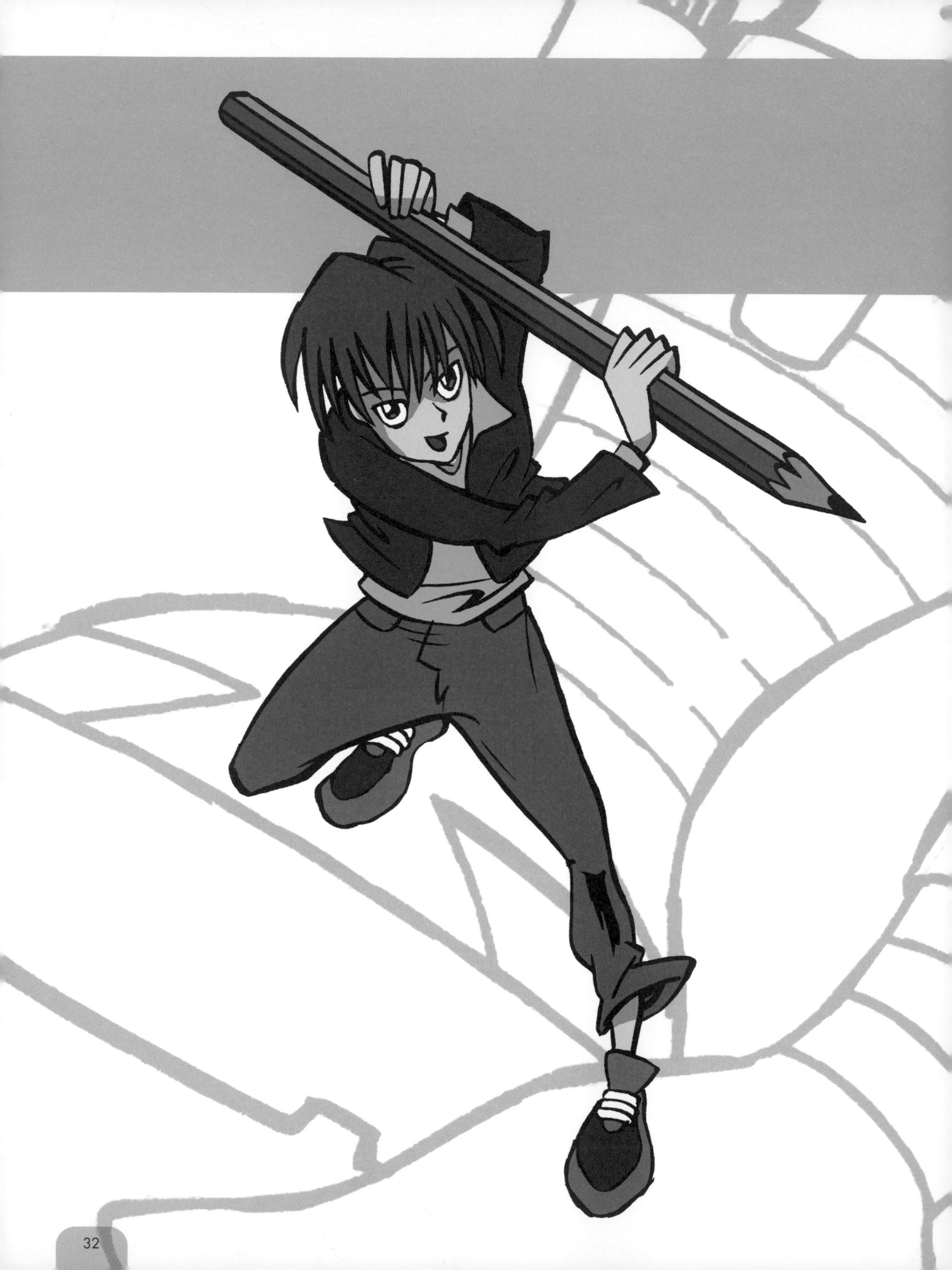

LET'S DRAW!

The first rule of drawing is that you must not be afraid to MAKE MISTAKES. With every error comes learning, and with learning comes improvement. When you begin your drawing, it's a good idea to sketch loosely in pencil. The lighter your initial sketch the better – this will make it easier to erase lines at a later stage. Build your drawing slowly, using stronger lines as you find the shapes you're happy with.

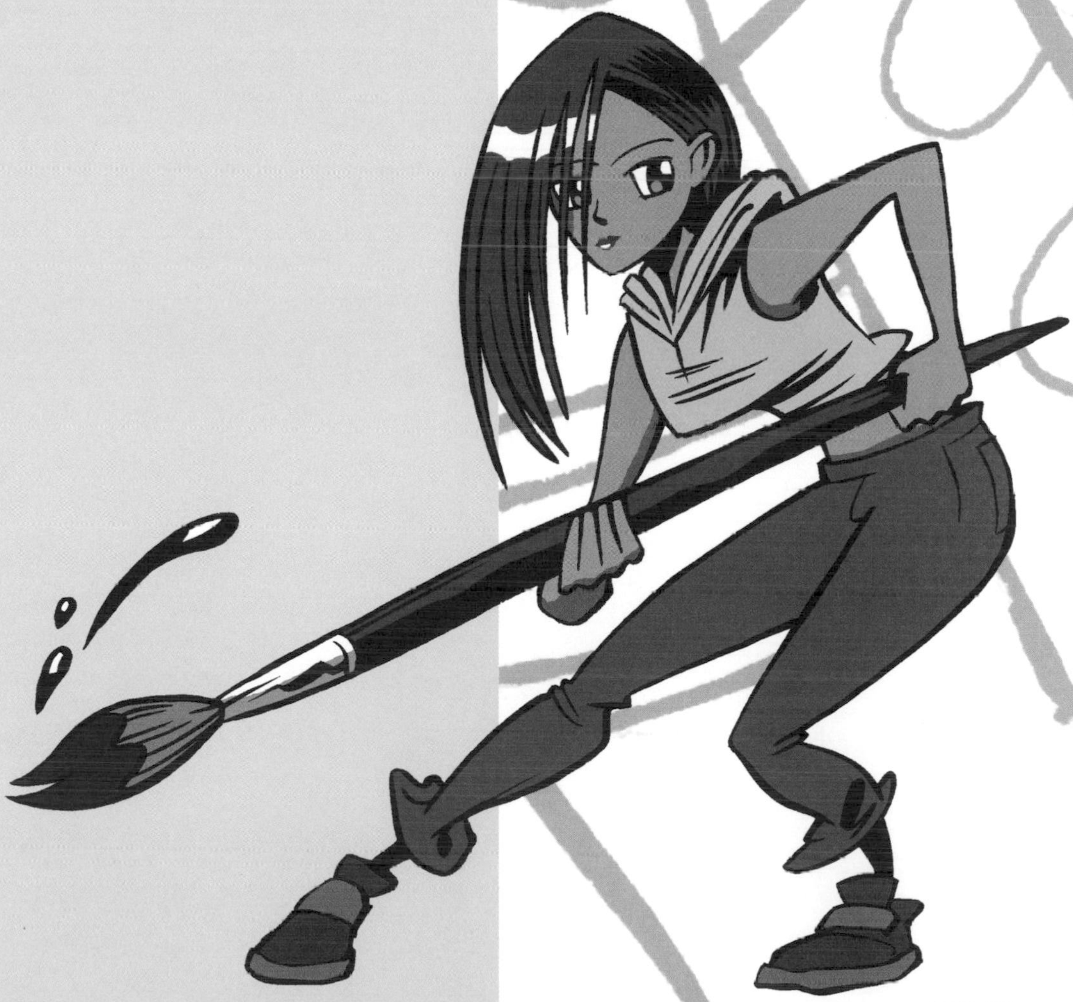

LEAPING PUNCH

A FUTURISTIC HERO GIVES A GIANT OGRE A FLYING UPPERCUT!

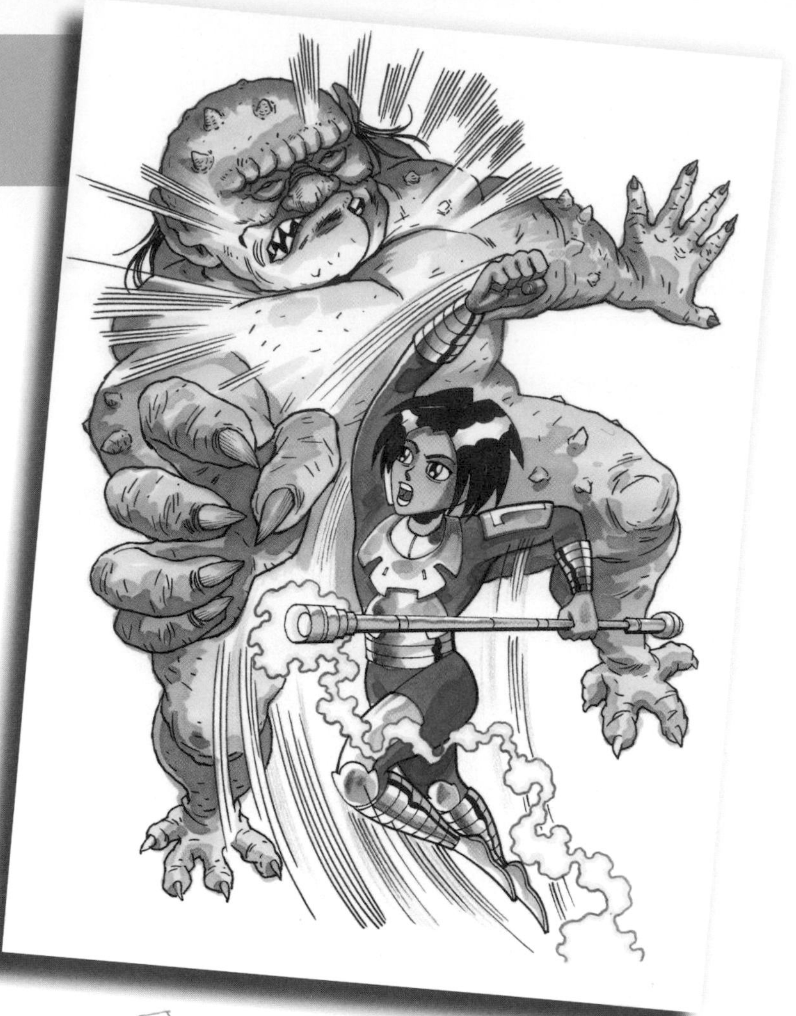

STAGE 1

Start with a wireframe sketch of a leaping hero character, in the bottom-right quarter of the page.

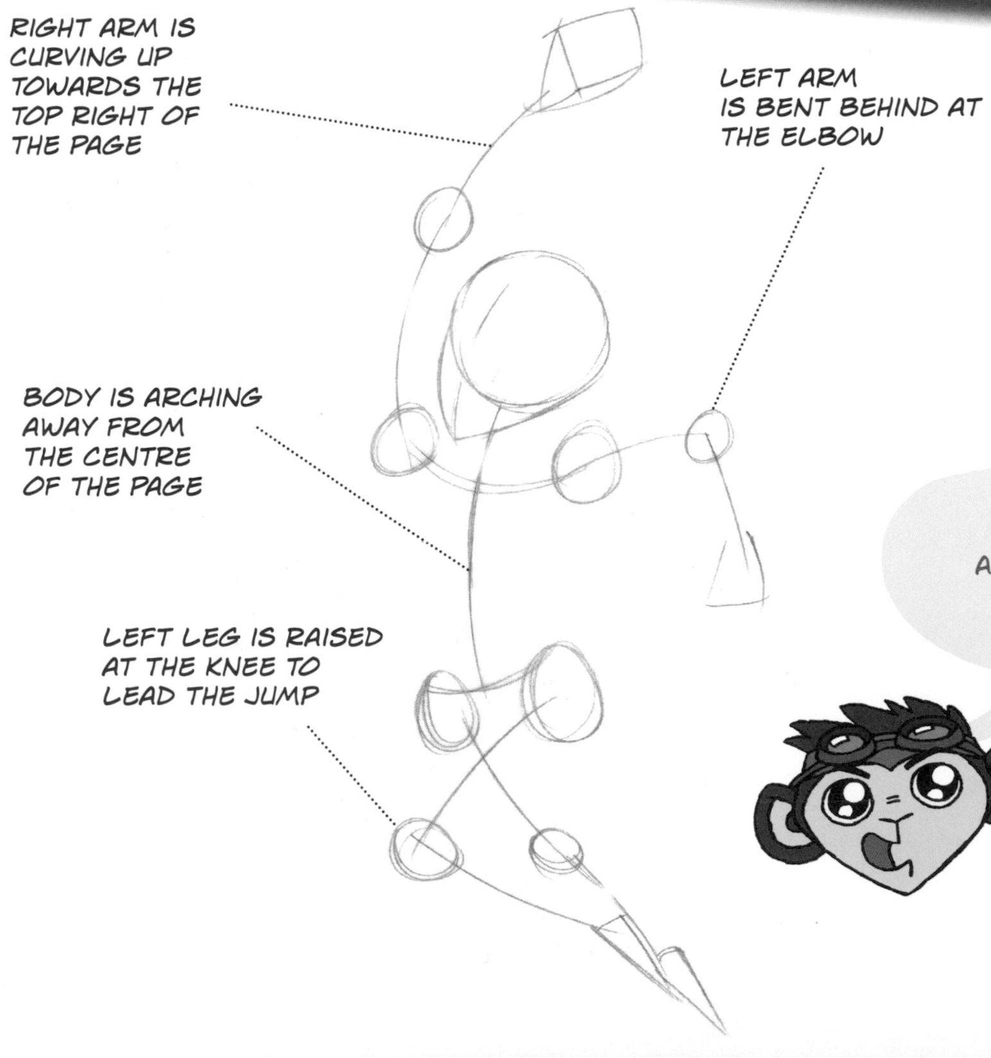
RIGHT ARM IS CURVING UP TOWARDS THE TOP RIGHT OF THE PAGE
LEFT ARM IS BENT BEHIND AT THE ELBOW
BODY IS ARCHING AWAY FROM THE CENTRE OF THE PAGE
LEFT LEG IS RAISED AT THE KNEE TO LEAD THE JUMP

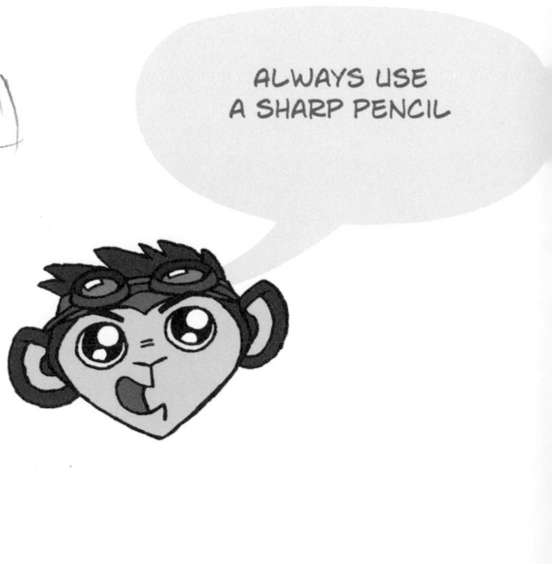
ALWAYS USE A SHARP PENCIL

STAGE 2

Outline the figure – use curving lines to create the shapes of the muscles. Add in facial features and hair.

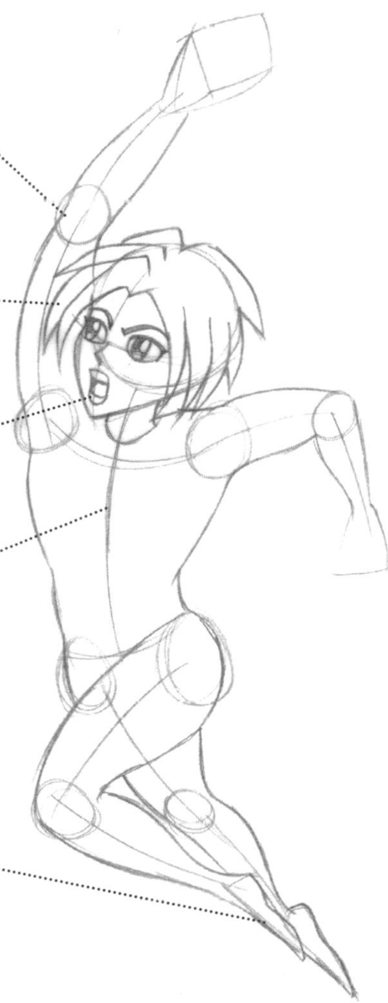
ARMS SHOULD BE THICKER AT THE FOREARM AND UPPER ARM AND THINNER AT THE WRIST AND ELBOW
HAIR IS FORMED OF LONG SPIKES THAT FALL DOWN FROM A CENTRE PARTING
MOUTH IS OPEN IN AN ATTACKING YELL
CHEST IS BROAD TO CONTAIN RIBCAGE, CURVING IN AT THE WAIST
FEET POINT DOWN TO INDICATE UPWARDS MOVEMENT

STAGE 3

Draw in a battle costume, the hands and a power staff.

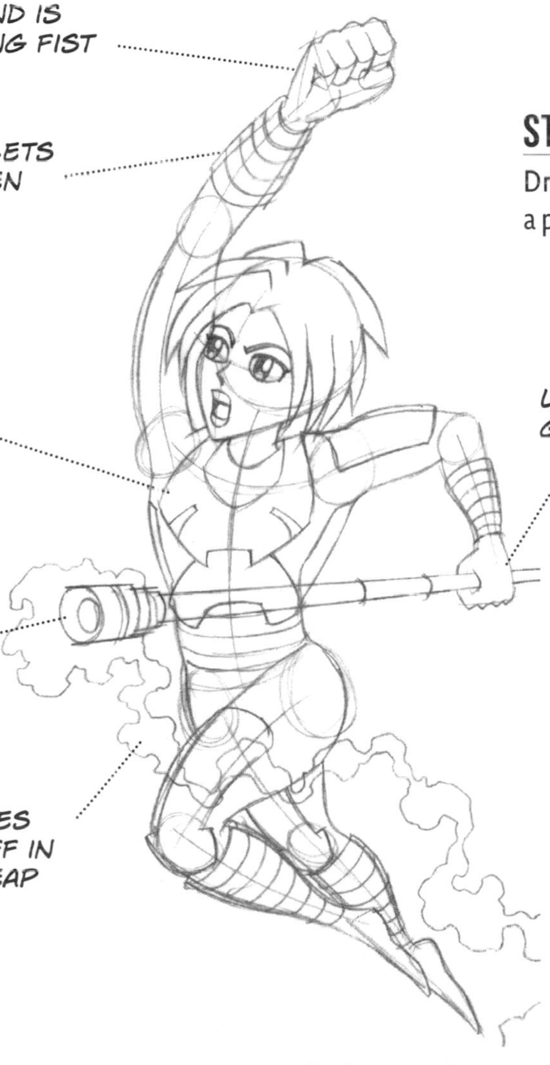
RIGHT HAND IS A PUNCHING FIST
LONG BRACELETS TO STRENGTHEN PUNCH POWER
ARMOURED BREAST PLATE
LEFT HAND IS A GRIPPING FIST
STAFF HAS A LARGE HEAD TO FOCUS ENERGY
ENERGY CRACKLES AWAY FROM STAFF IN DIRECTION OF LEAP

STAGE 4

Draw a wireframe for a large ogre from the centre to the top-left of the page.

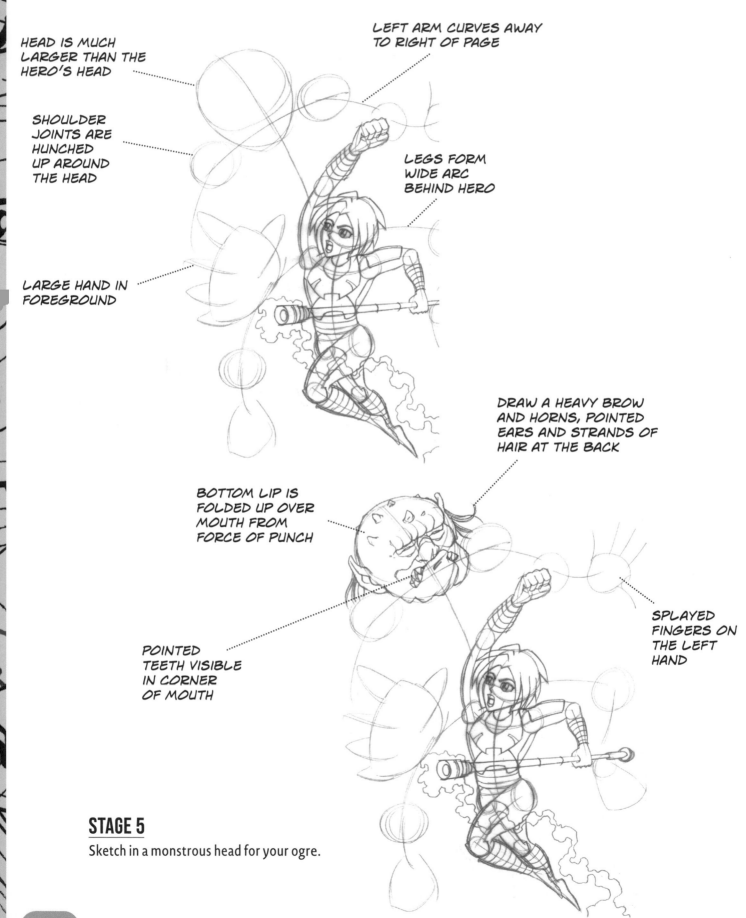

HEAD IS MUCH LARGER THAN THE HERO'S HEAD
LEFT ARM CURVES AWAY TO RIGHT OF PAGE
SHOULDER JOINTS ARE HUNCHED UP AROUND THE HEAD
LEGS FORM WIDE ARC BEHIND HERO
LARGE HAND IN FOREGROUND

DRAW A HEAVY BROW AND HORNS, POINTED EARS AND STRANDS OF HAIR AT THE BACK
BOTTOM LIP IS FOLDED UP OVER MOUTH FROM FORCE OF PUNCH
SPLAYED FINGERS ON THE LEFT HAND
POINTED TEETH VISIBLE IN CORNER OF MOUTH

STAGE 5

Sketch in a monstrous head for your ogre.

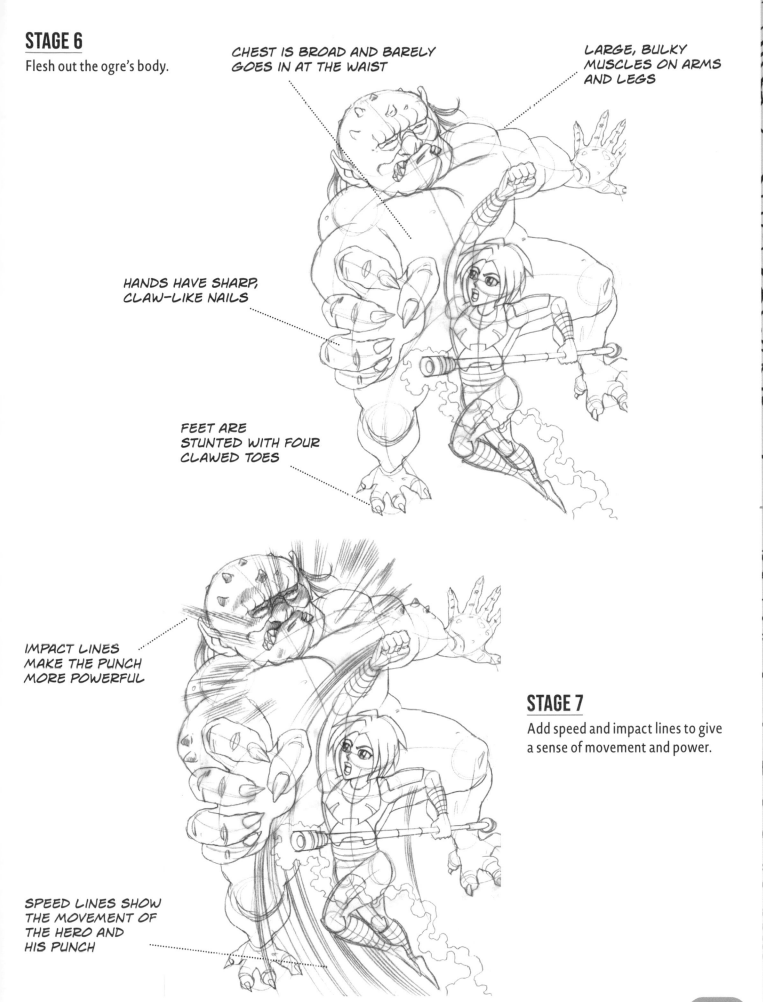

STAGE 6

Flesh out the ogre's body.

CHEST IS BROAD AND BARELY GOES IN AT THE WAIST
LARGE, BULKY MUSCLES ON ARMS AND LEGS
HANDS HAVE SHARP, CLAW-LIKE NAILS
FEET ARE STUNTED WITH FOUR CLAWED TOES

STAGE 7

Add speed and impact lines to give a sense of movement and power.

IMPACT LINES MAKE THE PUNCH MORE POWERFUL
SPEED LINES SHOW THE MOVEMENT OF THE HERO AND HIS PUNCH

STAGE 8

Ink your drawing.

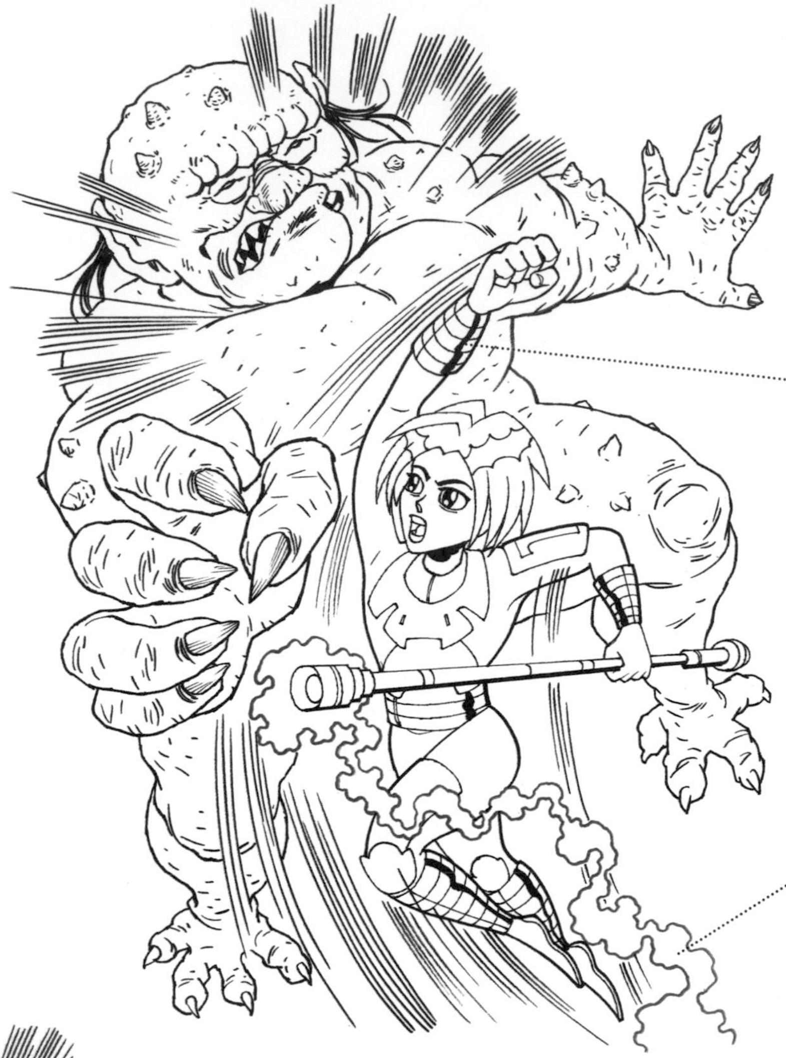
FILL IN AREAS OF SOLID BLACK
USE A BLUE PEN TO OUTLINE THE ENERGY FLOW

STAGE 9

Colour your hero with blue, grey and flesh-coloured markers, and colour your ogre with dull shades of beige and grey. Add shading using darker tones.

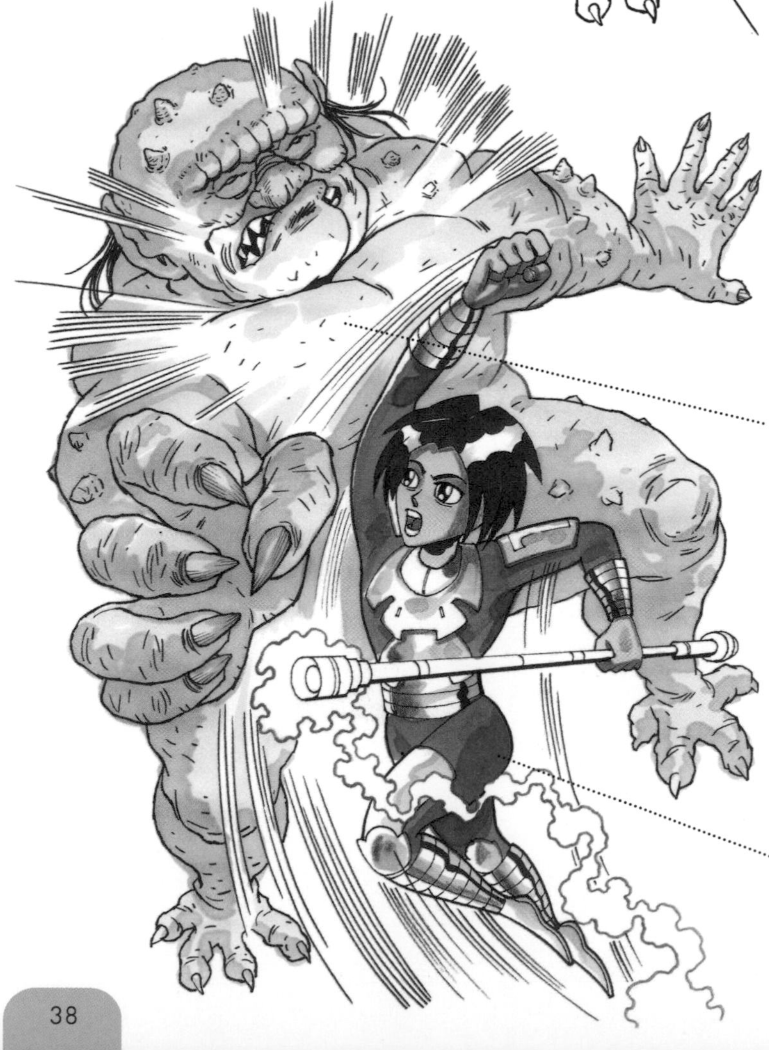
LEAVE THE AREA AROUND THE PUNCH WHITE TO DRAW THE EYE OF THE VIEWER
USE DARKER TINTS OF THE MAIN COLOURS TO ADD SHADING

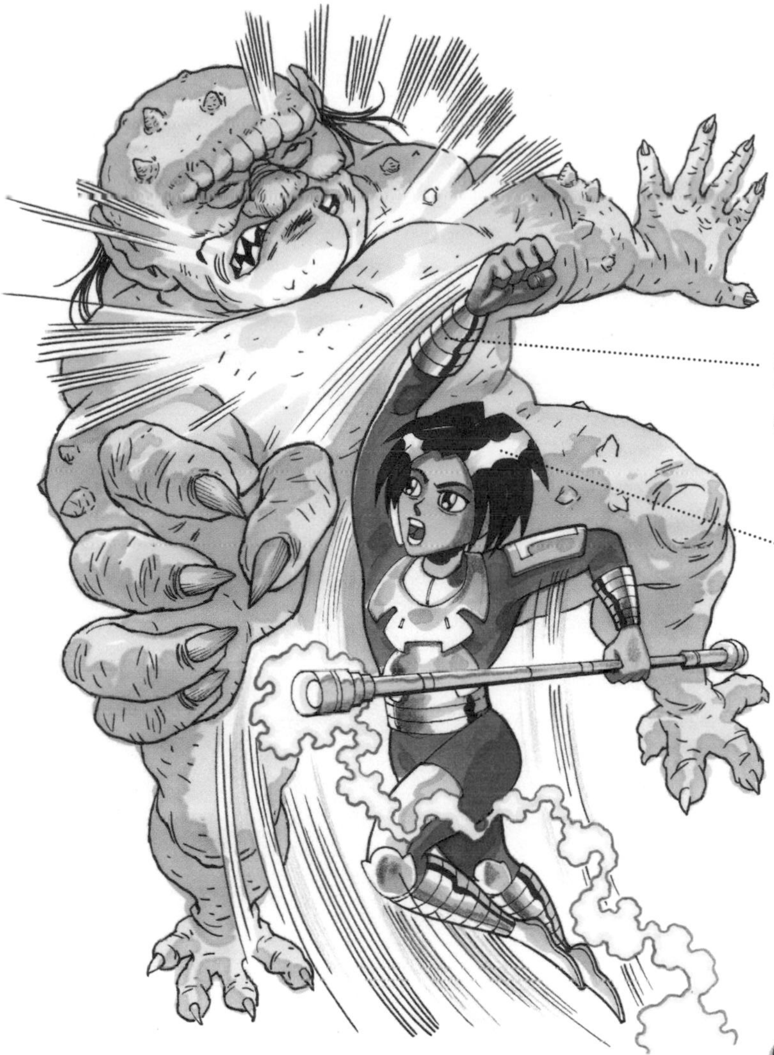

USE PALE BLUE TO REFLECT THE COLOUR OF THE HERO'S COSTUME
LEAVE WHITE AREAS AS HIGHLIGHTS

STAGE 10

Colour the power staff bright gold-yellow and the outline of the energy crackle pale blue. Add some faint colour to your speed lines.

STAGE 11

Finish by using dark greys to add shade to your ogre.

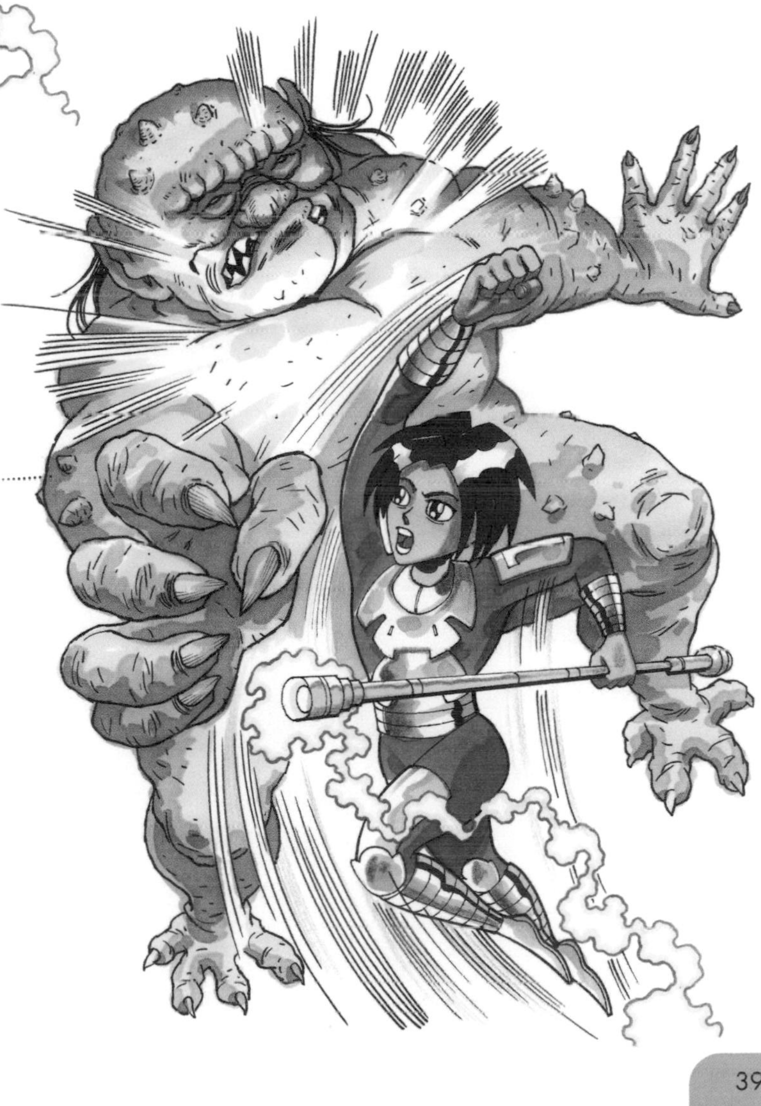

SHADOWS ON THE TOP OF THE ARMS AND HEAD PUSH THE VIEWER'S EYE TO THE IMPACT AREA

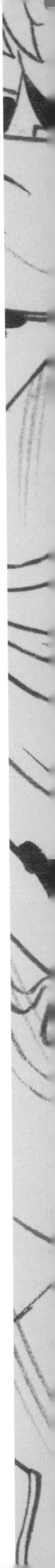

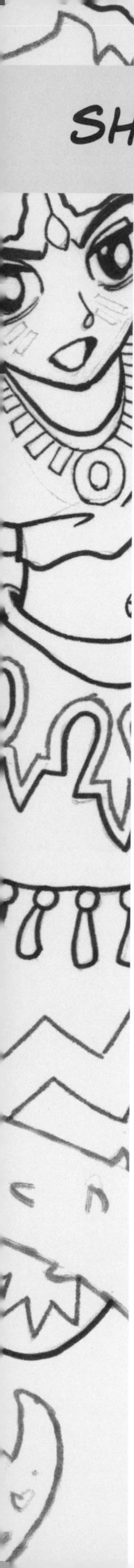

SHAMAN SPELL

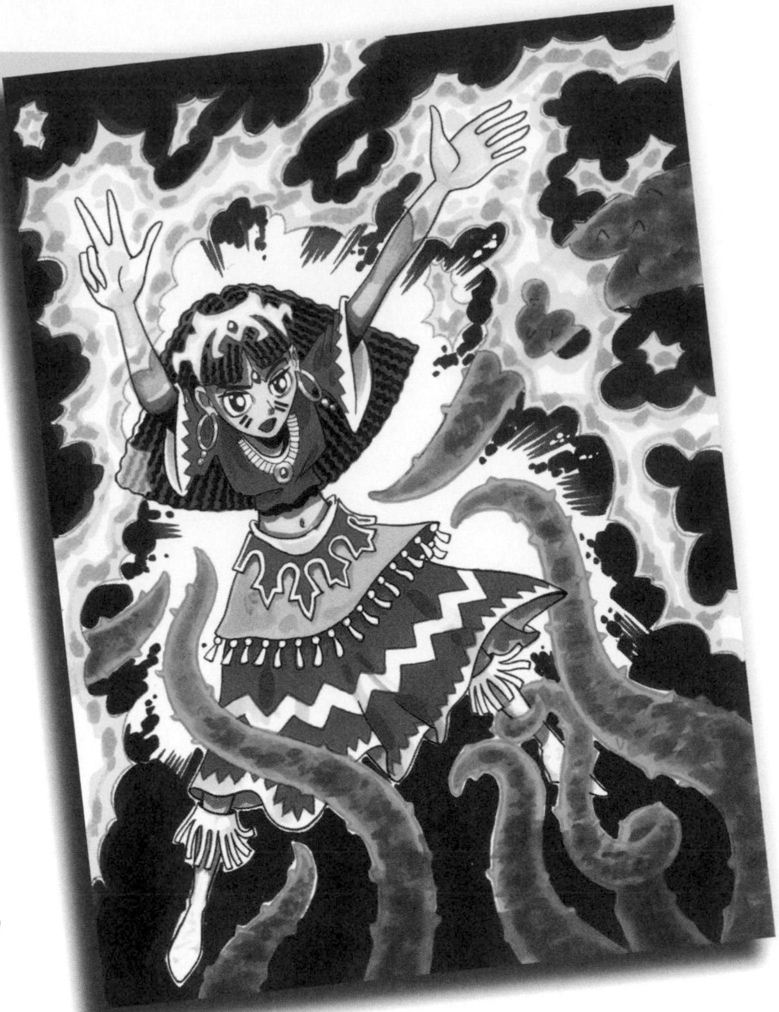

A MAGICAL SHAMAN GIRL DEFENDS HERSELF AGAINST A TENTACLED ATTACK!

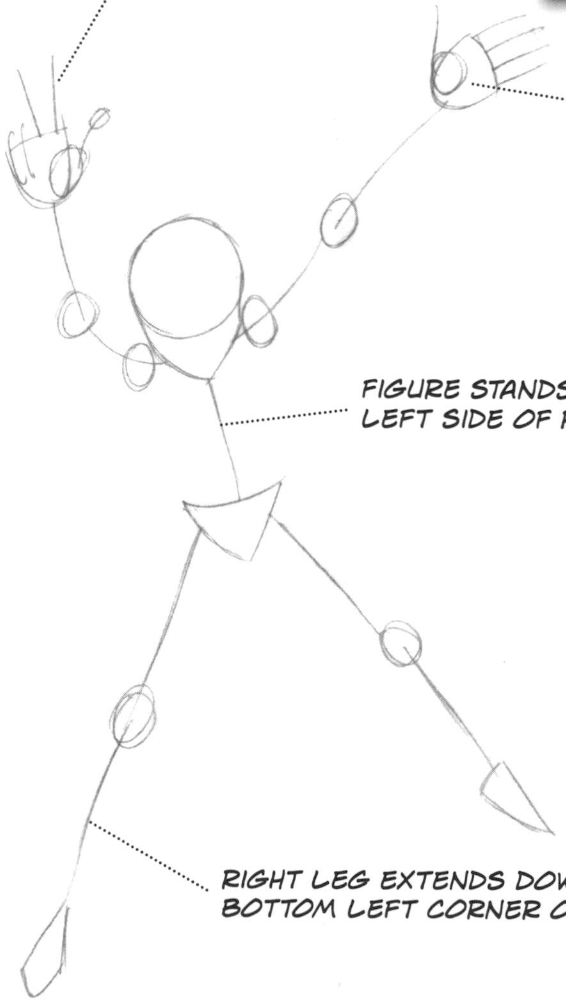

RIGHT HAND HAS INDEX AND SECOND FINGERS UP, WITH THIRD AND FOURTH FINGERS DOWN – A COMMON MANGA GESTURE
LEFT HAND IS OPEN WITH PALM FACING OUT
FIGURE STANDS TO THE LEFT SIDE OF PAGE
RIGHT LEG EXTENDS DOWN INTO BOTTOM LEFT CORNER OF PAGE

STAGE 1

Start with a wireframe for your figure, with legs apart and arms outstretched. The viewpoint is above and to the left, so the neck will be hidden from view.

STAGE 2

Flesh out your figure with smooth, curving lines.

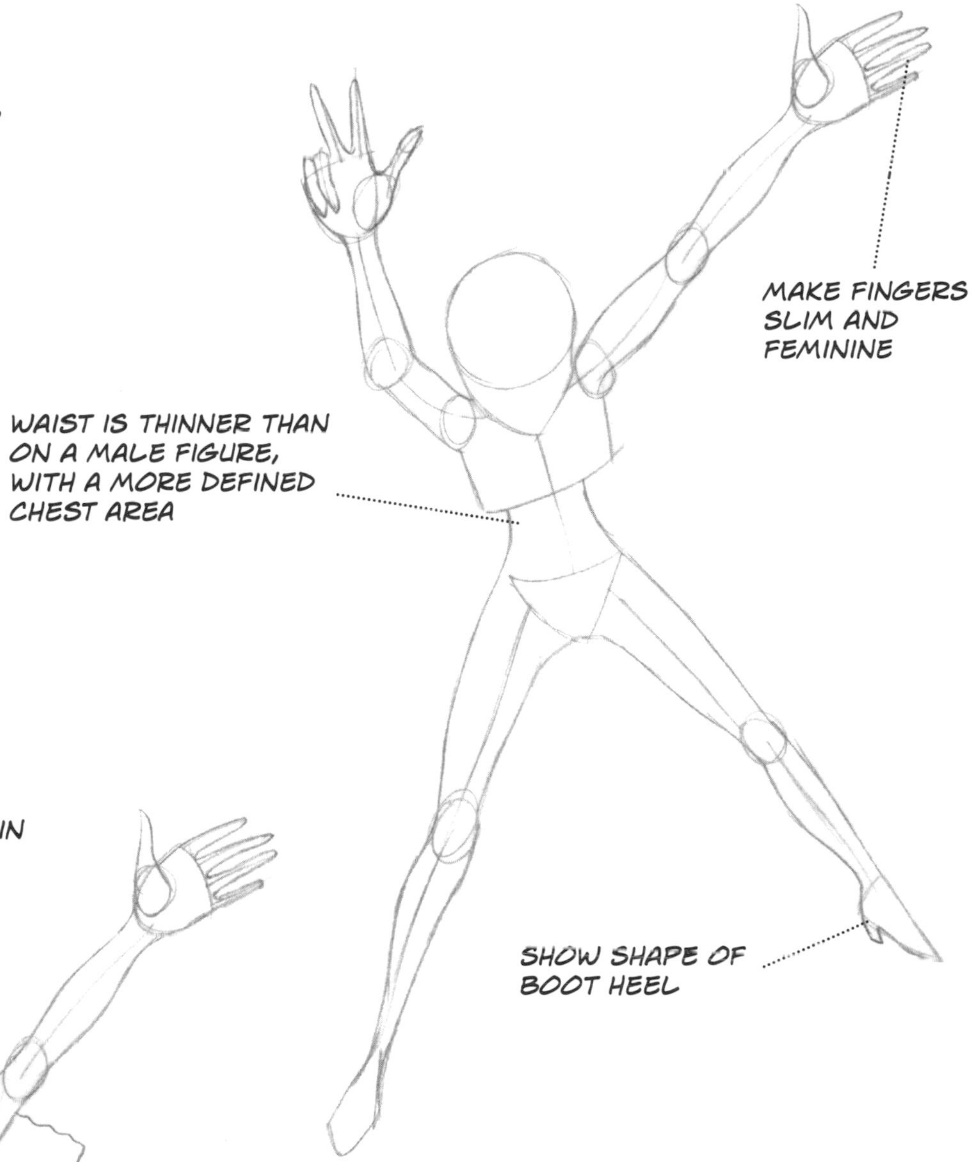
MAKE FINGERS SLIM AND FEMININE
WAIST IS THINNER THAN ON A MALE FIGURE, WITH A MORE DEFINED CHEST AREA
SHOW SHAPE OF BOOT HEEL

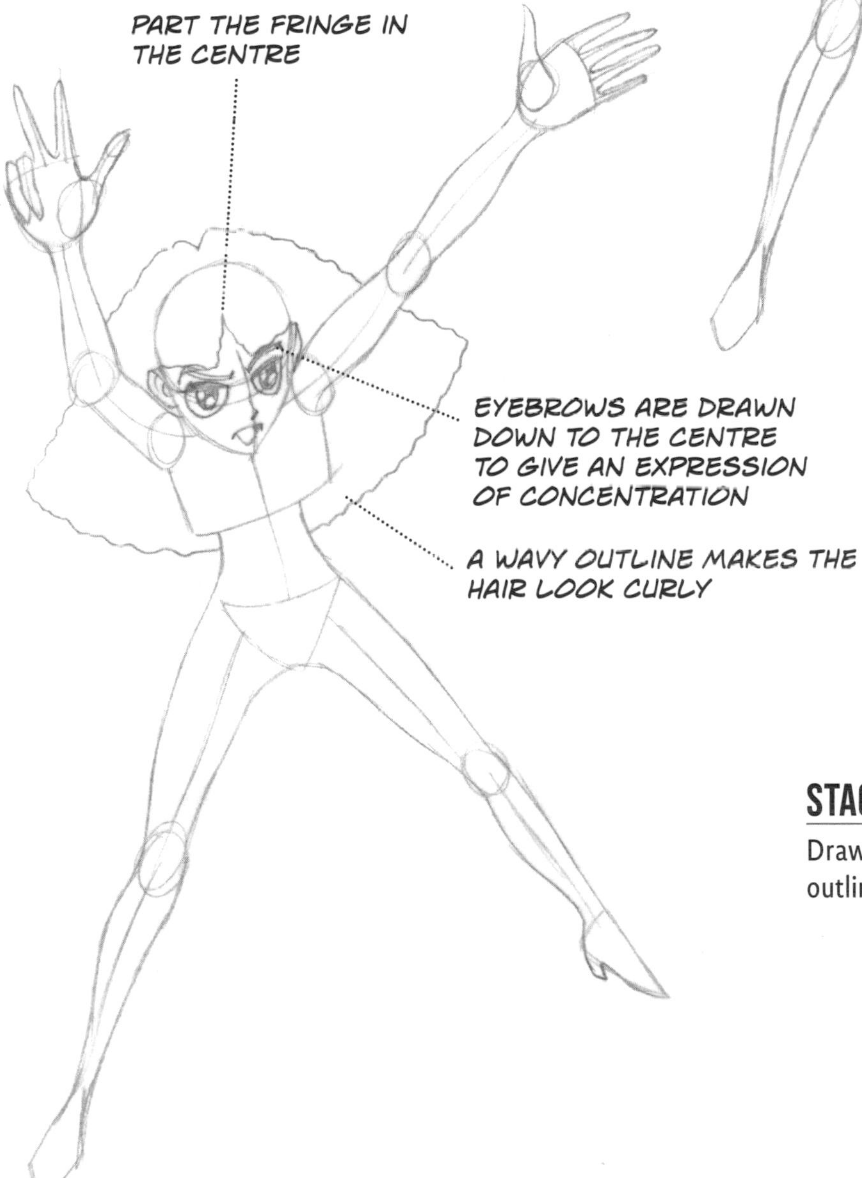
PART THE FRINGE IN THE CENTRE
EYEBROWS ARE DRAWN DOWN TO THE CENTRE TO GIVE AN EXPRESSION OF CONCENTRATION
A WAVY OUTLINE MAKES THE HAIR LOOK CURLY

STAGE 3

Draw in a face and a large, wavy outline of hair.

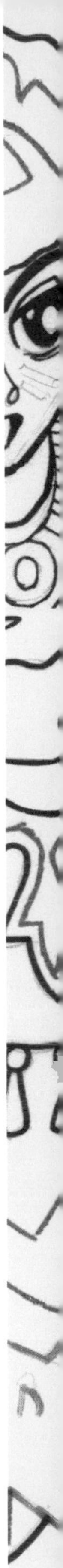

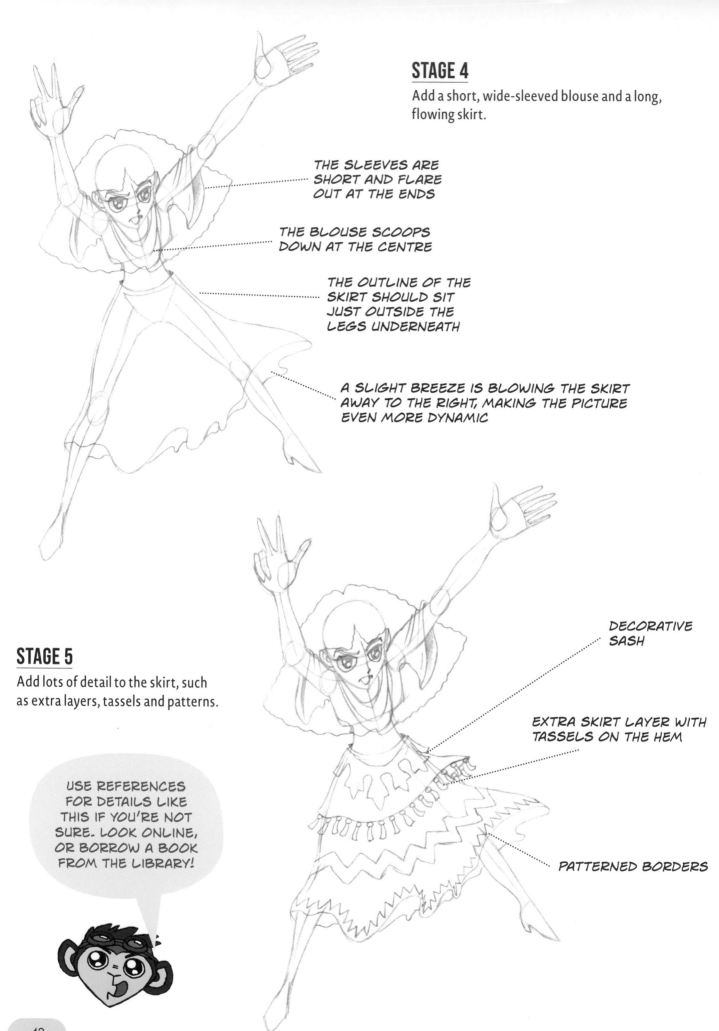

STAGE 4

Add a short, wide-sleeved blouse and a long, flowing skirt.

THE SLEEVES ARE SHORT AND FLARE OUT AT THE ENDS
THE BLOUSE SCOOPS DOWN AT THE CENTRE
THE OUTLINE OF THE SKIRT SHOULD SIT JUST OUTSIDE THE LEGS UNDERNEATH
A SLIGHT BREEZE IS BLOWING THE SKIRT AWAY TO THE RIGHT, MAKING THE PICTURE EVEN MORE DYNAMIC

STAGE 5

Add lots of detail to the skirt, such as extra layers, tassels and patterns.

DECORATIVE SASH
EXTRA SKIRT LAYER WITH TASSELS ON THE HEM
PATTERNED BORDERS

USE REFERENCES FOR DETAILS LIKE THIS IF YOU'RE NOT SURE. LOOK ONLINE, OR BORROW A BOOK FROM THE LIBRARY!

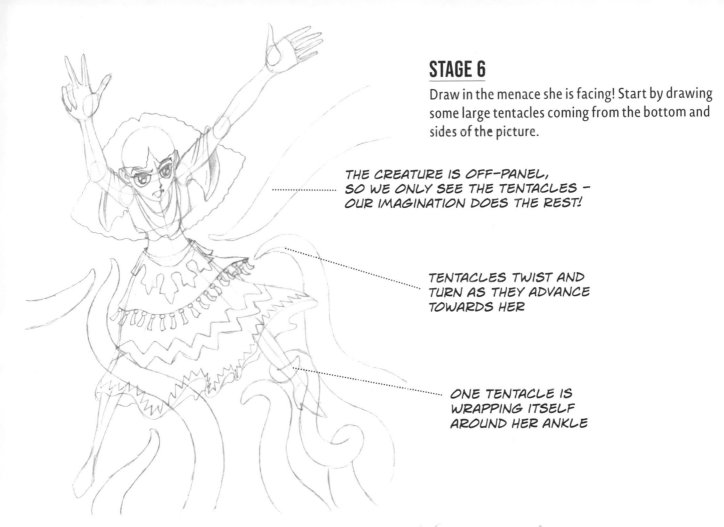

STAGE 6

Draw in the menace she is facing! Start by drawing some large tentacles coming from the bottom and sides of the picture.

THE CREATURE IS OFF-PANEL, SO WE ONLY SEE THE TENTACLES – OUR IMAGINATION DOES THE REST!

TENTACLES TWIST AND TURN AS THEY ADVANCE TOWARDS HER

ONE TENTACLE IS WRAPPING ITSELF AROUND HER ANKLE

STAGE 7

Add lots of crackling energy flowing from her hands and filling the surrounding air.

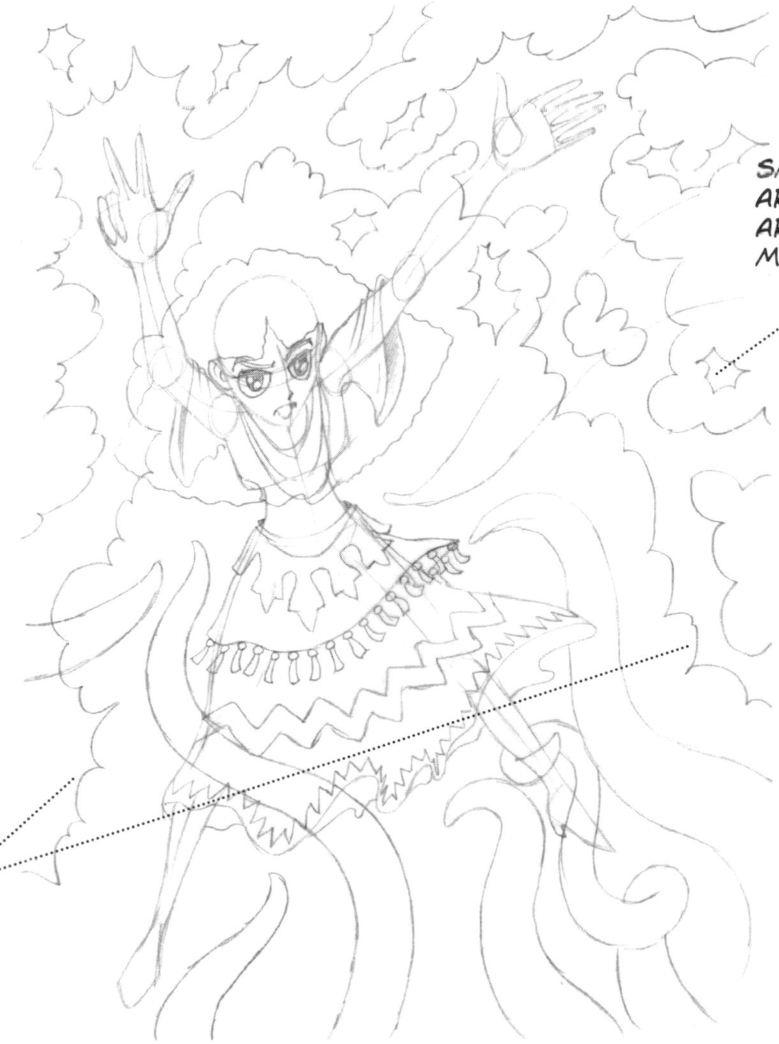

SMALL SPARKS ARE DOTTED AROUND THE MAIN STREAMS

THE MAIN STREAMS HEAD DOWN ON EITHER SIDE TOWARDS THE CREATURE

STAGE 8

Draw in some spiky details on the tentacles, and add some face markings and jewellery to the character.

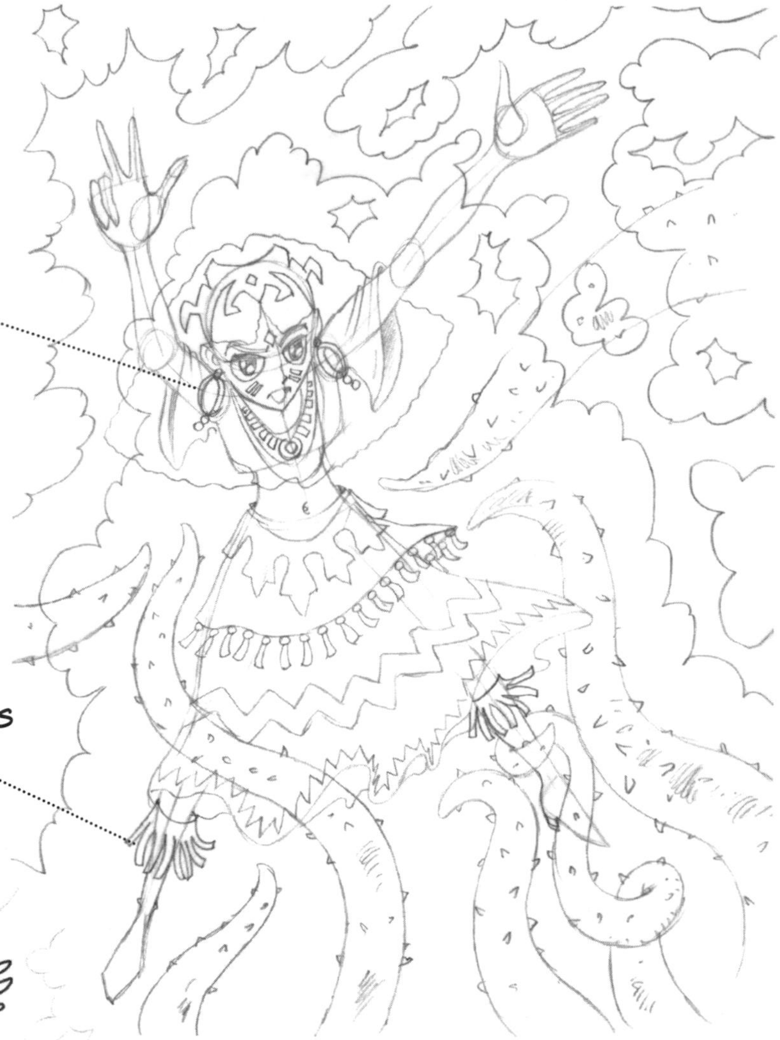
HEADPIECE, EARRINGS AND NECKLACE
ADD SOME TASSELLED BOOTS

STAGE 9

Ink your drawing, starting with the main character.

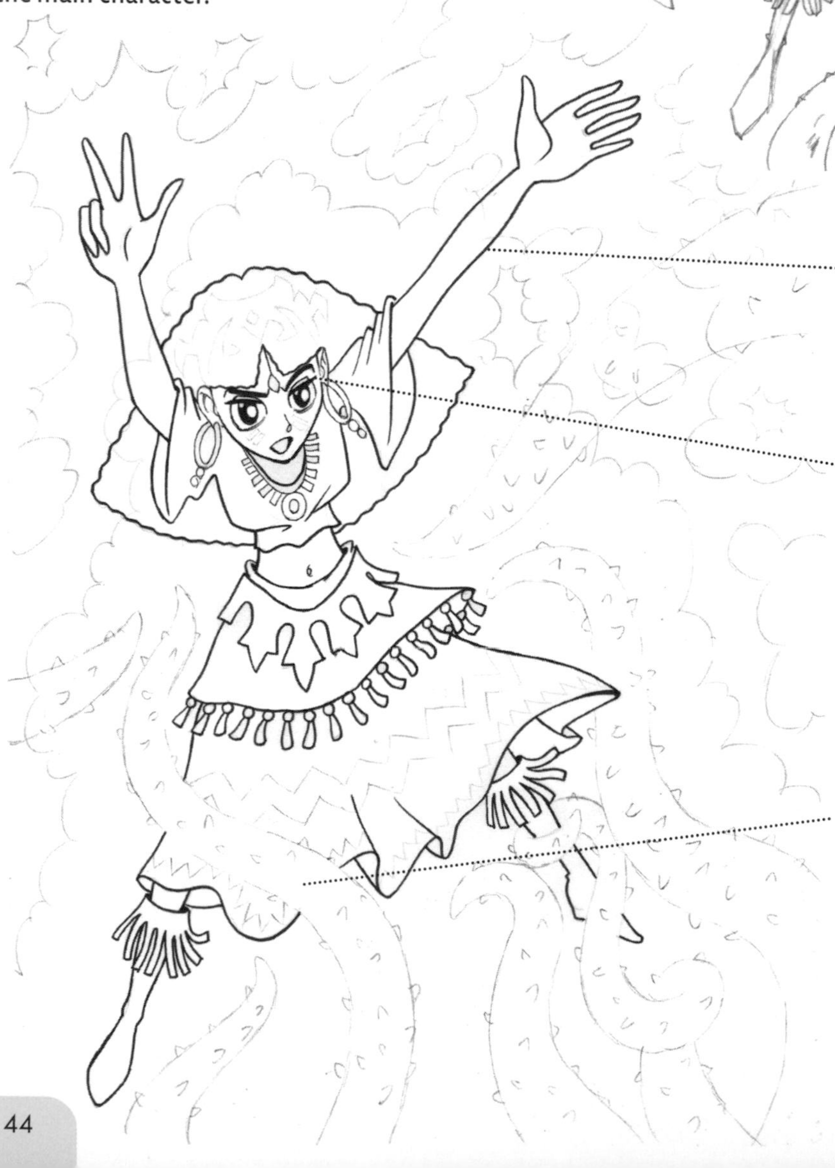
USE A BLACK FINEPOINT PEN
FILL IN THE EYES AND EYEBROWS
LEAVE BLANK THE AREAS WHERE THE TENTACLES ARE IN FRONT OF HER

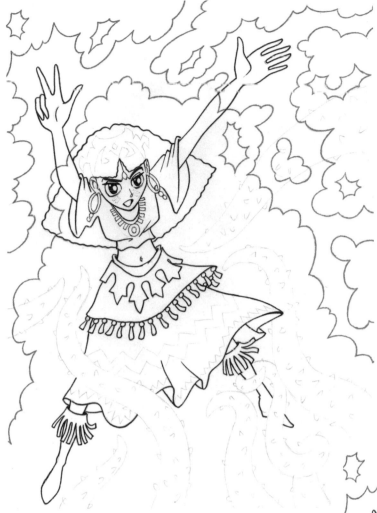

STAGE 10

Outline the crackling energy bands with a warm red fibre-tip pen.

STAGE 11

Outline the tentacles in green and the headpiece in blue.

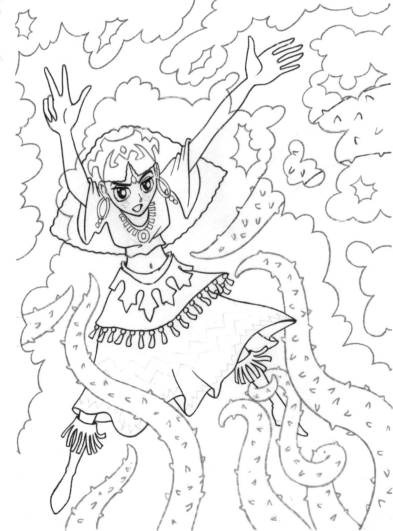

45

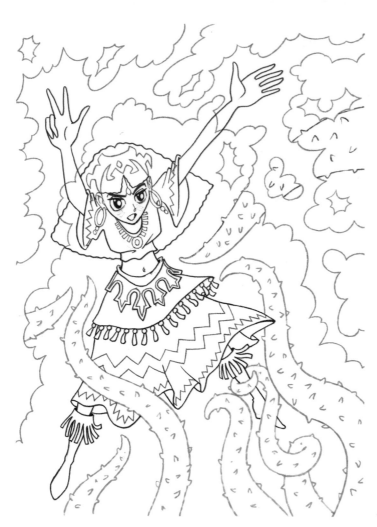

STAGE 12

Outline the patterns on the blouse and skirts with purple.

STAGE 13

Now colour the main character with flesh colours, pale blues, mauve and purple. Use yellow-gold for her jewellery.

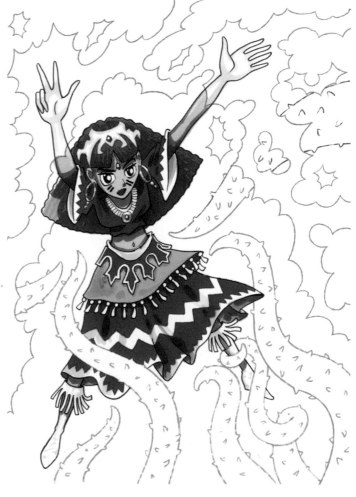

STAGE 14

Use yellow for the energy bolts, and green for the tentacles.

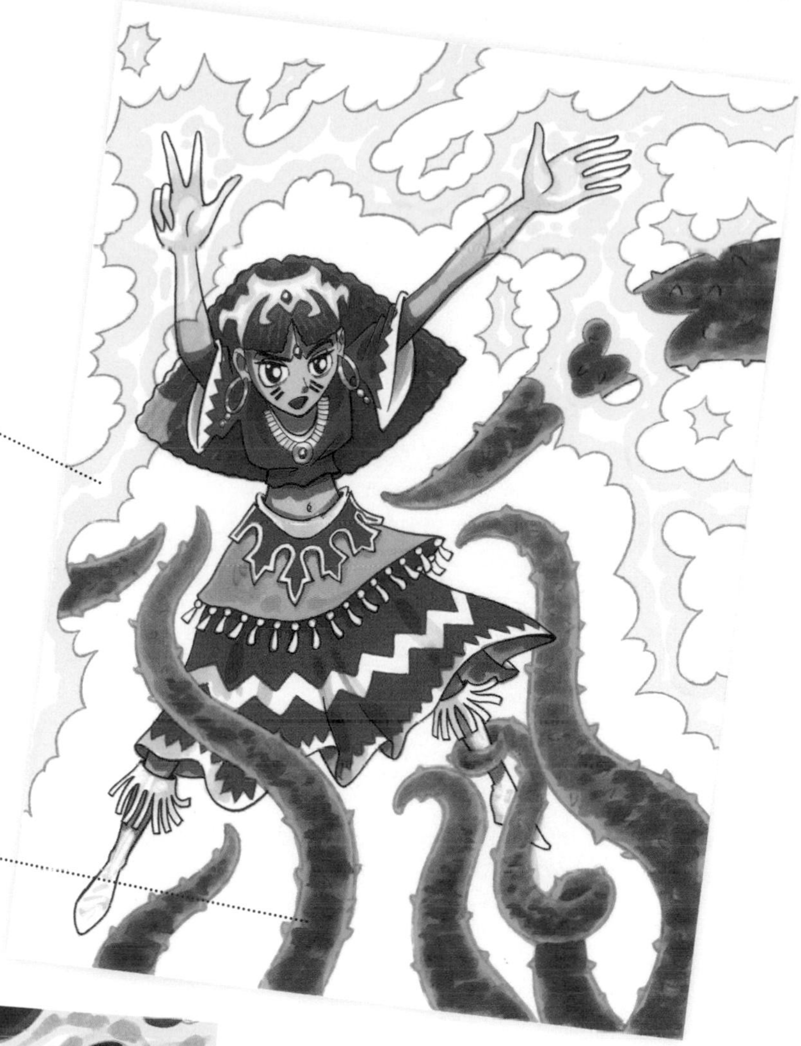
LEAVE WHITE GAPS IN THE YELLOW TO MAKE THE ENERGY GLOW
USE DARK GREEN AND BROWN TO ADD SHADOW TO THE TENTACLES

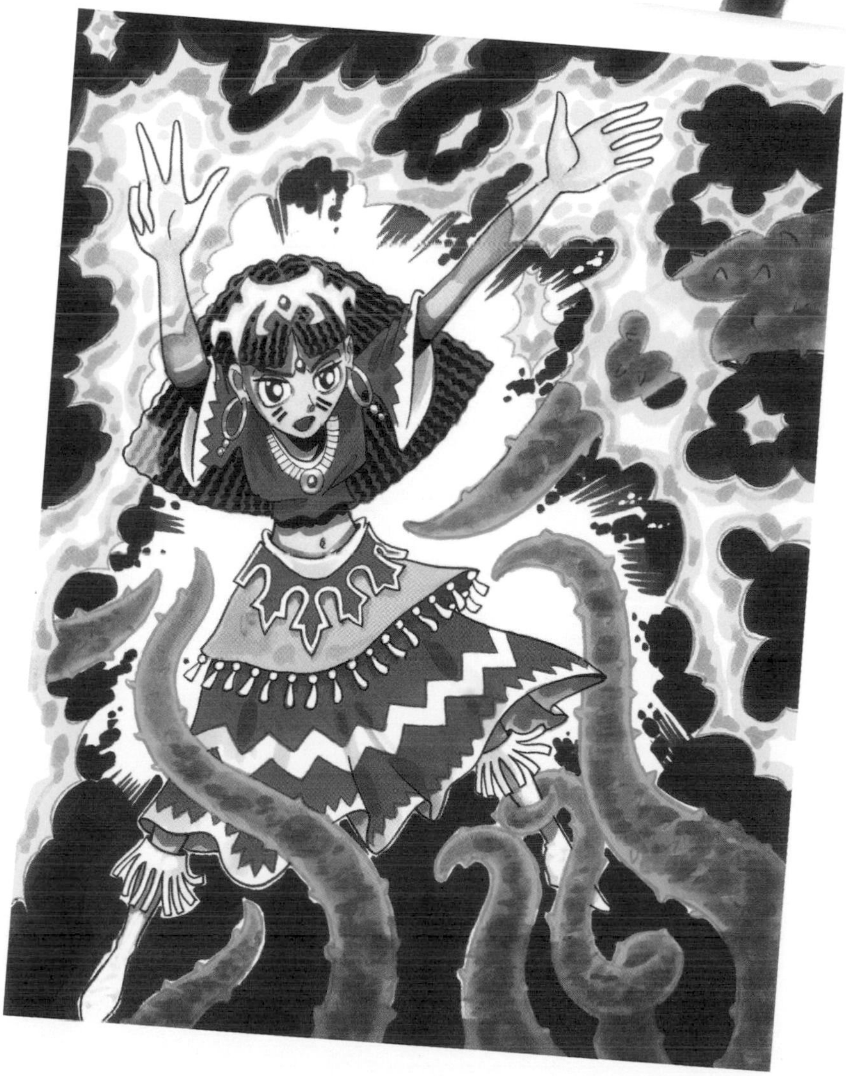

STAGE 15

Add some black shadows on the figure and wavy lines to the hair. Finish by filling in the background with a dark, rich brown colour, leaving a white centre behind the character.

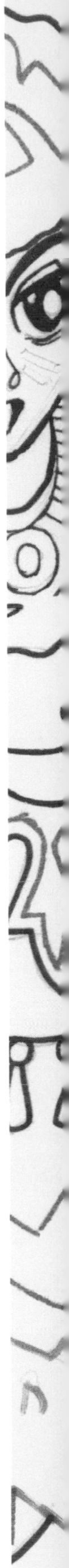

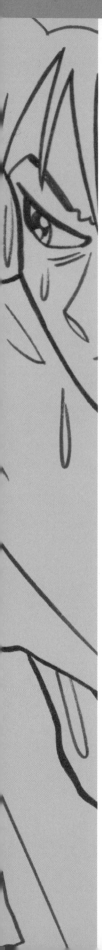

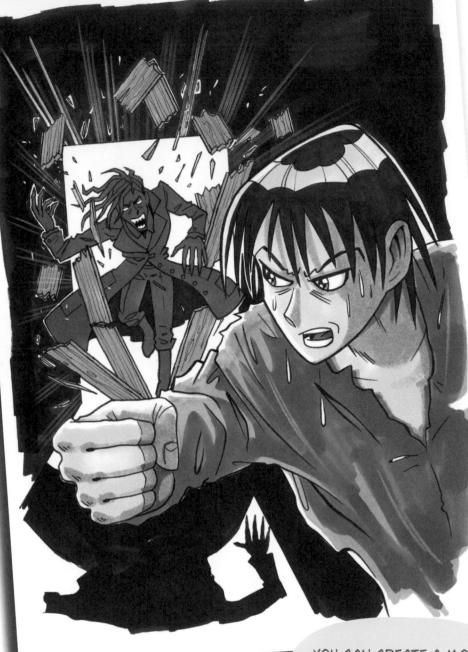

YOU CAN RUN, BUT YOU CAN'T HIDE FROM A GHOUL ATTACK!

YOU CAN CREATE A MOODY ATMOSPHERE BY USING JUST ONE OR TWO COLOURS, LIKE THIS BLACK AND BLUE SCENE!

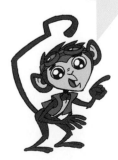

STAGE 1

Draw a large wireframe head and right arm, with the head roughly centre-right on the page with a large fist shape in the bottom-left.

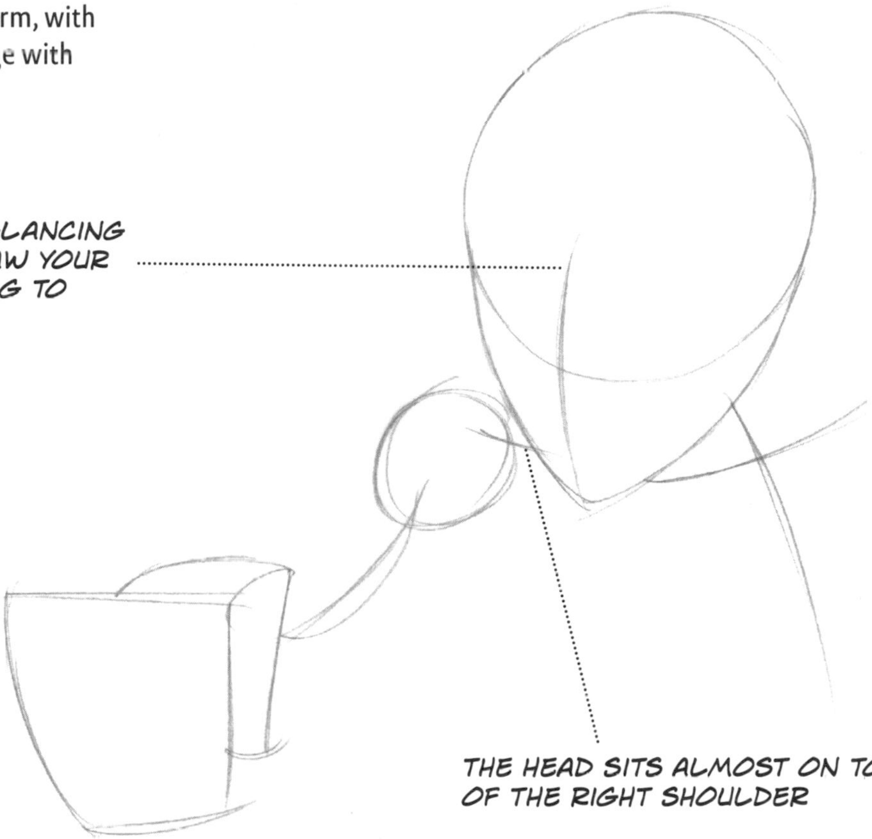
THE HEAD WILL BE GLANCING BACKWARDS, SO DRAW YOUR CENTRE LINE CURVING TO THE LEFT
THE HEAD SITS ALMOST ON TOP OF THE RIGHT SHOULDER

STAGE 2

Sketch in an angry, determined facial expression, with the eyes looking backwards over the right shoulder. Draw in long spikes of hair hanging down around the face.

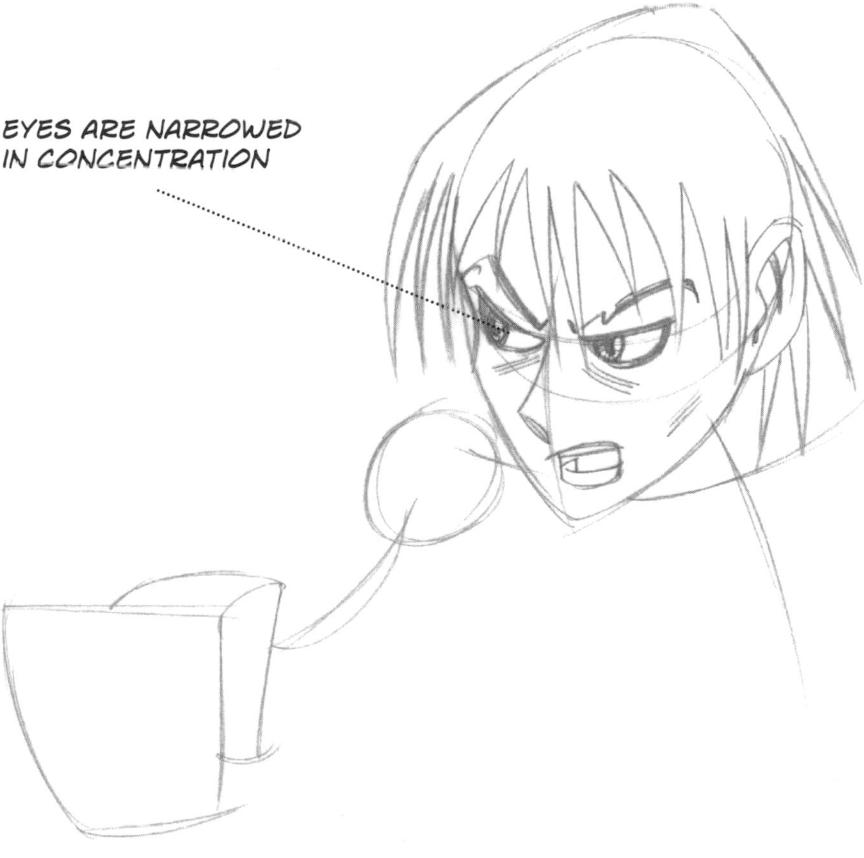
EYES ARE NARROWED IN CONCENTRATION

STAGE 3

Flesh out the figure, creating a shirt with a tattered, jagged outline to show that the character is in distress. Draw in the clenched right fist. Add some sweat drops on the face and dripping down towards the floor.

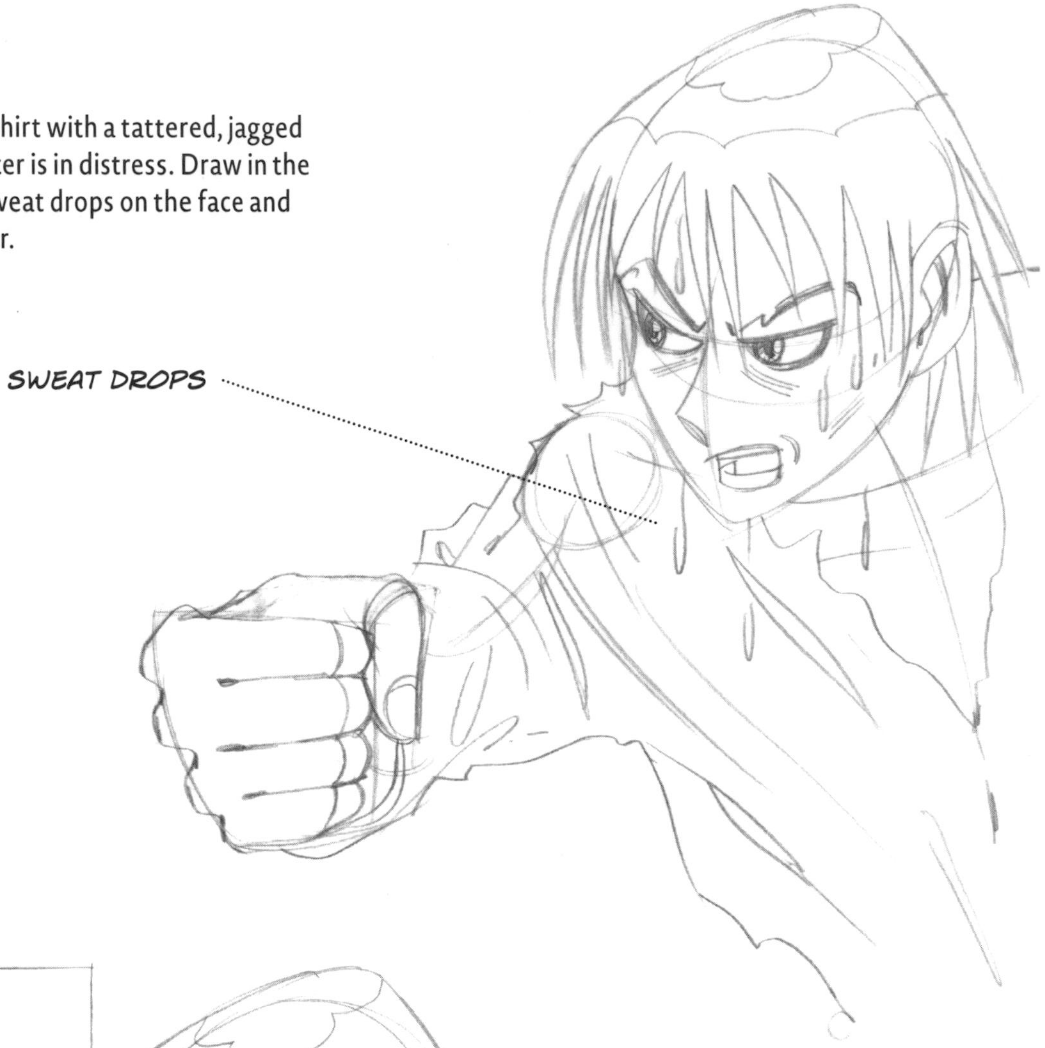
SWEAT DROPS

STAGE 4

In the background draw a rectangle for a door and sketch a wireframe for a second figure entering through it. The second figure's head is down and forwards, hiding the neck; its right leg is bent at the knee and it has longer than usual fingers.

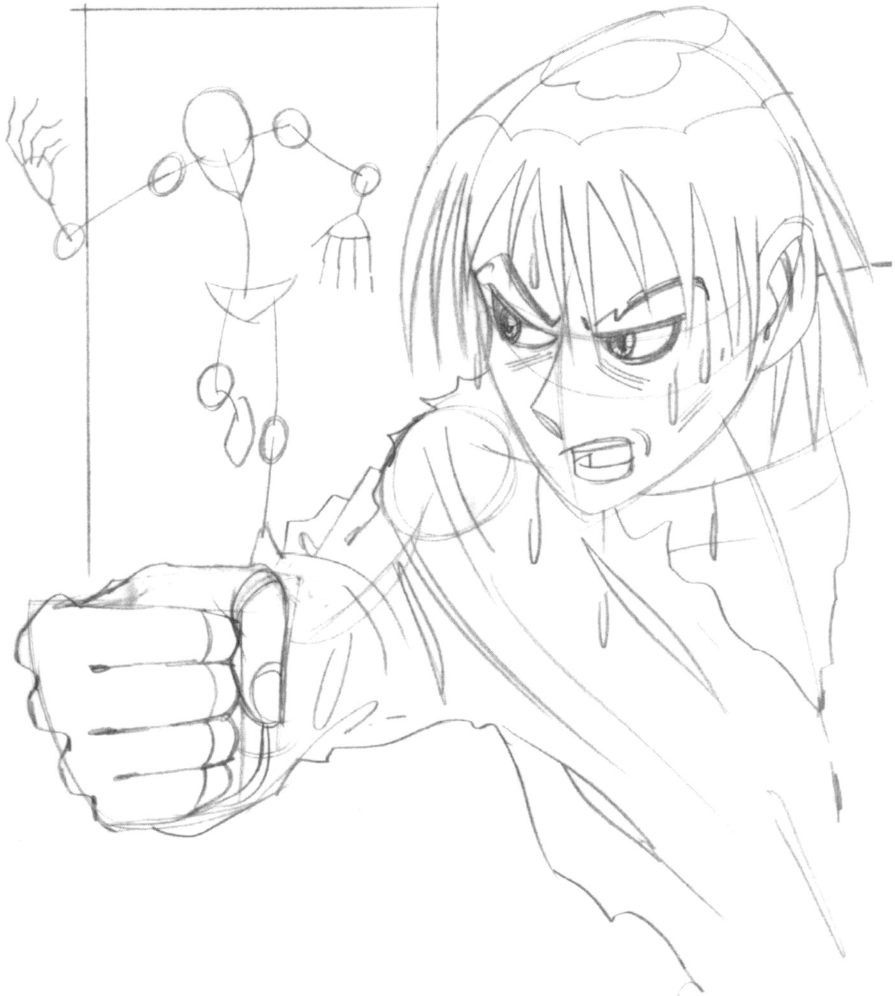

STAGE 5

Flesh out the second figure, giving it a trenchcoat, boots, long messy hair and spindly hands. Indicate sharp teeth and evil-looking eyes.

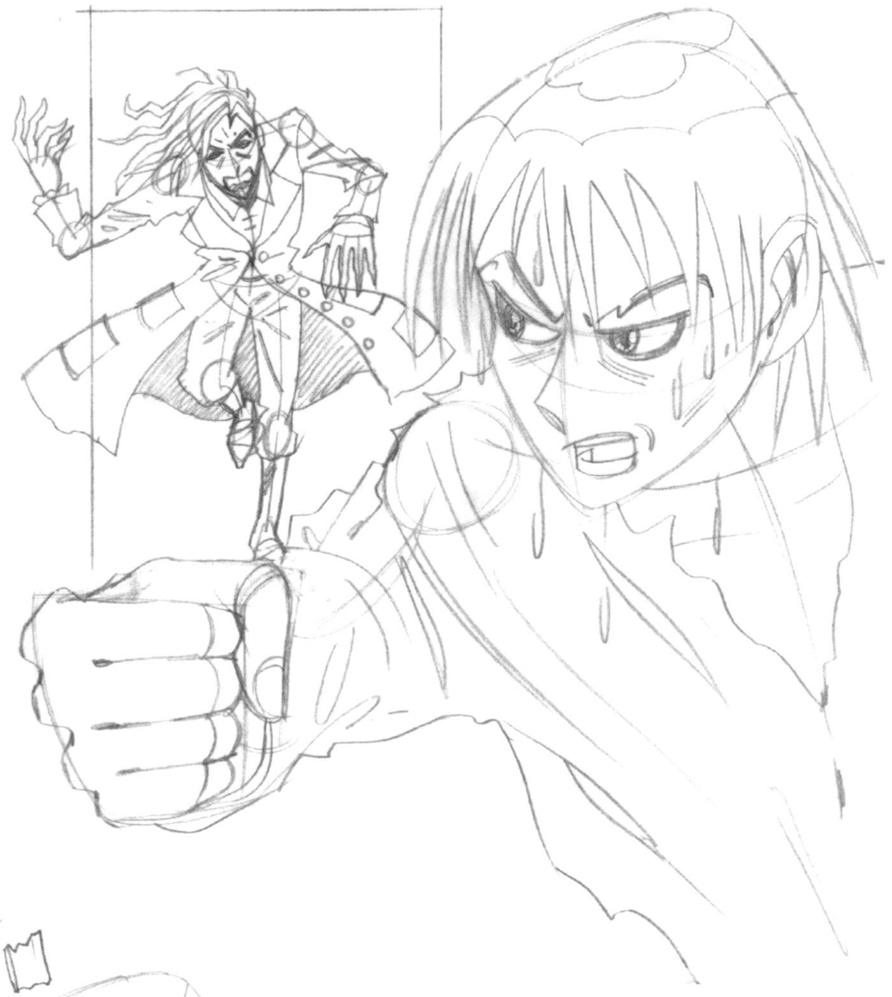

CREATE LOTS OF SMALL SPLINTERS AND FRAGMENTS OF WOODEN PLANKS

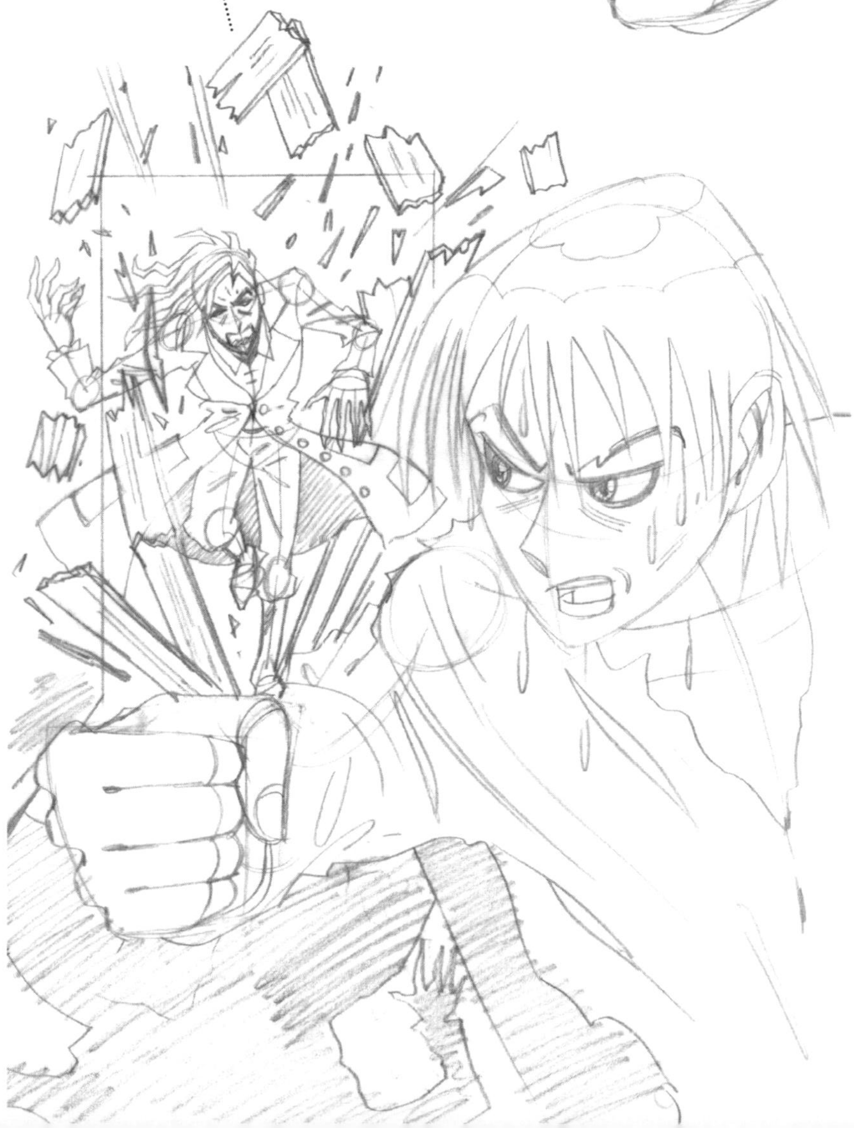

STAGE 6

Sketch in the splintered remains of the door the second figure is crashing through. The light source will be outside the door, so indicate the shadow he's casting at the bottom of the page.

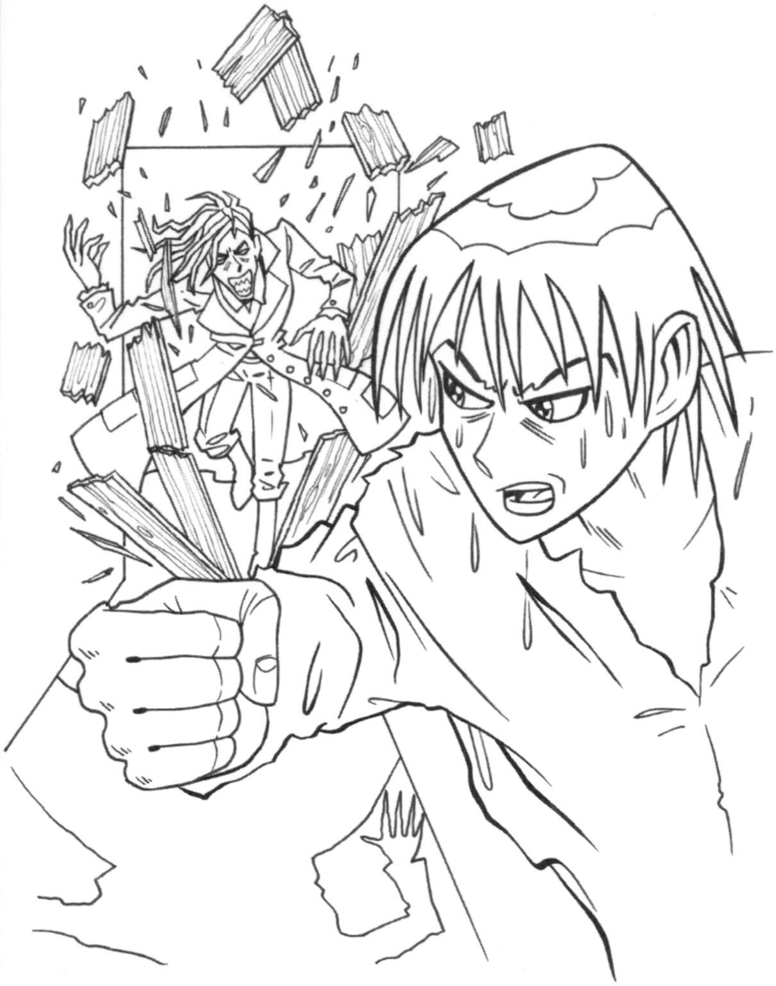

STAGE 7

Ink your drawing with black pen, using a thicker pen or brush pen on the foreground character to make him more dominant in the picture.

STAGE 8

Colour the foreground character: use pale blue on the face and hand, and mid-blue on the shirt. Leave a white highlight around the edge to show where the light is hitting him.

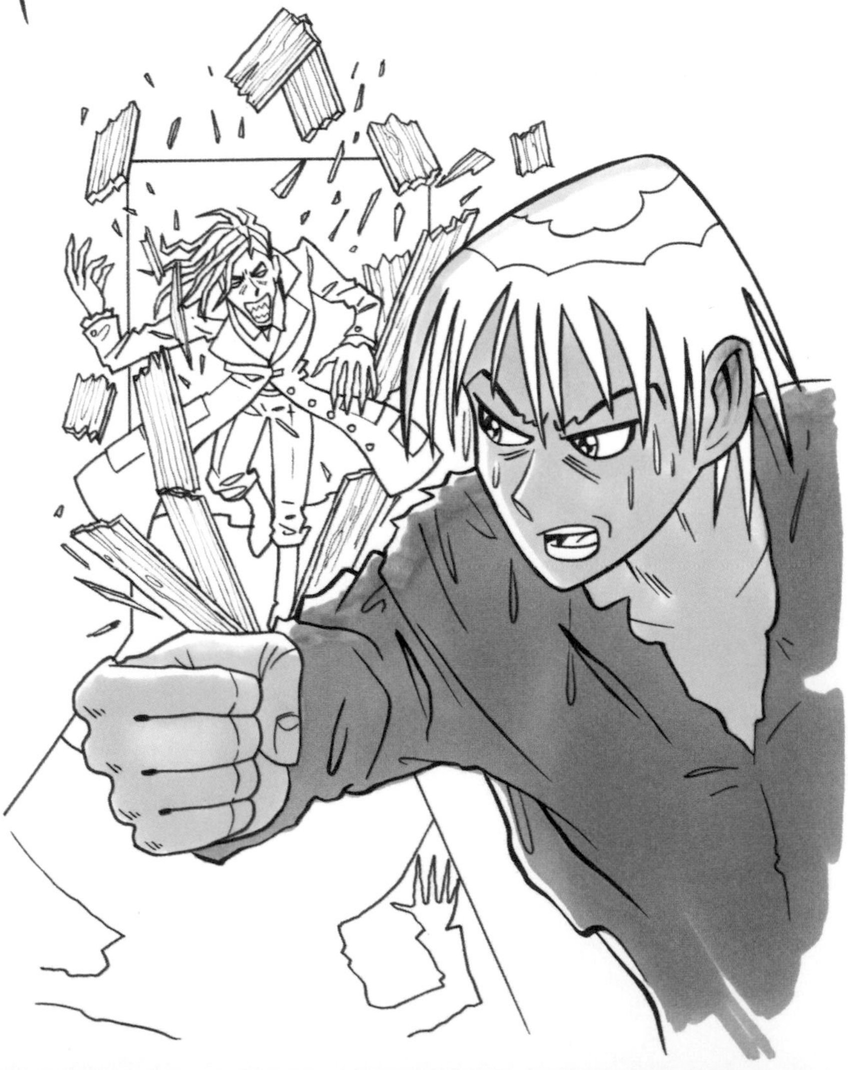

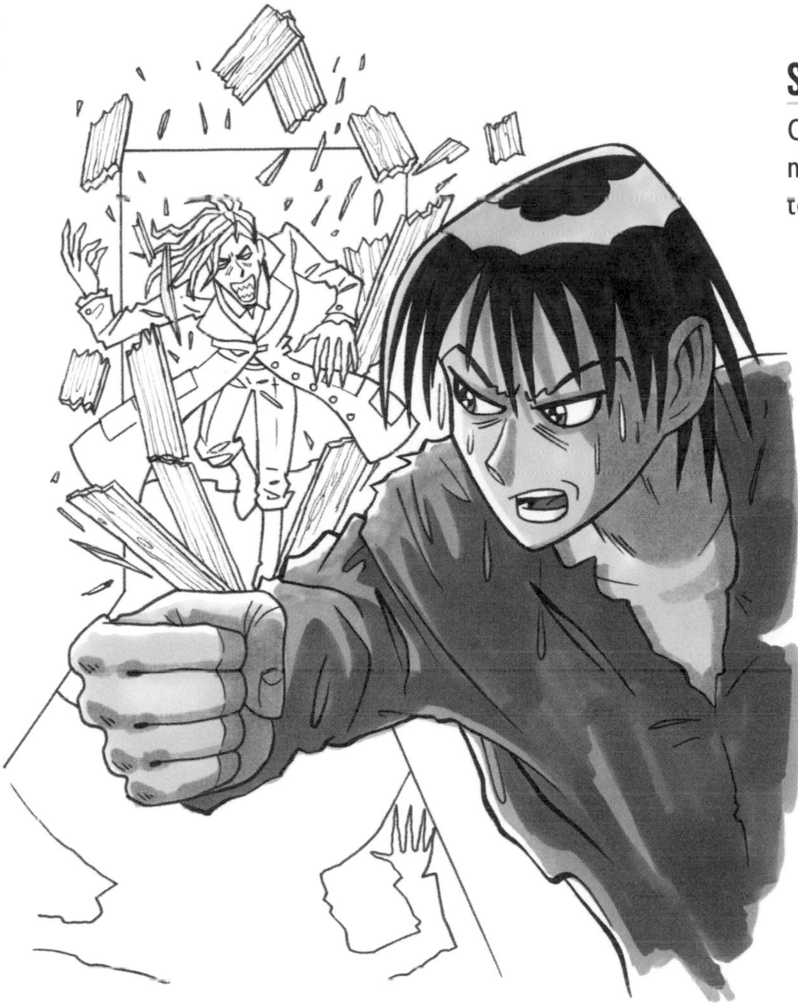

STAGE 9

Colour the hair black with a pale blue highlight, and add mid-grey shadows on the face and hands. Use a darker grey to put shadows on the shirt.

STAGE 10

Colour the second figure with dark blue, leaving the eyes and teeth white. Fill in the mouth and the inside of the coat black.

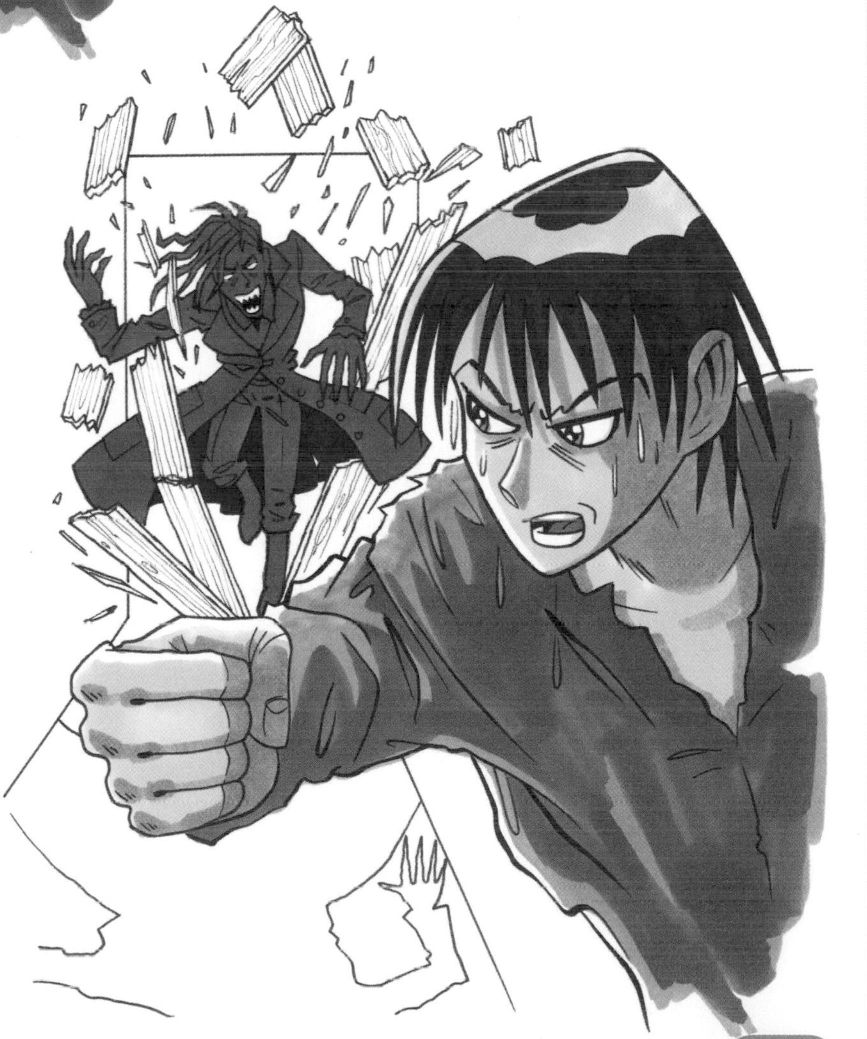

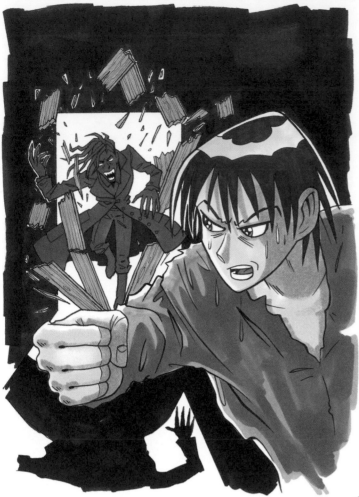

STAGE 11

Colour the background and the shadow on the floor black – the colour doesn't have to be neatly applied. Colour the splintered remains of the door with mid-grey.

STAGE 12

Use dark grey to add some final shadows and to draw in some texture lines on the hero's hair. Finish with some white paint: add impact lines coming out from the door, movement lines on the hero's body, and add a few more small splinters!

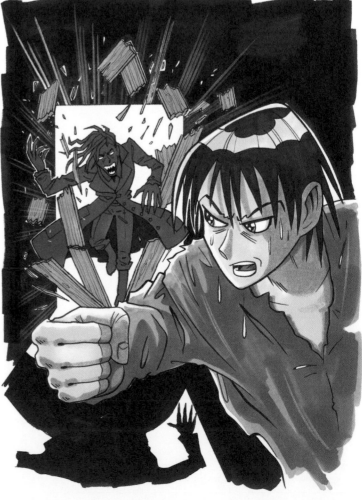

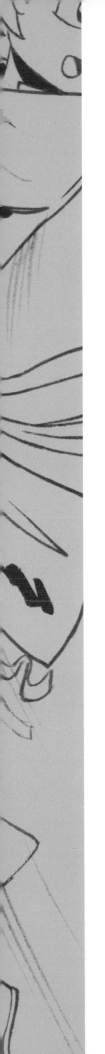

SWORDPLAY

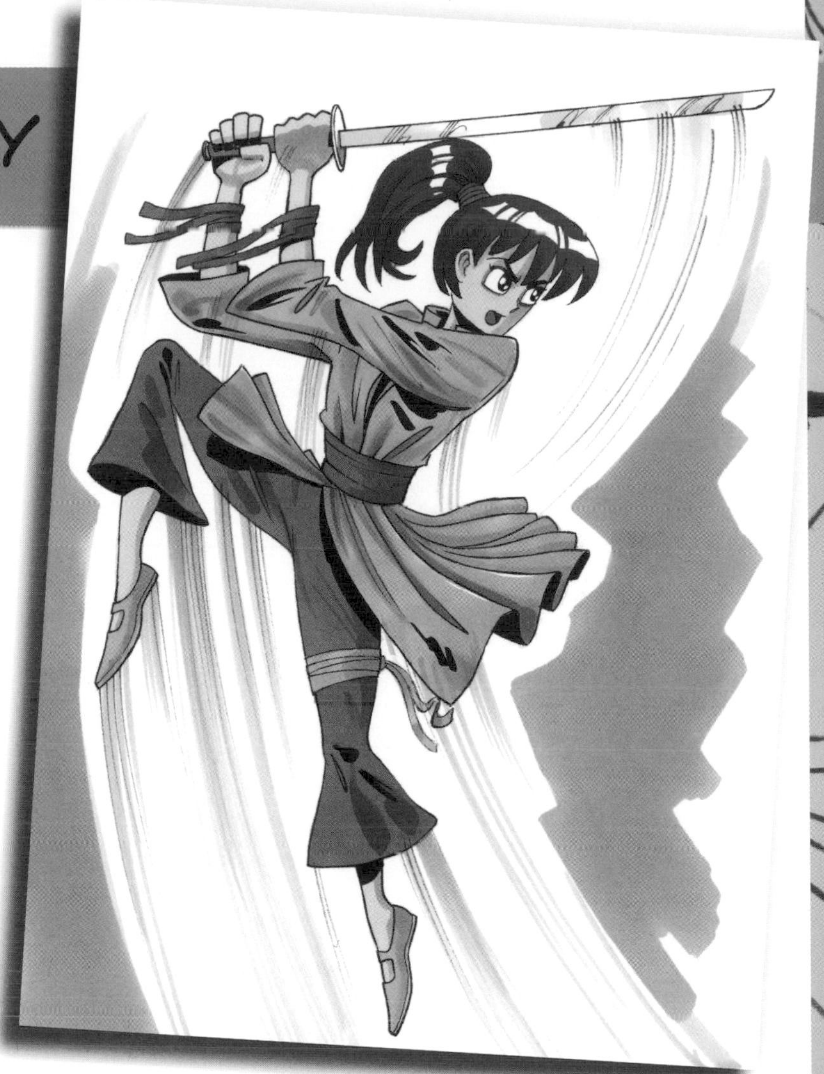

A TRADITIONAL-STYLE SWORDSWOMAN IN A LEAPING DEFENCE MOVE

STAGE 1

Start with a leaping wireframe for your figure.

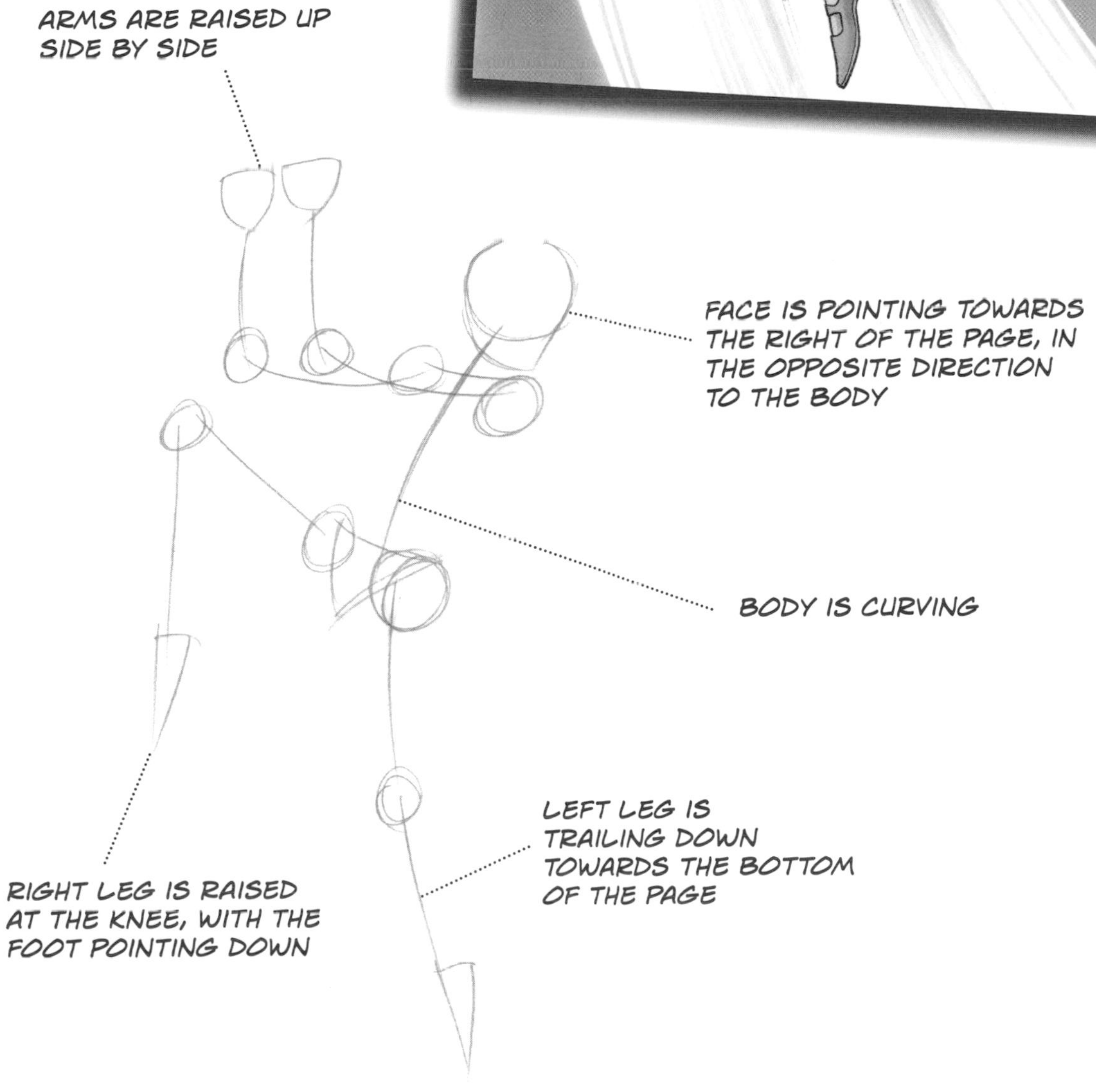

ARMS ARE RAISED UP SIDE BY SIDE
FACE IS POINTING TOWARDS THE RIGHT OF THE PAGE, IN THE OPPOSITE DIRECTION TO THE BODY
BODY IS CURVING
LEFT LEG IS TRAILING DOWN TOWARDS THE BOTTOM OF THE PAGE
RIGHT LEG IS RAISED AT THE KNEE, WITH THE FOOT POINTING DOWN

STAGE 2

Flesh out your figure with smooth, graceful lines.

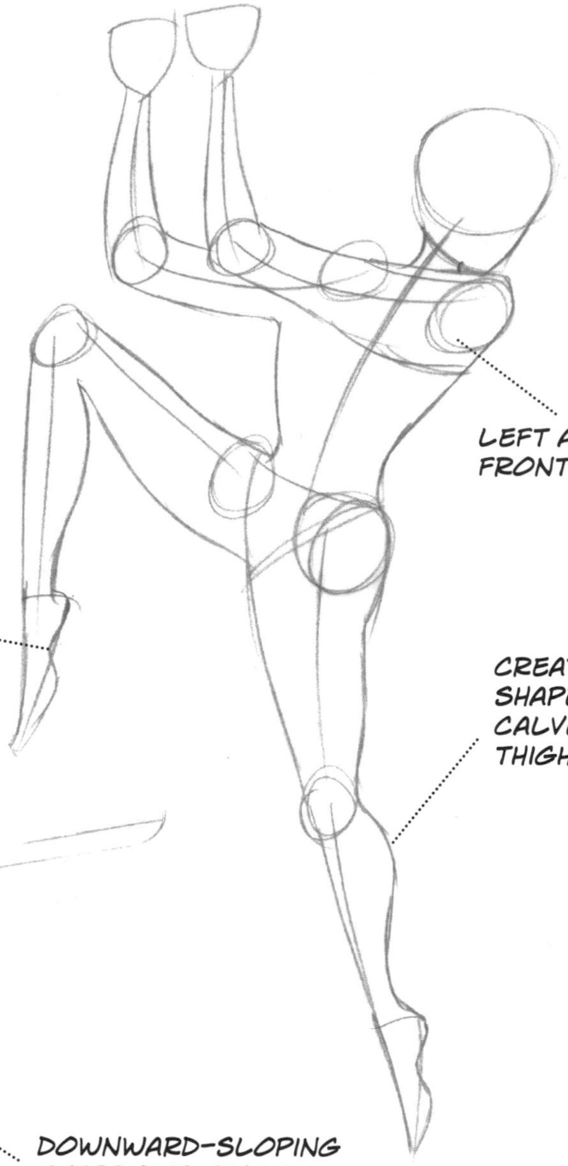
LEFT ARM IS IN FRONT OF RIGHT
SHOW CURVE OF HEEL AND SOLE OF FOOT
CREATE MUSCLE SHAPES ON CALVES AND THIGHS

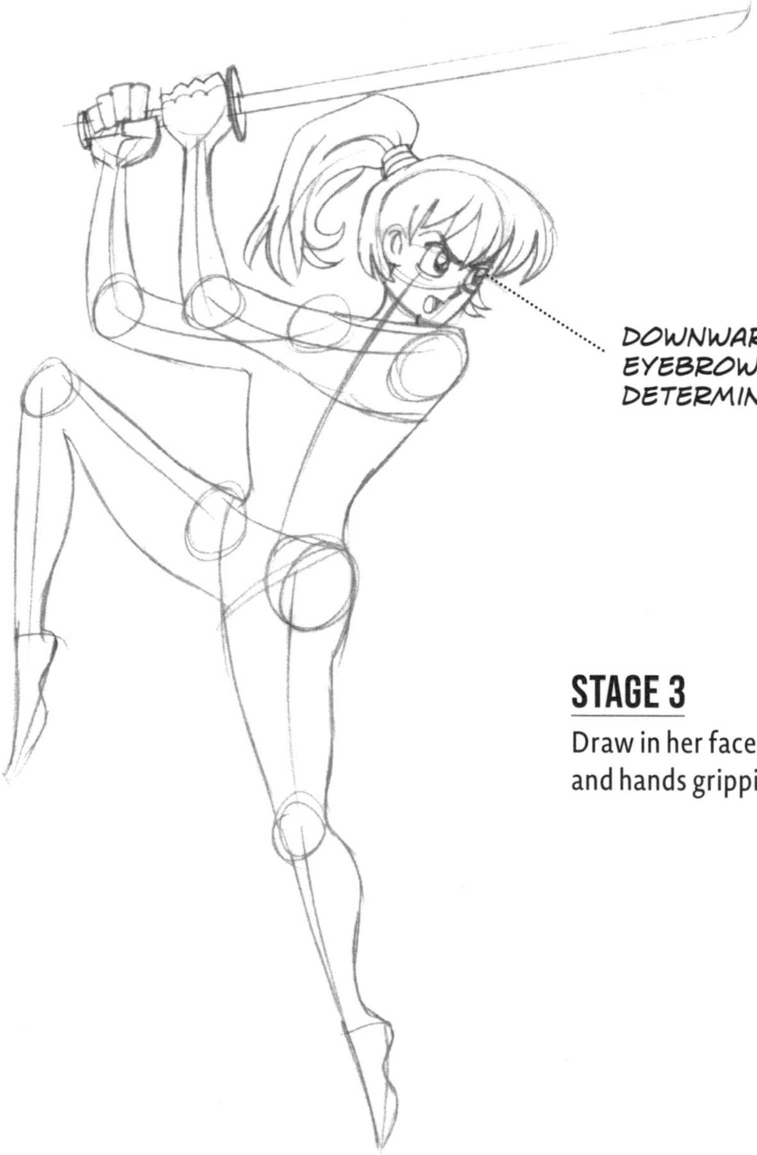
DOWNWARD-SLOPING EYEBROWS GIVE A DETERMINED LOOK

STAGE 3

Draw in her face, long hair in a ponytail, and hands gripping a long sword.

STAGE 4

Add a traditional-style tunic and calf-length trousers.

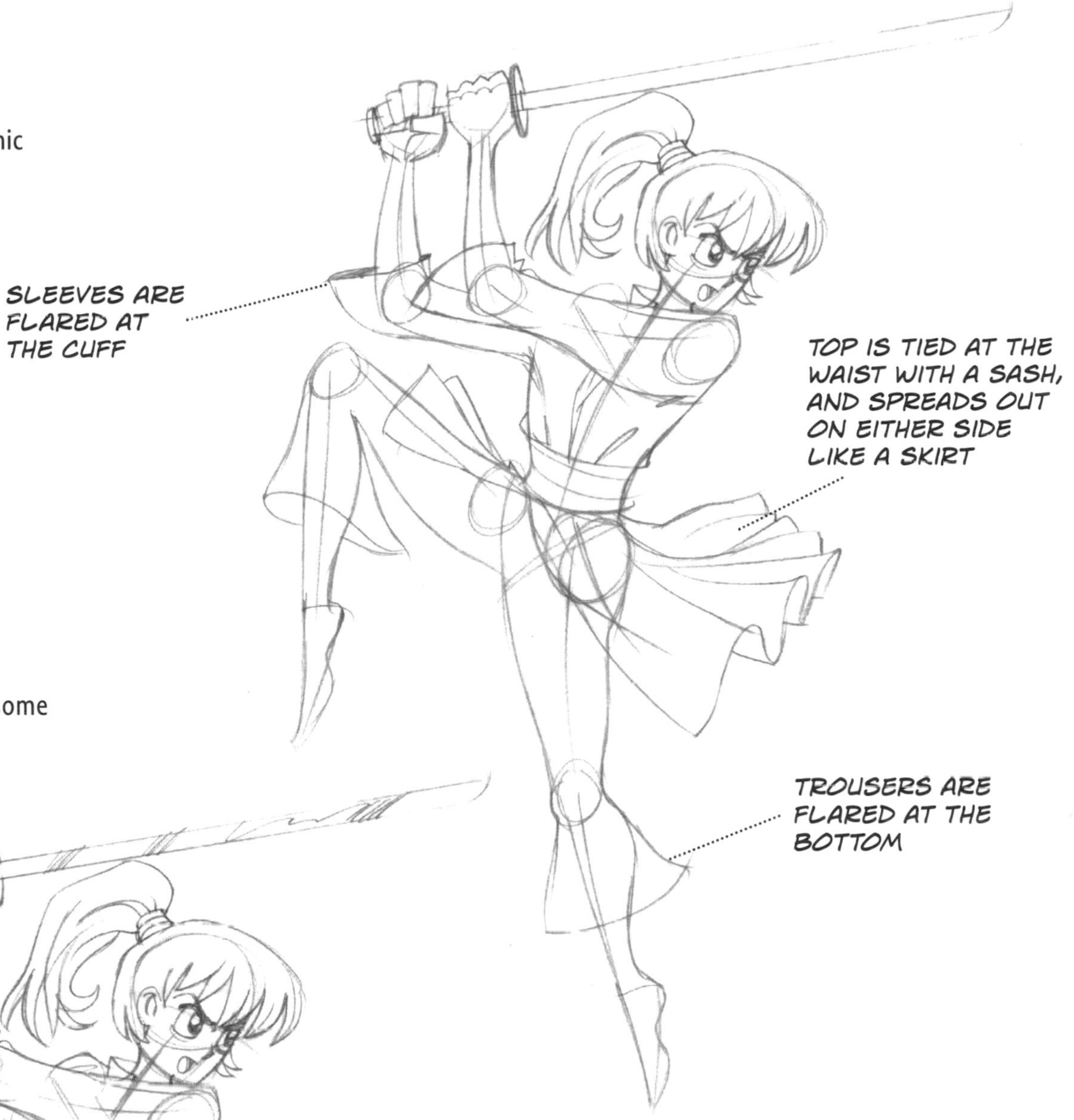
SLEEVES ARE FLARED AT THE CUFF
TOP IS TIED AT THE WAIST WITH A SASH, AND SPREADS OUT ON EITHER SIDE LIKE A SKIRT
TROUSERS ARE FLARED AT THE BOTTOM

STAGE 5

Add in further detail and some movement lines.

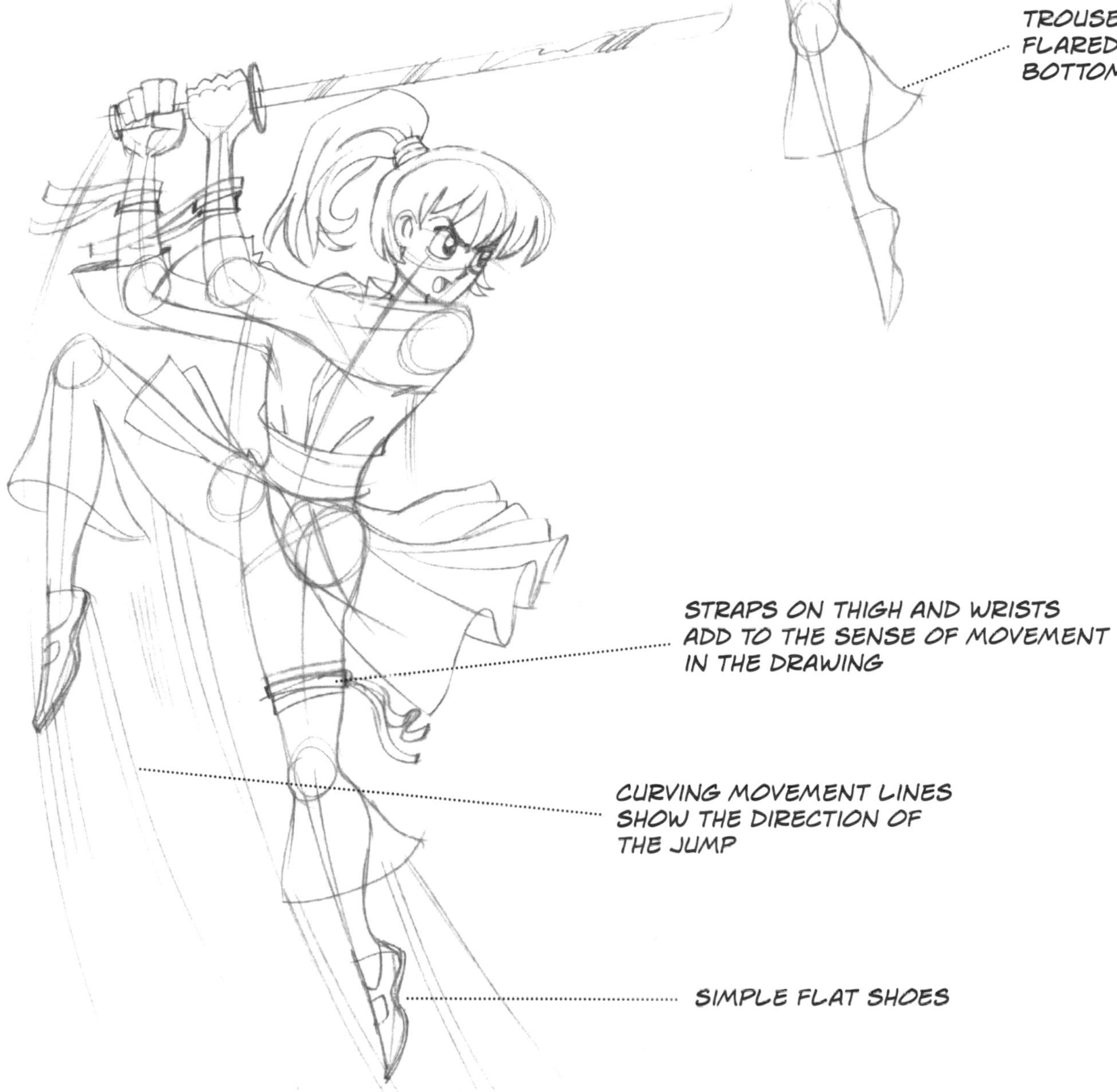
STRAPS ON THIGH AND WRISTS ADD TO THE SENSE OF MOVEMENT IN THE DRAWING
CURVING MOVEMENT LINES SHOW THE DIRECTION OF THE JUMP
SIMPLE FLAT SHOES

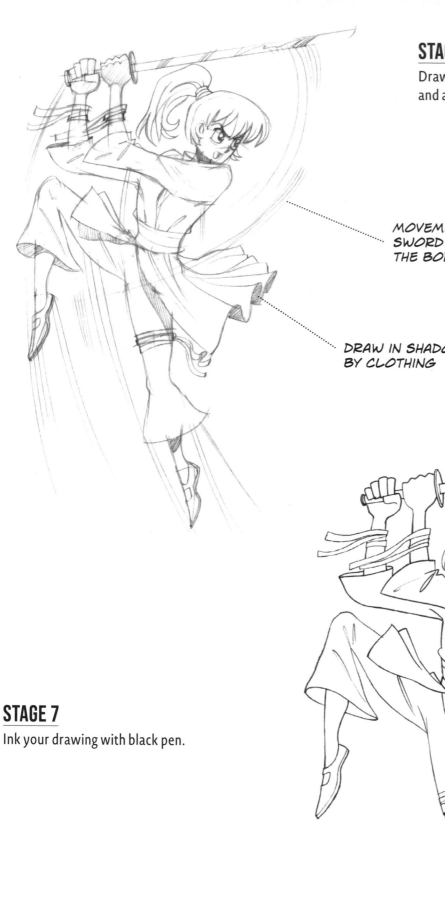

STAGE 6

Draw movement lines on the blade of the sword, and add a few shadows.

MOVEMENT LINES OF SWORD ARC ACROSS THE BODY

DRAW IN SHADOWS CAST BY CLOTHING

STAGE 7

Ink your drawing with black pen.

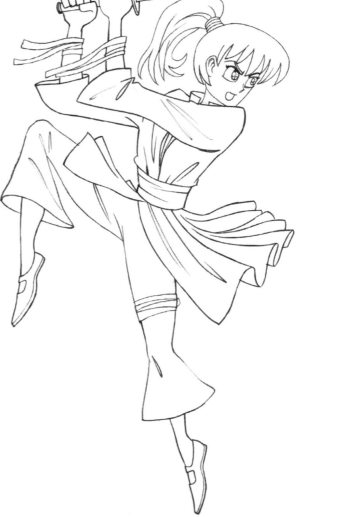

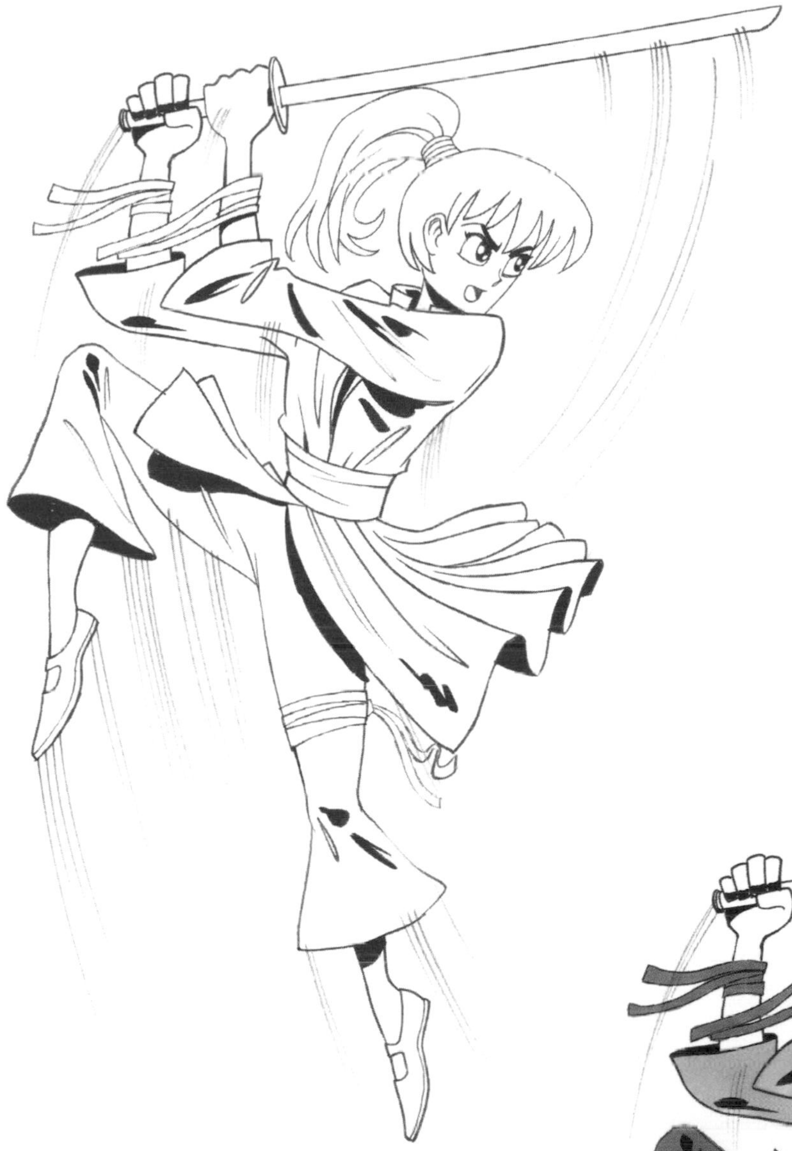

STAGE 8

Create some solid black shadows in the folds of the fabric, under the chin and on the hands.

STAGE 9

Fill in areas of flat colour.

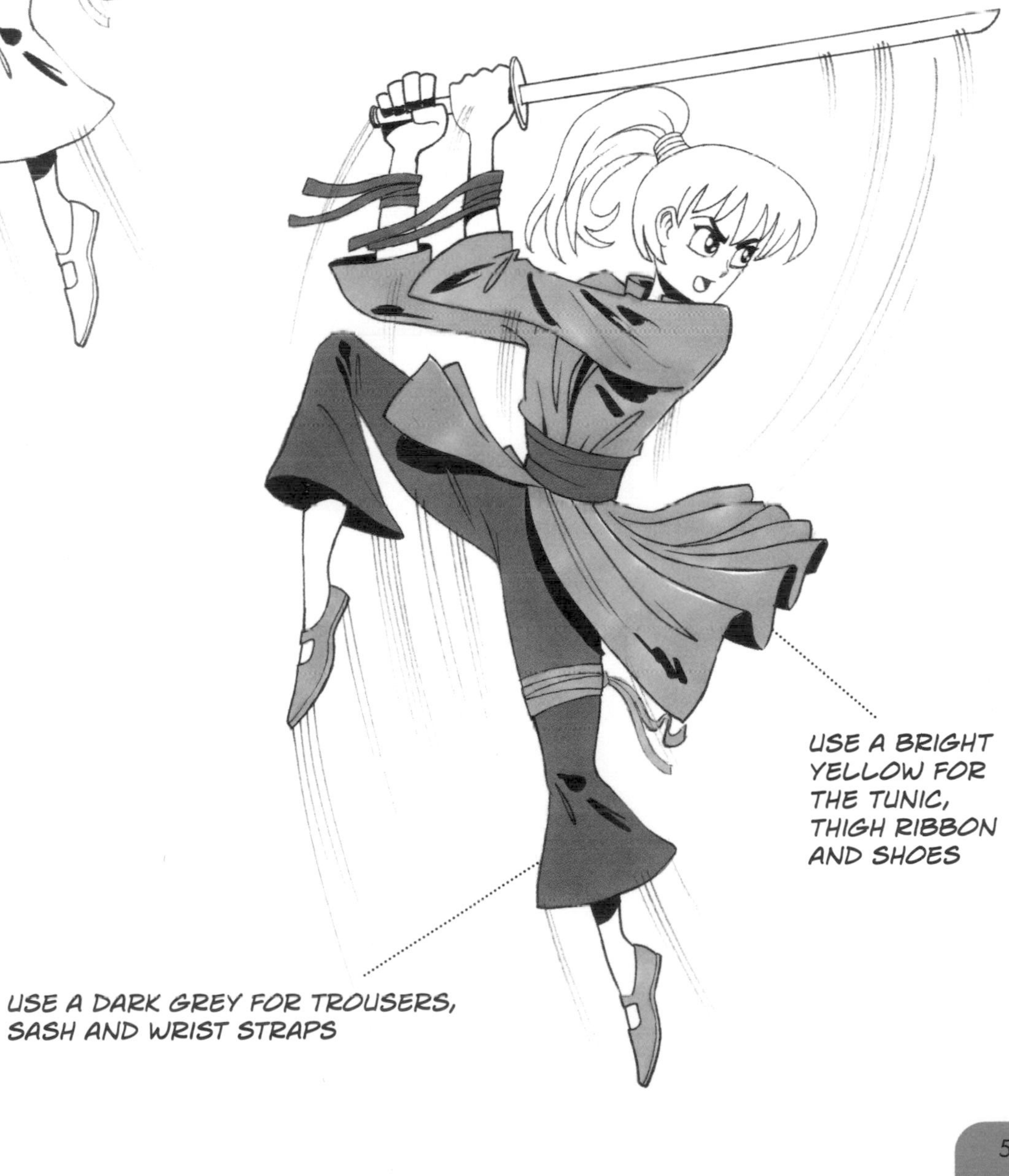
USE A BRIGHT YELLOW FOR THE TUNIC, THIGH RIBBON AND SHOES
USE A DARK GREY FOR TROUSERS, SASH AND WRIST STRAPS

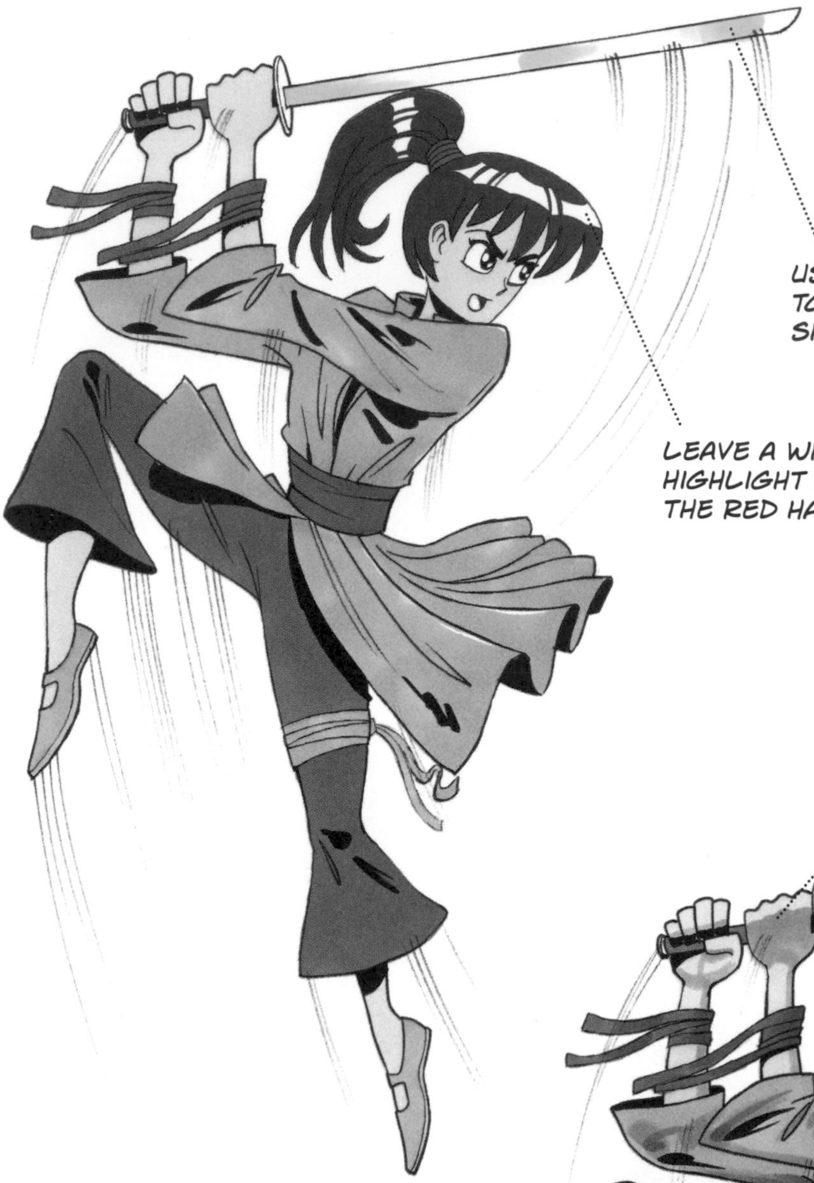
USE PALE BLUE
TO GIVE A METALLIC
SHEEN TO THE BLADE
LEAVE A WHITE
HIGHLIGHT ON
THE RED HAIR

STAGE 10

Colour in her skin and hair, and add blue highlights to the sword.

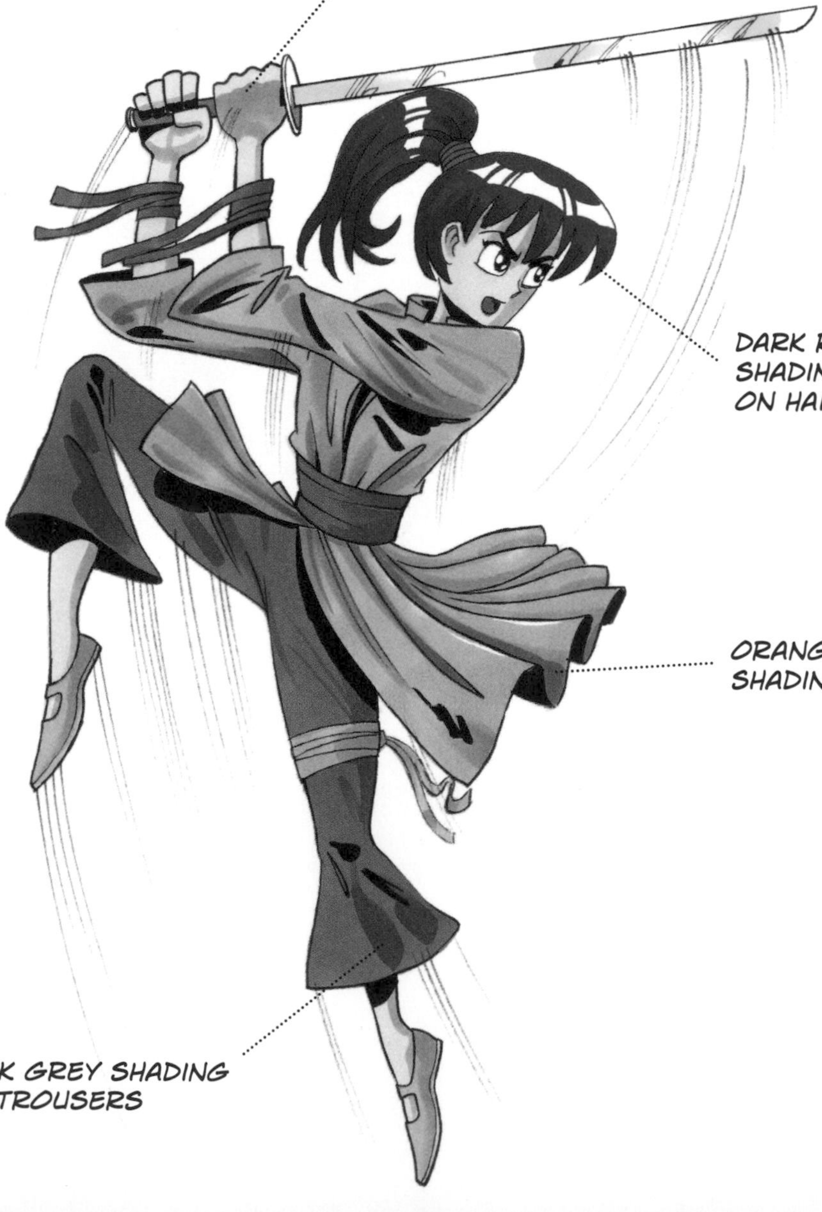
DARK FLESH TONE
DARK RED
SHADING
ON HAIR
ORANGE
SHADING
DARK GREY SHADING
ON TROUSERS

STAGE 11

Add some darker shading to each area of colour to create shadows.

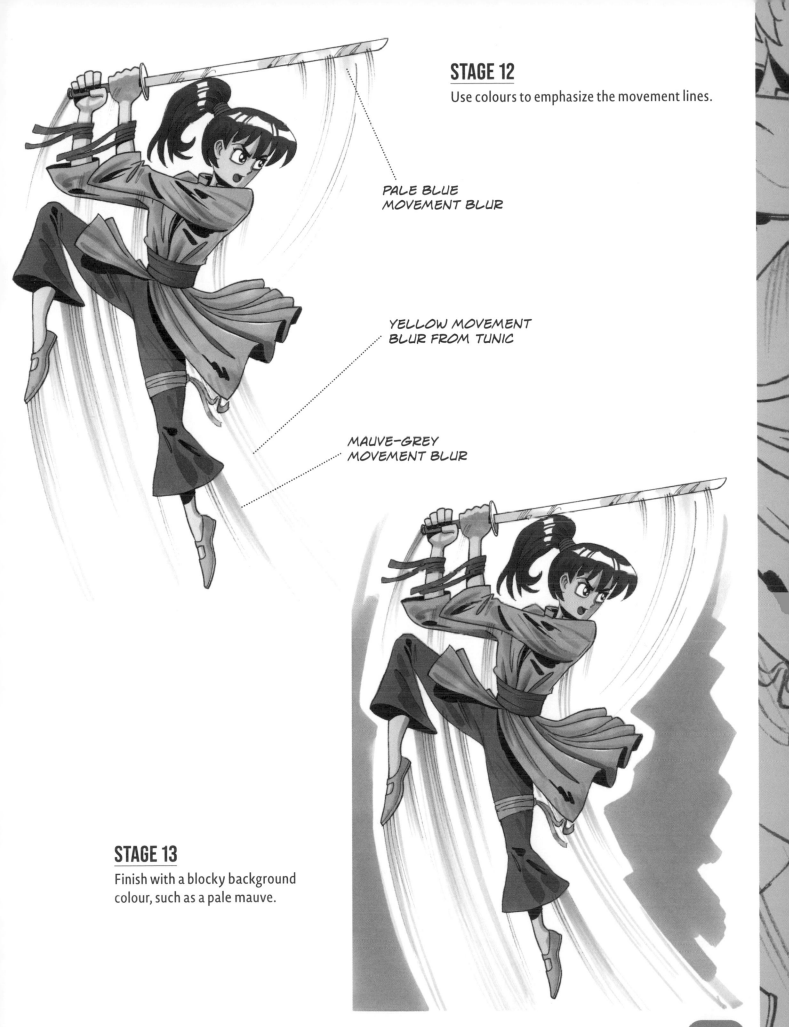

STAGE 12

Use colours to emphasize the movement lines.

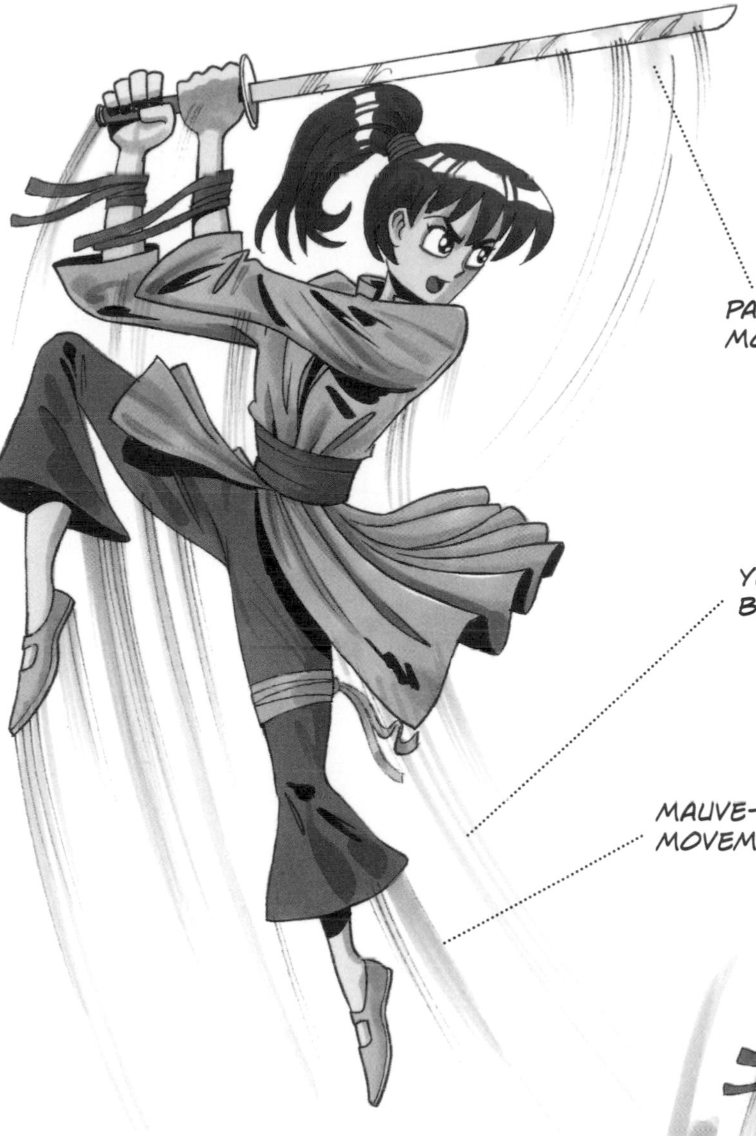
PALE BLUE MOVEMENT BLUR
YELLOW MOVEMENT BLUR FROM TUNIC
MAUVE-GREY MOVEMENT BLUR

STAGE 13

Finish with a blocky background colour, such as a pale mauve.

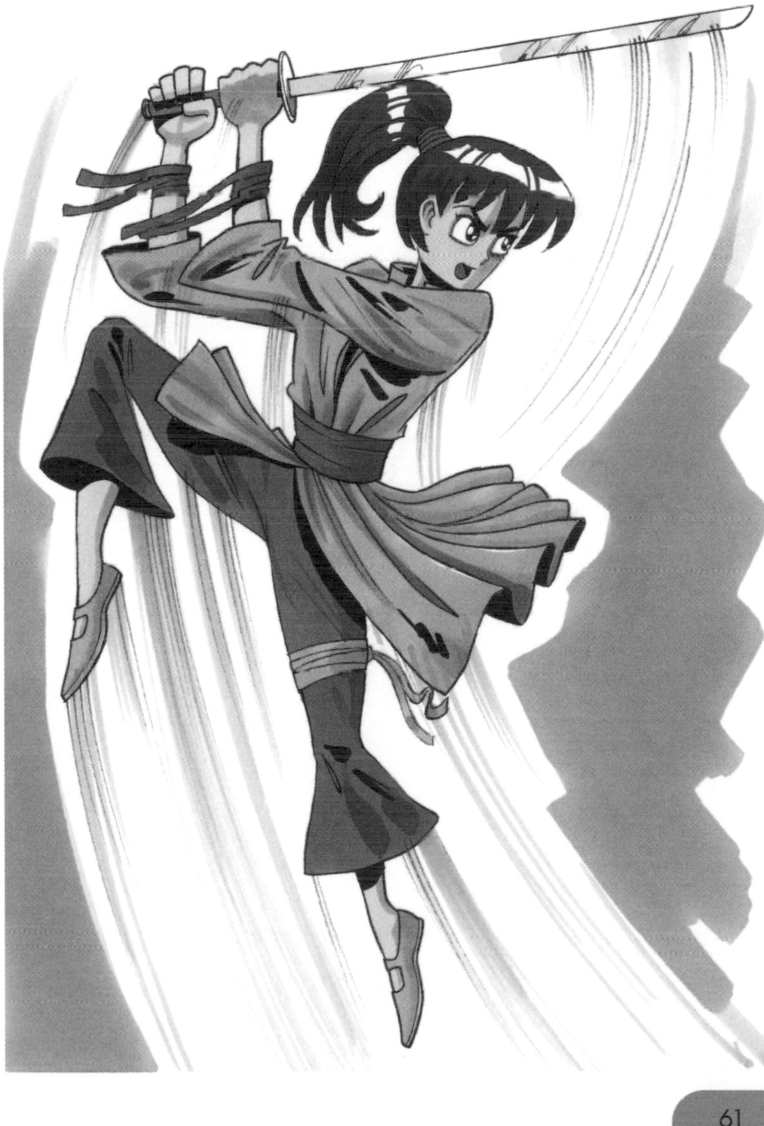

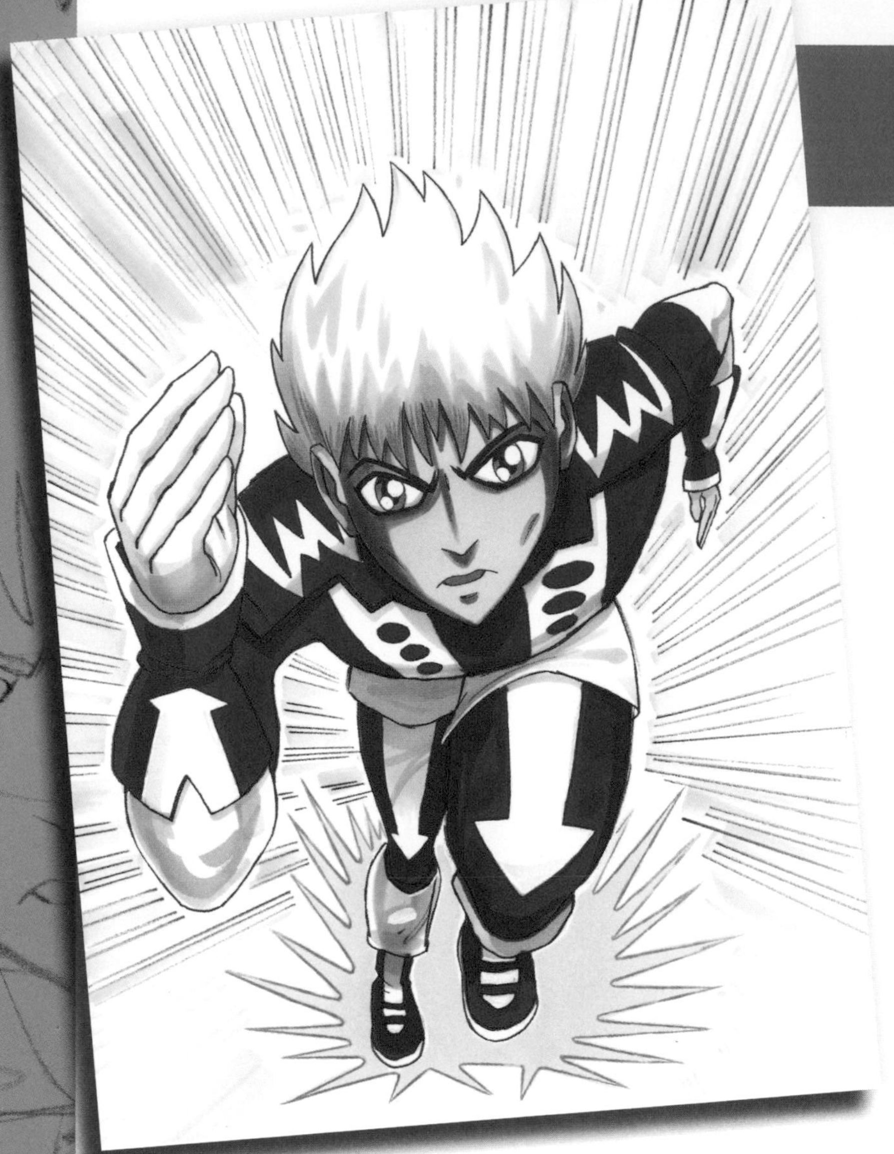

SPRINT!

A FORESHORTENED IMAGE OF A SPRINTING HERO

STAGE 1

Draw a wireframe structure for a large head, sloping shoulders and upper arms.

LEFT ARM IS RAISED UP AND AWAY FROM THE BODY, SO THE UPPER ARM IS SHORTENED

SHOULDER IS ROUGHLY IN LINE WITH THE CENTRE OF THE HEAD, AS IT IS TILTING FORWARDS

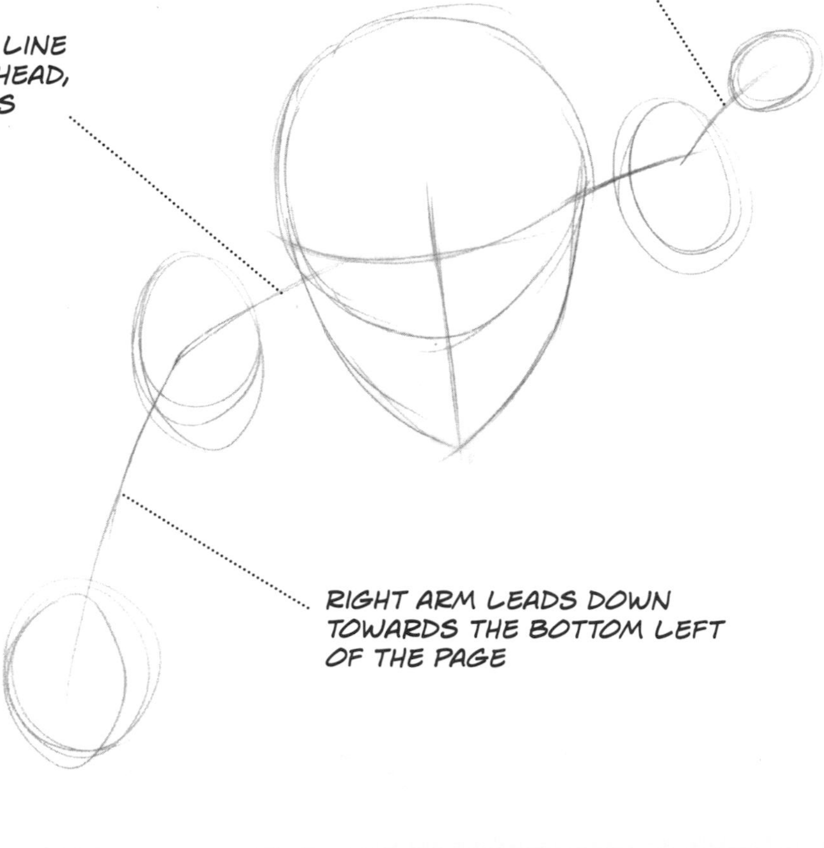

RIGHT ARM LEADS DOWN TOWARDS THE BOTTOM LEFT OF THE PAGE

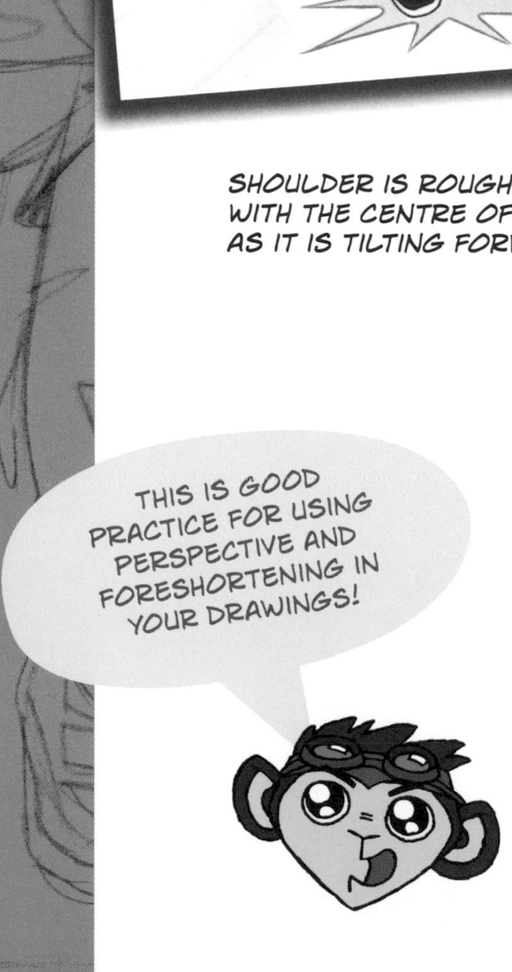
THIS IS GOOD PRACTICE FOR USING PERSPECTIVE AND FORESHORTENING IN YOUR DRAWINGS!

STAGE 2

Draw in a large wireframe forearm and hand on the figure's right side, and a small forearm and hand on the left. Sketch in the upper torso.

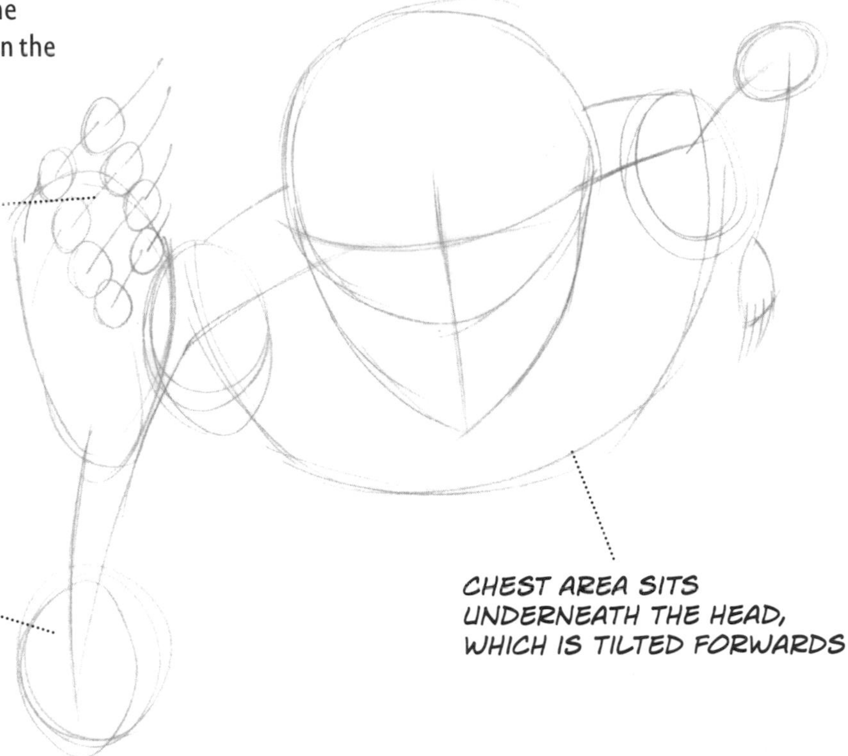
FINGERS ARE CLOSED AND ANGLED INWARDS
RIGHT ARM IS RAISED AT THE ELBOW
CHEST AREA SITS UNDERNEATH THE HEAD, WHICH IS TILTED FORWARDS

STAGE 3

Draw in wireframe legs. The perspective means that the legs will appear much smaller than the top part of the body.

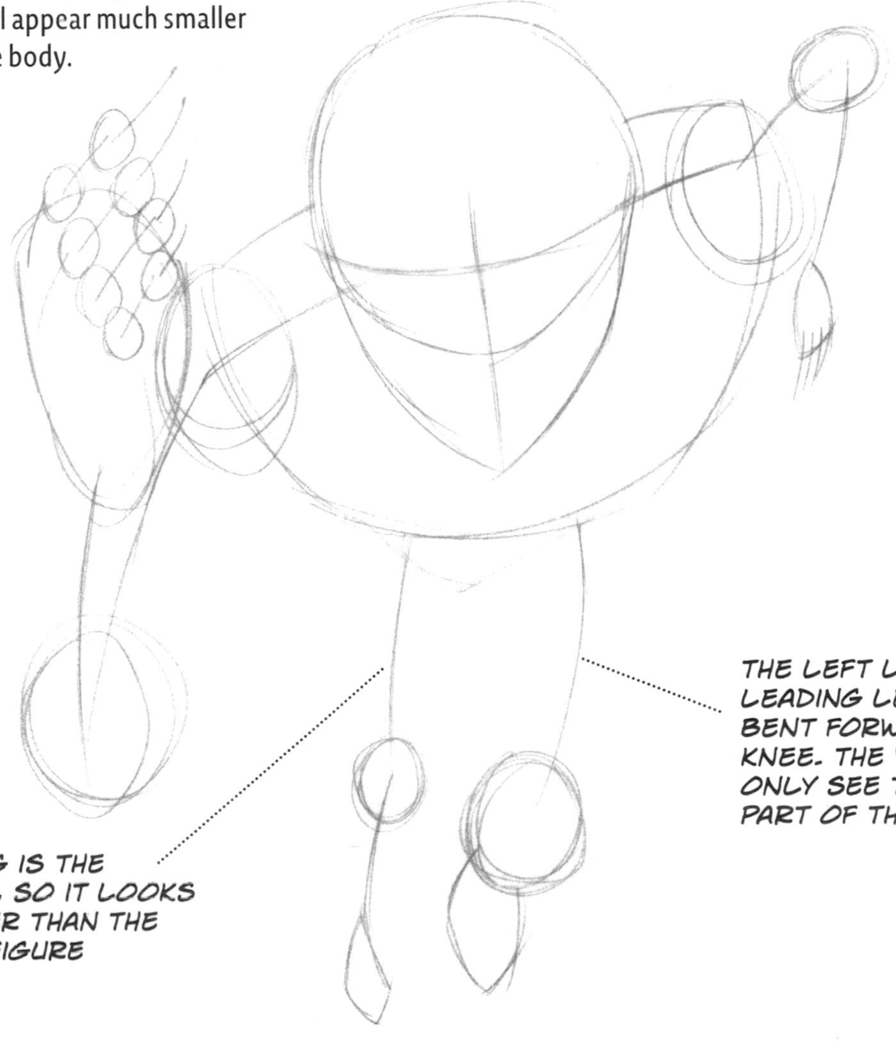
THE LEFT LEG IS THE LEADING LEG, SO IT'S BENT FORWARDS AT THE KNEE. THE VIEWER WILL ONLY SEE THE THIGH AND PART OF THE FOOT
THE RIGHT LEG IS THE TRAILING LEG, SO IT LOOKS MUCH SMALLER THAN THE REST OF THE FIGURE

STAGE 4

Flesh out your figure with curving lines as shown. Note how large the character's right forearm is in comparison to the left.

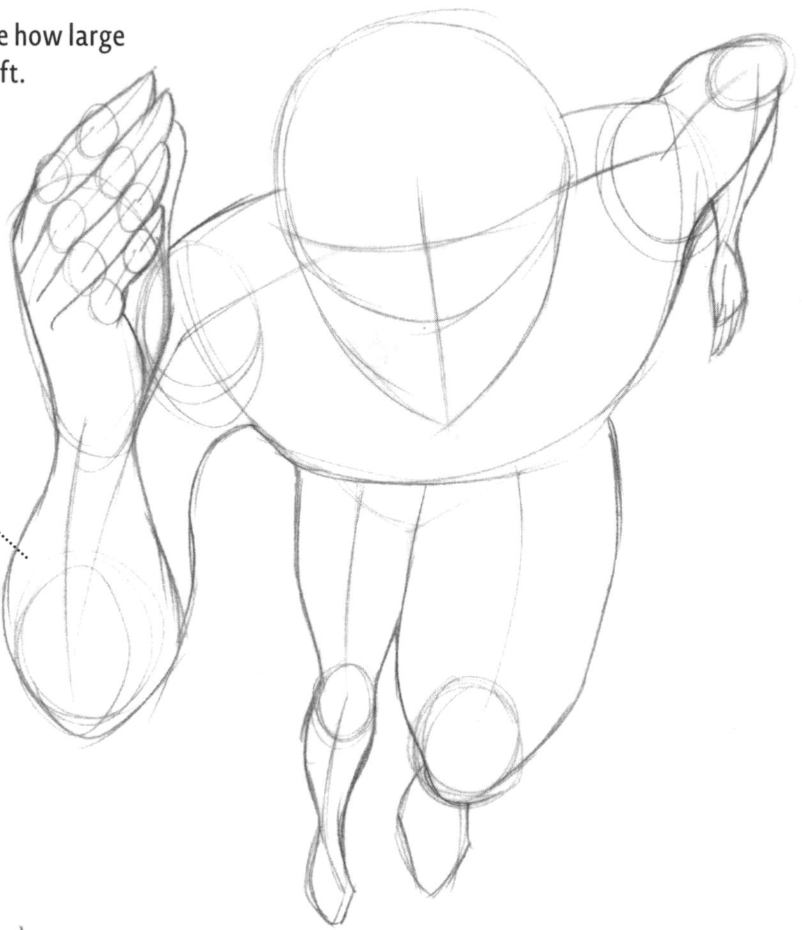
SEE HOW THE OPPOSITE ARM AND LEG ARE FORWARD IN THE SPRINT: THE RIGHT ARM AND LEFT LEG ARE IN FRONT, THE LEFT ARM AND RIGHT LEG ARE BEHIND

STAGE 5

Draw in a determined face with a sharp, pointed chin and spiky hair.

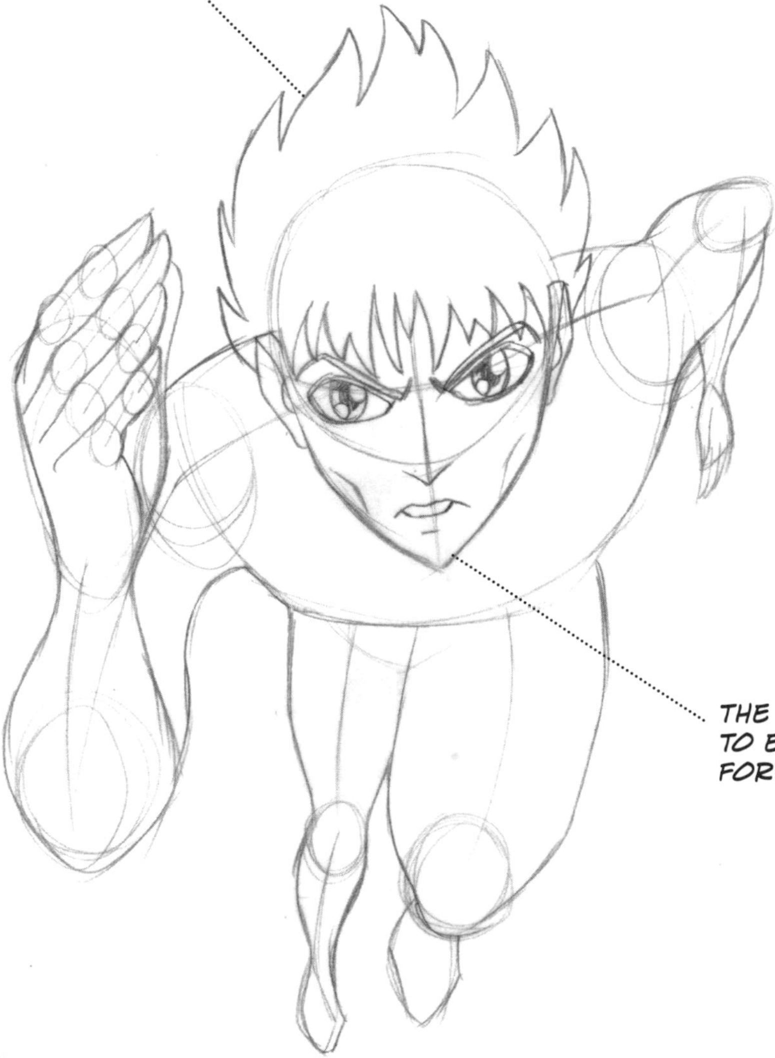
THE HAIR STYLE RESEMBLES A FLAME, WHICH CAN SUGGEST HEAT AND SPEED TO THE VIEWER
THE CHIN IS POINTED TO EMPHASIZE THE FORWARD MOVEMENT

STAGE 6

Add a costume with lots of detail to your figure.

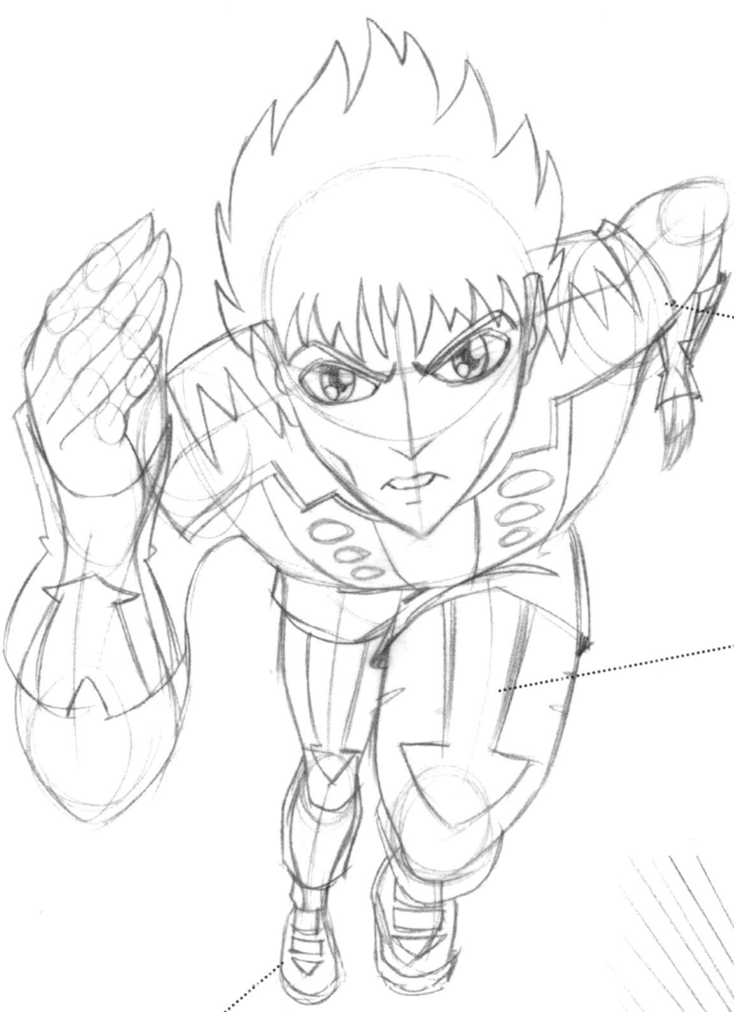

USE THE COSTUME DECORATION TO GIVE A SUGGESTION OF PADDING OR ARMOUR
ARROW SHAPES ON THE COSTUME GIVE A SENSE OF DIRECTION
THE SHOES SHOULD LOOK SUITABLE FOR RUNNING

STAGE 7

Draw a flash shape around the feet, and add in speed lines. The speed lines should all come from the centre of the page and radiate out towards the edge.

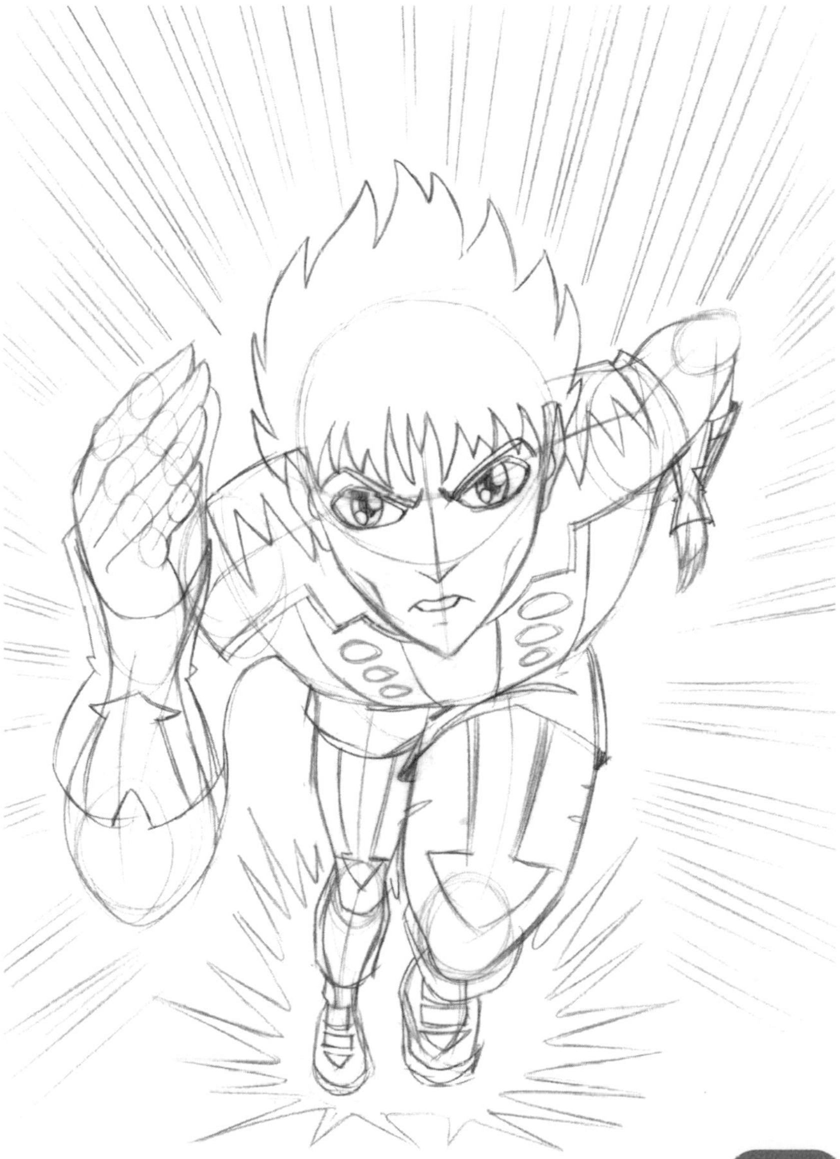

STAGE 8

Outline the character in black, leaving the costume details blank.

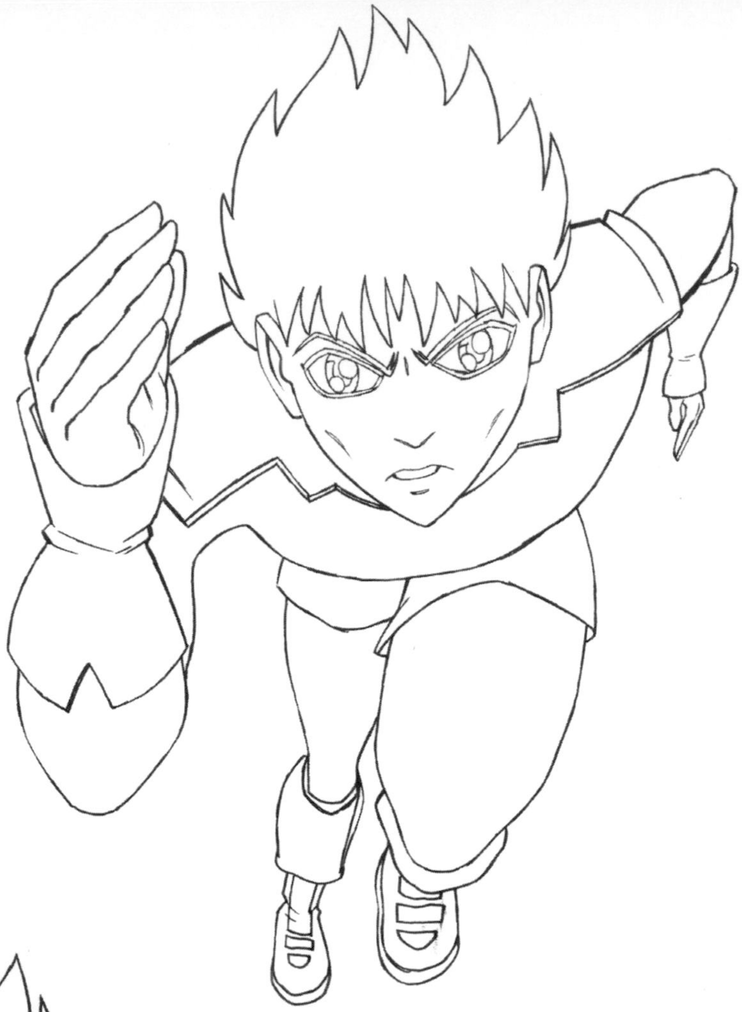

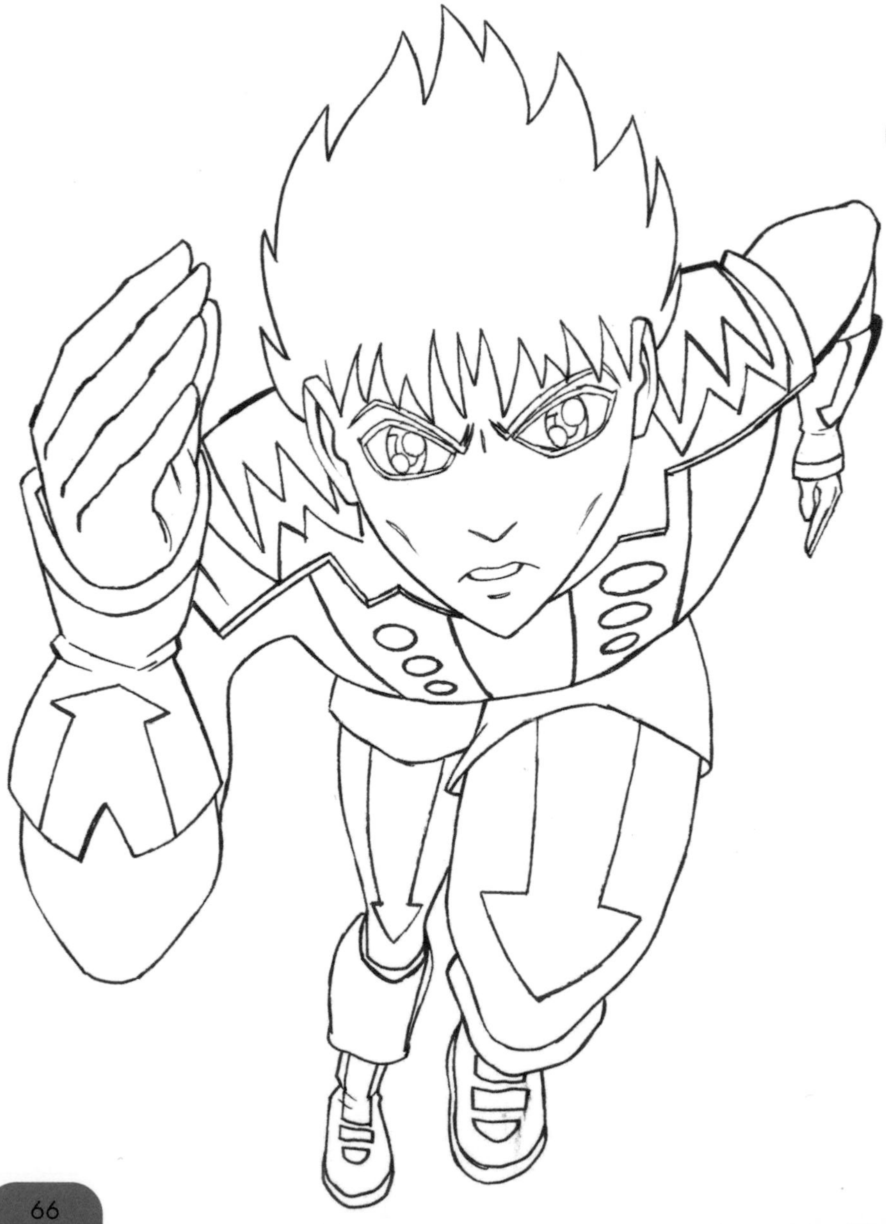

STAGE 9

Use a red fibre-tip pen to draw in the costume details.

STAGE 10

Colour parts of the costume pattern in red, and use a pale blue to shade the bottom part of the hair. Colour in the face with a flesh tone.

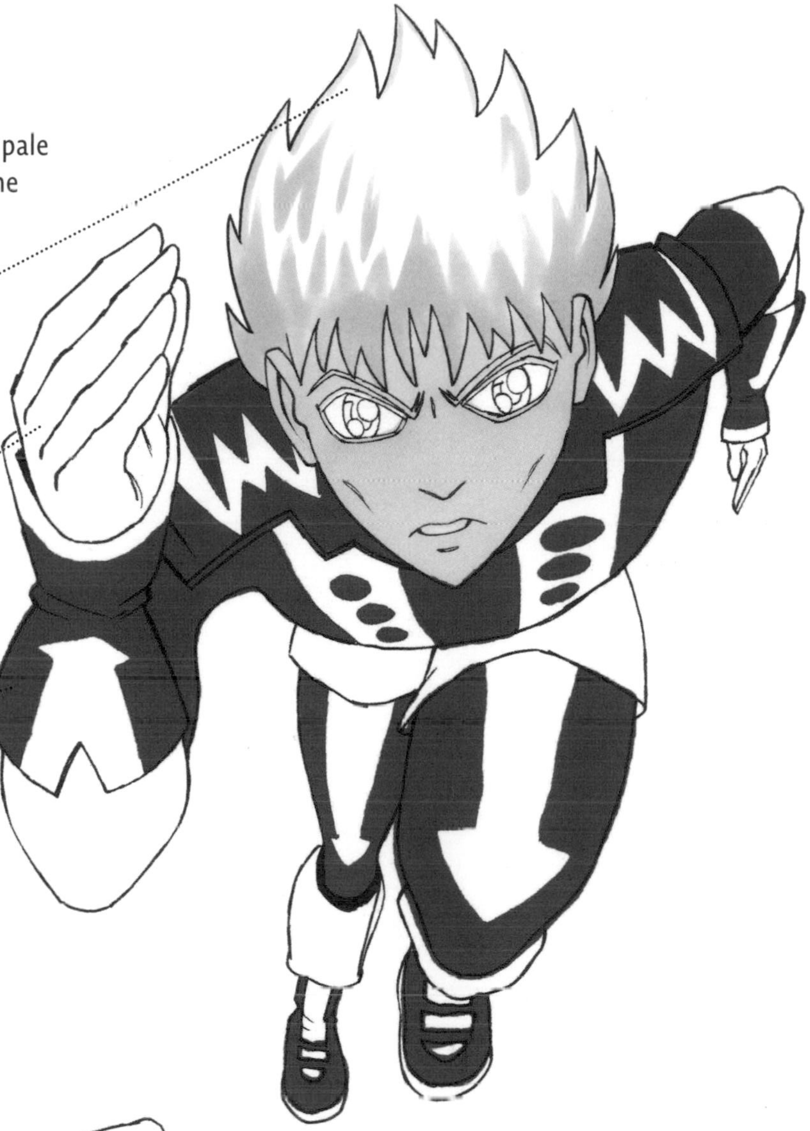
LEAVE THE TOP PARTS OF THE HAIR WHITE
LEAVE THE HANDS WHITE FOR NOW, AS THE CHARACTER IS WEARING GLOVES
CAREFULLY FILL IN SOLID RED AREAS, LEAVING THE ARROW SHAPES WHITE

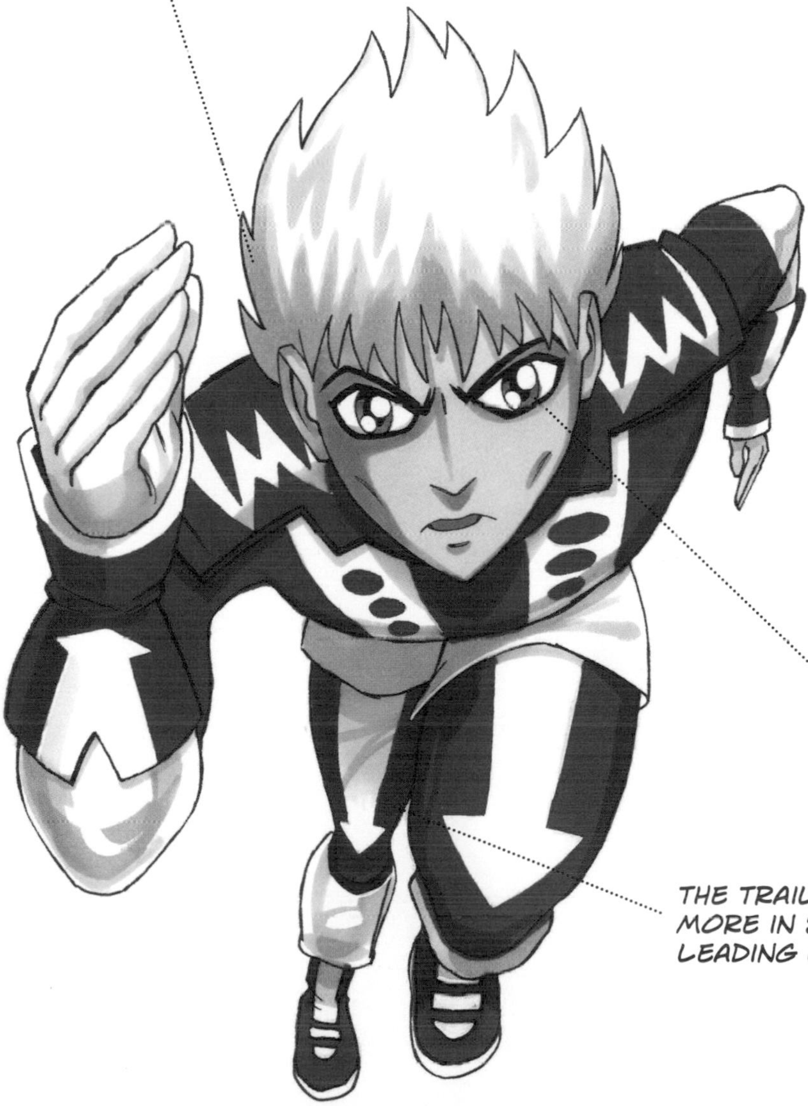
MAUVE ON PALE BLUE IS GOOD FOR SHADING WHITE OBJECTS
COLOUR THE EYES WITH STRONG ORANGE
THE TRAILING LEG SHOULD BE MORE IN SHADOW THAN THE LEADING LEG

STAGE 11

Add shading to the face and body with darker tints of red, grey and mauve, and colour in the eyes and mouth.

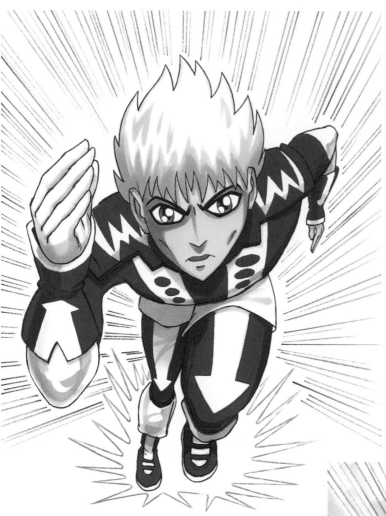

STAGE 12

Use a dark grey or black finepoint pen to draw in the speed lines with a ruler, and outline the flash in yellow.

STAGE 13

Finish with some pale blue marker to add depth to the speed lines, and fill in the flash with bright yellow. Add some more shadow to the face and body.

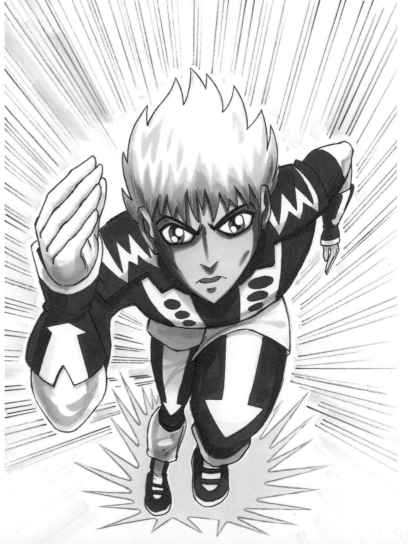

JUMPING ATTACK!

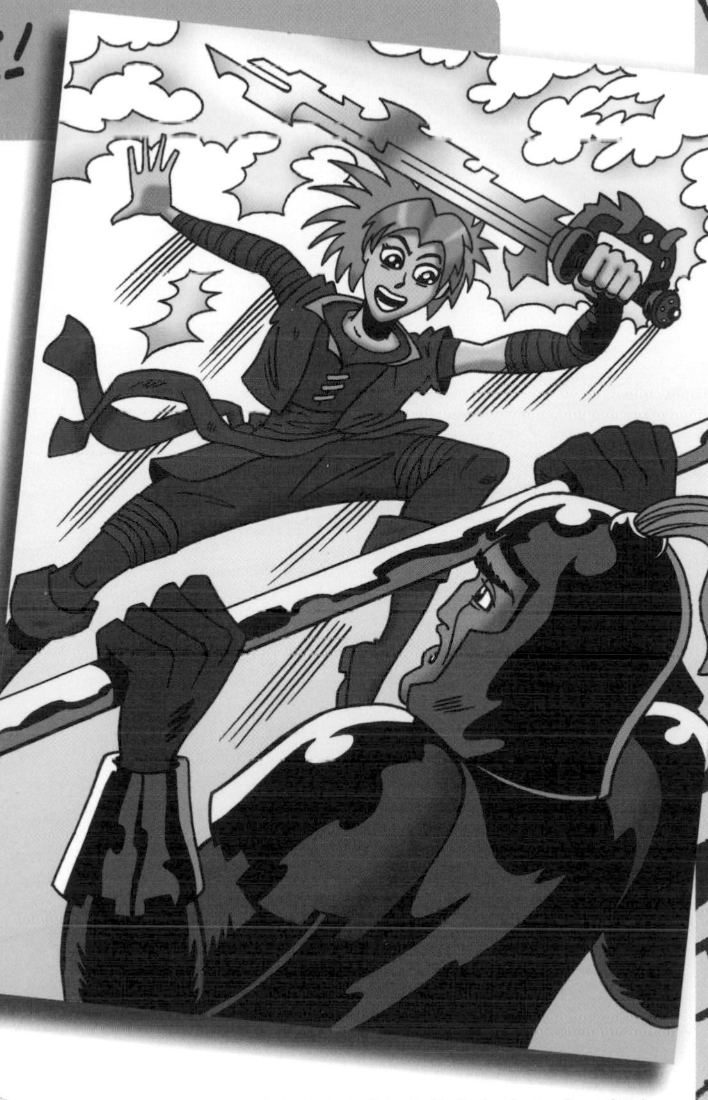

A SWORD-WIELDING HEROINE TAKES ON A HULKING GUARD

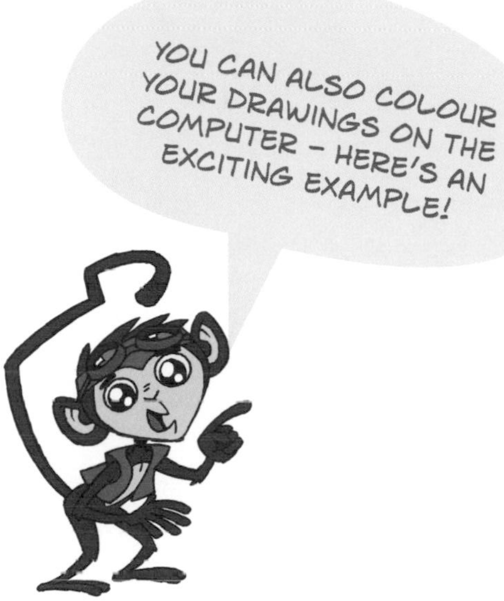
YOU CAN ALSO COLOUR YOUR DRAWINGS ON THE COMPUTER – HERE'S AN EXCITING EXAMPLE!

STAGE 1

Create a wireframe guide for a leaping figure in the top half of the page.

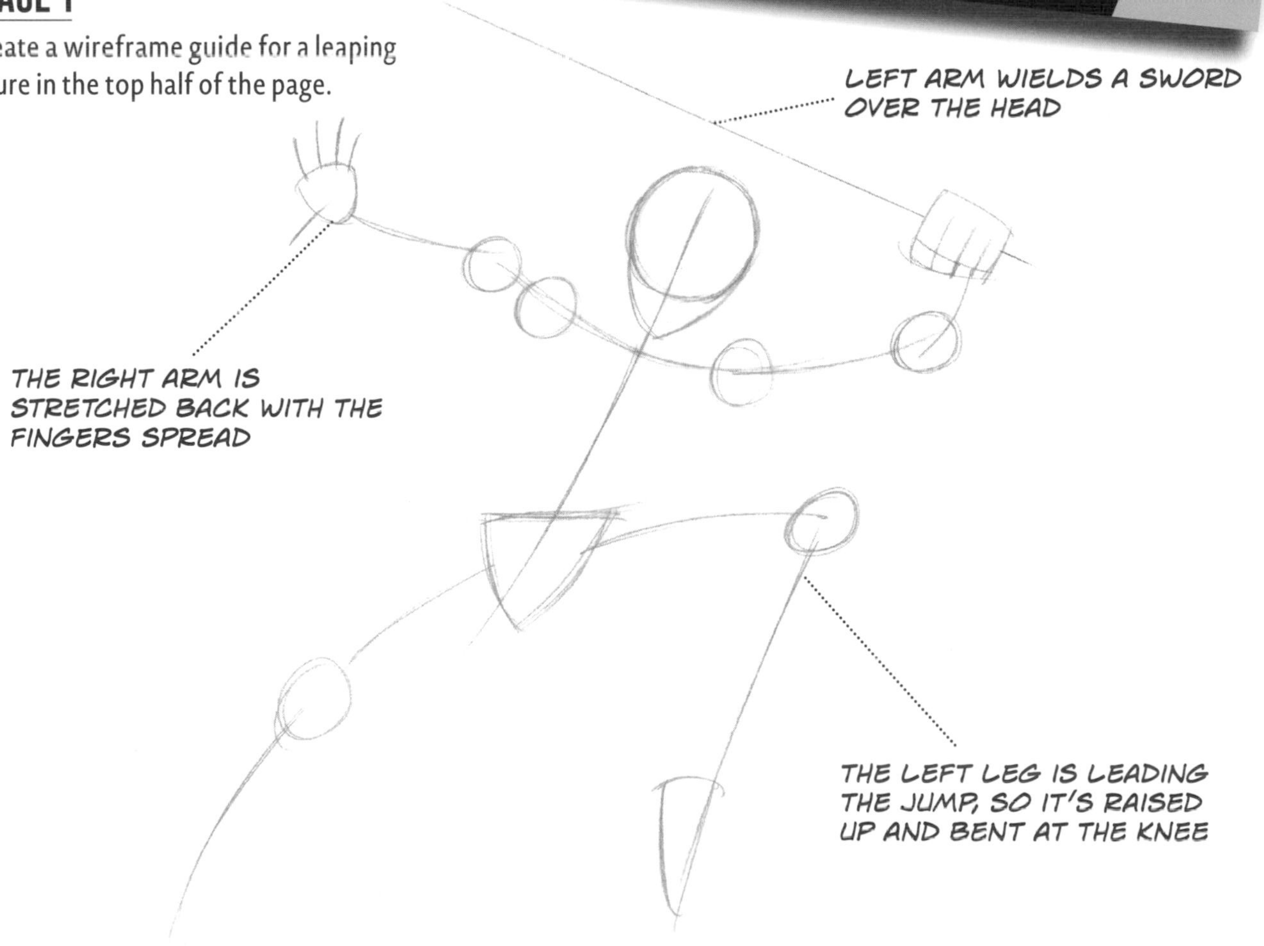
LEFT ARM WIELDS A SWORD OVER THE HEAD
THE RIGHT ARM IS STRETCHED BACK WITH THE FINGERS SPREAD
THE LEFT LEG IS LEADING THE JUMP, SO IT'S RAISED UP AND BENT AT THE KNEE

STAGE 2

Add a wireframe guard at the bottom-right. He's in the foreground so will be bigger than the first figure. This gives depth and perspective to the drawing.

THE GUARD IS HOLDING UP A STAFF TO DEFEND HIMSELF – DRAW THIS WITH A RULER, DIAGONALLY ACROSS THE PAGE

NOTE HOW THE FINGERS ARE HOLDING THE STAFF

SHOULDERS ARE HUNCHED UP TO THE HEAD IN A DEFENSIVE POSITION

HER LEFT FOOT IS POINTING STRAIGHT DOWN

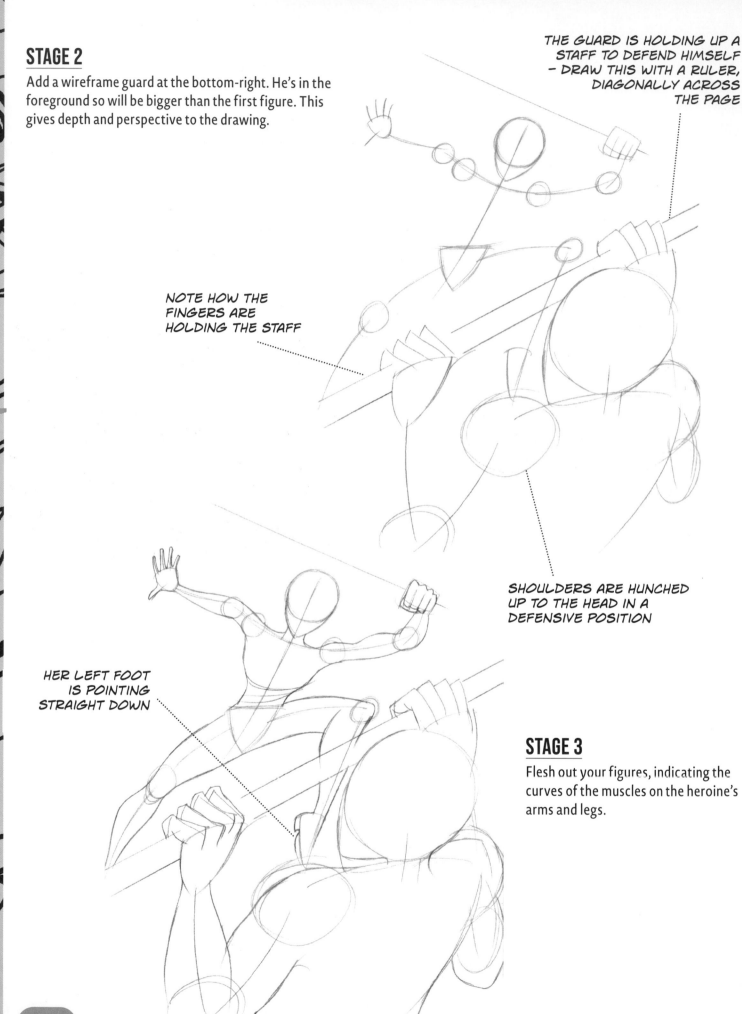

STAGE 3

Flesh out your figures, indicating the curves of the muscles on the heroine's arms and legs.

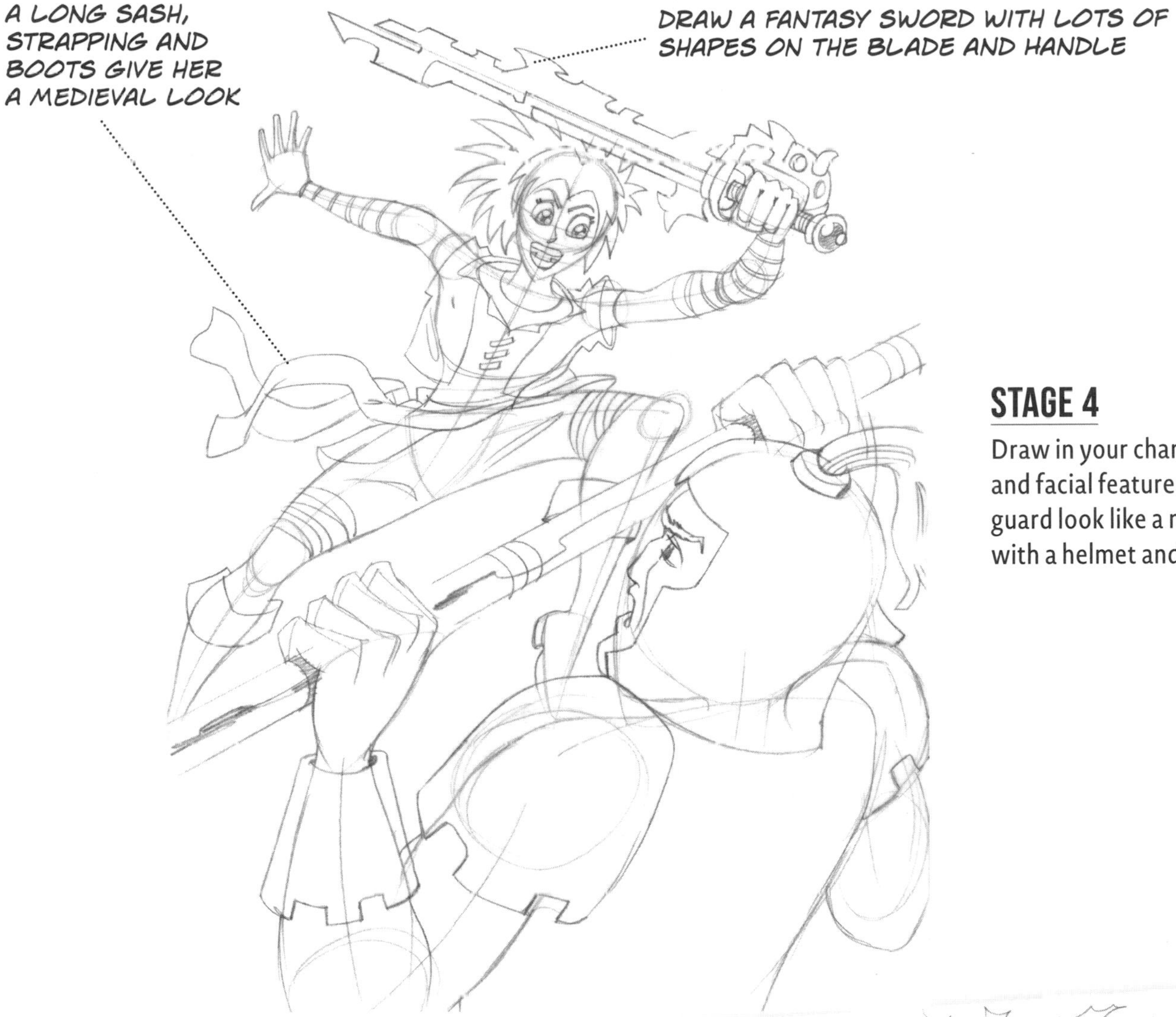
A LONG SASH, STRAPPING AND BOOTS GIVE HER A MEDIEVAL LOOK
DRAW A FANTASY SWORD WITH LOTS OF SHAPES ON THE BLADE AND HANDLE

STAGE 4

Draw in your characters' clothing and facial features. Make the guard look like a medieval knight with a helmet and plume.

STAGE 5

Add shading suggestions, speed lines and a crackling burst of energy around the sword.

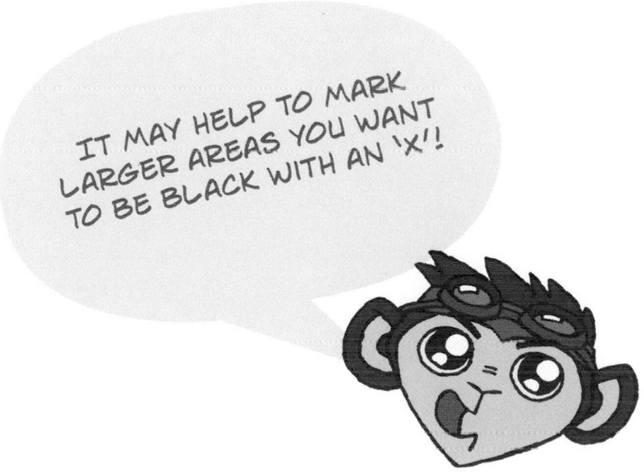
IT MAY HELP TO MARK LARGER AREAS YOU WANT TO BE BLACK WITH AN 'X'!

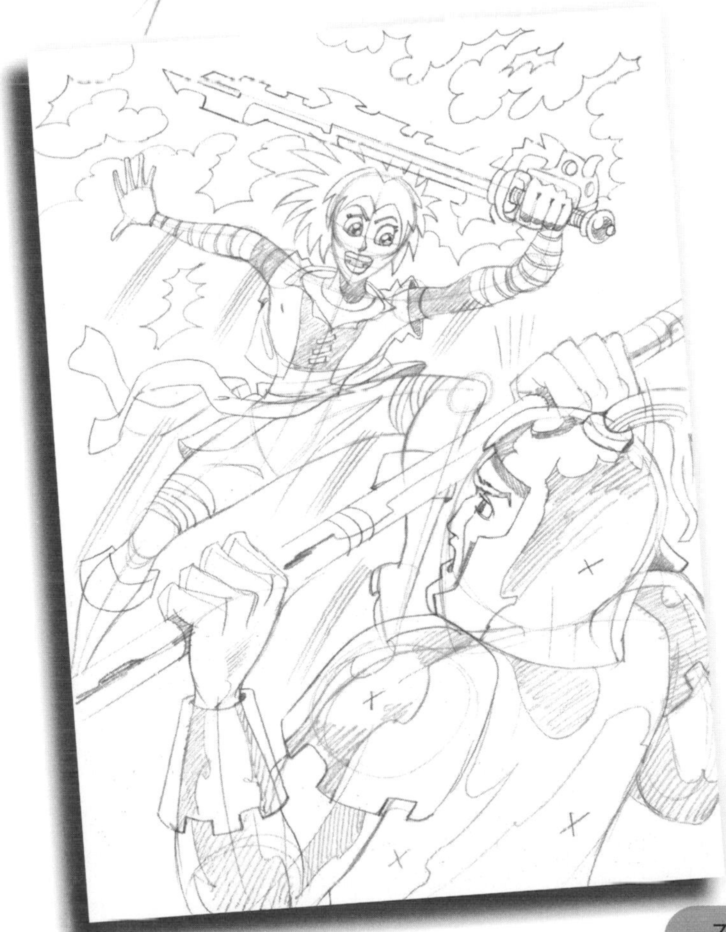

STAGE 6

Outline your characters with black pen and fill in solid areas of black.

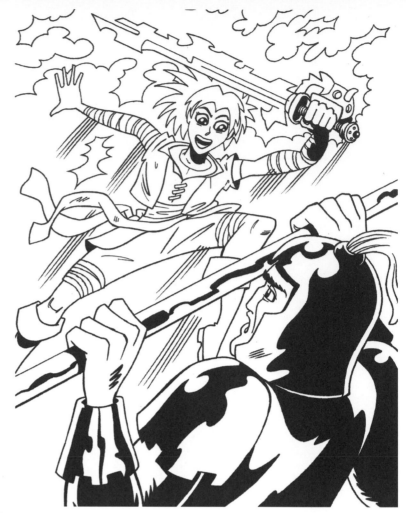

STAGE 7

If you are using a computer, scan your linework and make the contrast 100 per cent, then add colour (see page 11). Use a darker colour for the guard to draw the eye to the heroine. If you don't wish to use a computer, colour using markers instead.

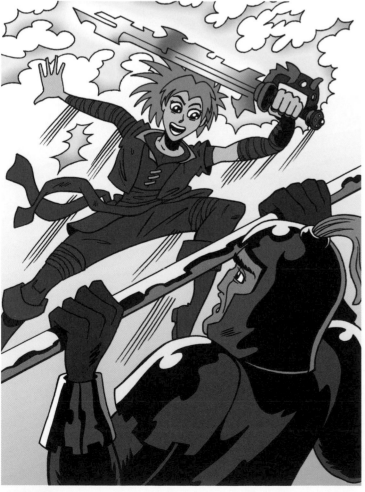

STAGE 8

Finish by adding some shading, using darker tones, and some white highlights, such as those on the heroine's hair. These final touches are really important: computer programs can give a very 'polished' look, but can make the drawing a little flat.

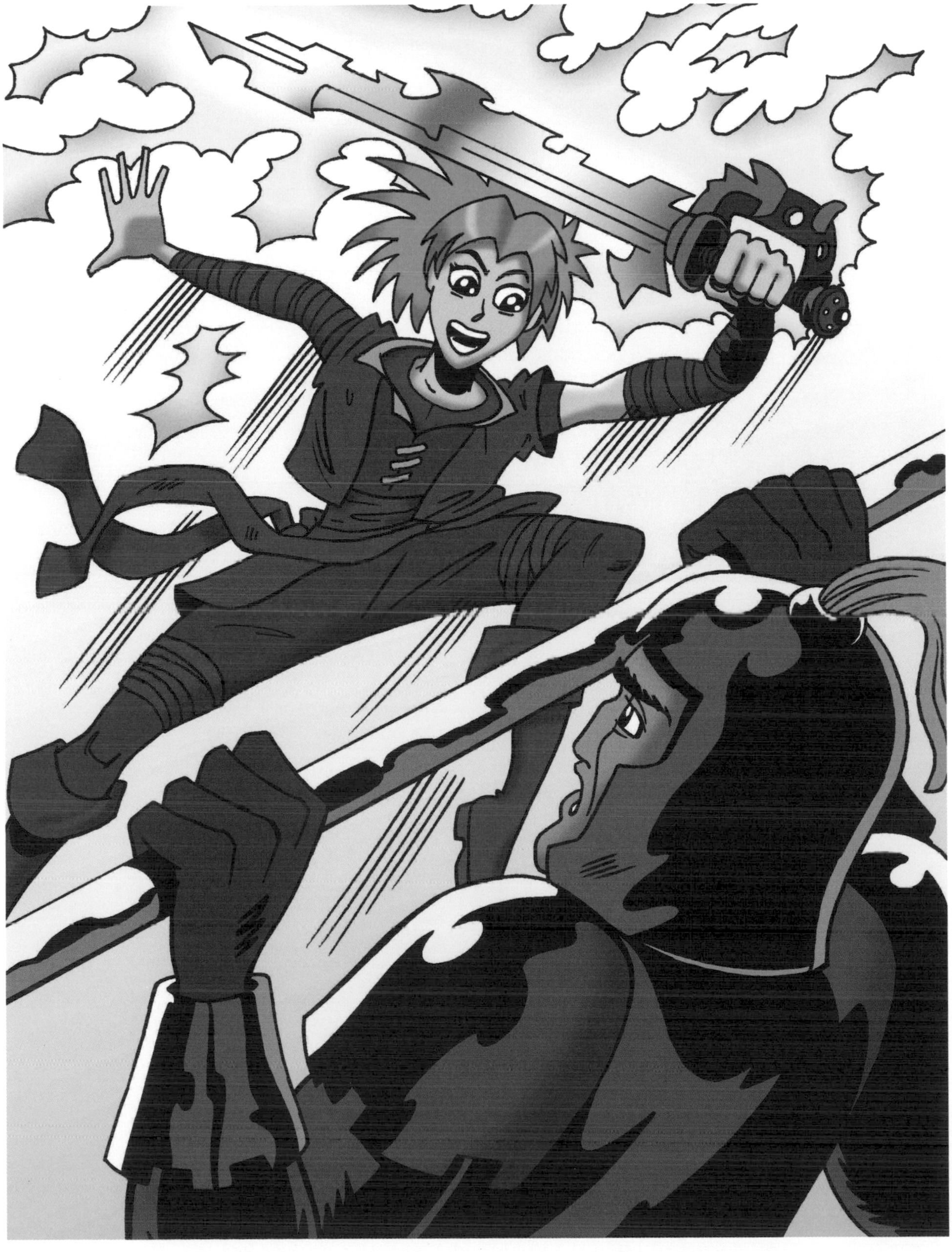

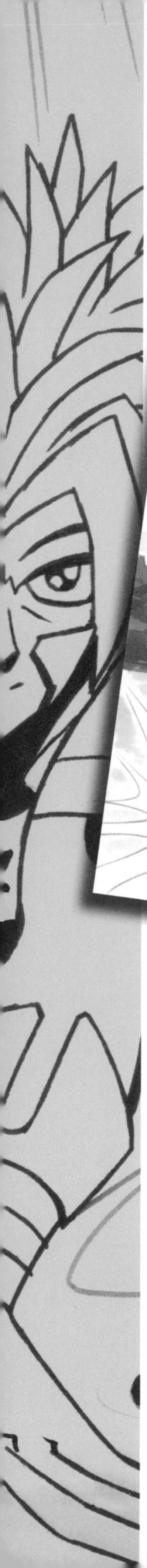

READY FOR ACTION!

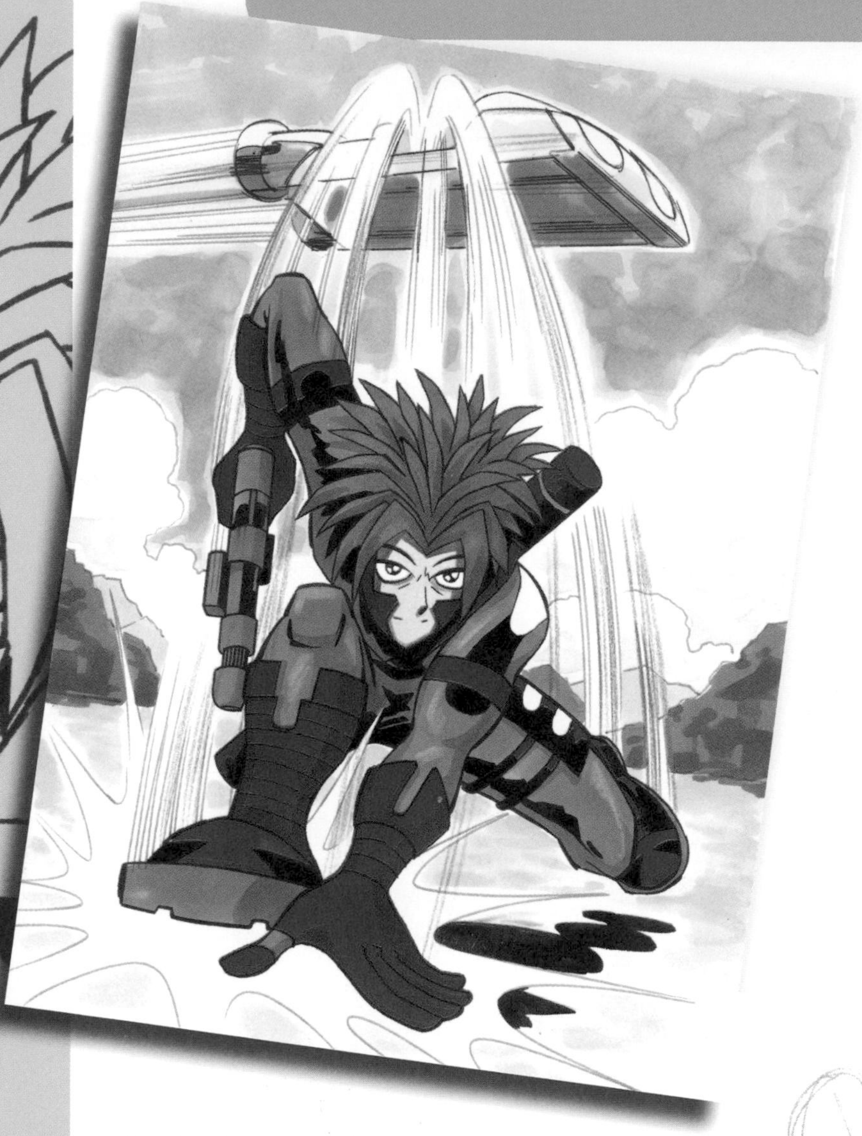

A FUTURISTIC AGENT LANDS IN ENEMY TERRITORY

STAGE 1

Start by sketching a wireframe head shape, with shoulder joints and upper arms.

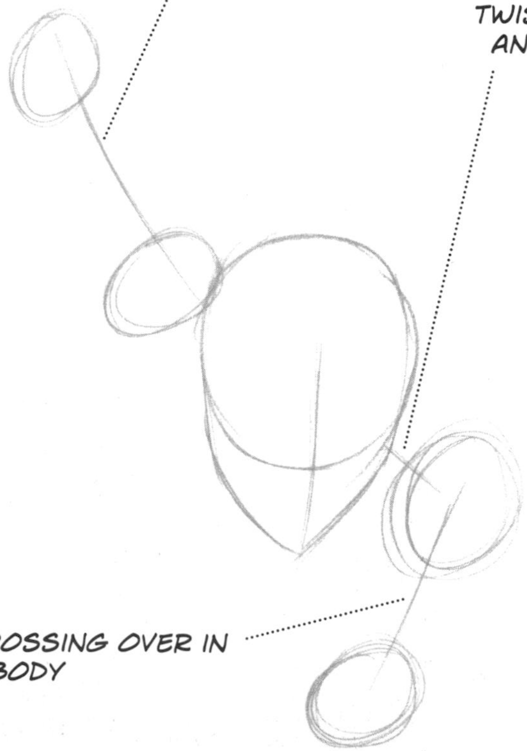
RIGHT ARM IS TUCKED BACK BEHIND THE BODY
SHOULDERS ARE TWISTED AT AN ANGLE
LEFT ARM IS CROSSING OVER IN FRONT OF THE BODY

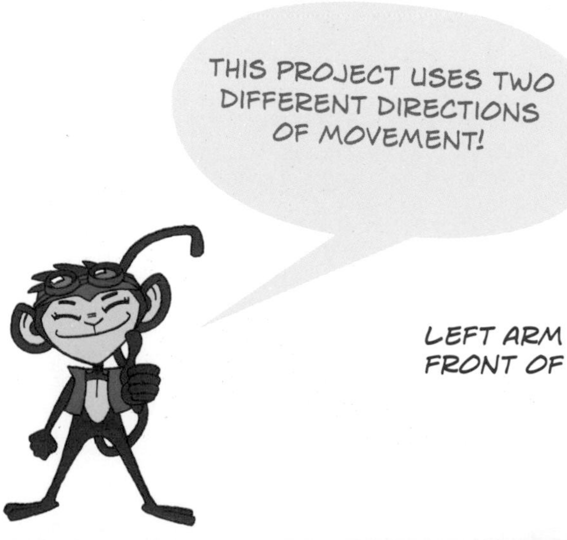
THIS PROJECT USES TWO DIFFERENT DIRECTIONS OF MOVEMENT!

STAGE 2

Draw in wireframe forearms and the leading left hand, which is spread out on the floor. Add crouching legs, with the right knee close to the chin.

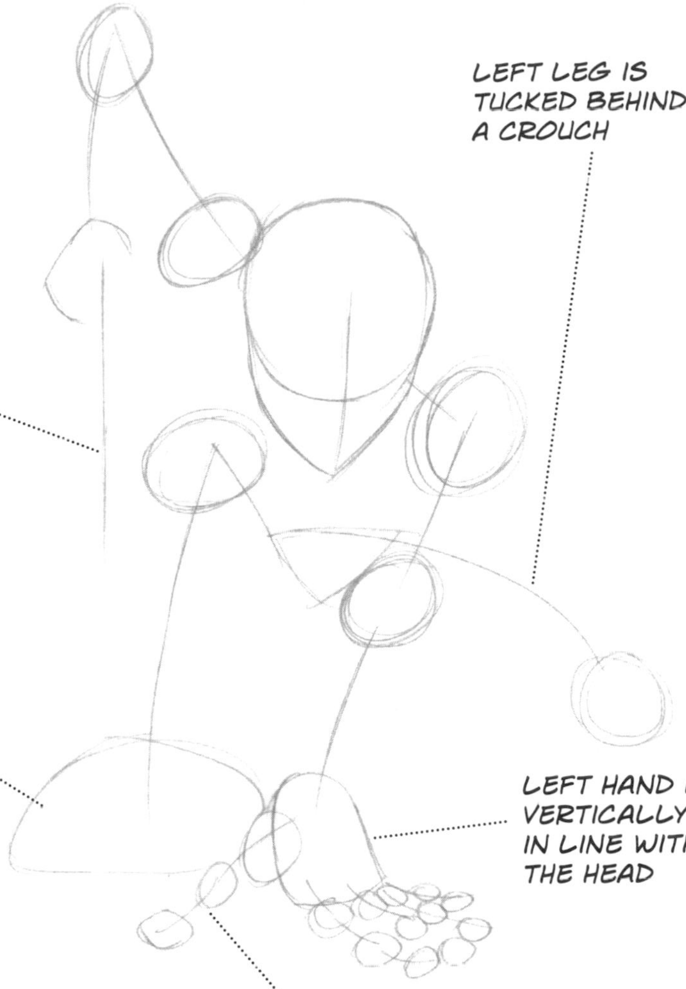
LEFT LEG IS TUCKED BEHIND IN A CROUCH
THE RIGHT HAND WILL BE HOLDING A WEAPON – SKETCH IN THE POSITION OF THE HAND, WITH A VERTICAL LINE FOR THE WEAPON
RIGHT FOOT IS SET JUST BEHIND THE LEFT HAND IN THE FOREGROUND OF THE FRAME
LEFT HAND IS VERTICALLY IN LINE WITH THE HEAD
THE THUMB AND FINGERS SUPPORT THE HAND'S WEIGHT

STAGE 3

Flesh out your figure, adding lots of spiky hair, a determined expression and a futuristic-looking hand gun.

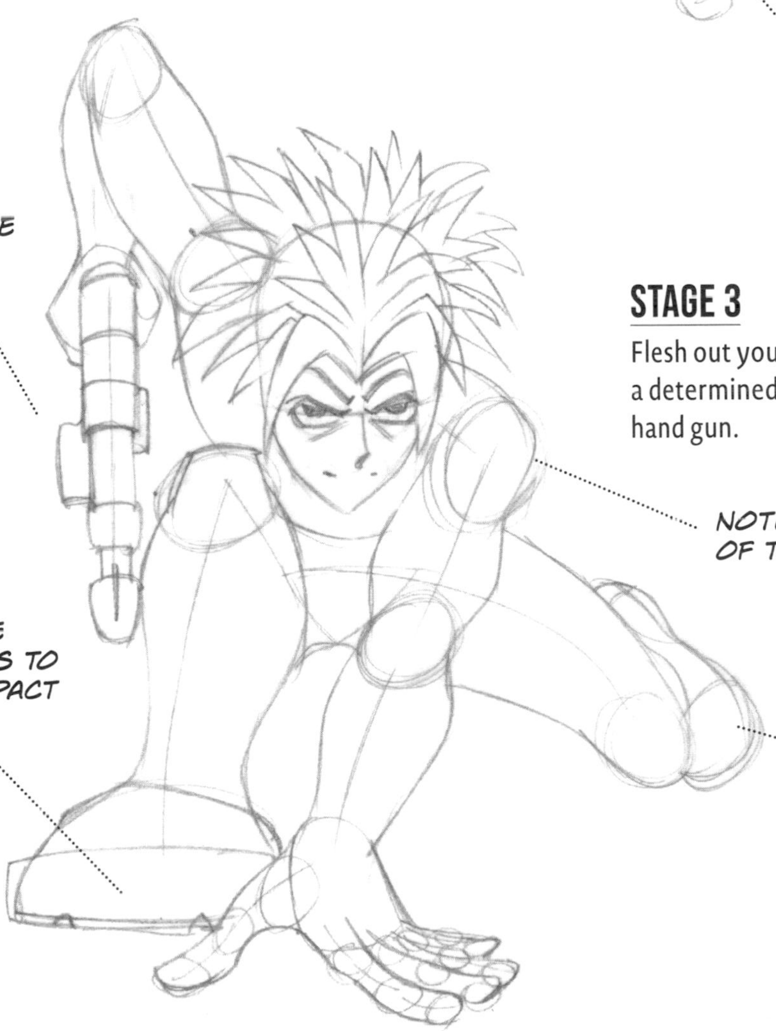
WEAPON IS AIMED STRAIGHT DOWN AT THE GROUND
NOTE THE CURVE OF THE MUSCLES
BOOTS HAVE THICK SOLES TO CUSHION IMPACT
LEFT FOOT IS PARTLY CONCEALED BEHIND THE FOLDED LEG

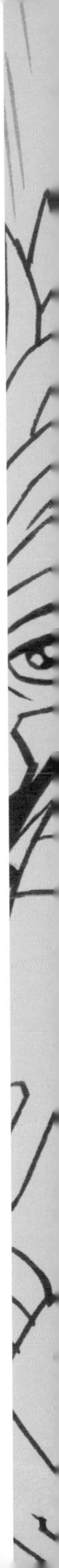

STAGE 4

Draw three straight lines above the figure, coming from a vanishing point to the left of the page, then bisect them with two diagonal lines.

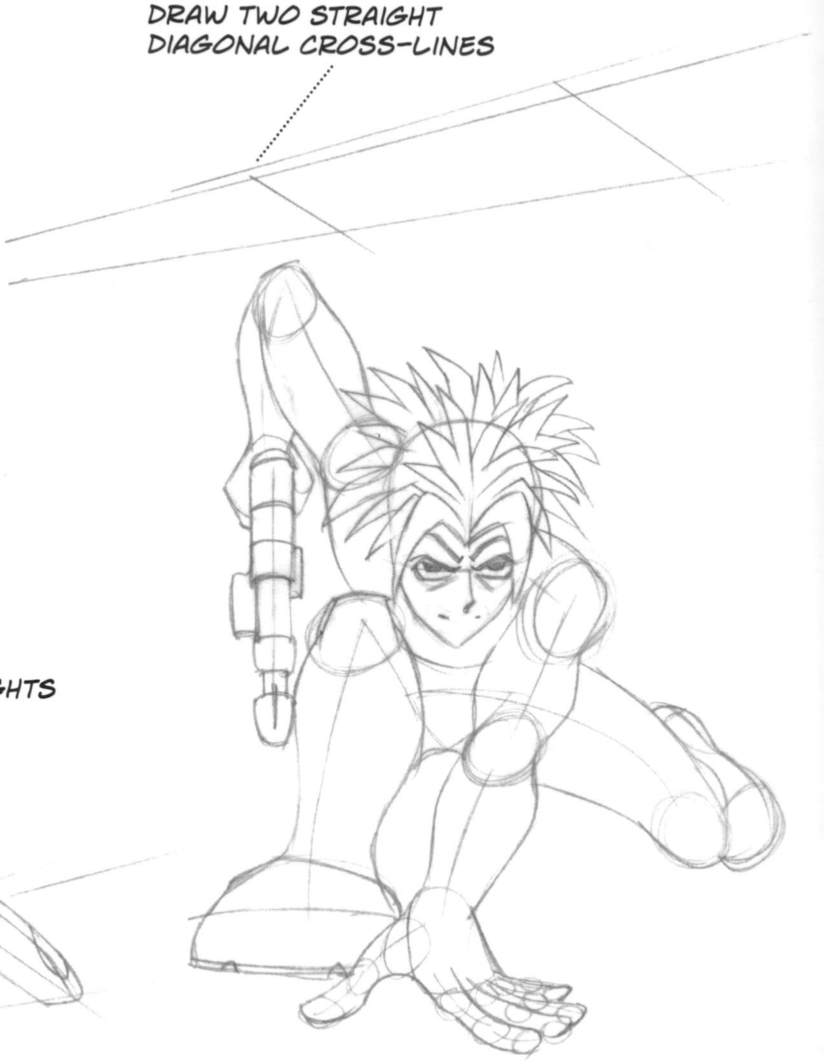
DRAW TWO STRAIGHT DIAGONAL CROSS-LINES
LINES MEET AT A VANISHING POINT OFF THE PAGE

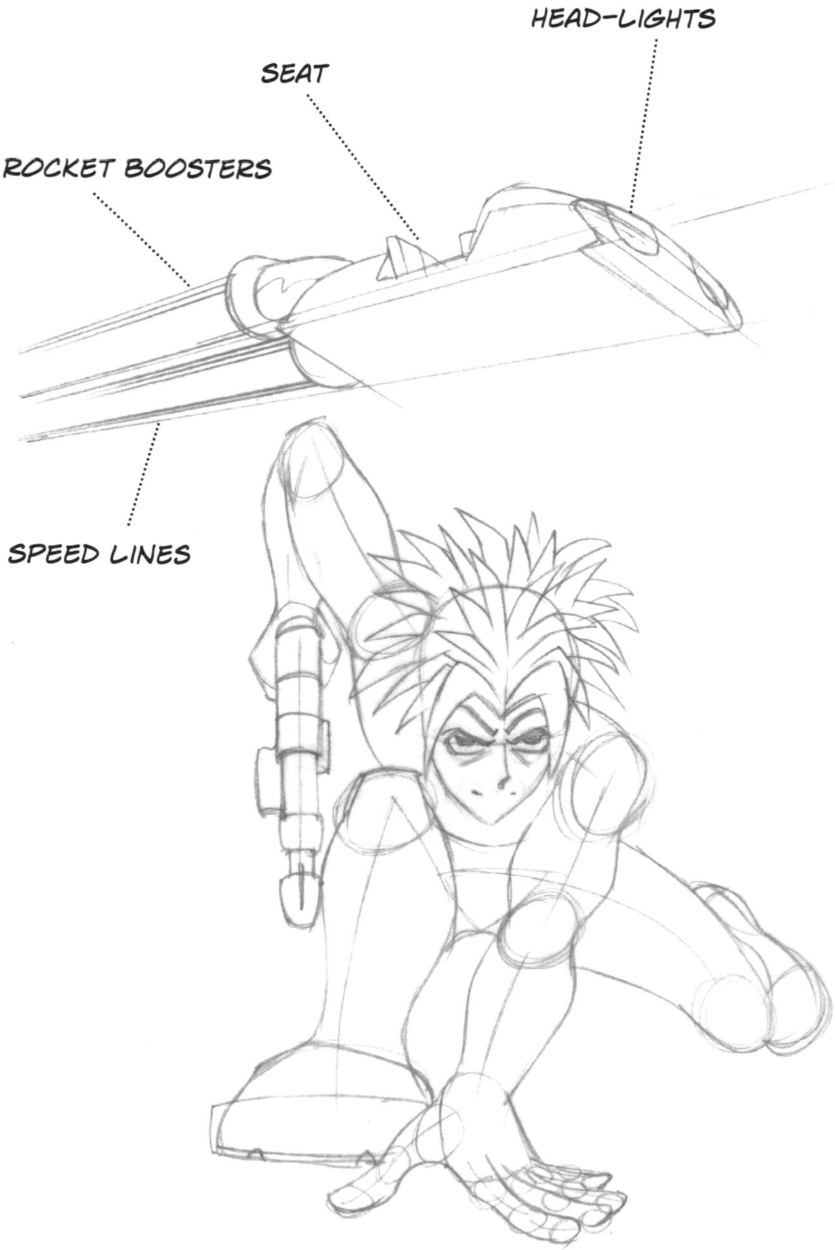
HEAD-LIGHTS
SEAT
ROCKET BOOSTERS
SPEED LINES

STAGE 5

Use your guidelines to draw in a futuristic flying vehicle.

STAGE 6

Use speed lines to show that the figure has jumped from the moving vehicle, and an impact burst to show he's landed with a thump!

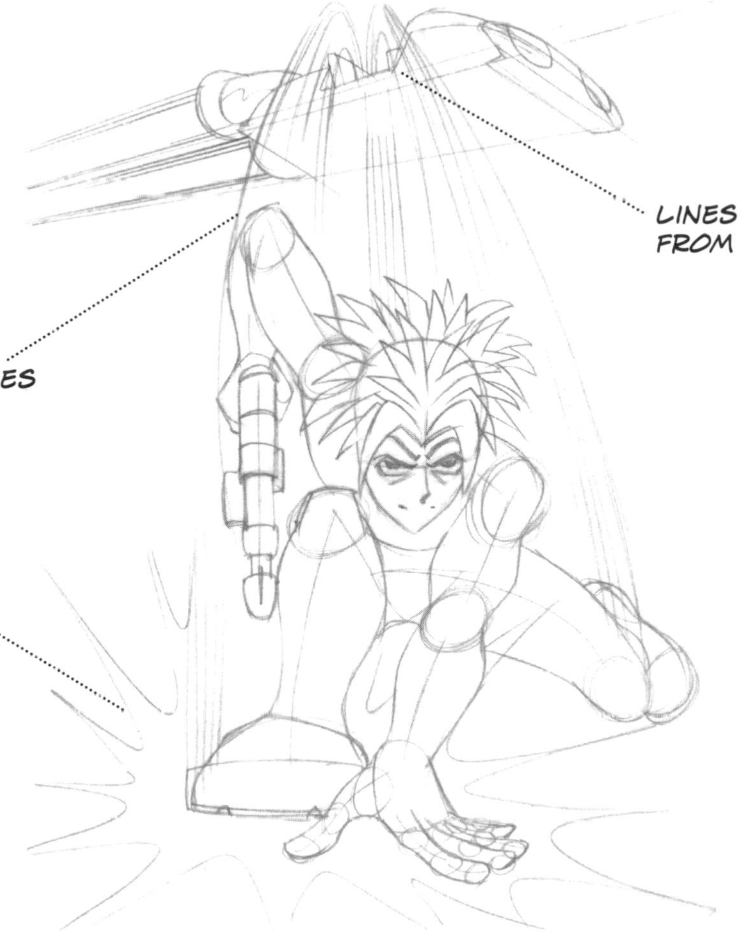
LINES COMING FROM SEAT
SPEED LINES
IMPACT BURST

STAGE 7

Add some background and costume details.

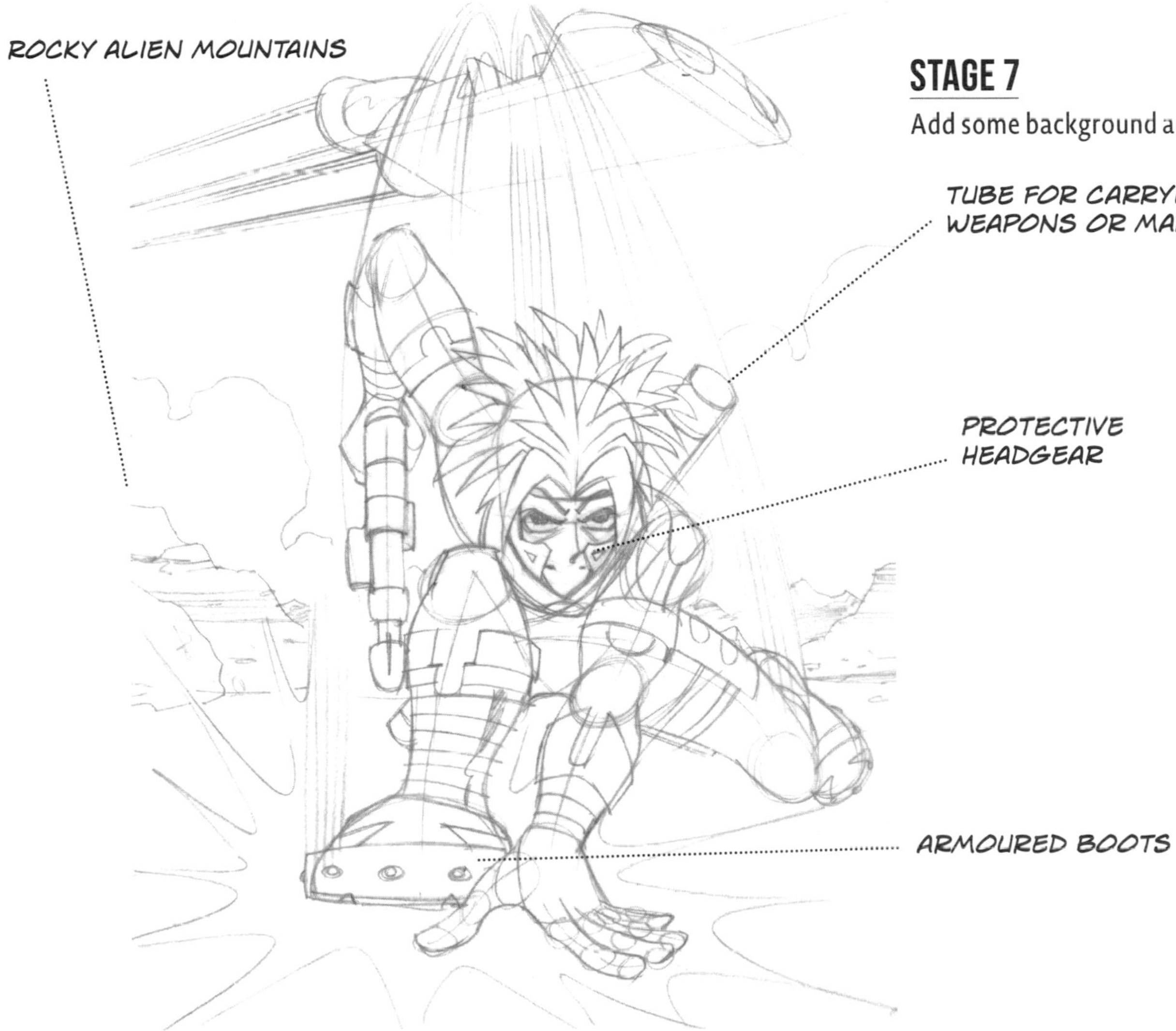
ROCKY ALIEN MOUNTAINS
TUBE FOR CARRYING WEAPONS OR MAPS
PROTECTIVE HEADGEAR
ARMOURED BOOTS

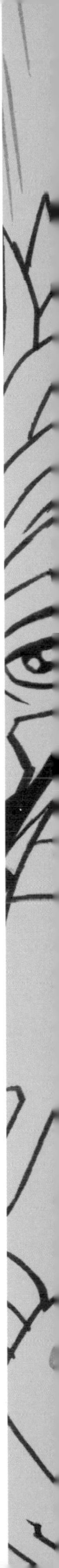

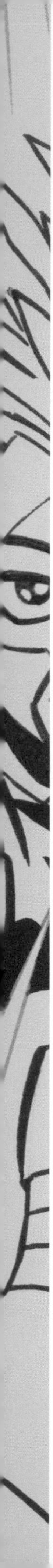

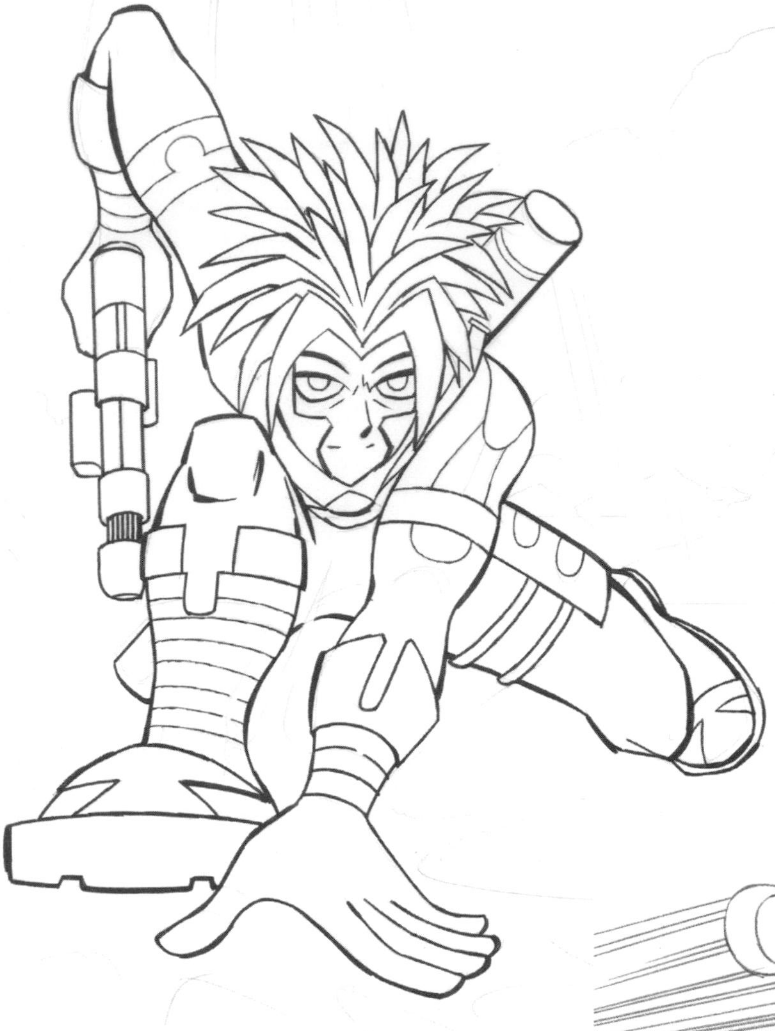

STAGE 8

Outline your figure in black. I've used a combination of black fine pen and brush pen here to give a variety to the line weight.

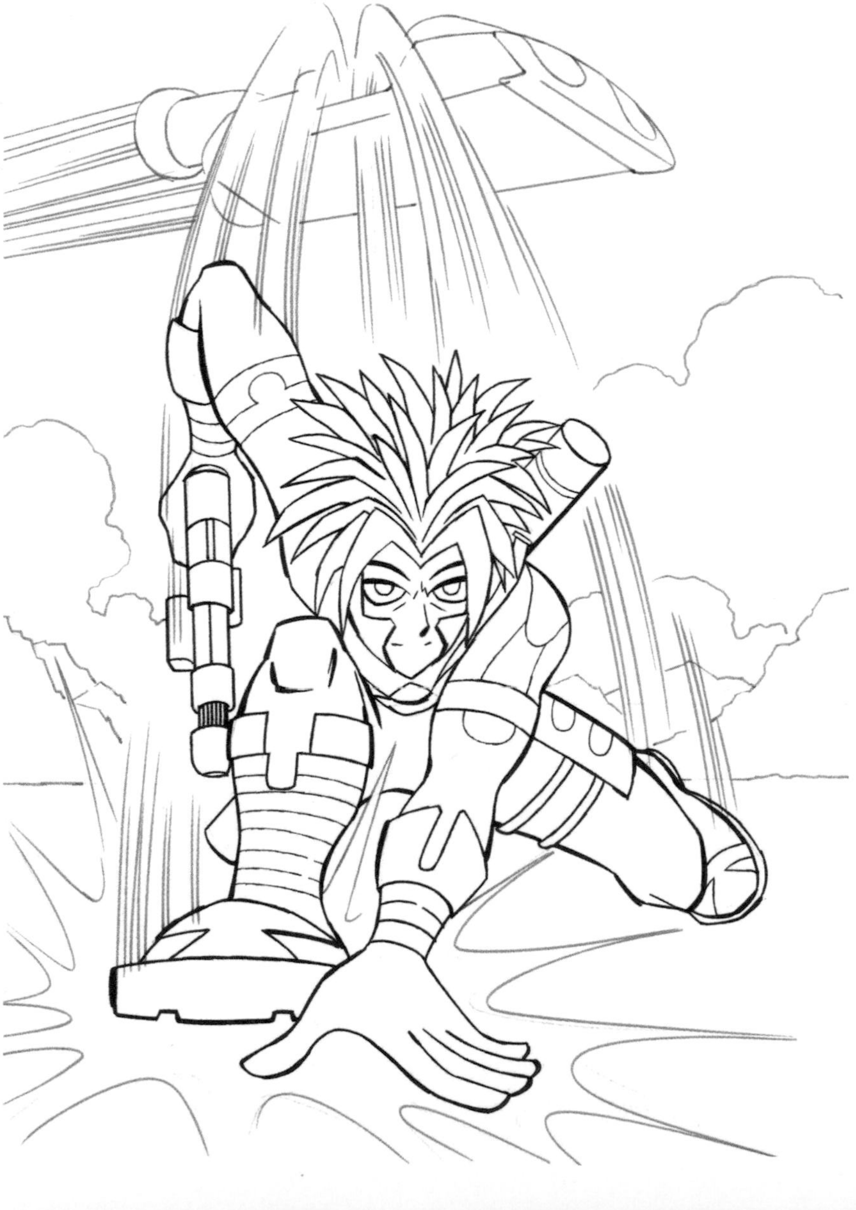

STAGE 9

Outline the rest of the drawing in a mid-grey or brown pen to make the figure stand out.

STAGE 10

Fill in a few solid black areas to give some body to the drawing.

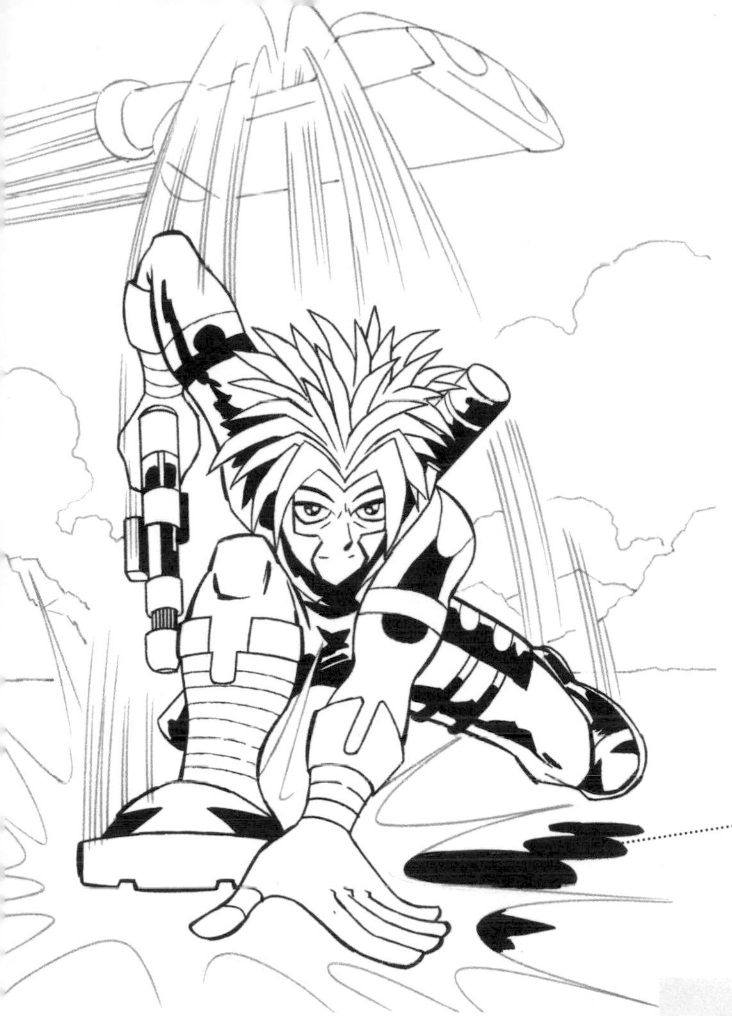
ADD A BLACK SHADOW UNDERNEATH THE CHARACTER

STAGE 11

Use a pale, creamy yellow to fill in the sky, then add in some darker orange tones. Use a pale brown on the ground before adding in some darker tones.

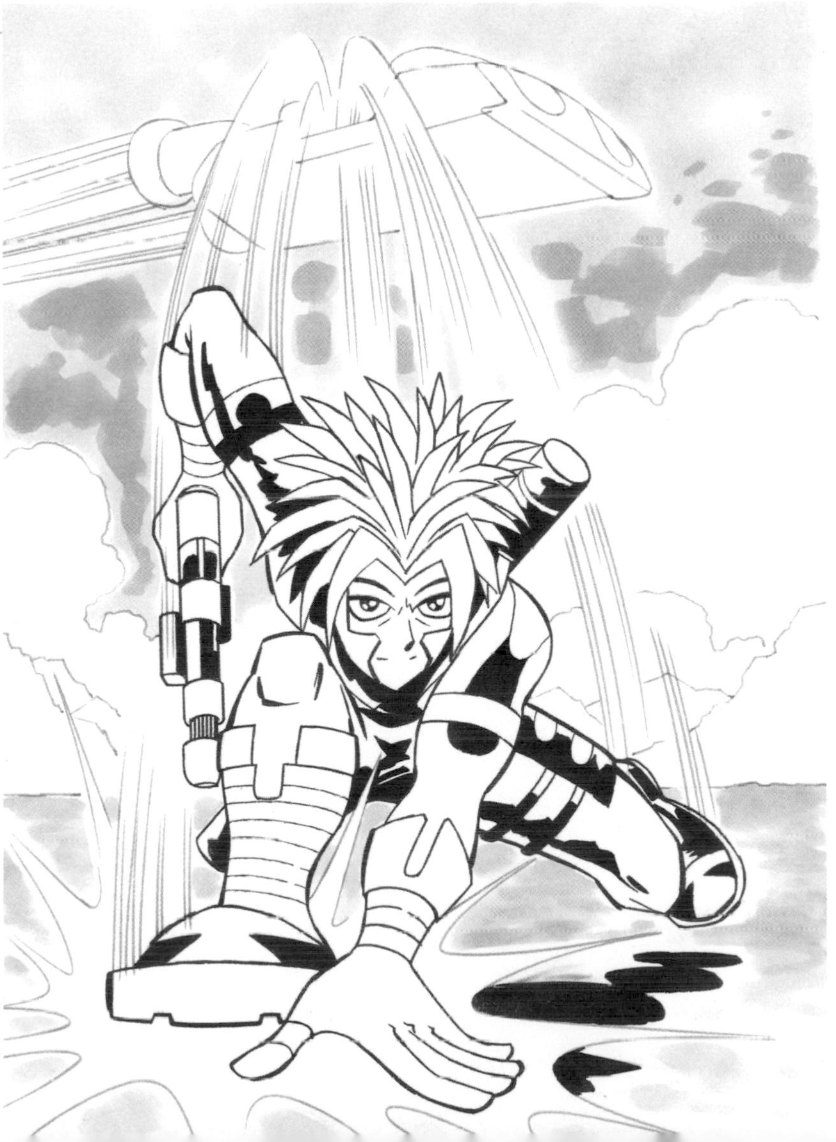

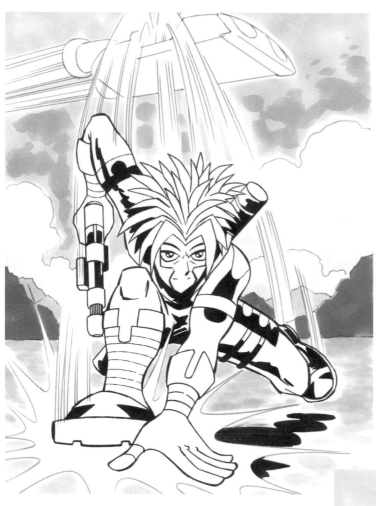

STAGE 12

Use a mid-grey for the mountains, with a paler grey for the ones further back. Add some pale cream to the base of the clouds, leaving the upper parts white.

STAGE 13

Colour your character's costume, hair and face.

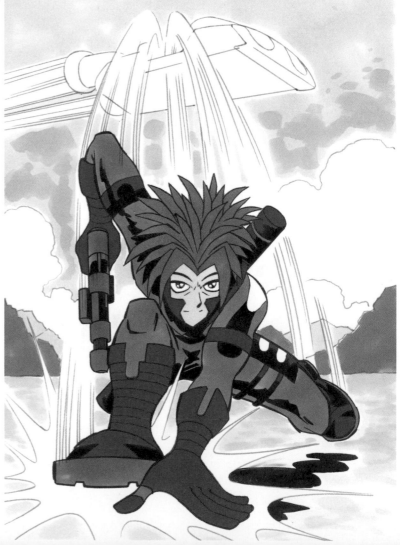

STAGE 14

Add some blue, grey and mauve to the vehicle, and use darker tones to shade the background and figure.

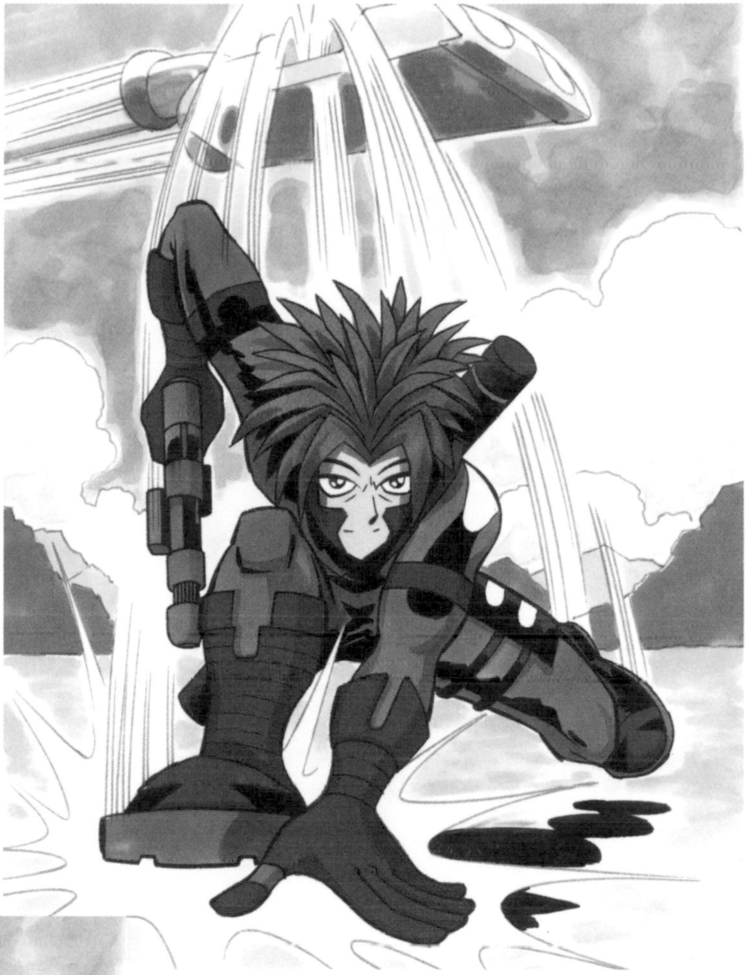

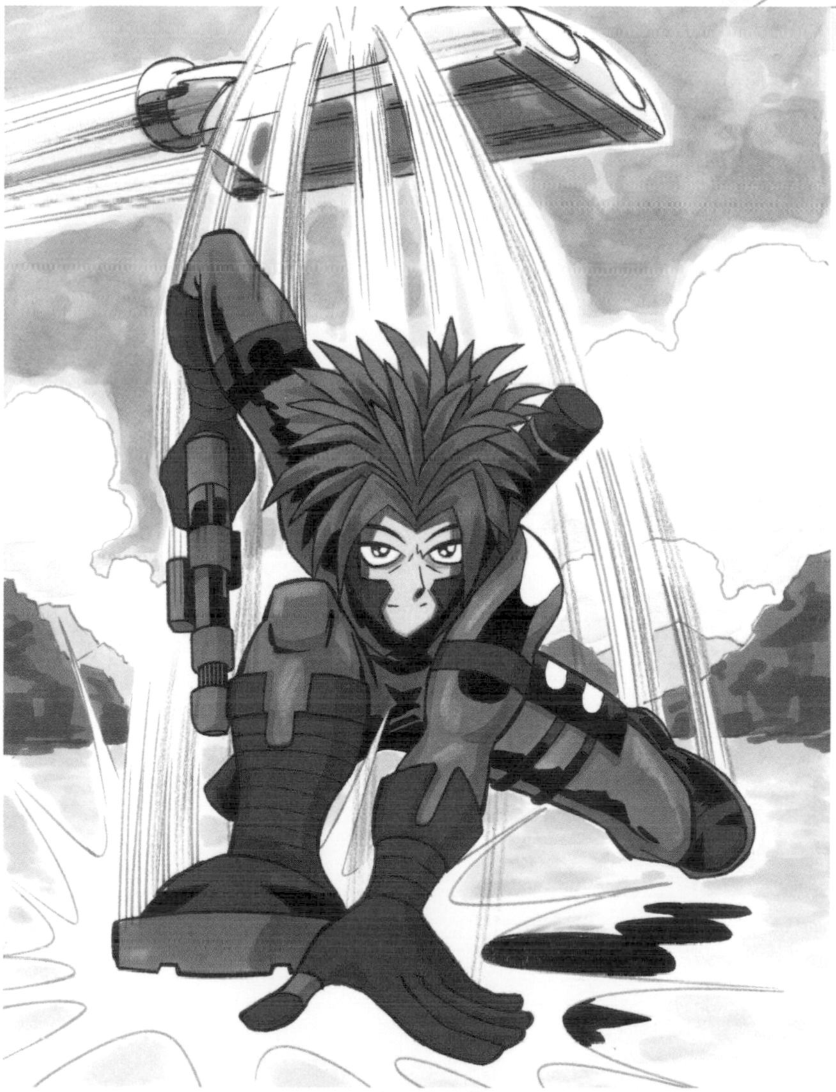

STAGE 15

Add colour to the speed lines and finish by putting in some more dark and light tones to make your drawing really dynamic!

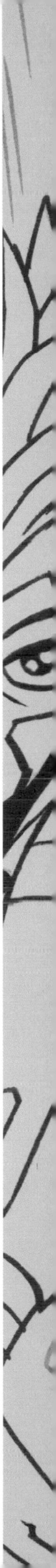

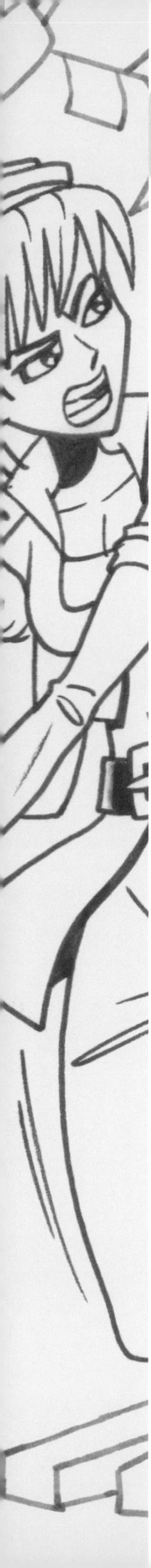

GET YOUR KICKS!

A ROBOT DEVELOPS
A SUDDEN HEADACHE!

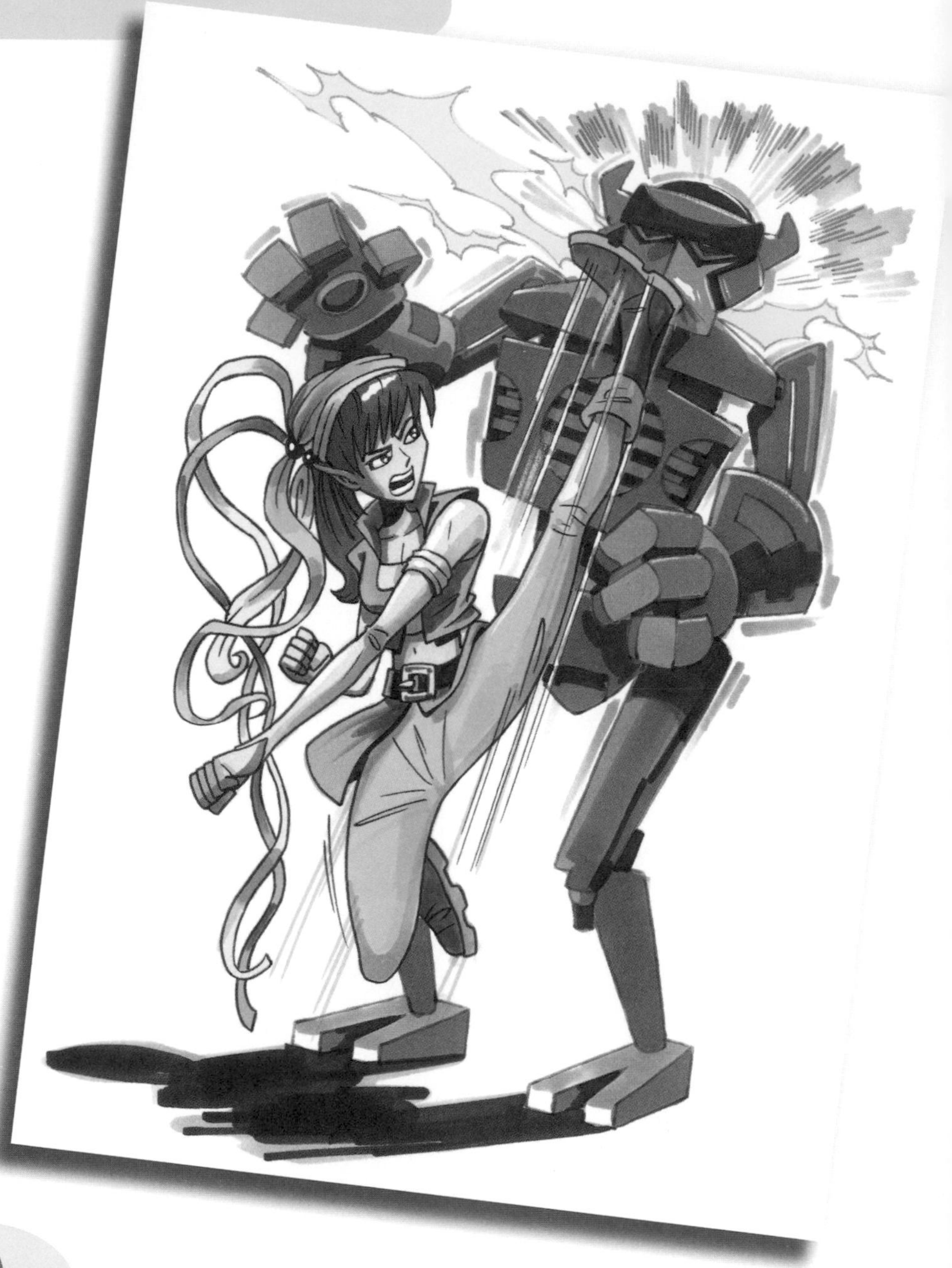

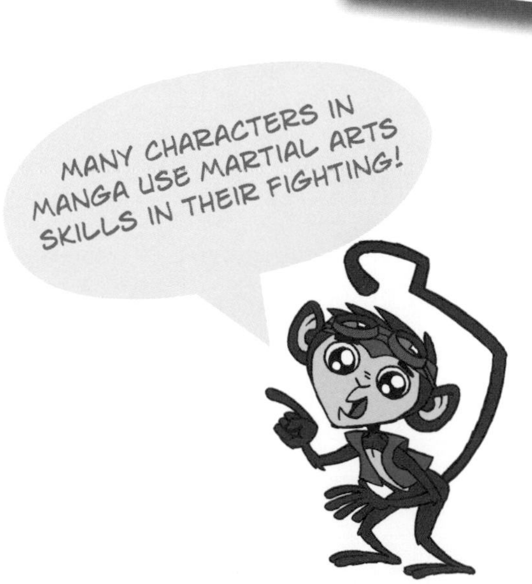
MANY CHARACTERS IN MANGA USE MARTIAL ARTS SKILLS IN THEIR FIGHTING!

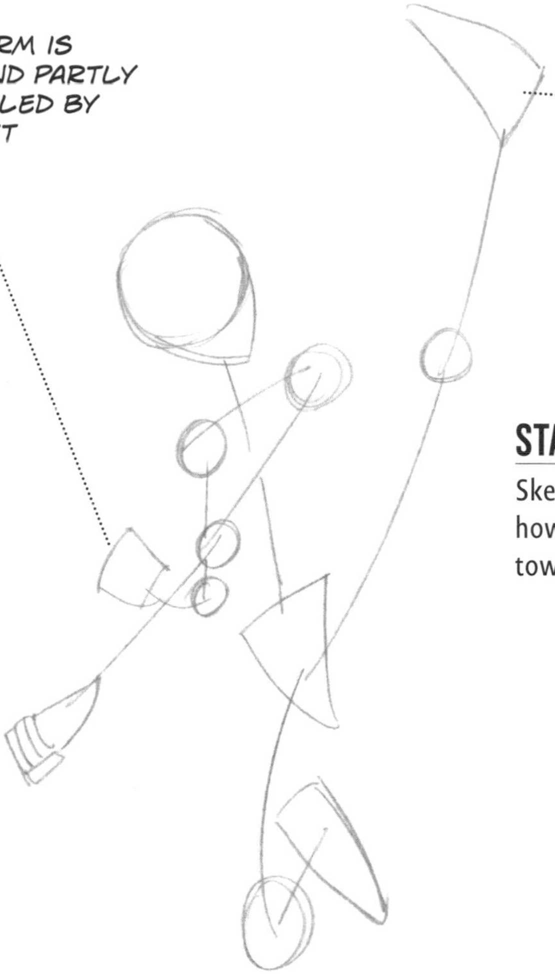
RIGHT ARM IS BENT AND PARTLY CONCEALED BY THE LEFT
THE BOTTOM OF THE FOOT FACES UPWARDS

STAGE 1

Sketch a leaping, kicking wireframe figure – notice how her left arm passes across her chest and towards the floor.

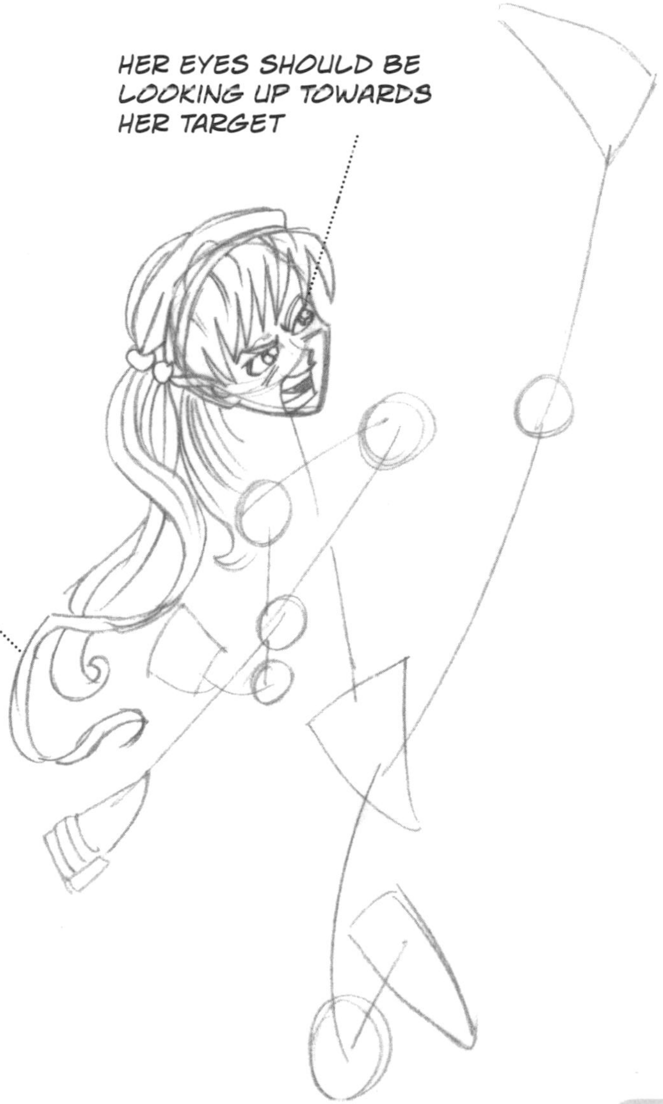
HER EYES SHOULD BE LOOKING UP TOWARDS HER TARGET
RIBBONS CAN EXTEND DOWN AS FAR AS HER HANDS

STAGE 2

Add an angry facial expression and hair. Also draw in a cap with long ribbons attached – make these twist and turn in an interesting way.

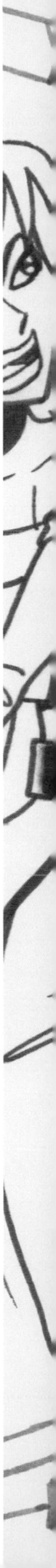

STAGE 3

Flesh out the figure and give her leggings, boots, a small jacket, belt and skirt. Add a sleeve garment to her left arm.

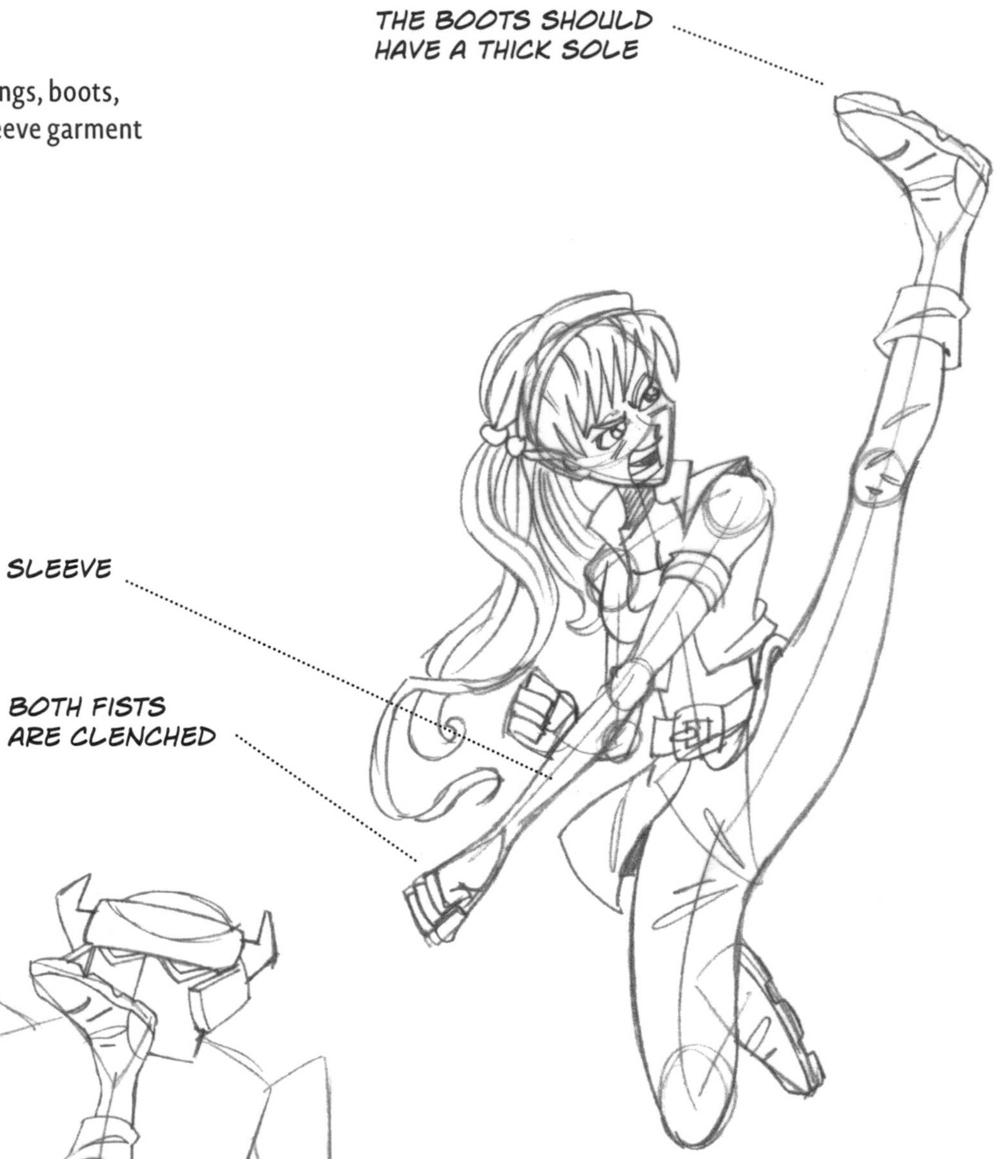
THE BOOTS SHOULD HAVE A THICK SOLE
SLEEVE
BOTH FISTS ARE CLENCHED

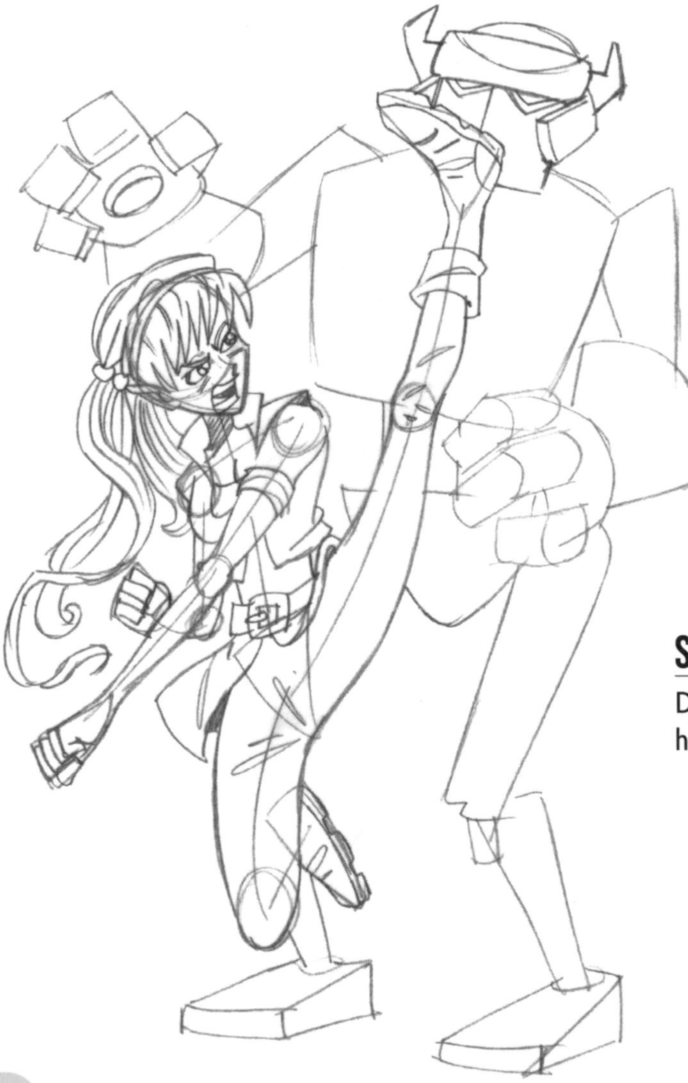

STAGE 4

Draw in a blocky outline for the robot – make sure its head is partly concealed by the girl's foot.

STAGE 5

Add some extra ribbons to the girl's cap and draw speed lines for her legs. Add impact lines and electricity bursts coming from the robot's head and fill in more detail on its bodywork.

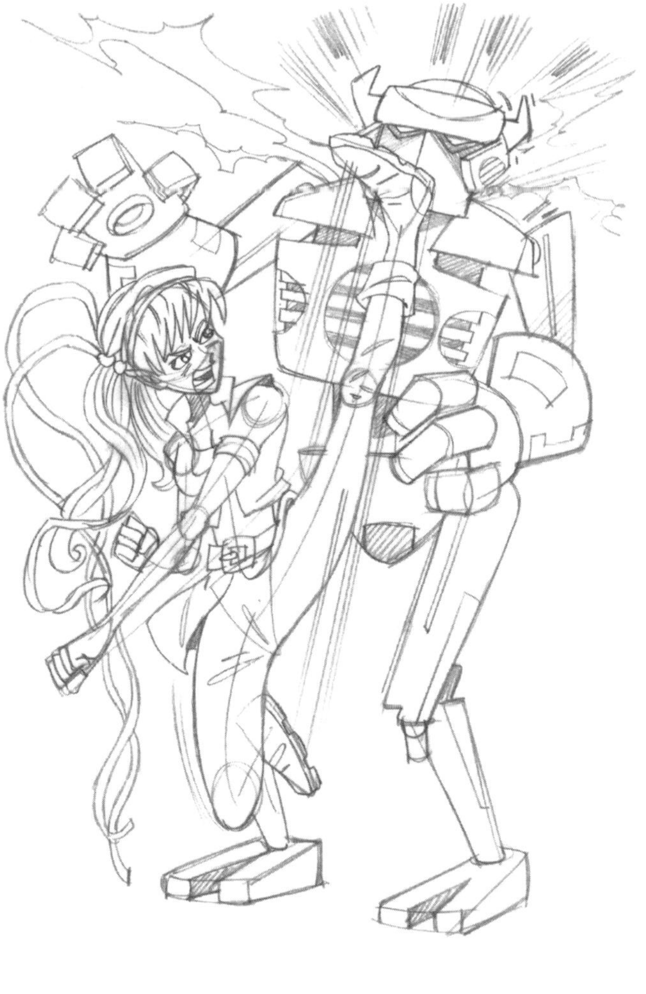

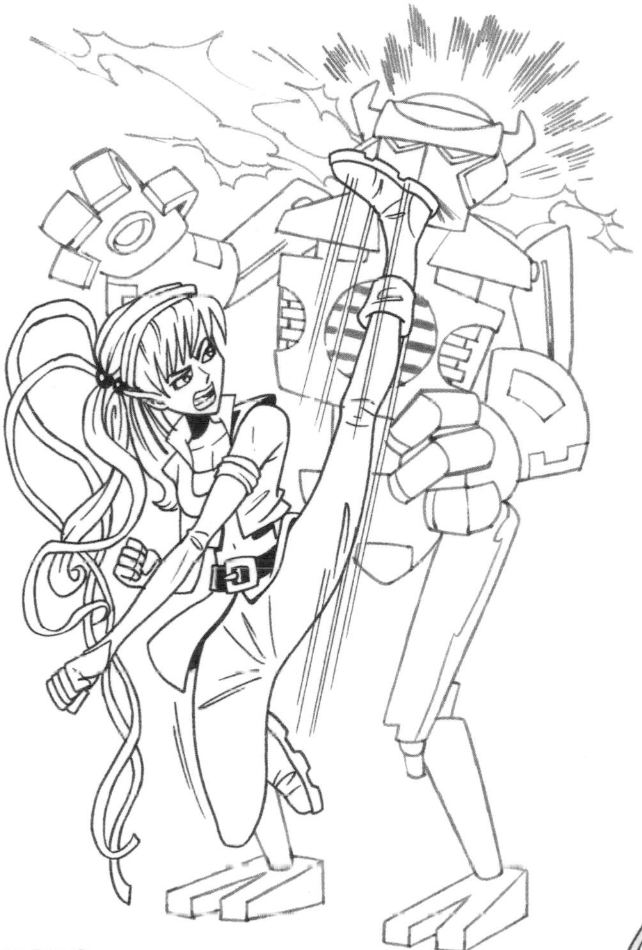

STAGE 6

Outline the girl in black and the robot in grey. Use a red pen to outline the electricity bursts.

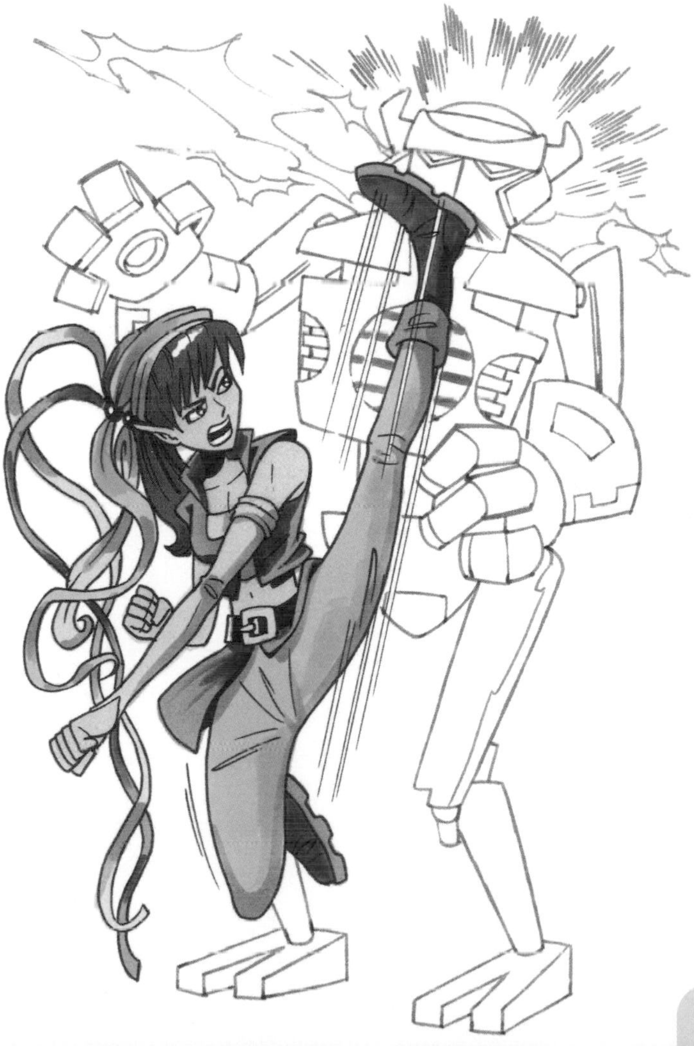

STAGE 7

Colour the girl's skin tone and hair. Fill in her clothes with greens and yellows, then shade with darker tones.

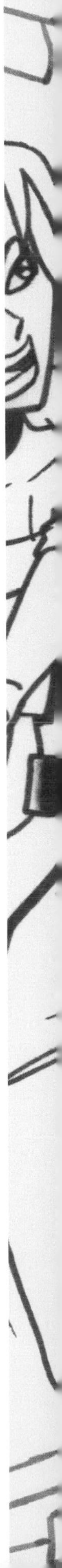

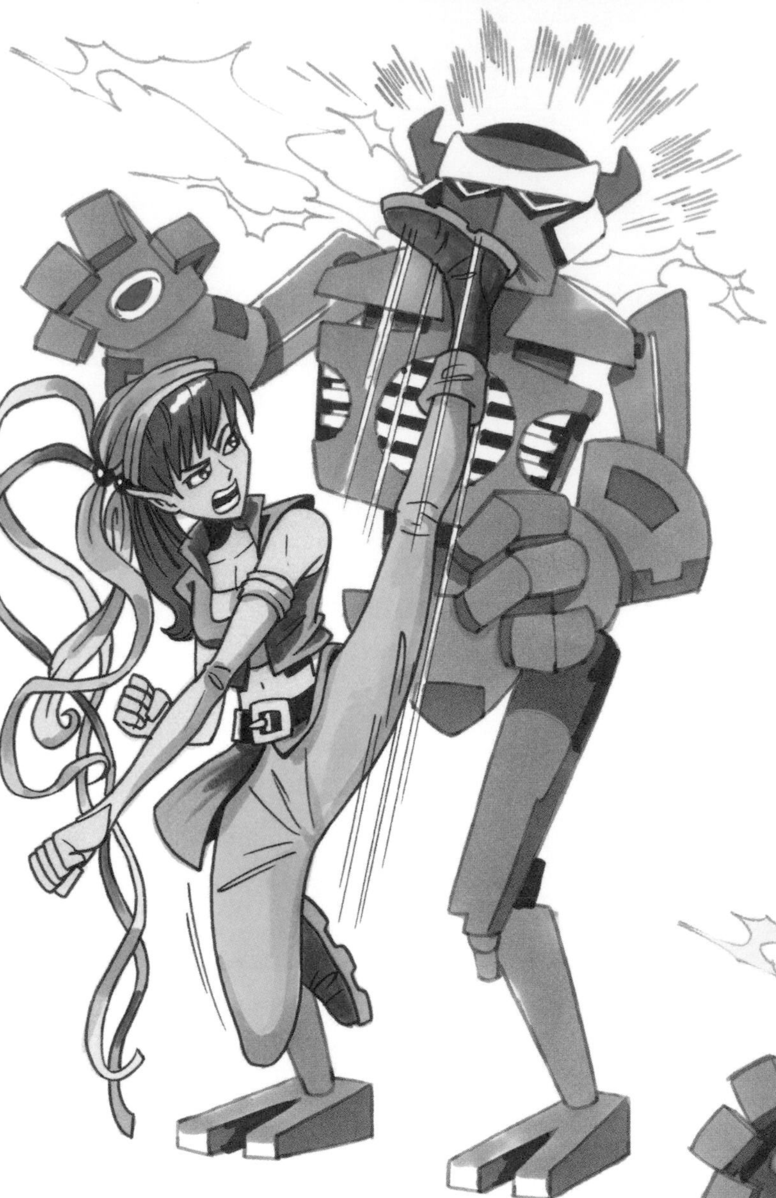

STAGE 8

Colour the robot with mid-grey, adding some darker grey detailing, red eyes and an orange palm laser.

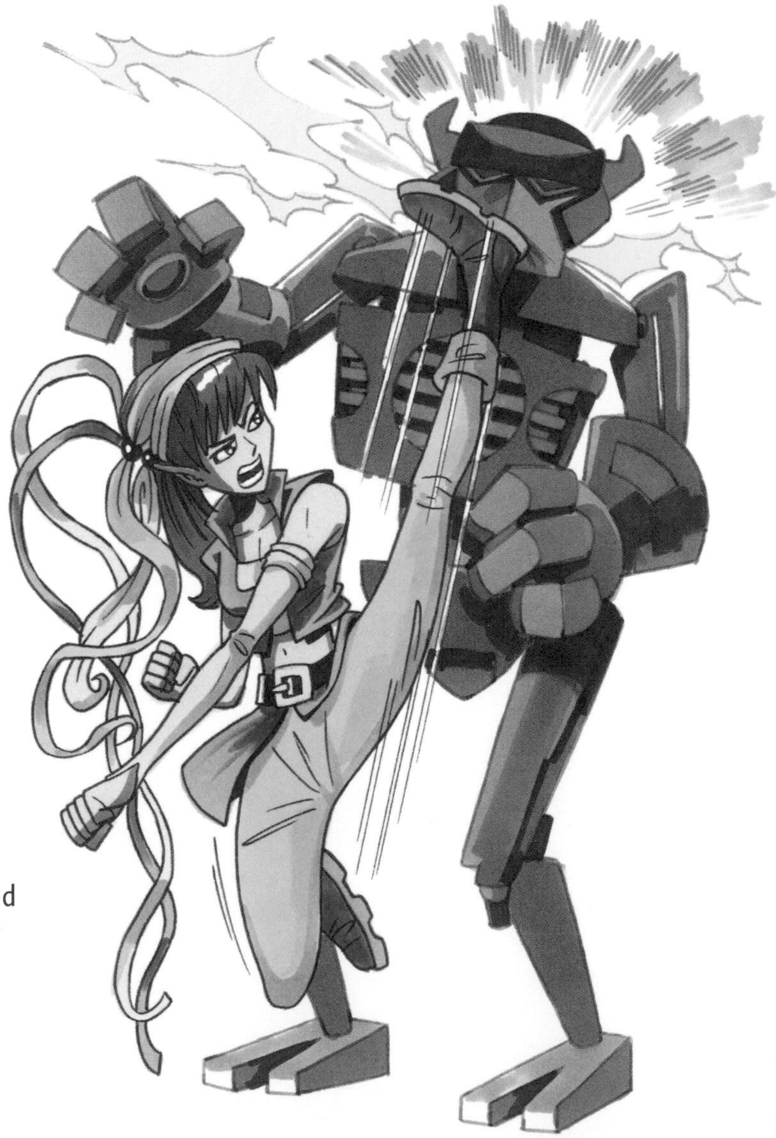

STAGE 9

Work in some darker greys and black on the robot and add blue to the chest grill area. Colour the electricity bursts in yellow and use a pale grey to highlight the impact lines behind the robot's head.

STAGE 10
Finish by adding some more movement lines to the girl's legs in green pencil and white paint, grey 'shudder' lines around the edges of the robot, and a dark grey-black shadow on the ground.

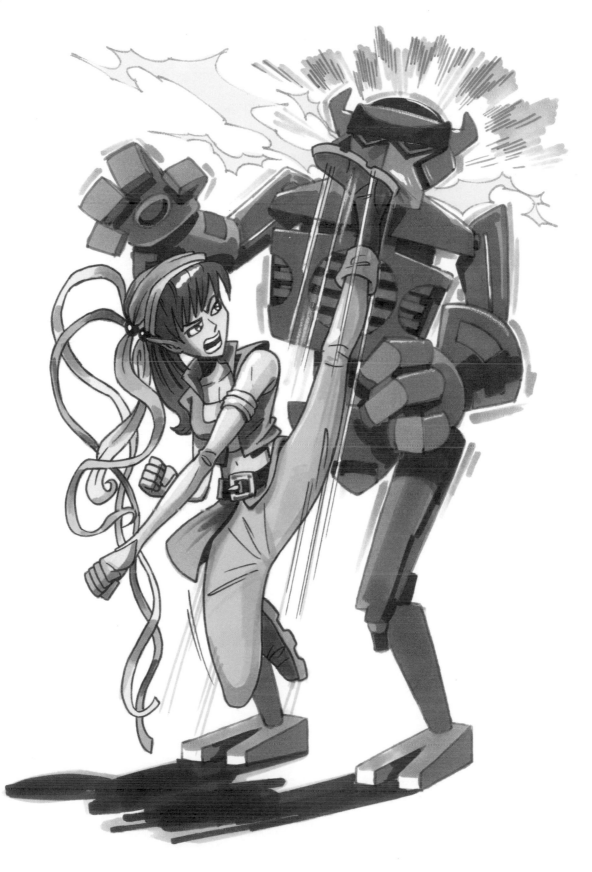

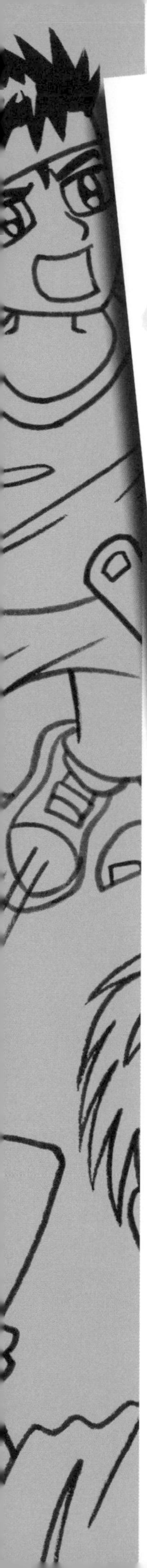

SLAM DUNK!

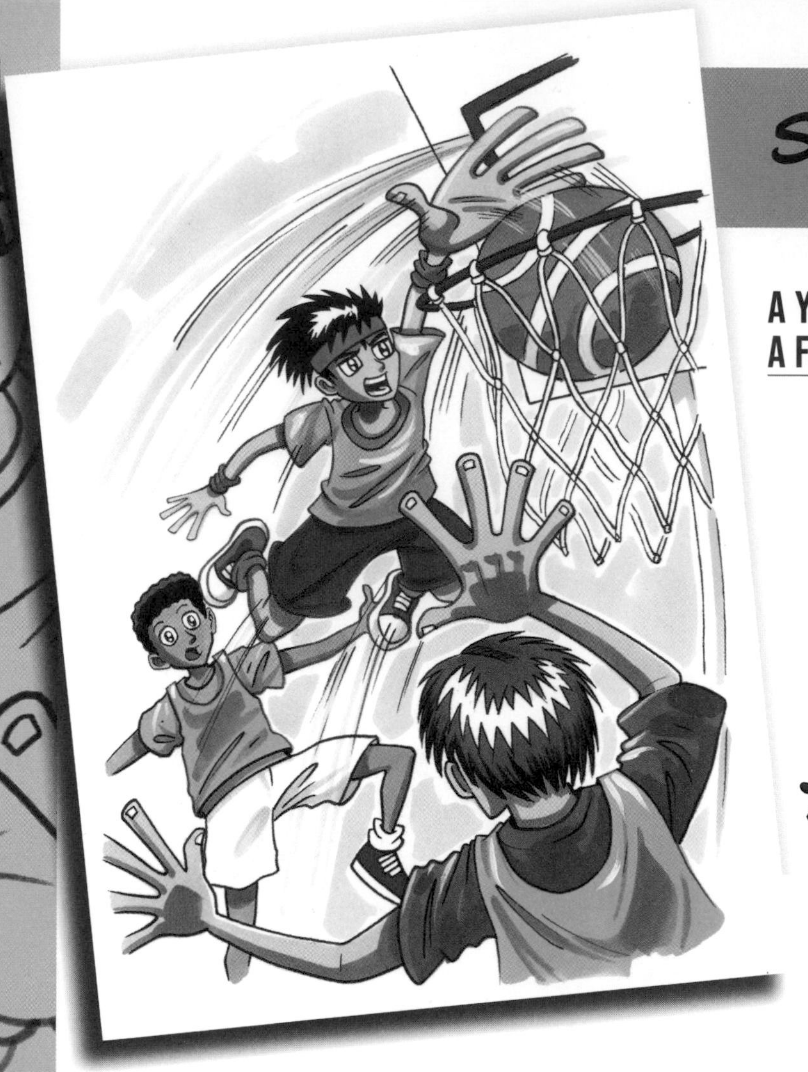

A YOUNG PLAYER LEAPS TO SCORE A FLYING BASKET!

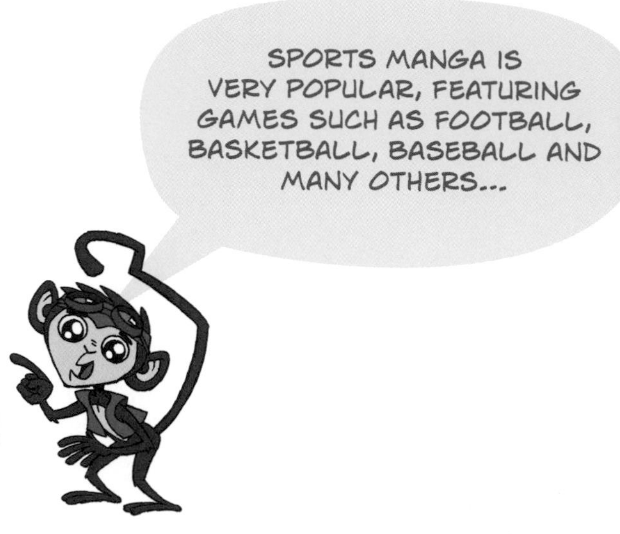
SPORTS MANGA IS VERY POPULAR, FEATURING GAMES SUCH AS FOOTBALL, BASKETBALL, BASEBALL AND MANY OTHERS...

STAGE 1

Draw a wireframe in the top half of the page for the main figure leaping in mid-air. The left arm is raised up away from the body, stretching into the top-right foreground.

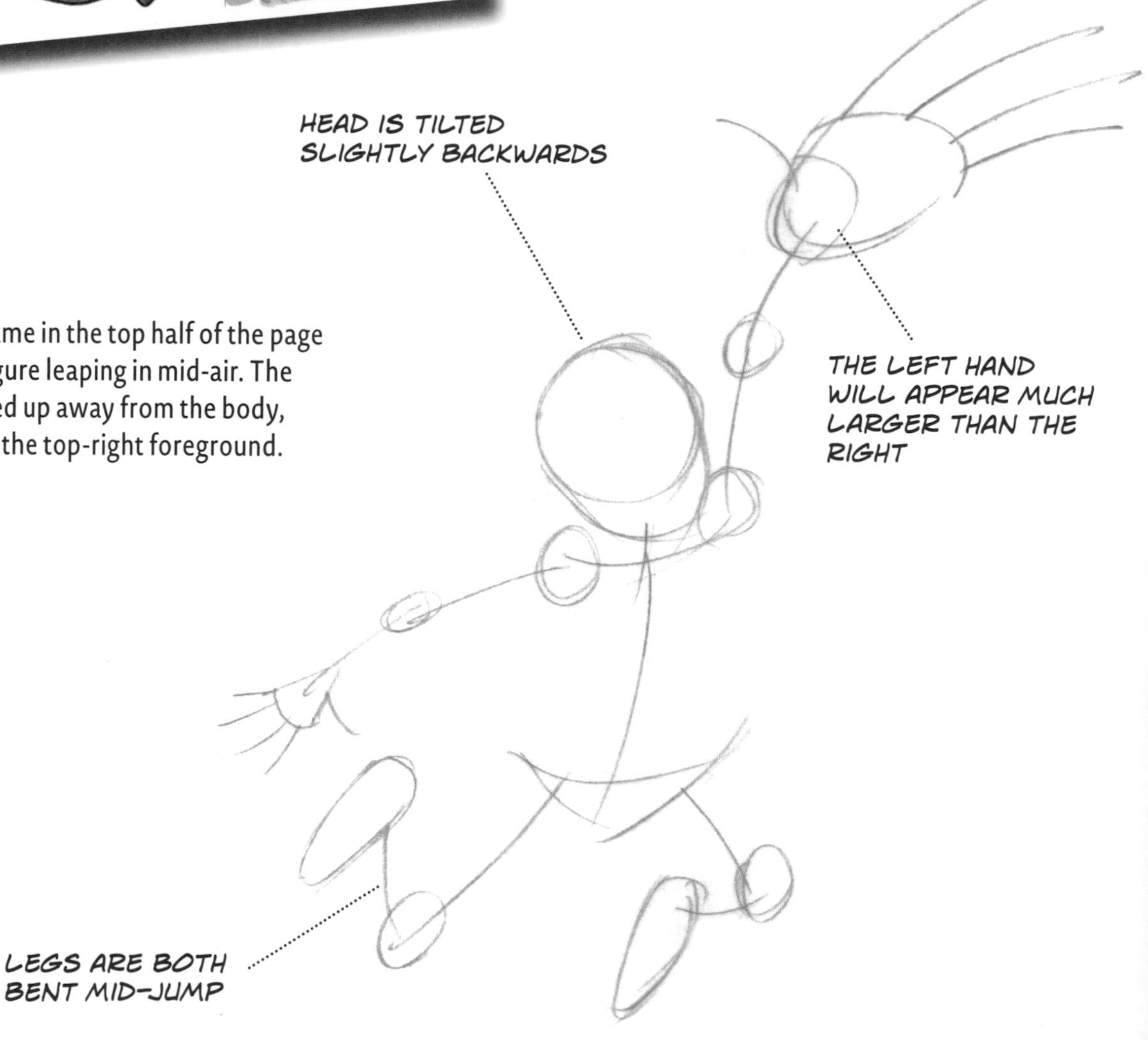
HEAD IS TILTED SLIGHTLY BACKWARDS
THE LEFT HAND WILL APPEAR MUCH LARGER THAN THE RIGHT
LEGS ARE BOTH BENT MID-JUMP

STAGE 2

Sketch in a face with a determined expression. Add spiky hair and a sweatband across his forehead.

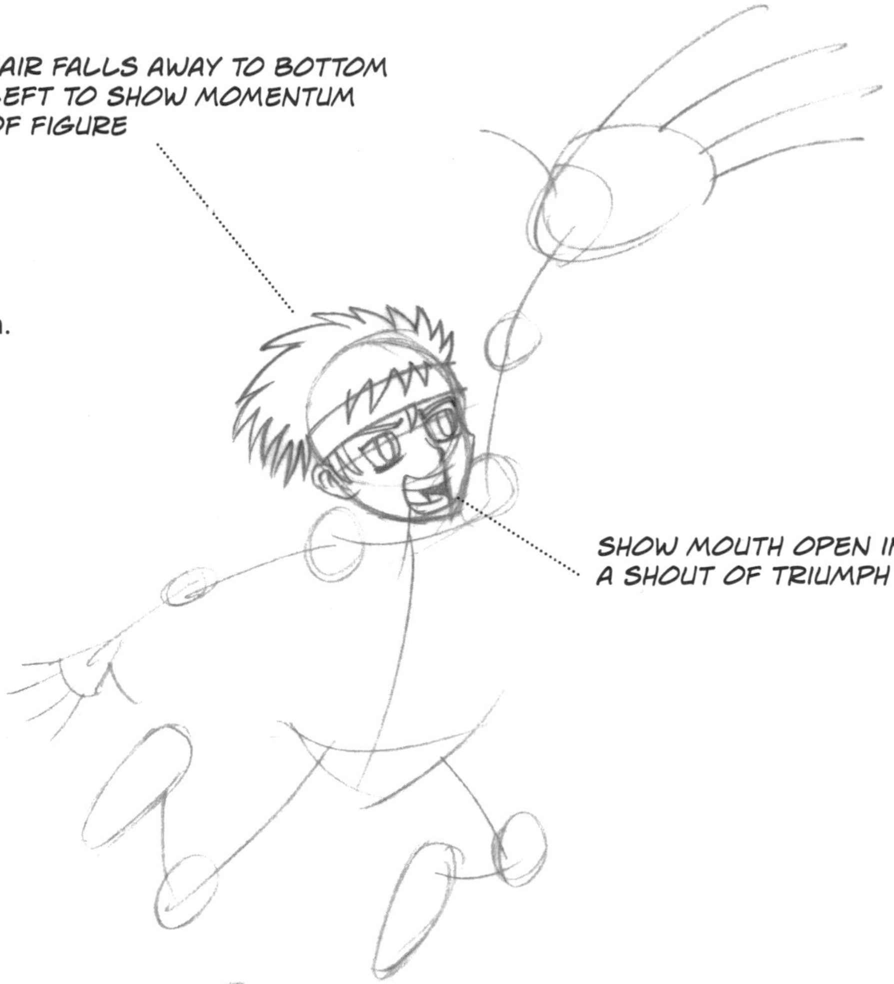
HAIR FALLS AWAY TO BOTTOM LEFT TO SHOW MOMENTUM OF FIGURE
SHOW MOUTH OPEN IN A SHOUT OF TRIUMPH

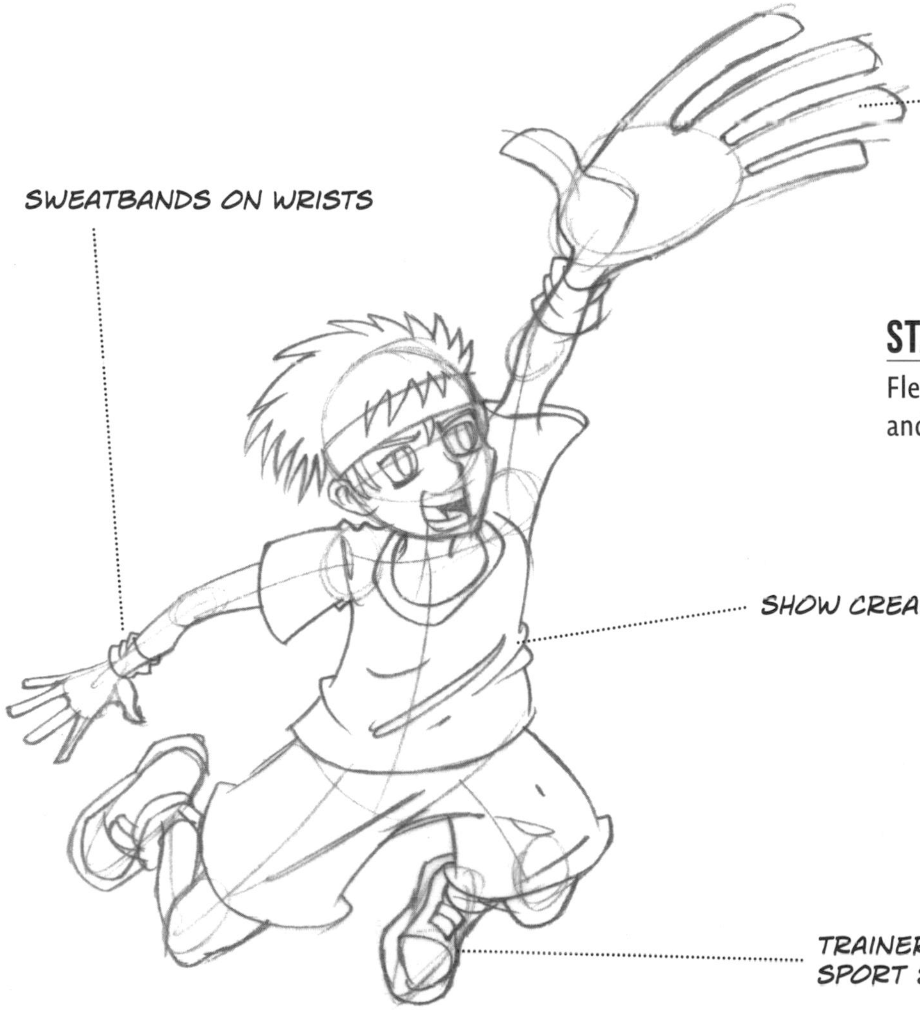
THE FINGERS ARE DISTORTED IN A CURVING STRETCH
SWEATBANDS ON WRISTS
SHOW CREASES
TRAINER-STYLE SPORT SHOES

STAGE 3

Flesh out your figure and add shoes, sweatbands and a loose-fitting T-shirt and shorts.

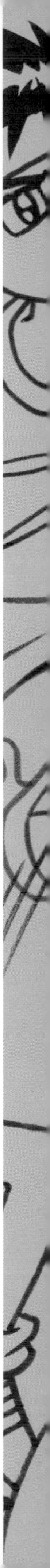

STAGE 4

Draw an ellipse shape under the hand for the basketball hoop.

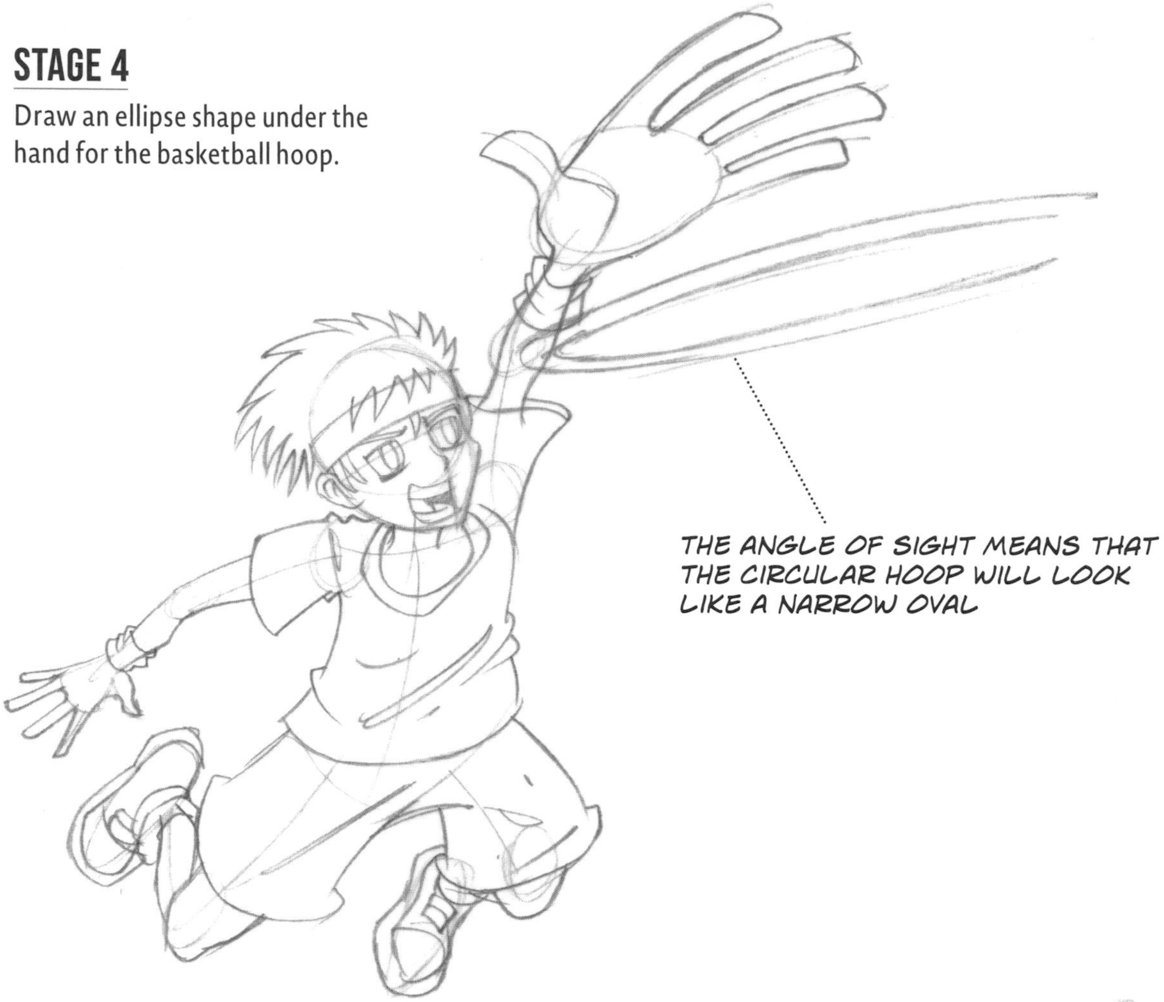
THE ANGLE OF SIGHT MEANS THAT THE CIRCULAR HOOP WILL LOOK LIKE A NARROW OVAL

STAGE 5

Add a circular basketball shape dropping through the hoop.

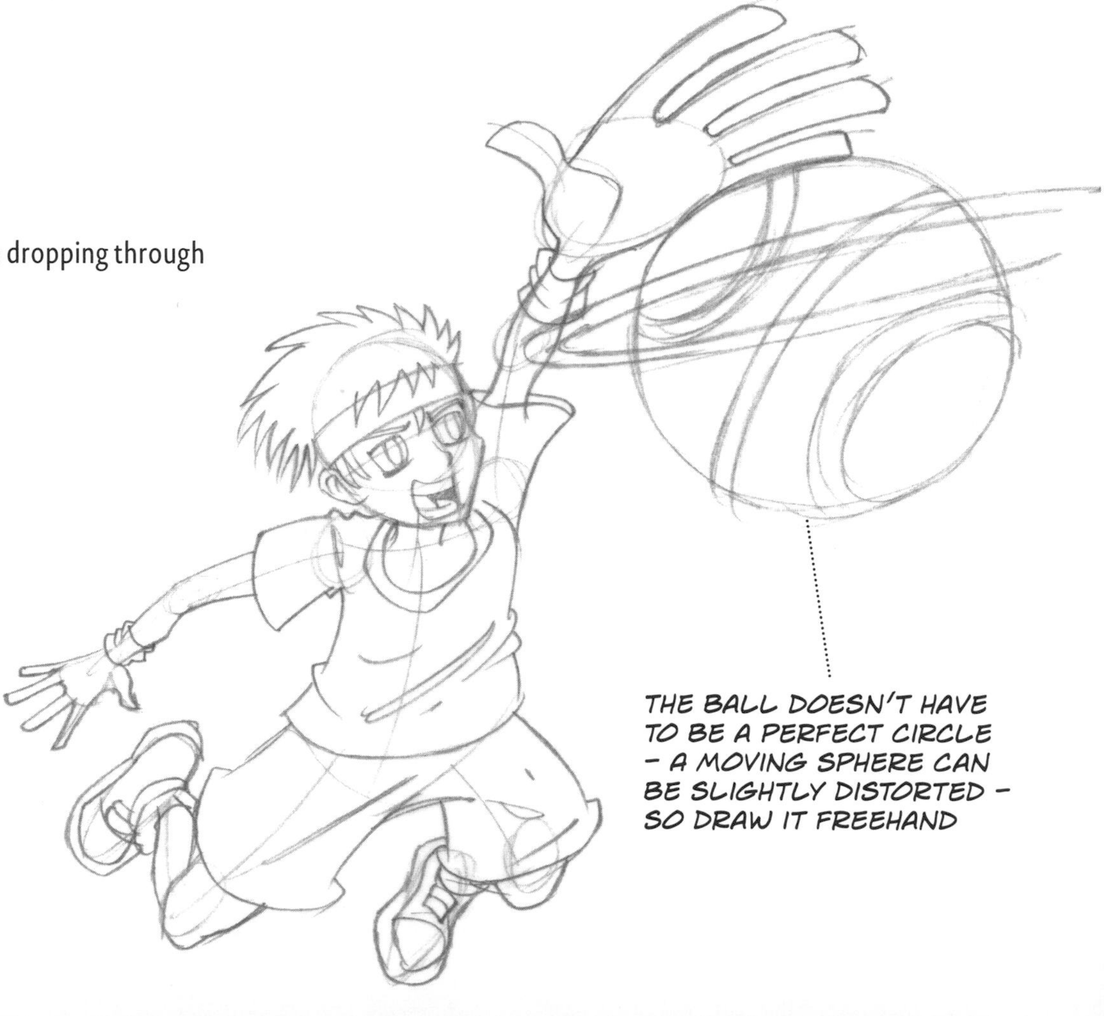
THE BALL DOESN'T HAVE TO BE A PERFECT CIRCLE – A MOVING SPHERE CAN BE SLIGHTLY DISTORTED – SO DRAW IT FREEHAND

STAGE 6

Sketch in the net, a backboard and a curving support pole.

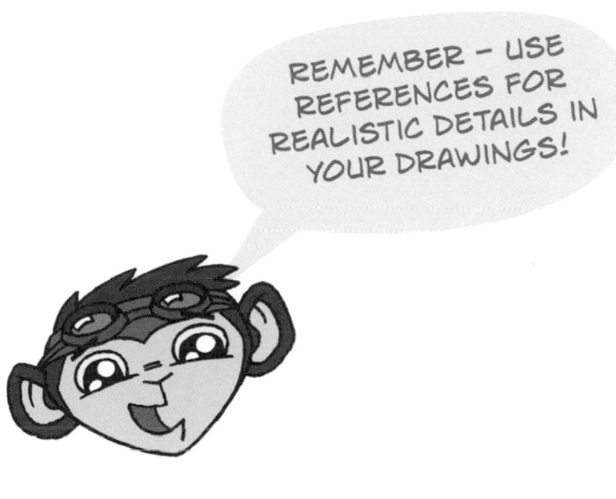
REMEMBER – USE REFERENCES FOR REALISTIC DETAILS IN YOUR DRAWINGS!

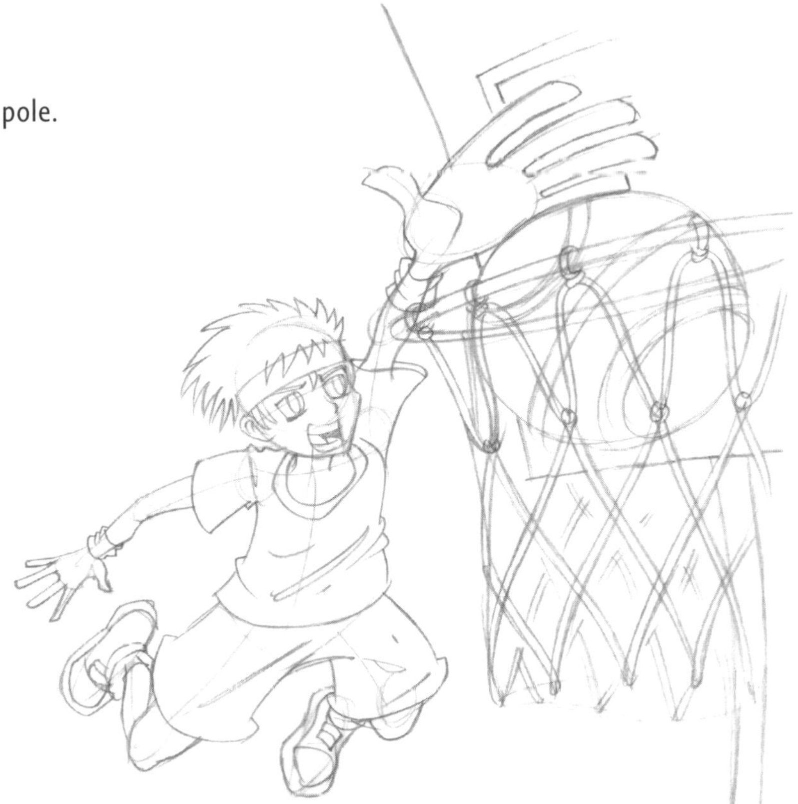

THE CURVE OF THE BACKBOARD AND POLE GIVES A SLIGHT DISTORTION AND FEELING OF MOVEMENT

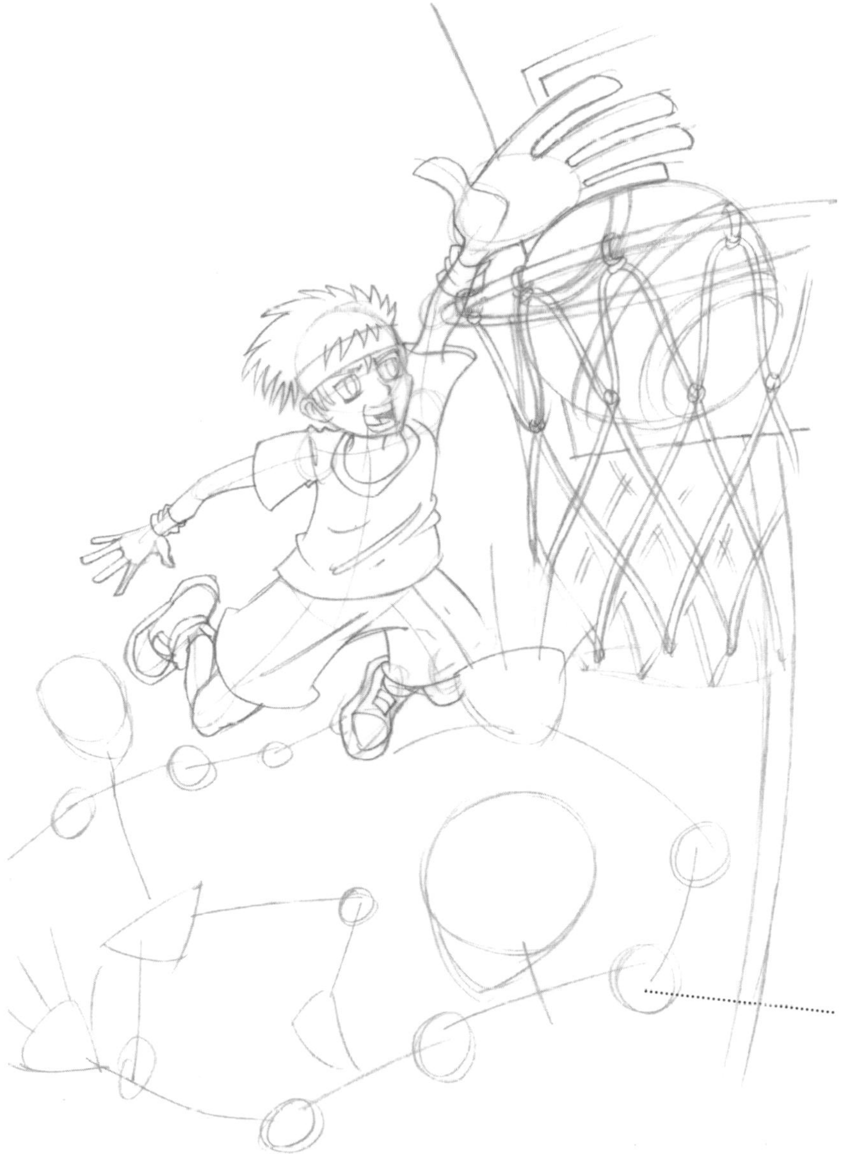

STAGE 7

Sketch in wireframes for two blocking figures at the bottom of the page – one is behind the main figure, one in front.

THE BACKGROUND FIGURE IS SMALLER THAN THE MAIN FIGURE; THE FOREGROUND FIGURE IS LARGER

STAGE 8

Flesh out the two opposing defenders trying to block the attack.

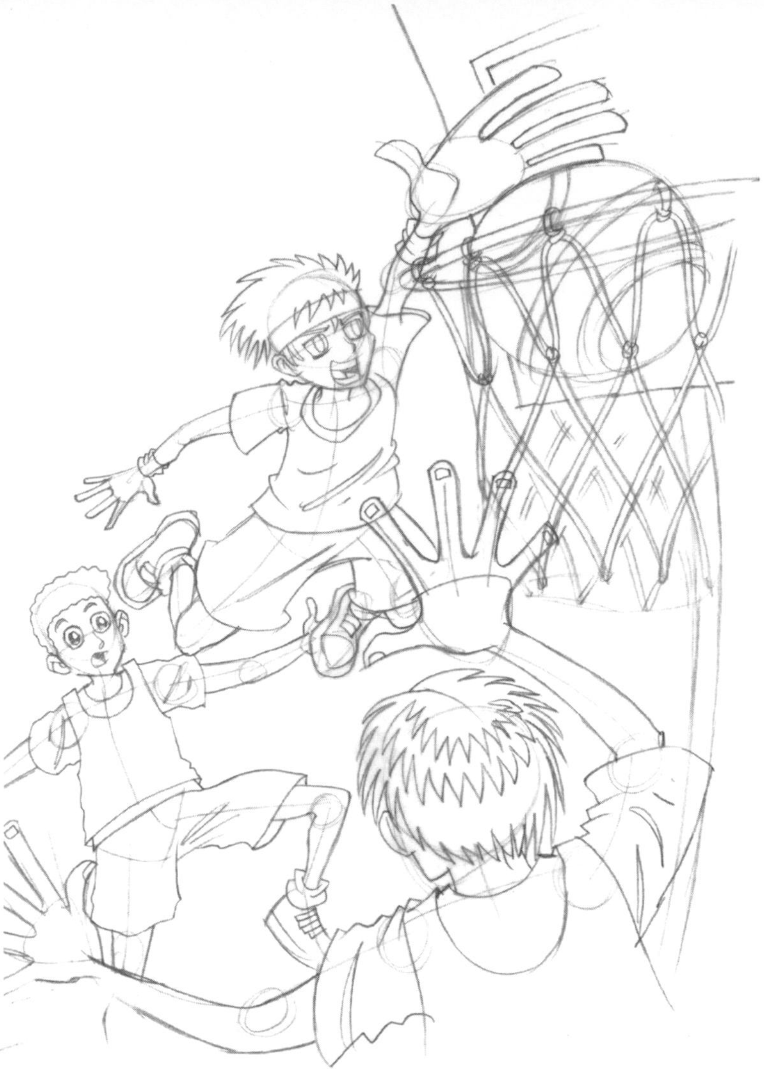

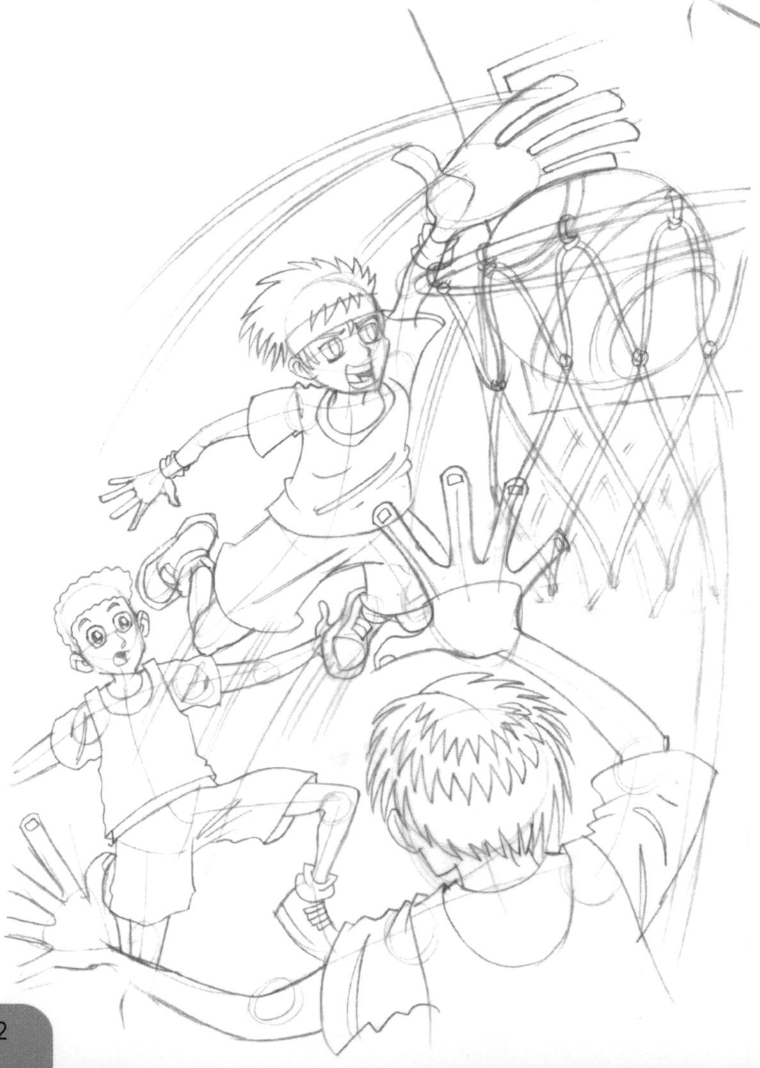

STAGE 9

Finish the pencil stage with some speed lines showing the direction of the leap.

STAGE 10

Ink your drawing with black.

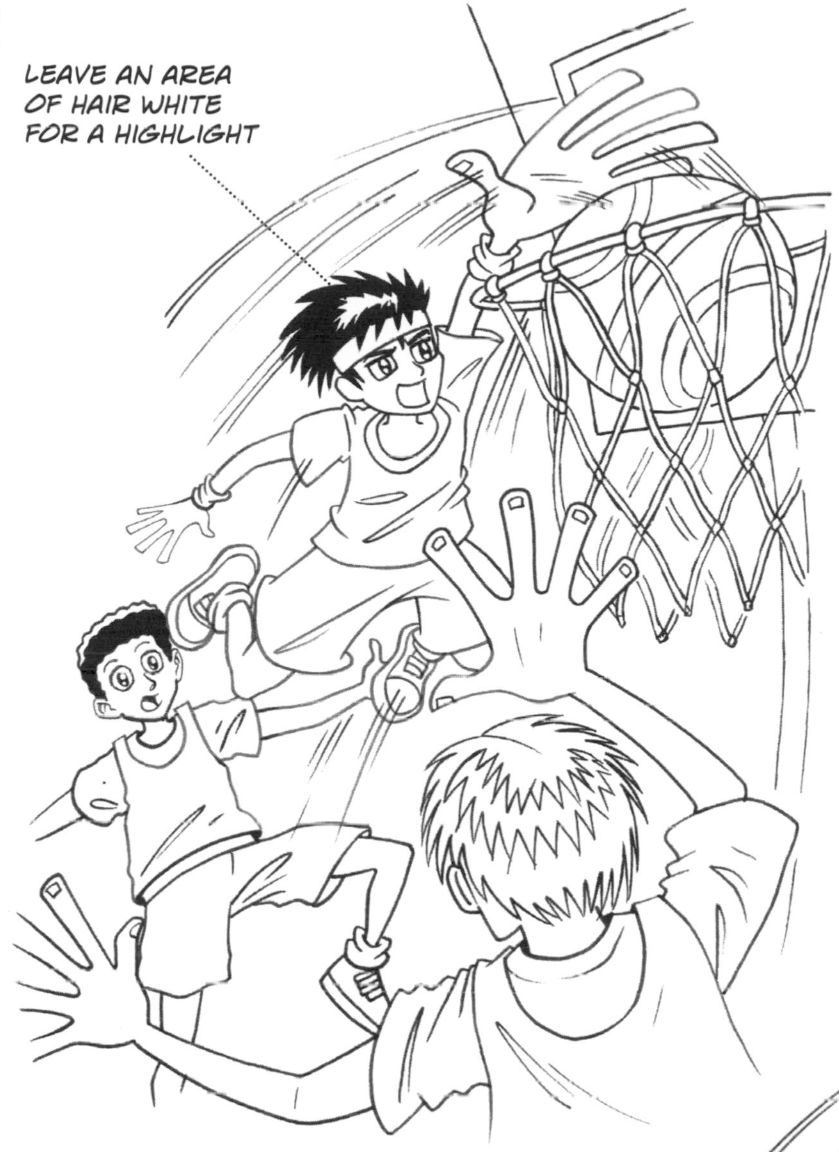
LEAVE AN AREA OF HAIR WHITE FOR A HIGHLIGHT

STAGE 11

Fill in the characters' flesh tones.

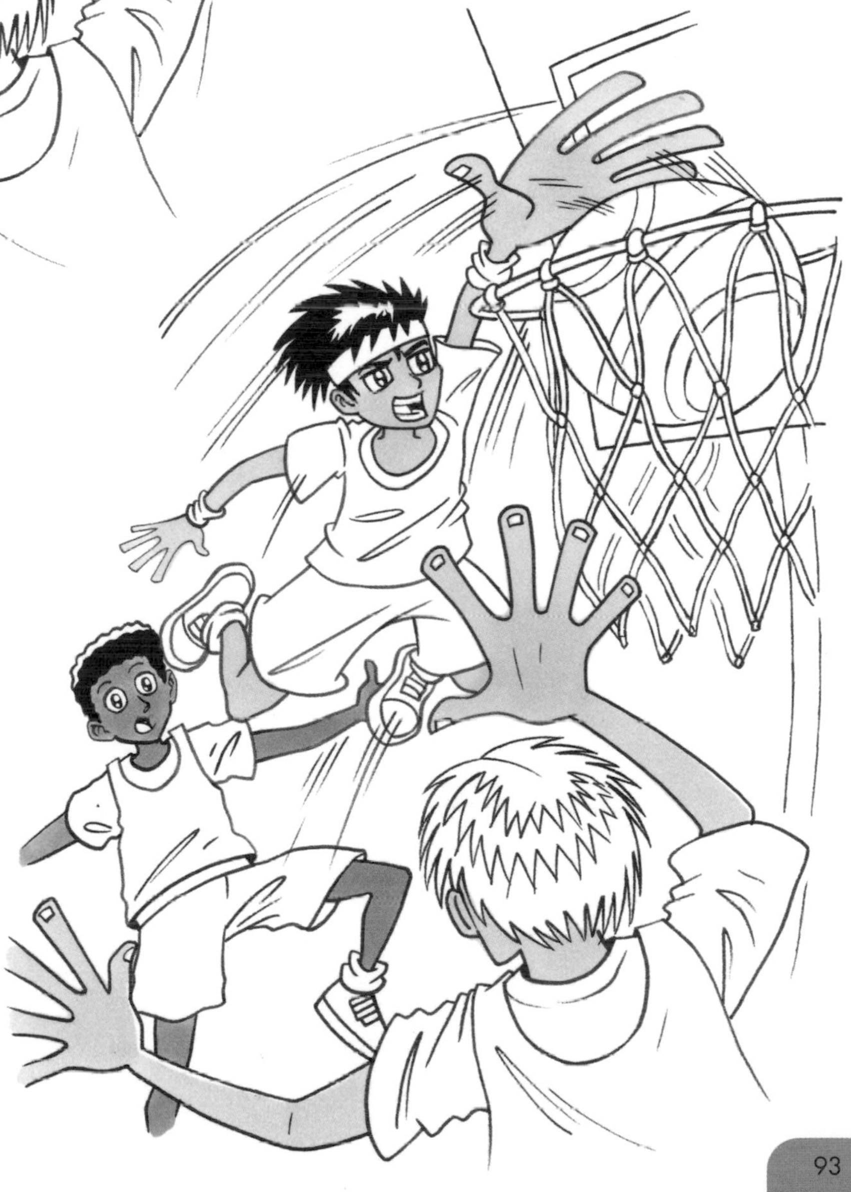

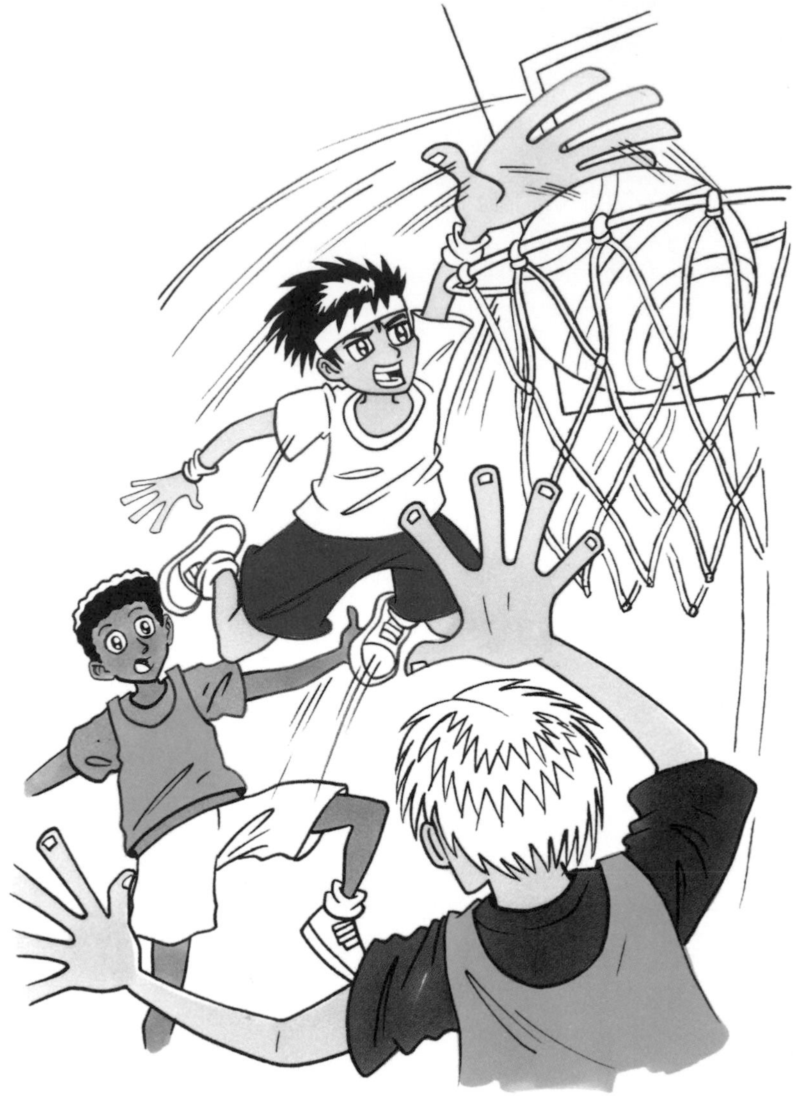

STAGE 12

Use bold colours on the clothes, with matching green vests on the opposition players.

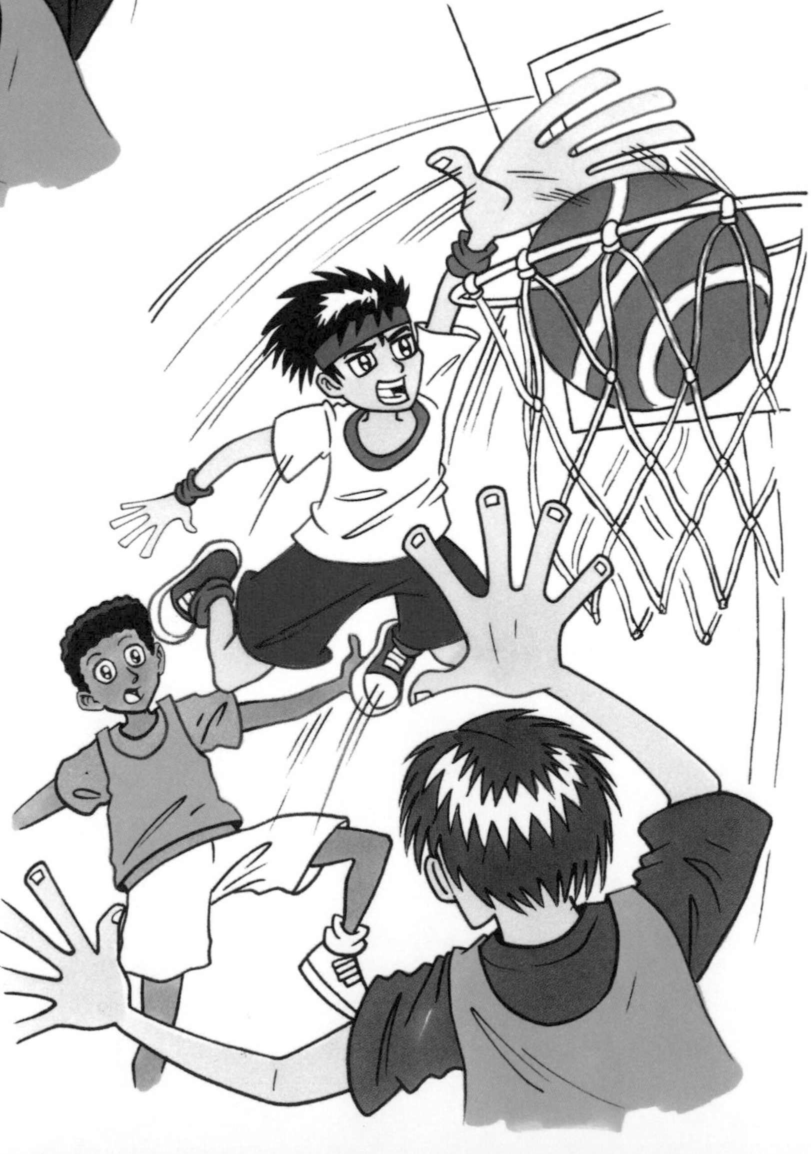

STAGE 13

Continue to add in bold colours, using orange for the ball, blue for the sweatband and brown for the foreground character's hair.

STAGE 14

Build up the shape and depth by adding some bold shadows on the characters, and add red to the hoop and backboard.

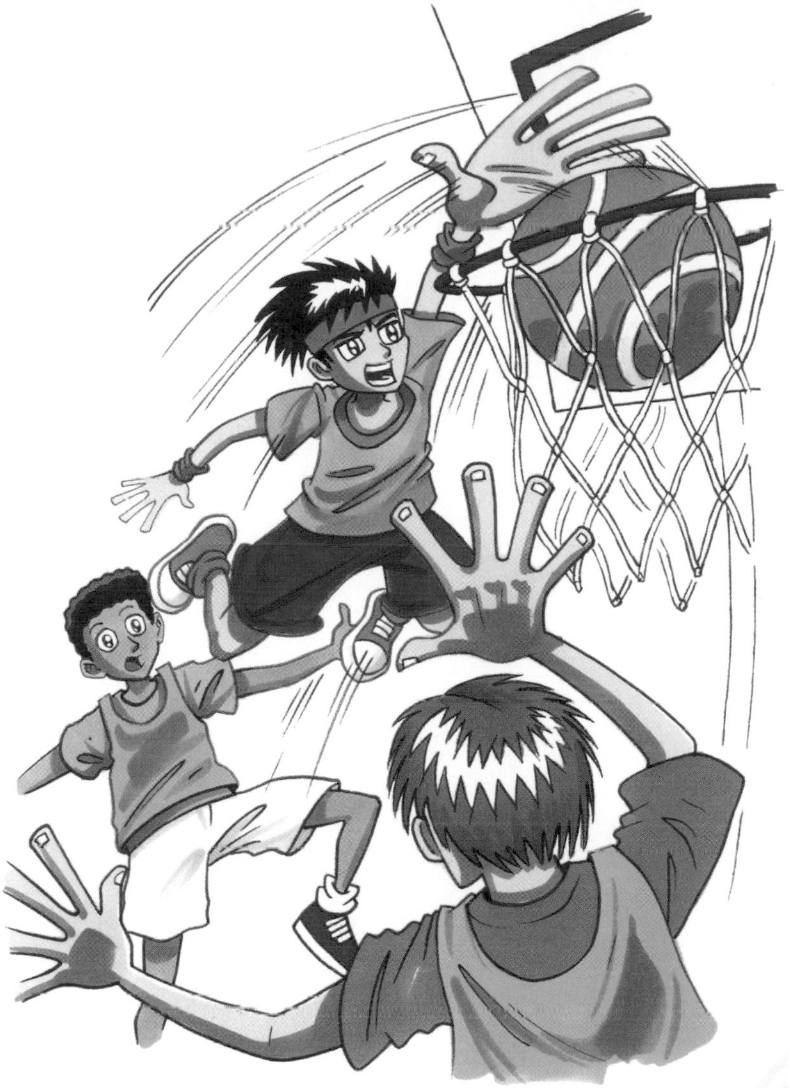

STAGE 15

Finish with more shading, warm beige strokes to the background, and colour on the speed lines. Tidy any colour bleed with white bleed-proof paint and add in a few white highlights.

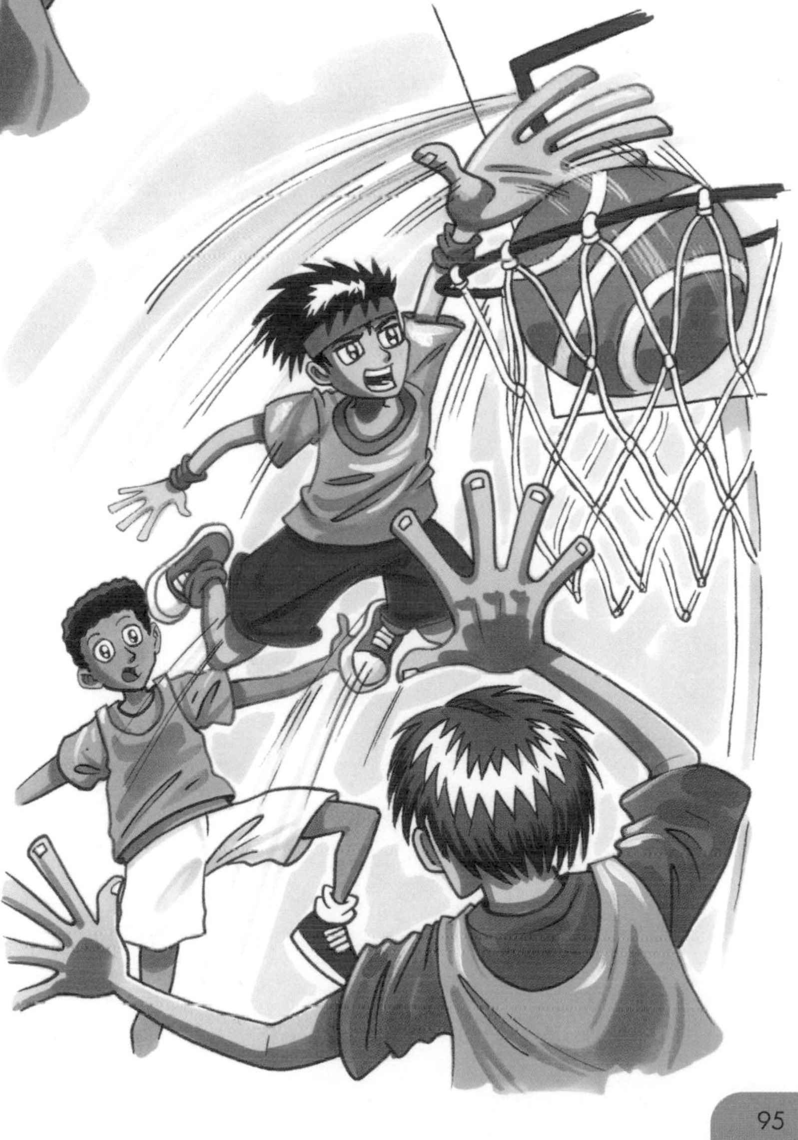

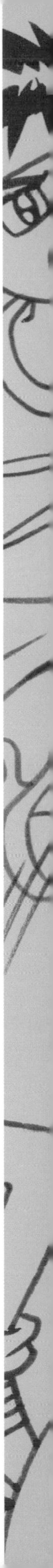

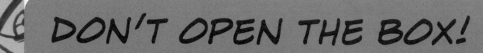

DON'T OPEN THE BOX!

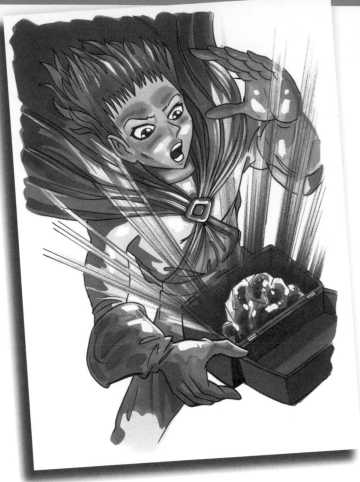

TOO LATE! A CASKET REVEALS ITS DEADLY TREASURE!

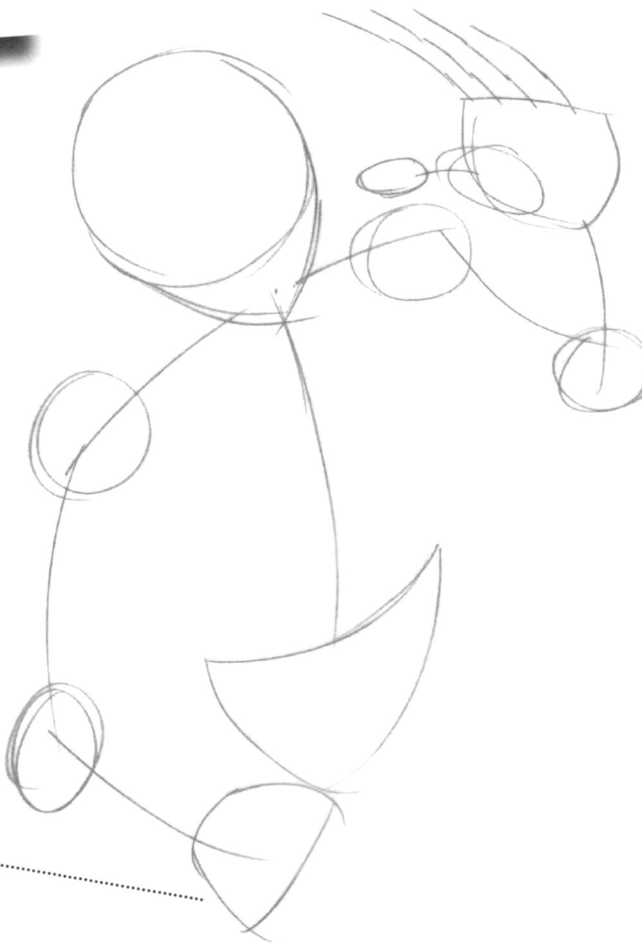

LEFT HAND IS RAISED UP TO HEAD LEVEL
RIGHT HAND EXTENDS TOWARDS THE BOTTOM OF THE PAGE – DON'T DRAW IN THE FINGERS YET

STAGE 1

Draw a wireframe head, upper body and arms that fill most of the page.

STAGE 2

Sketch in the character's hair and face. Draw an open mouth and a surprised expression, with the eyes looking down to the bottom right of the page.

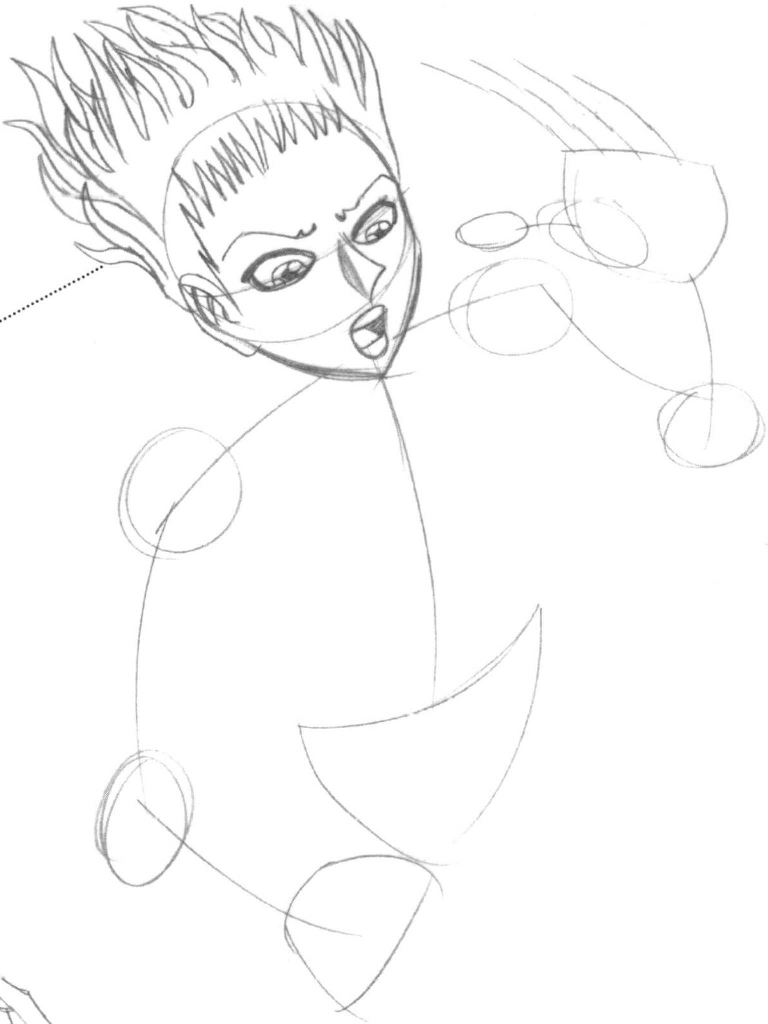
DRAW SOFT SPIKES OF HAIR FLOWING UP AND TO THE LEFT

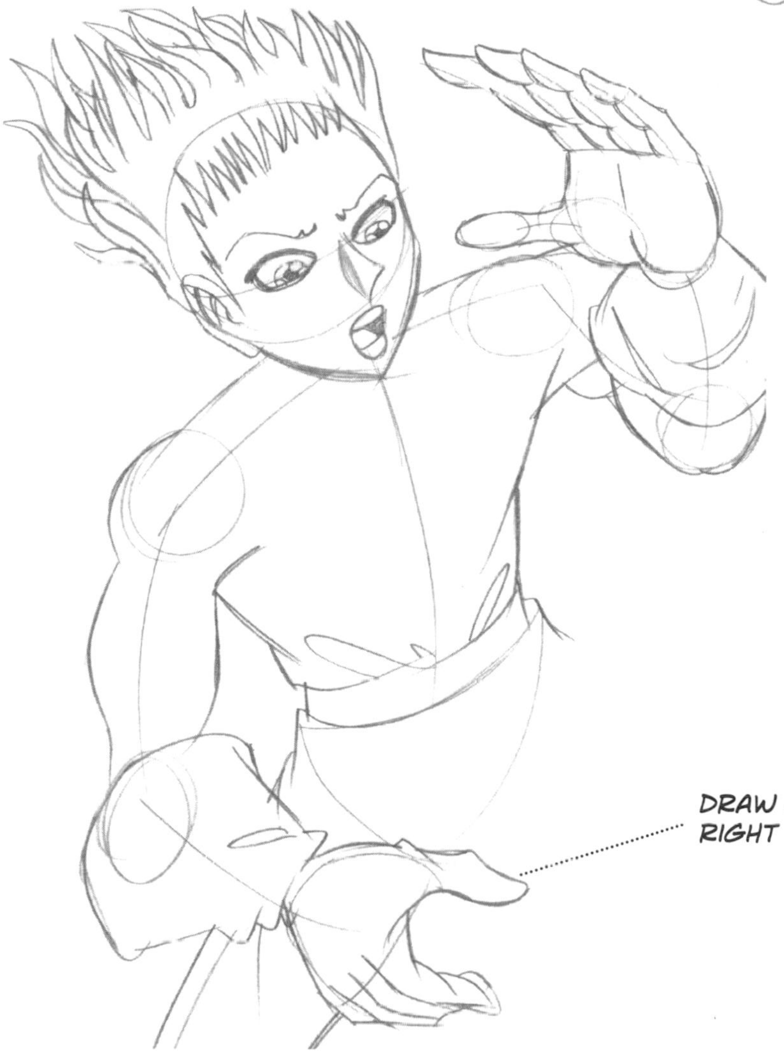
DRAW A LOOSE-GRIPPING RIGHT HAND

STAGE 3

Flesh out the torso, arms and right leg, and add gloved hands.

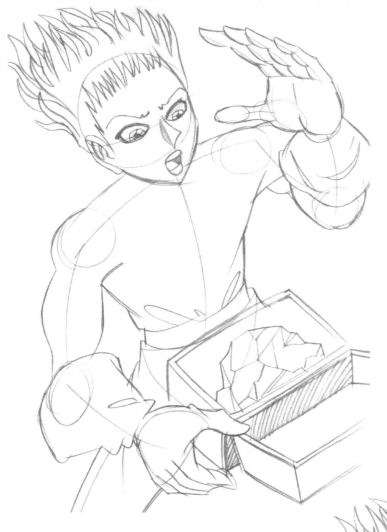

STAGE 4

Draw a casket with an open lid, revealing a jagged piece of rock.

STAGE 5

Add a cloak flowing up towards the top-left.

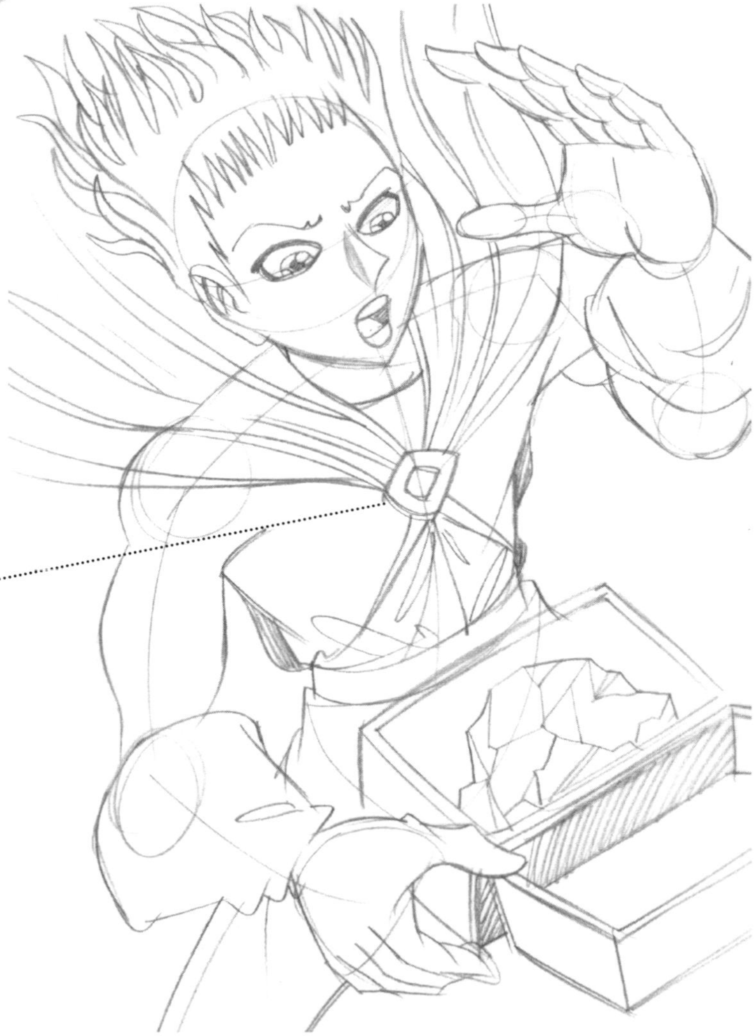

THE CLOAK IS FASTENED IN THE CENTRE OF THE CHEST

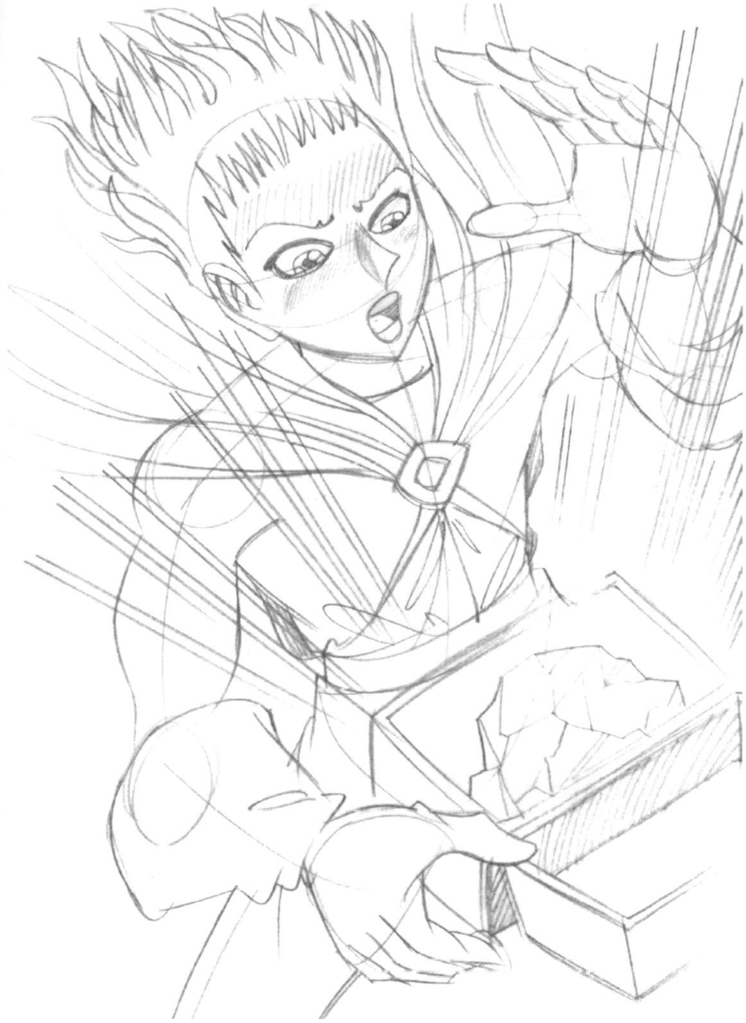

STAGE 6

Use a ruler to draw straight lines radiating from the rock.

STAGE 7

Ink the figure in black, and the rock and rays in red.

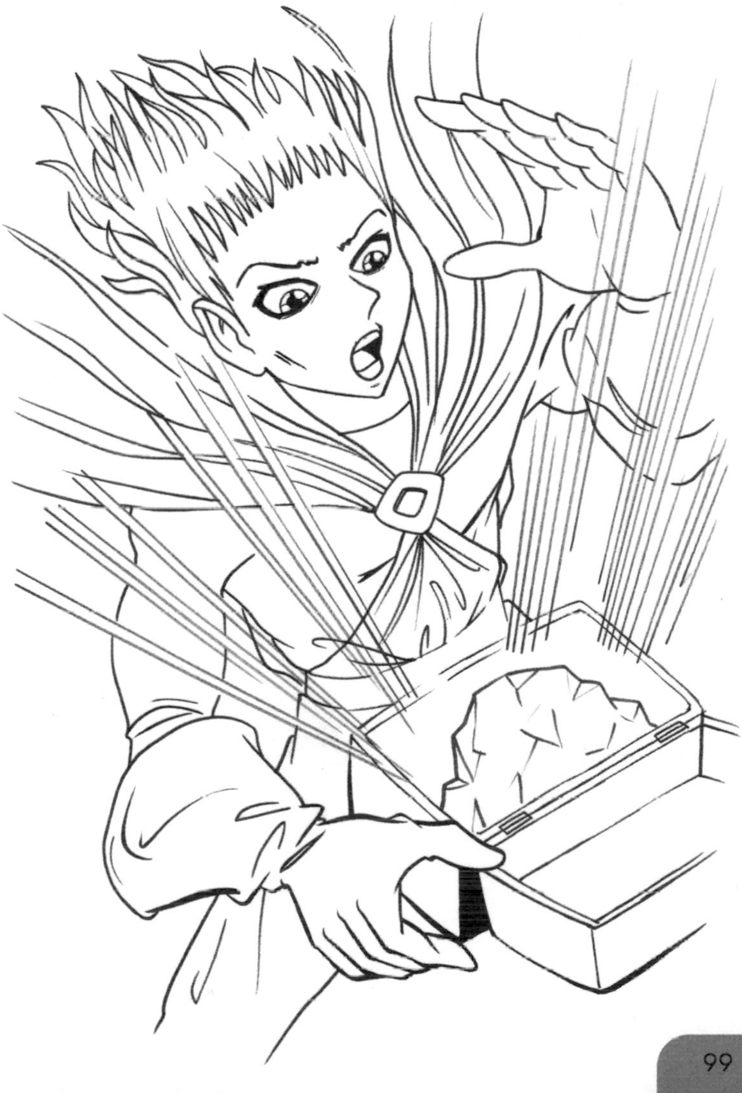

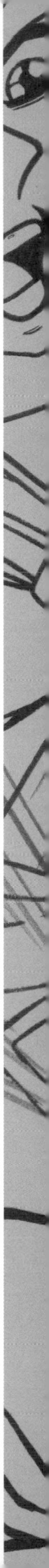

STAGE 8

Colour in the rock with reds and pinks, then use pale pinks and reds to create the rays.

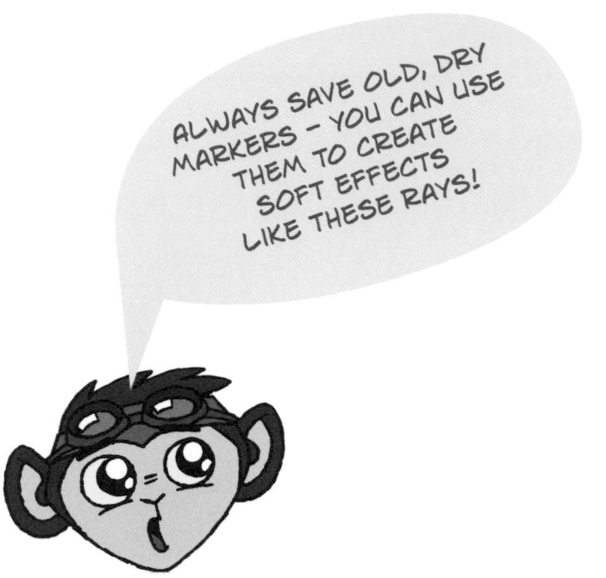
ALWAYS SAVE OLD, DRY MARKERS – YOU CAN USE THEM TO CREATE SOFT EFFECTS LIKE THESE RAYS!

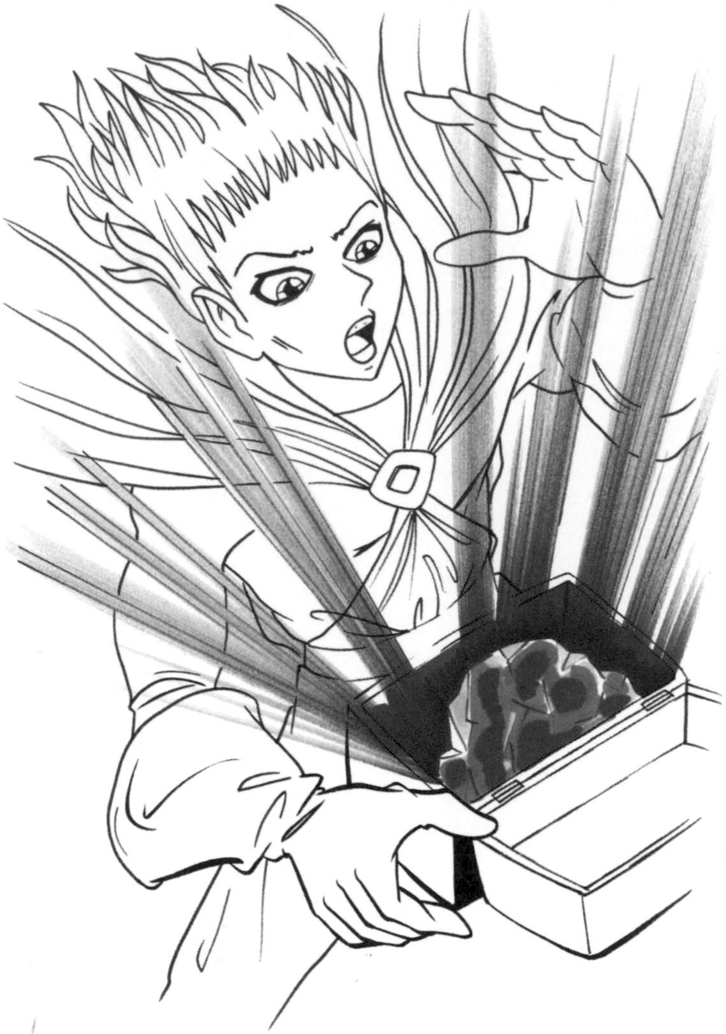

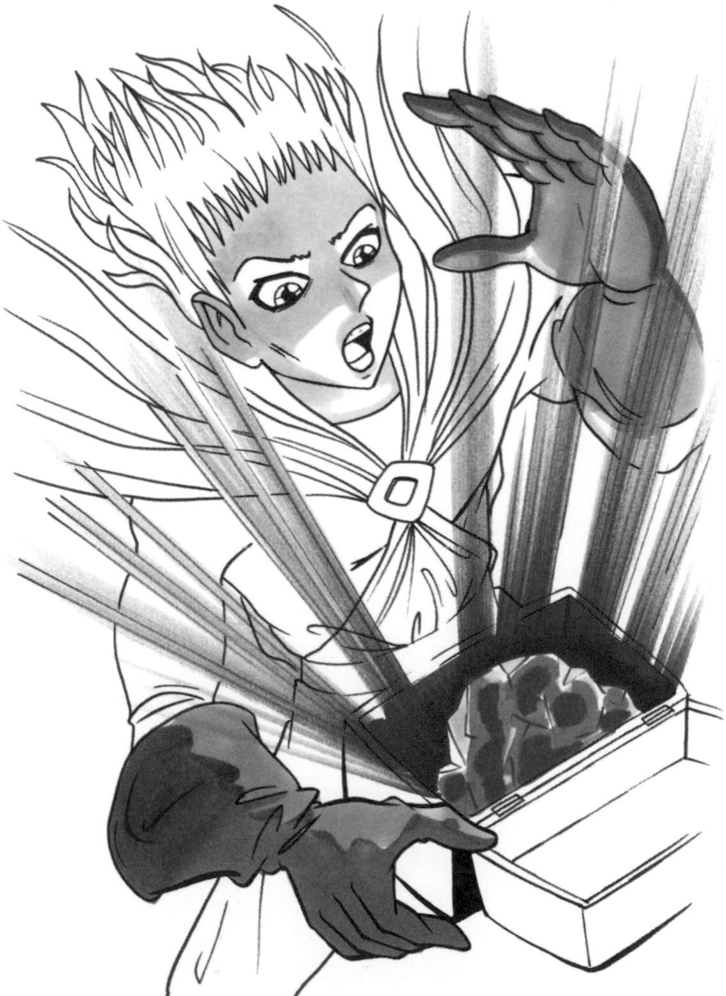

STAGE 9

Add flesh tone to the face, leaving white highlight areas, and use mid-grey and pink on the gloves.

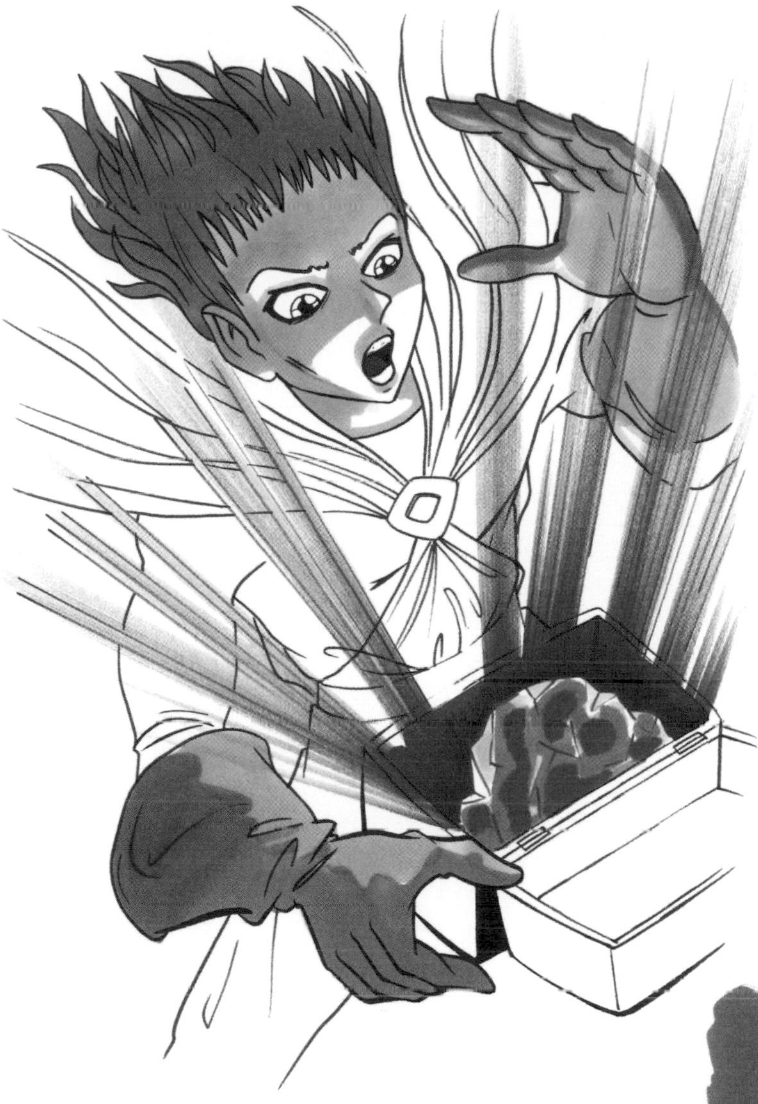

STAGE 10

Use dark grey on the hair and red on the tongue, and use a mid-grey to darken the face colour.

STAGE 11

Colour the tunic and leggings mauve, and the cape dark green.

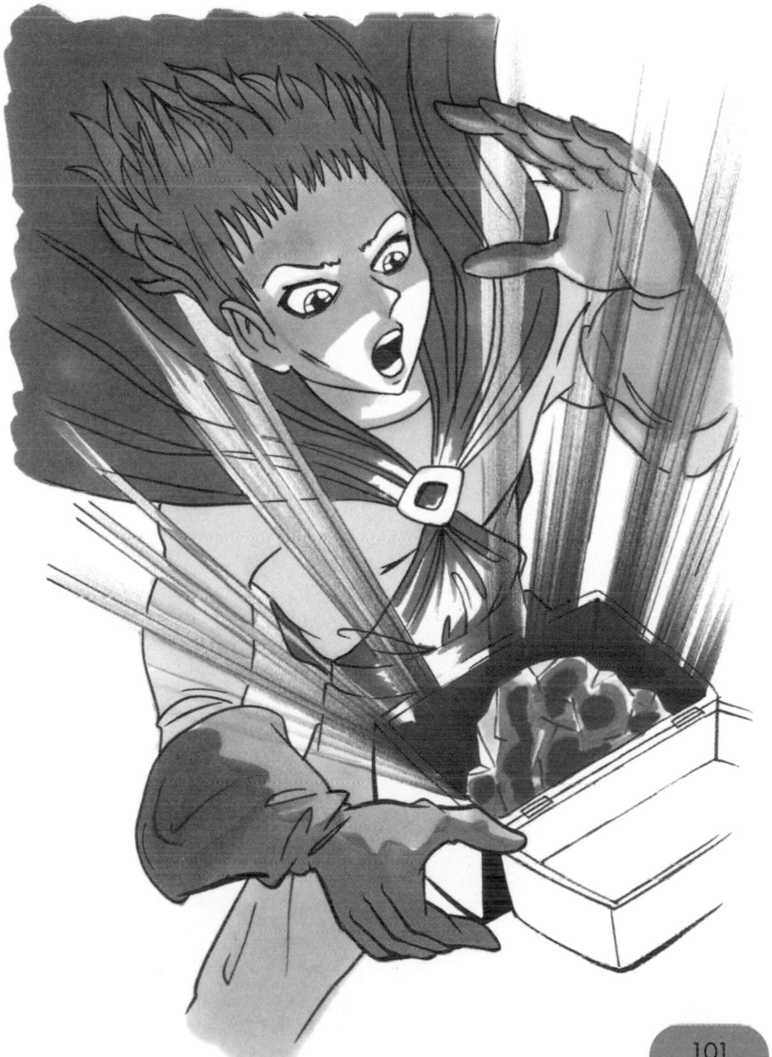

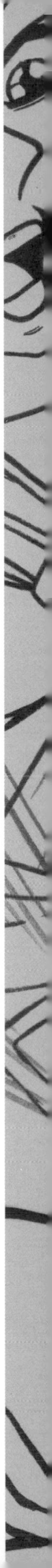

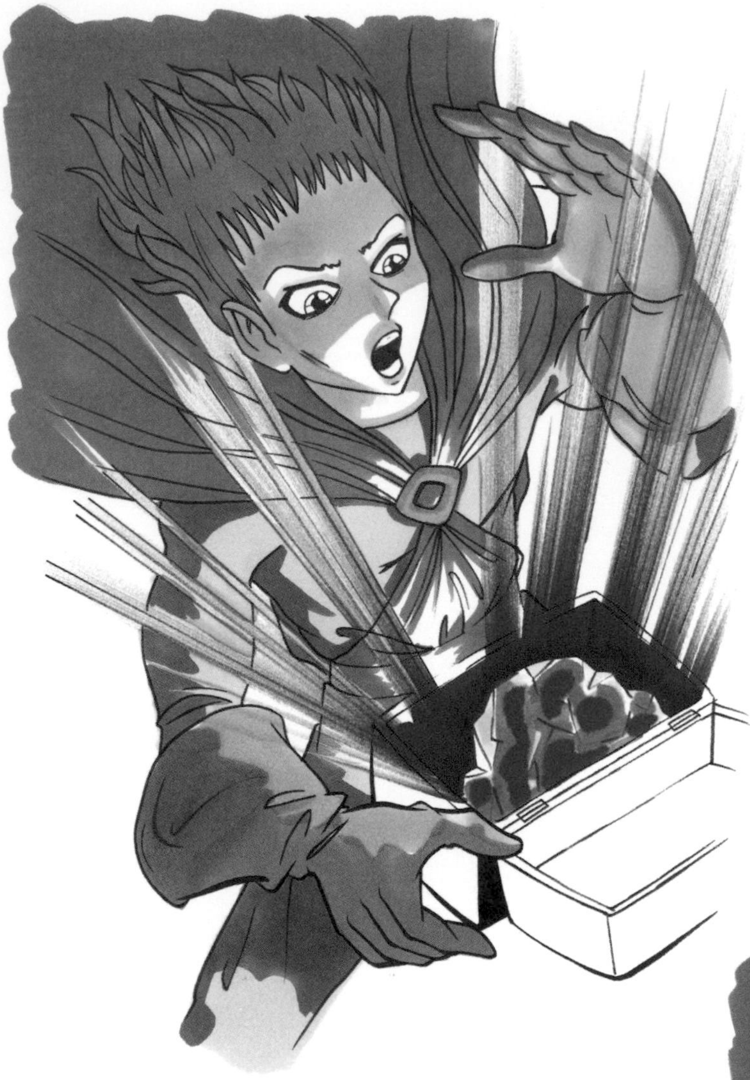

STAGE 12

Add a darker grey tone to the outer edges of the tunic and leggings. Use this to help define the shape of the body.

STAGE 13

Colour the casket with brown tones. Add red to the eyes and pink to the highlights on the face and cape to reflect the glow of the rock. Add some darker tones to the gloves and add some dark green streaks to the front of the cape.

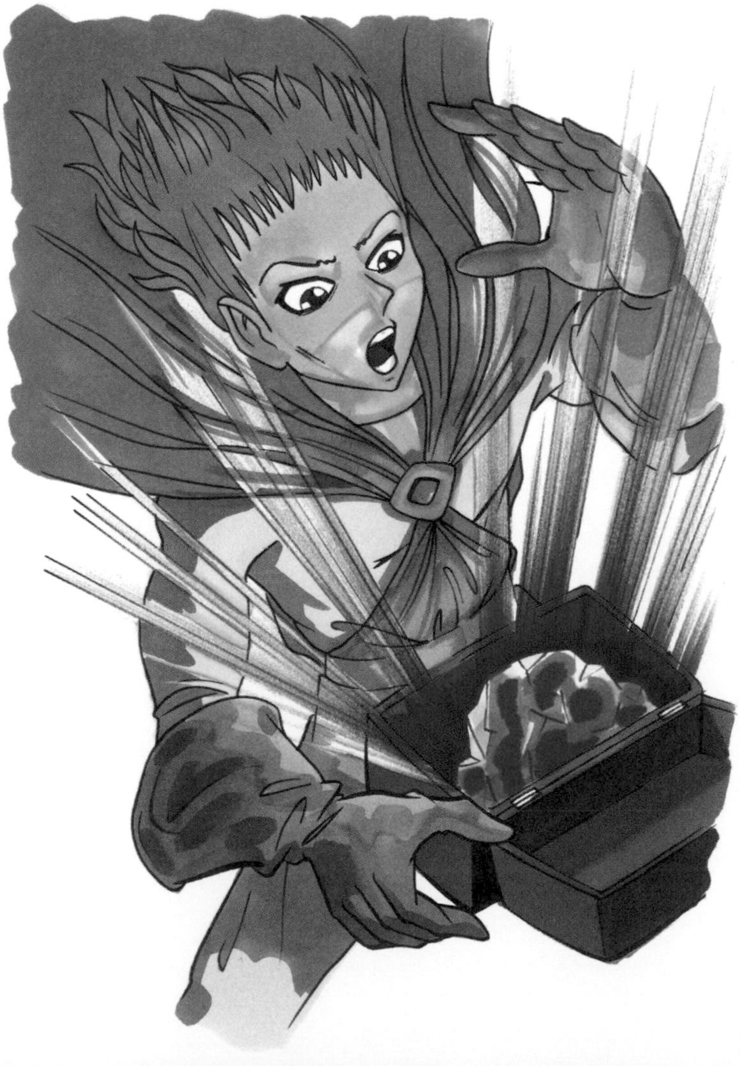

STAGE 14

Build up the colour on the cape and hair with darker tones, and add deeper shadows to the face.

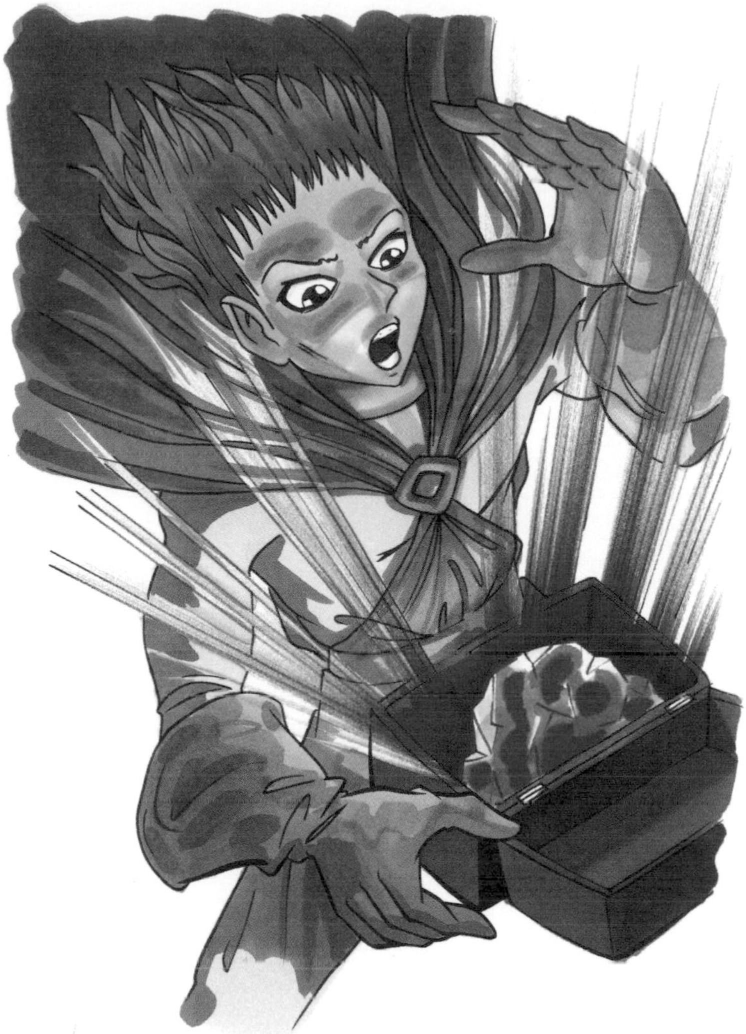

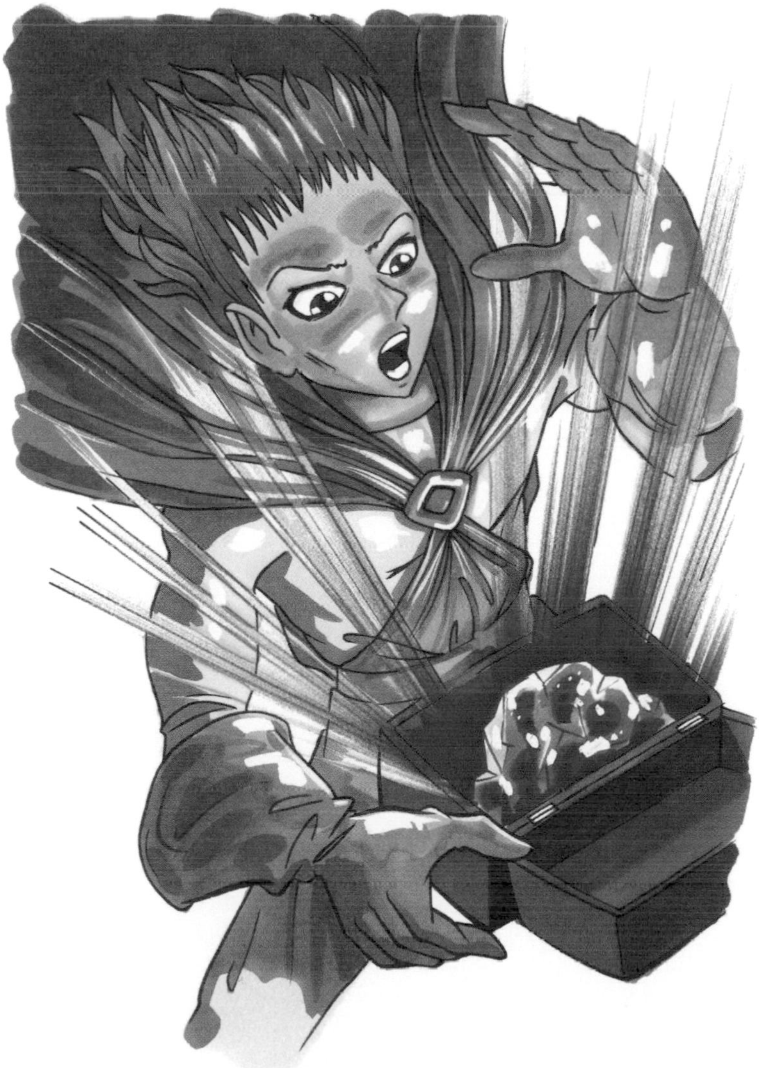

STAGE 15

Finish with some small areas of white paint on the hands, rock and clothes, to add extra punch to the highlights.

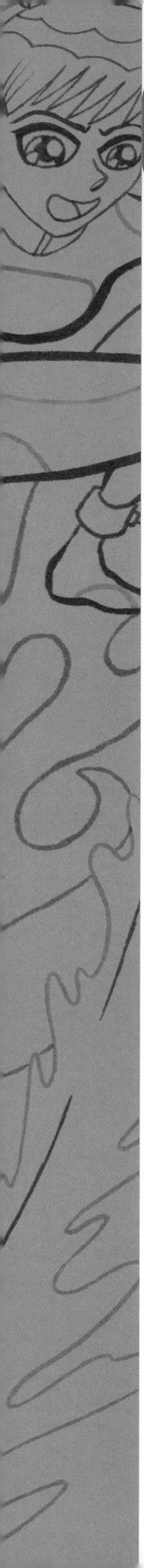

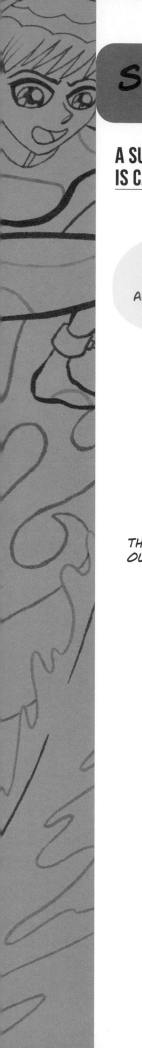

SURF'S UP!

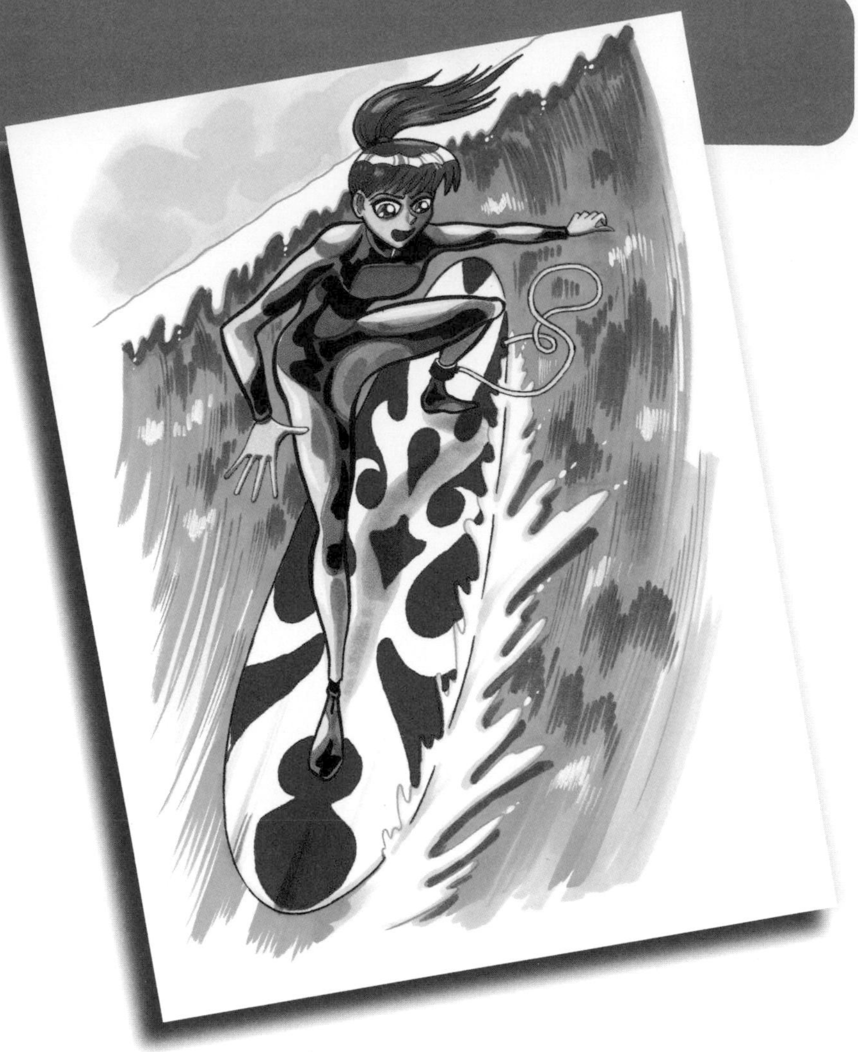

A SURFER GIRL IS CATCHING A BIG WAVE!

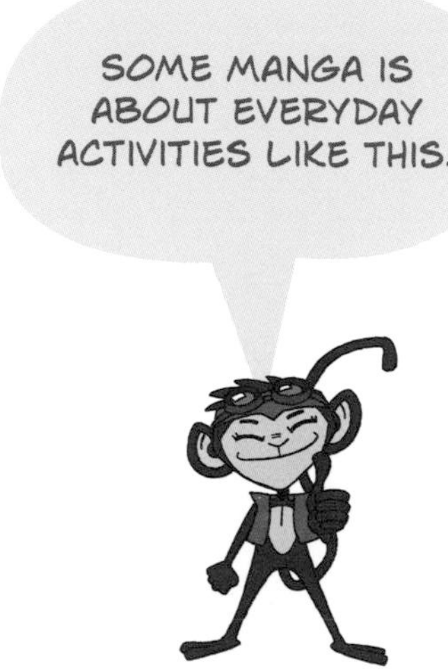
SOME MANGA IS ABOUT EVERYDAY ACTIVITIES LIKE THIS!

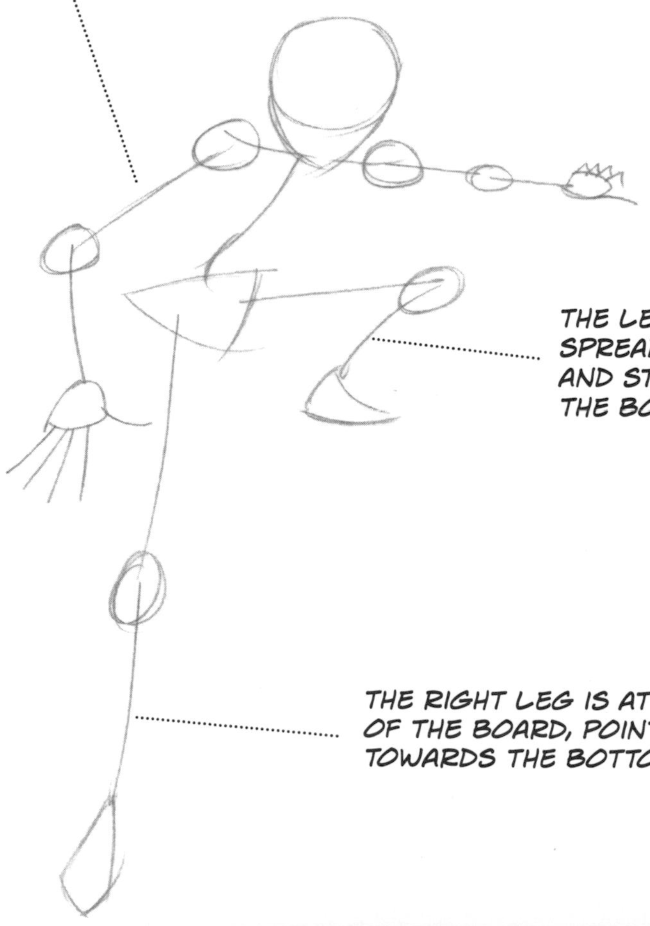
THE ARMS ARE STRETCHED OUT FOR BALANCE
THE LEFT LEG IS BENT, SPREADING THE GIRL'S WEIGHT AND STEADYING THE REAR OF THE BOARD
THE RIGHT LEG IS AT THE FRONT OF THE BOARD, POINTING DOWN TOWARDS THE BOTTOM OF THE PAGE

STAGE 1

Start by creating a crouching wireframe figure in the centre of the page.

STAGE 2

Flesh out the figure and add facial features and hair.

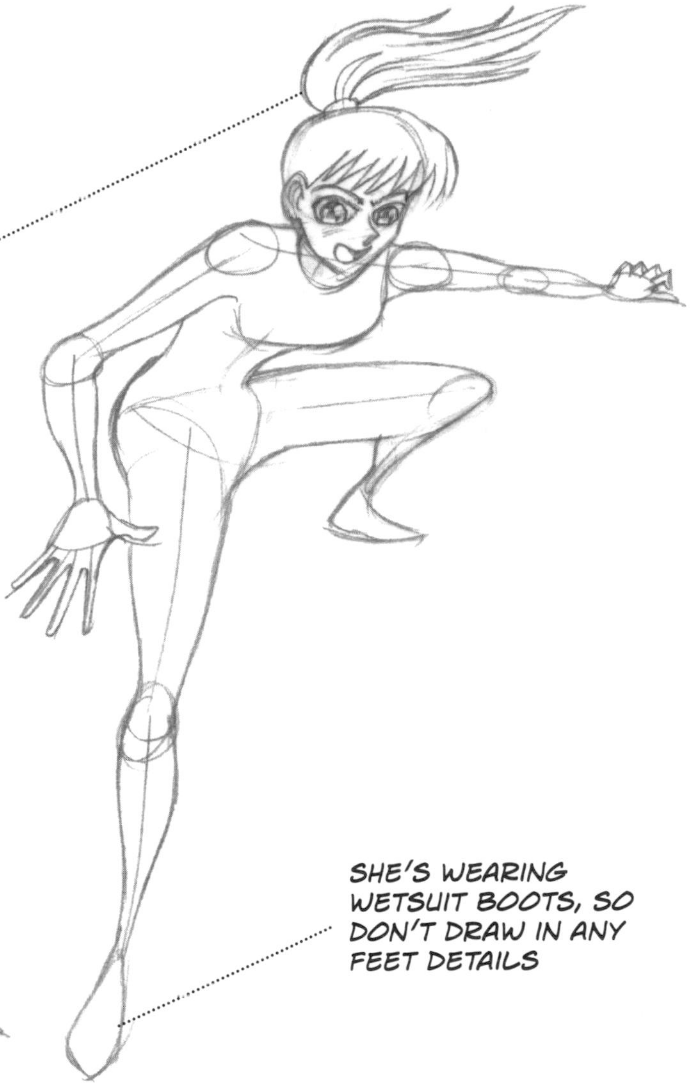
ADD A PONYTAIL TRAILING UP AND TO THE RIGHT
SHE'S WEARING WETSUIT BOOTS, SO DON'T DRAW IN ANY FEET DETAILS

STAGE 3

Draw in the board: create a long, thin teardrop shape that runs diagonally underneath the surfer girl.

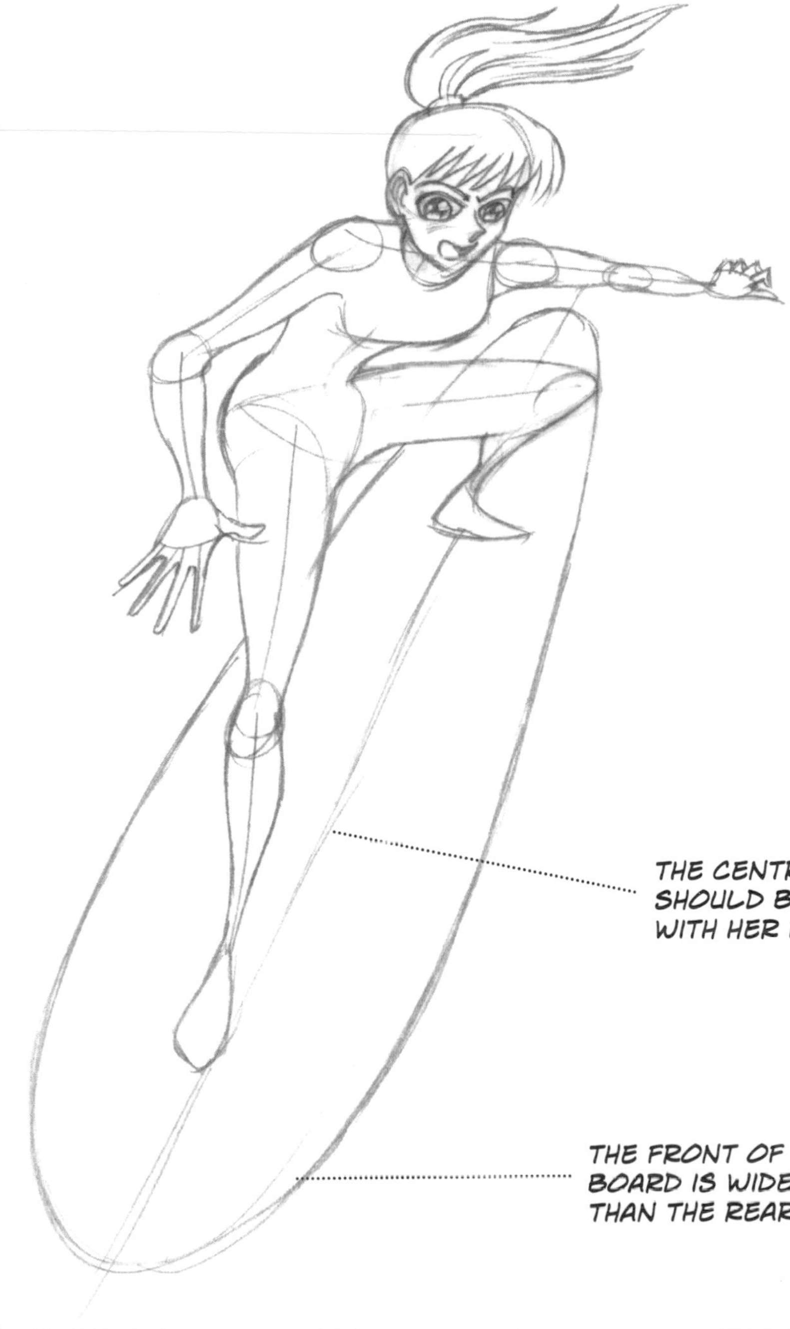
THE CENTRE OF THE BOARD SHOULD BE ROUGHLY IN LINE WITH HER FEET
THE FRONT OF THE BOARD IS WIDER THAN THE REAR

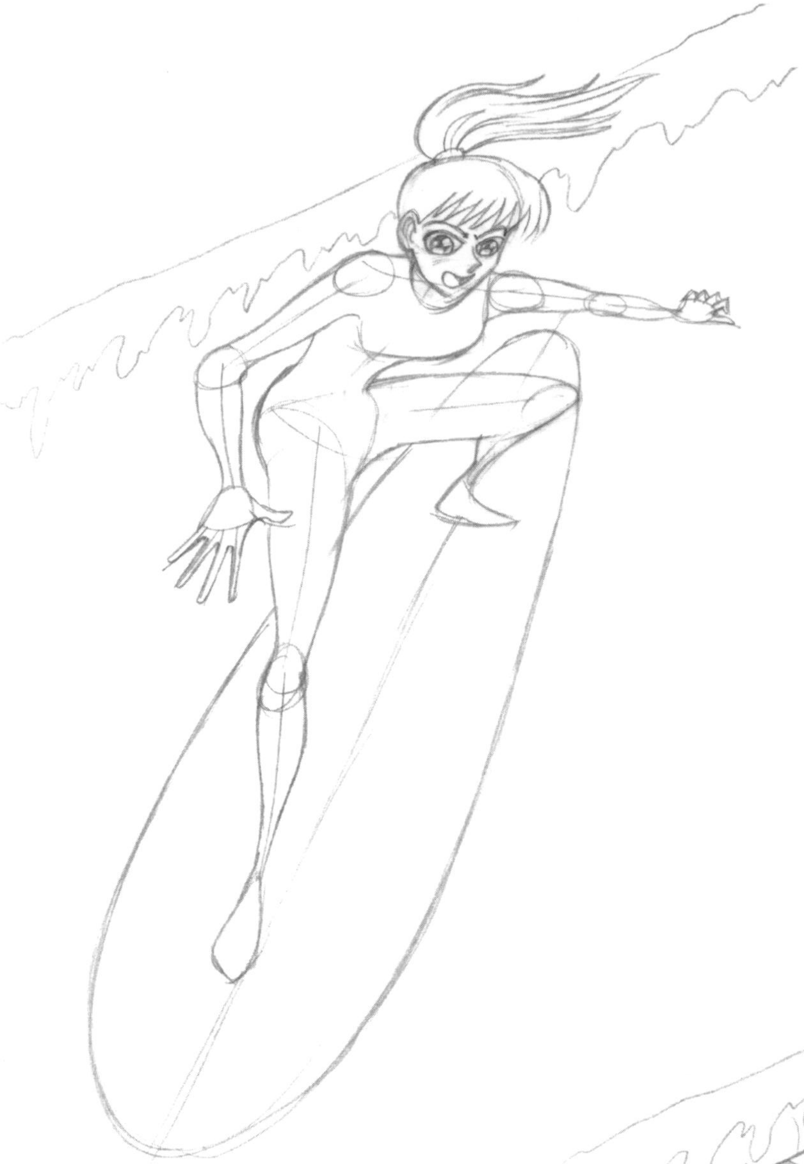

STAGE 4

Draw the lip of the wave running diagonally from the top-right of the page, down to roughly the level of her right elbow.

STAGE 5

Sketch a few sweeping lines to represent the moving water. These run at an angle, as shown, and curl slightly, just under the lip. Also add a few wavy lines to show the sheets of water dripping down the wave.

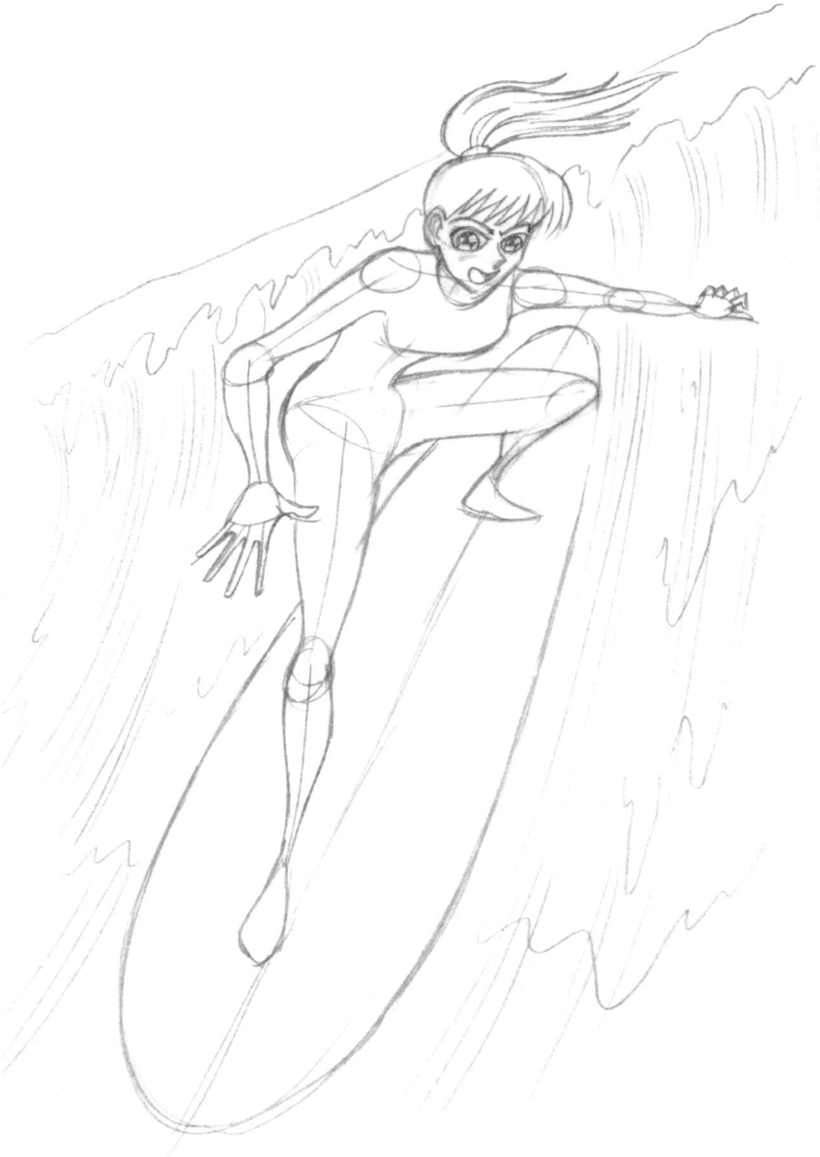

STAGE 6

Add a splash of water running along the edge of the surfboard.

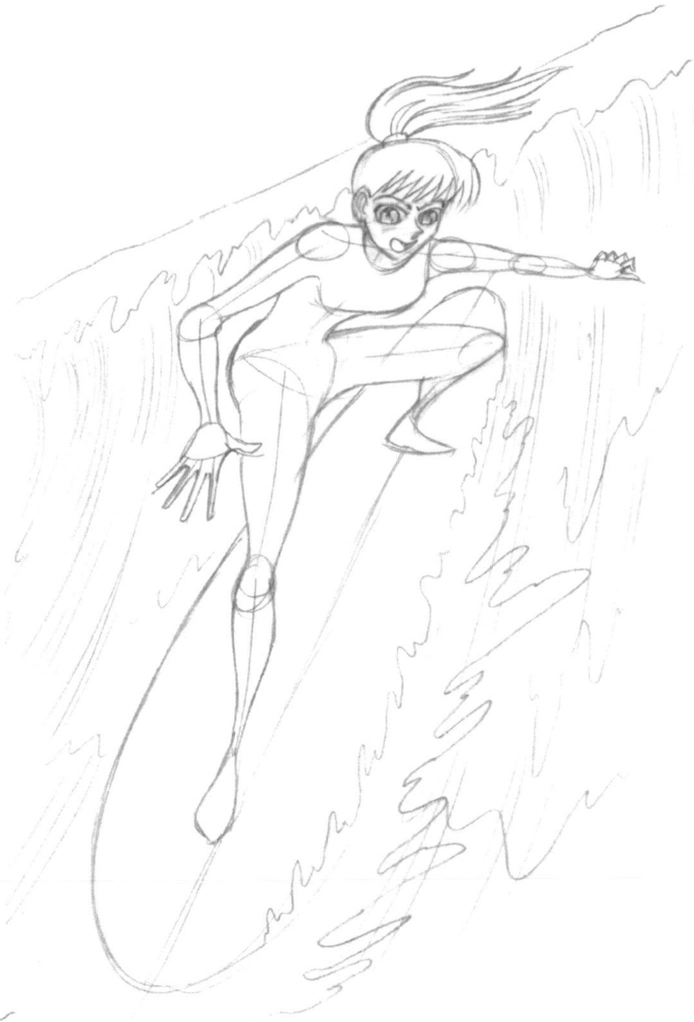

STAGE 7

Draw some details on the wetsuit and add a cord attaching her ankle to the board.

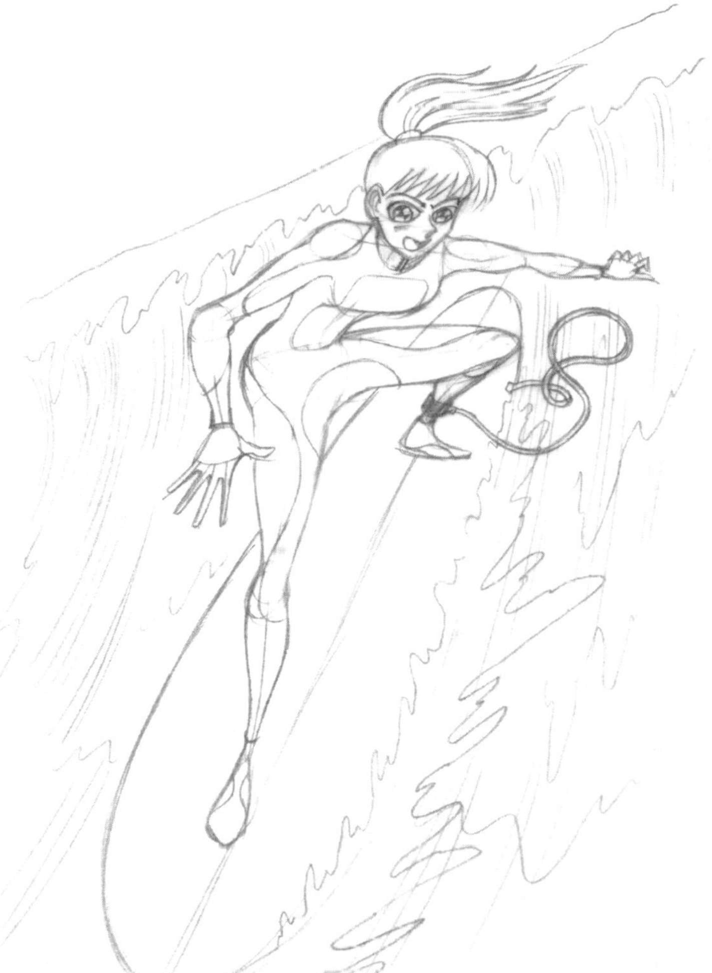

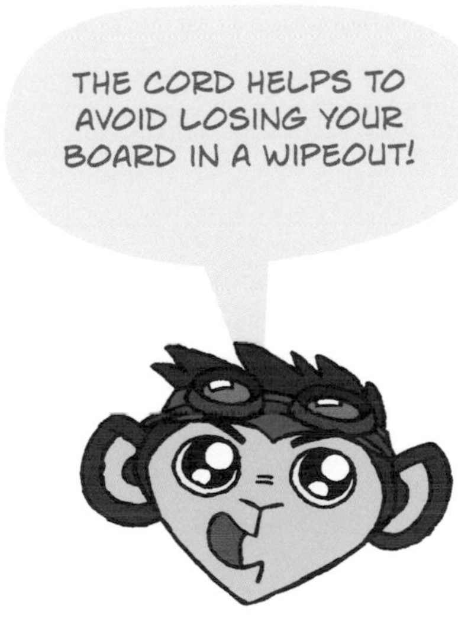
THE CORD HELPS TO AVOID LOSING YOUR BOARD IN A WIPEOUT!

STAGE 8

To finish the pencil stage, draw a funky pattern on the surfboard.

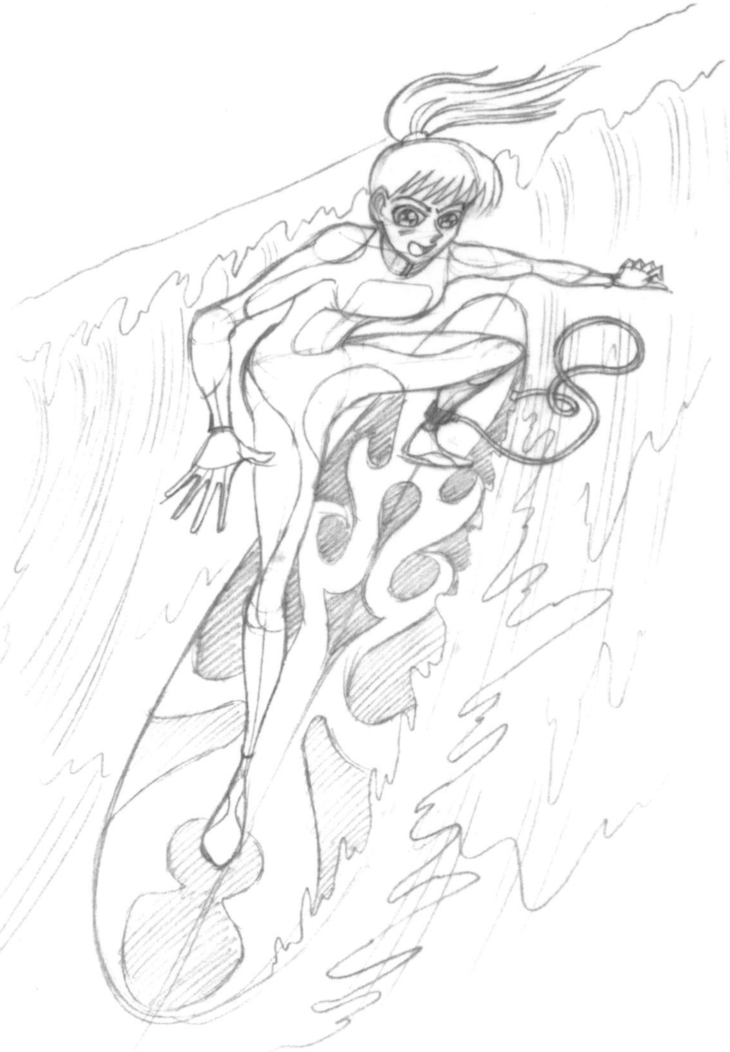

STAGE 9

Outline your figure with black. Use a yellow pen to outline the wetsuit pattern, a red pen for the board design and a blue pen for the water.

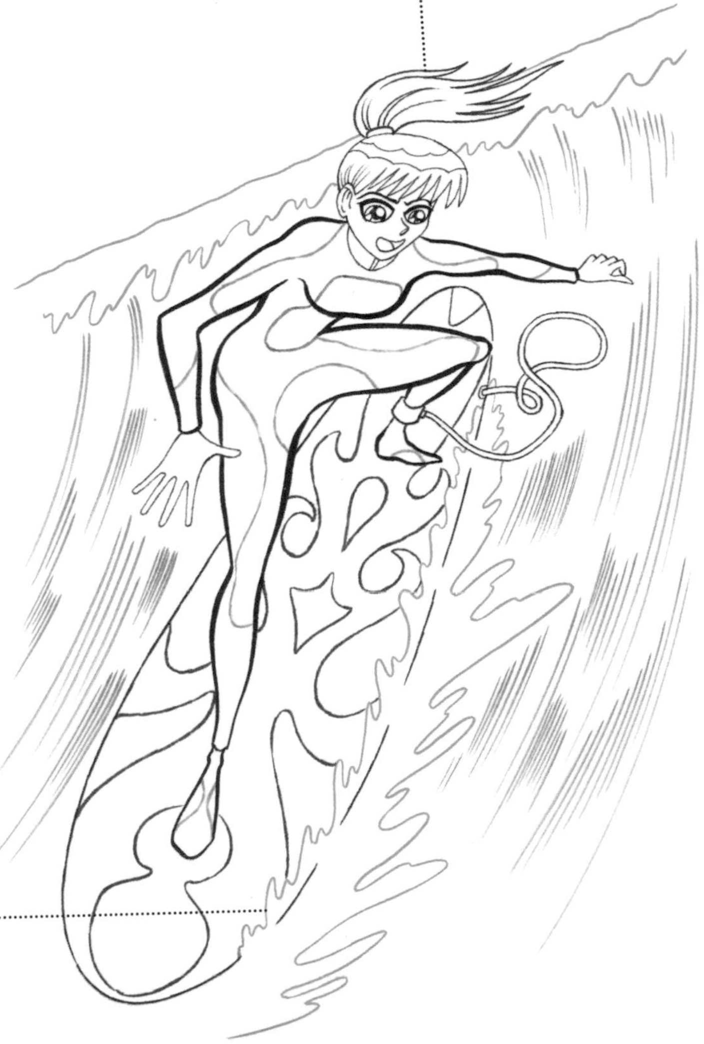
USE A BLACK BRUSH PEN ON THE BODY AND A FINE BLACK PEN FOR THE HEAD AND HANDS
DRAW THE RIGHT SIDE OF THE BOARD AS A BROKEN LINE, TO SHOW THAT WATER IS SPLASHING OVER IT

STAGE 10

Colour the wetsuit with yellow and dark grey – outline the yellow shapes with a fine orange line. Fill in the surfboard design with bright red.

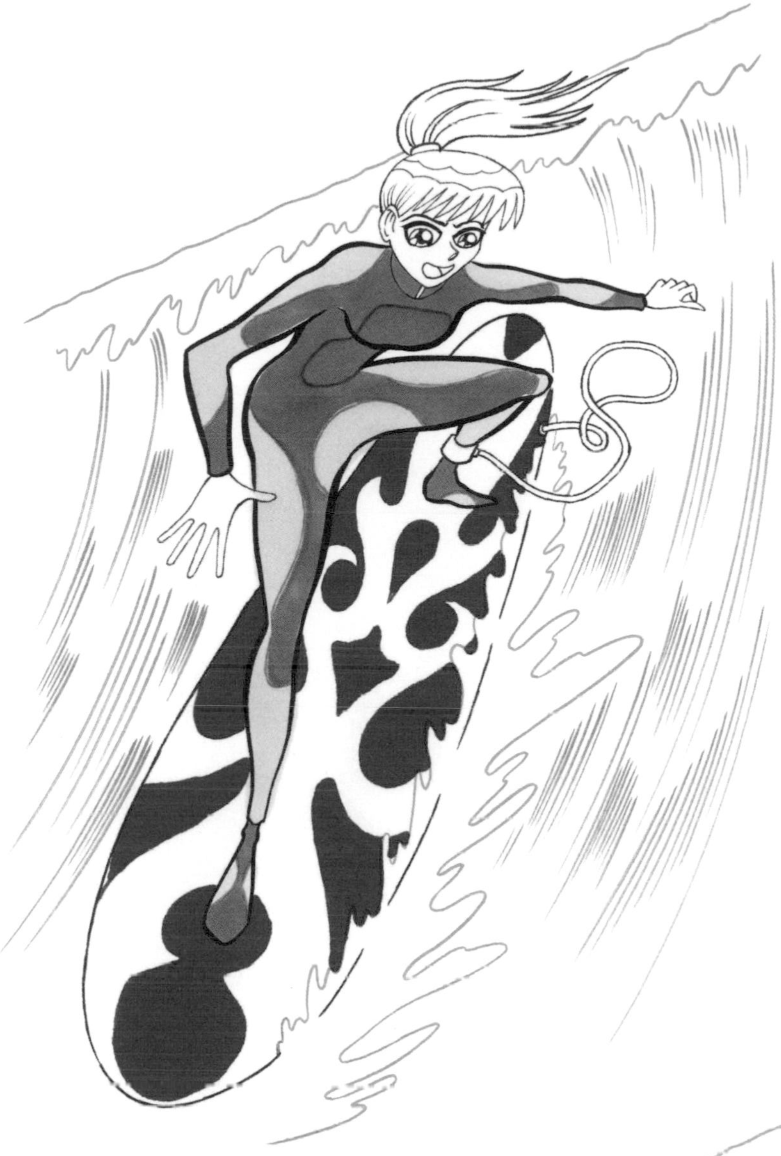

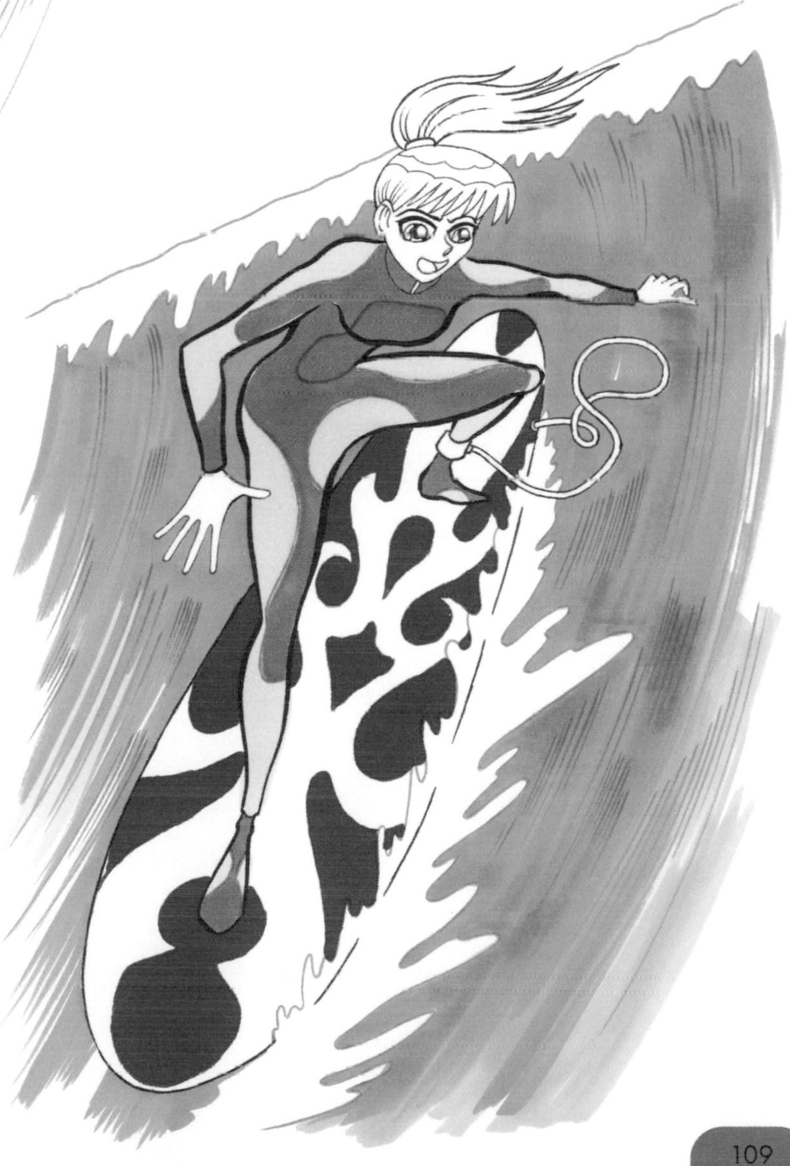

STAGE 11

Use medium and dark green-blues on the water, following the curve of the wave.

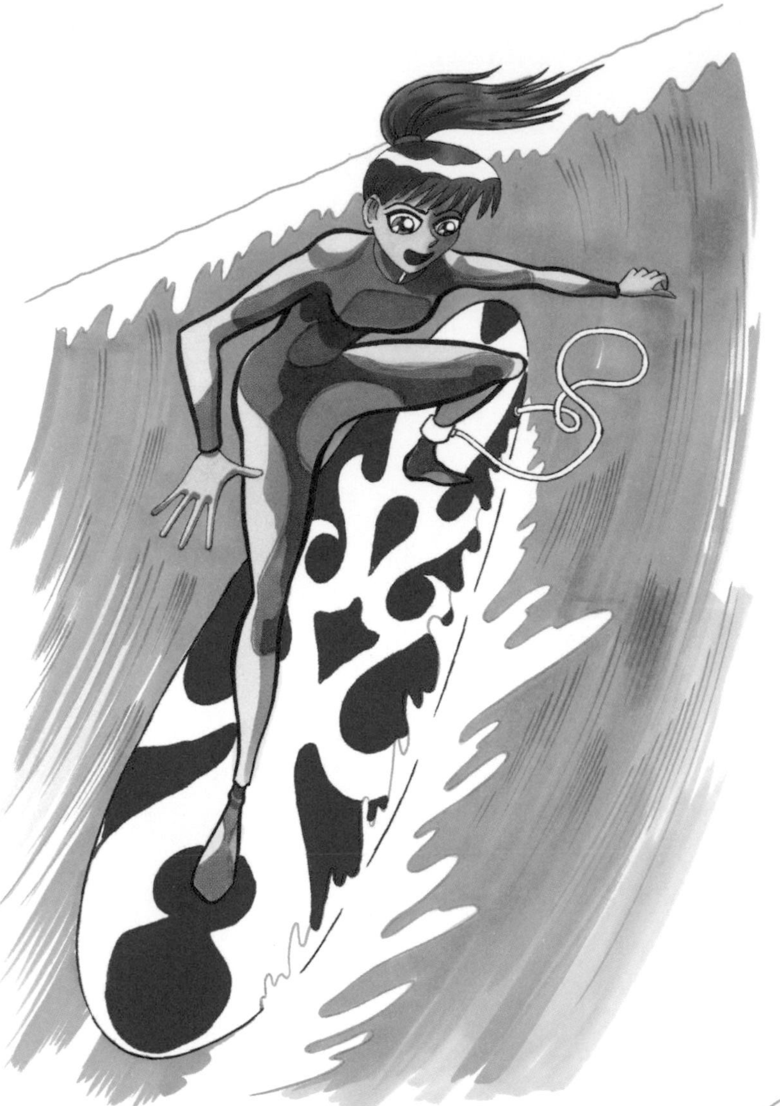

STAGE 12

Add flesh colour to the face and hands and orange to the hair. Use darker tones to add shading to the face, hair and body.

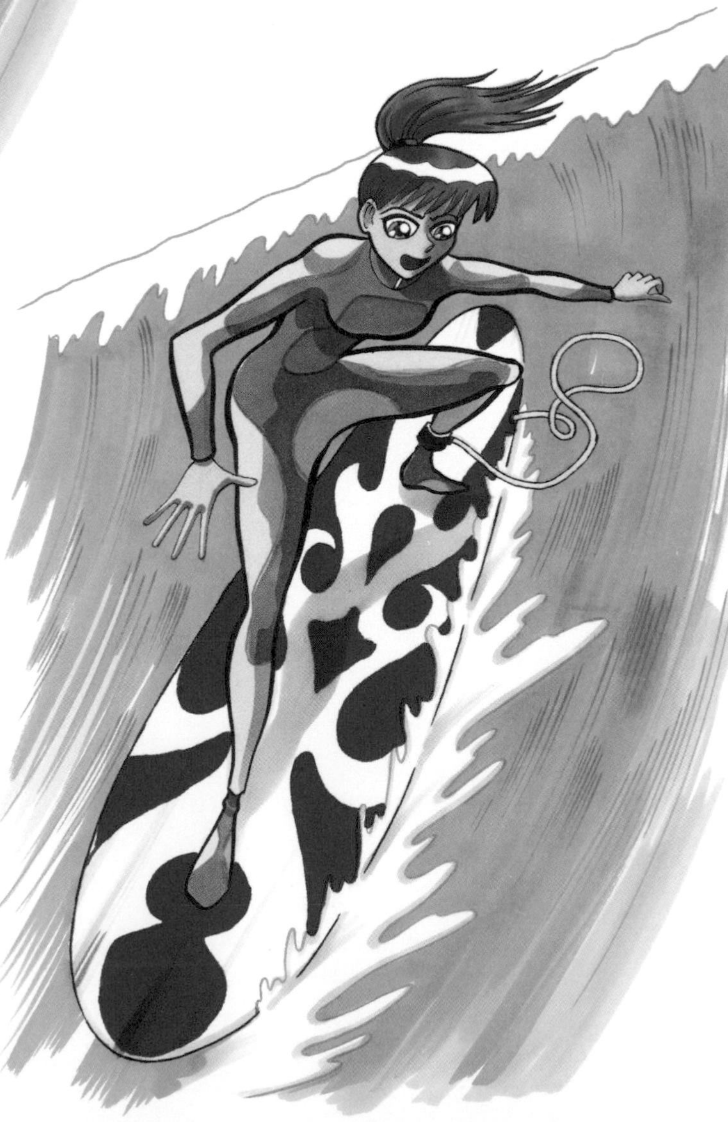

STAGE 13

Add a light blue-grey shadow on the board, and use pale blue to line the edge of the splash. Colour the cord.

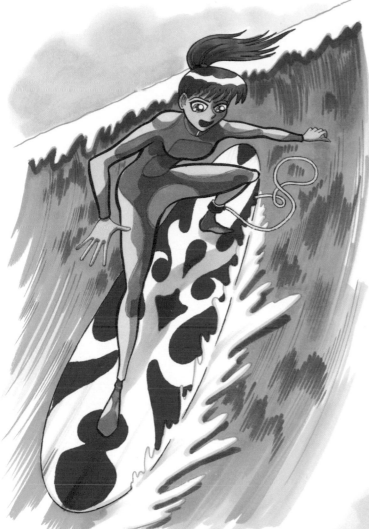

STAGE 14

Add some darker blue tones to the water and under the lip of the wave and splash line. Colour the sky area with mid-grey and pale blue.

STAGE 15

Finish by adding some solid blacks to the figure and white detailing on the water to make your drawing really pop!

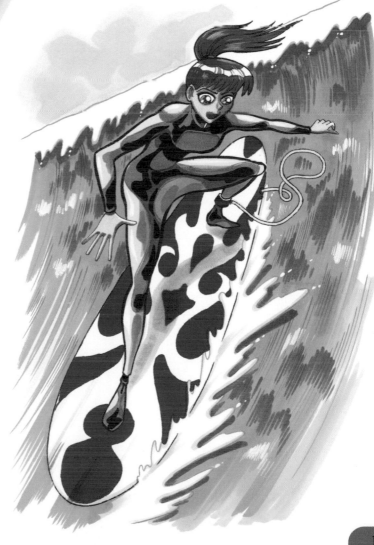

MECHA WAR!

A MECHA WARRIOR IN FLYING COMBAT!

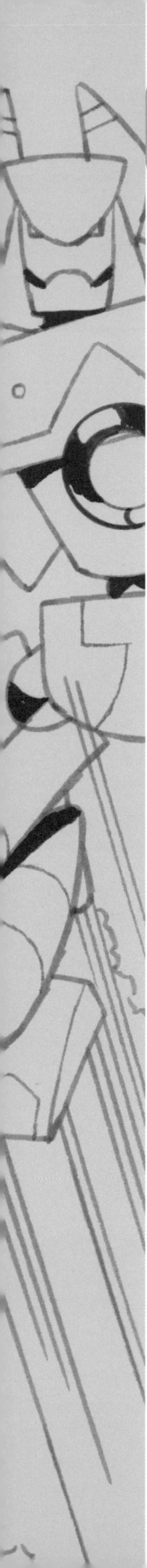

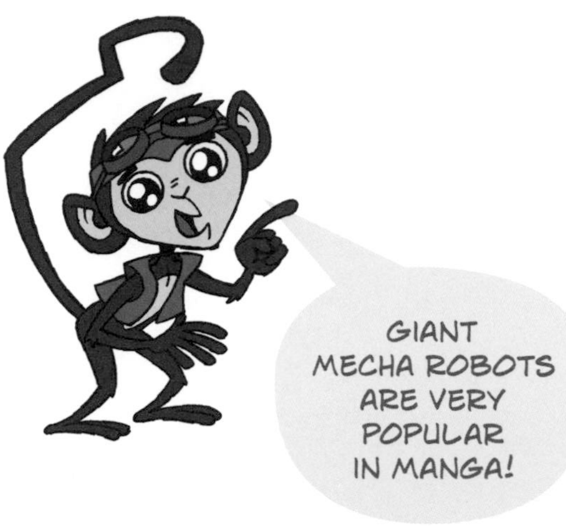
GIANT MECHA ROBOTS ARE VERY POPULAR IN MANGA!

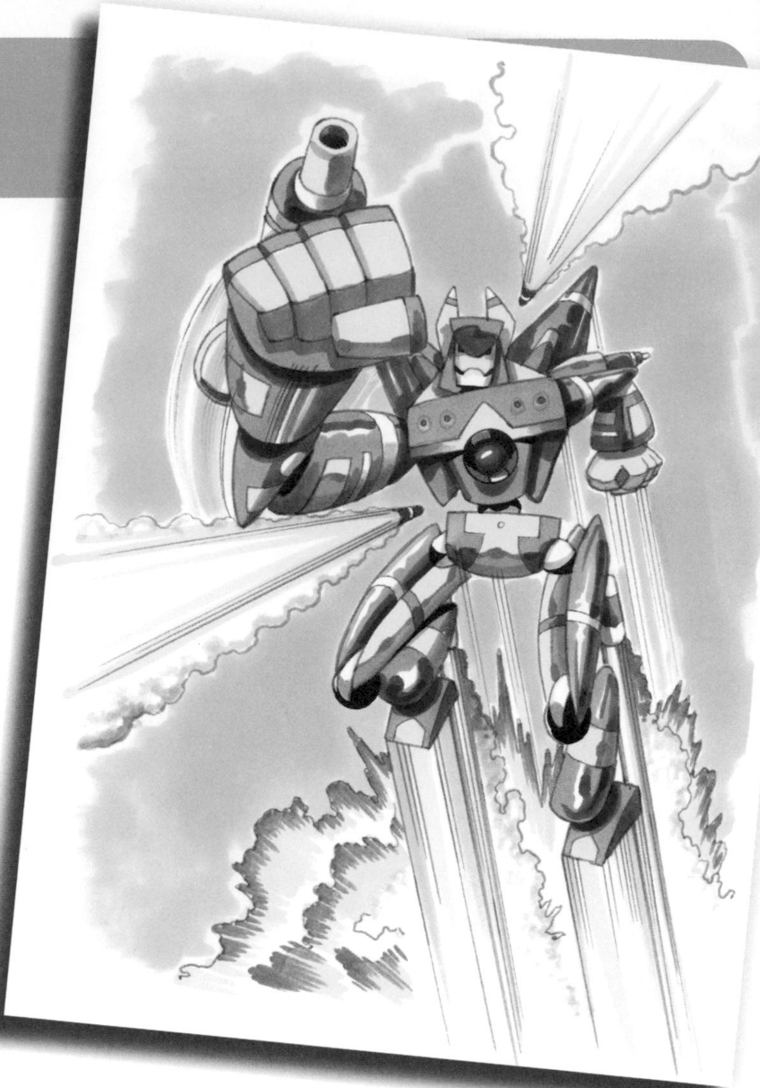

STAGE 1

Start with a leaping, punching wireframe shape for your mecha character.

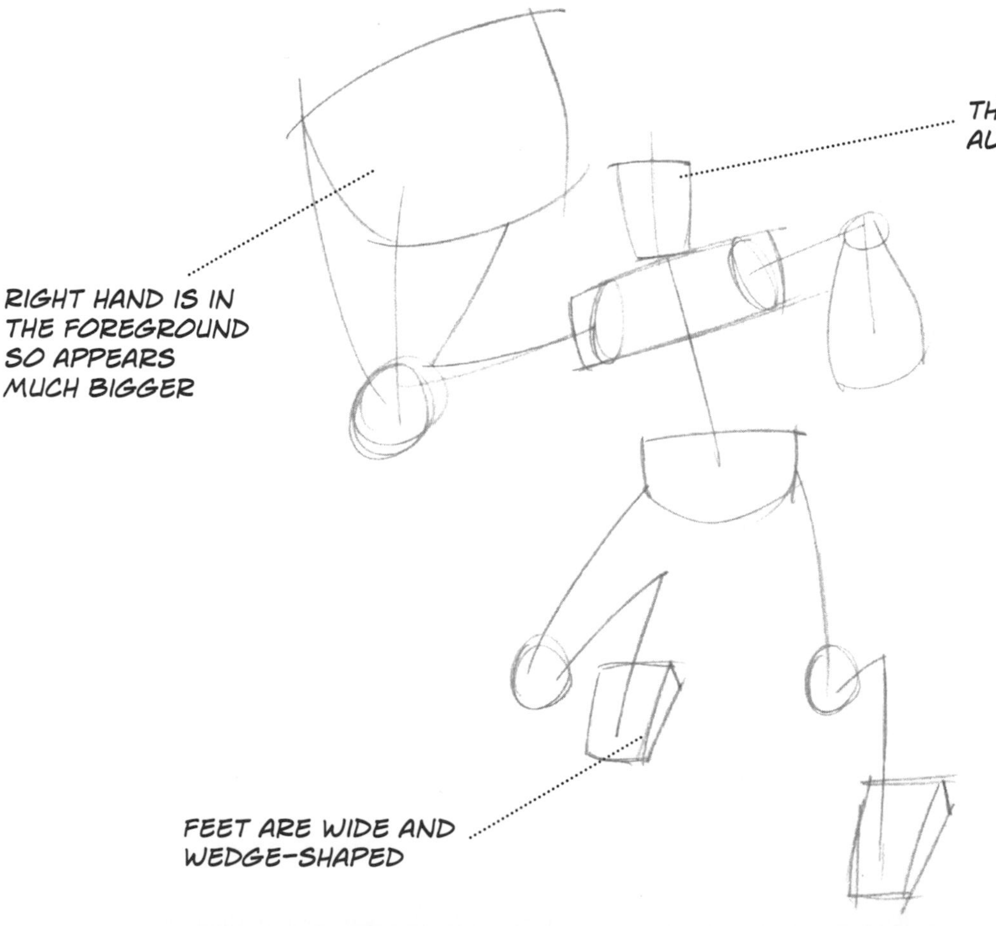
THE HEAD IS ALMOST CYLINDRICAL
RIGHT HAND IS IN THE FOREGROUND SO APPEARS MUCH BIGGER
FEET ARE WIDE AND WEDGE-SHAPED

STAGE 2

Sketch in both hands as clenched fists; the right hand will appear much larger than the left. Continue to flesh out the character, adding a block shape in the stomach area, to sit under the breast-plate, and wide forearm shapes.

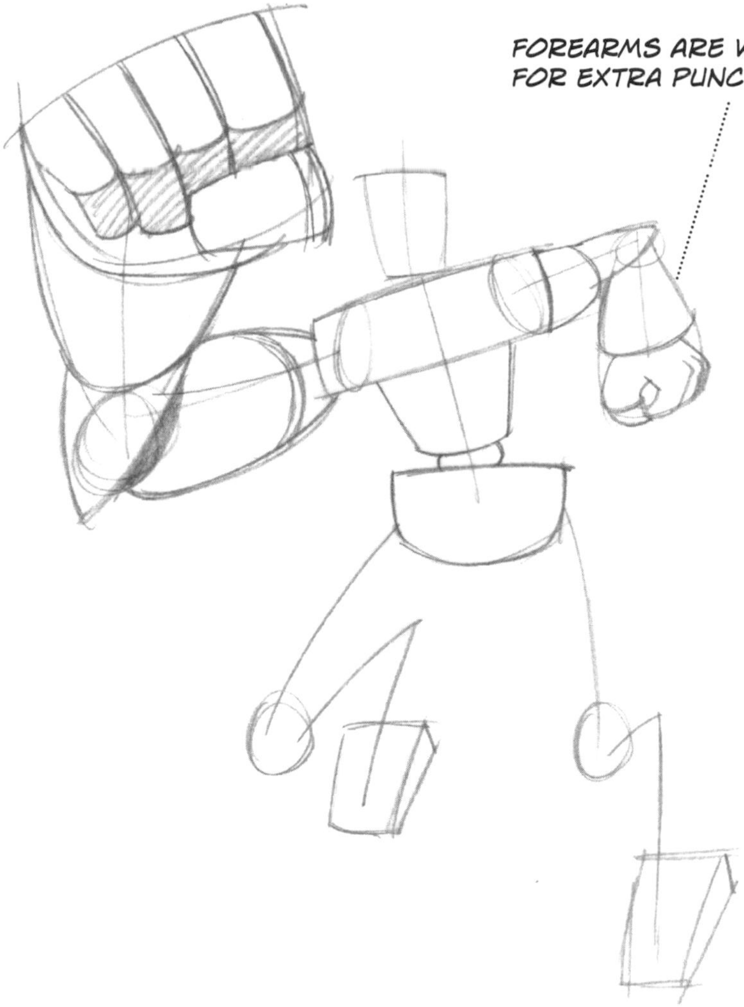
FOREARMS ARE WIDE FOR EXTRA PUNCH POWER

STAGE 3

Create curving upper and lower leg shapes. Keeping the sections detached slightly from each other gives a robotic, non-human appearance.

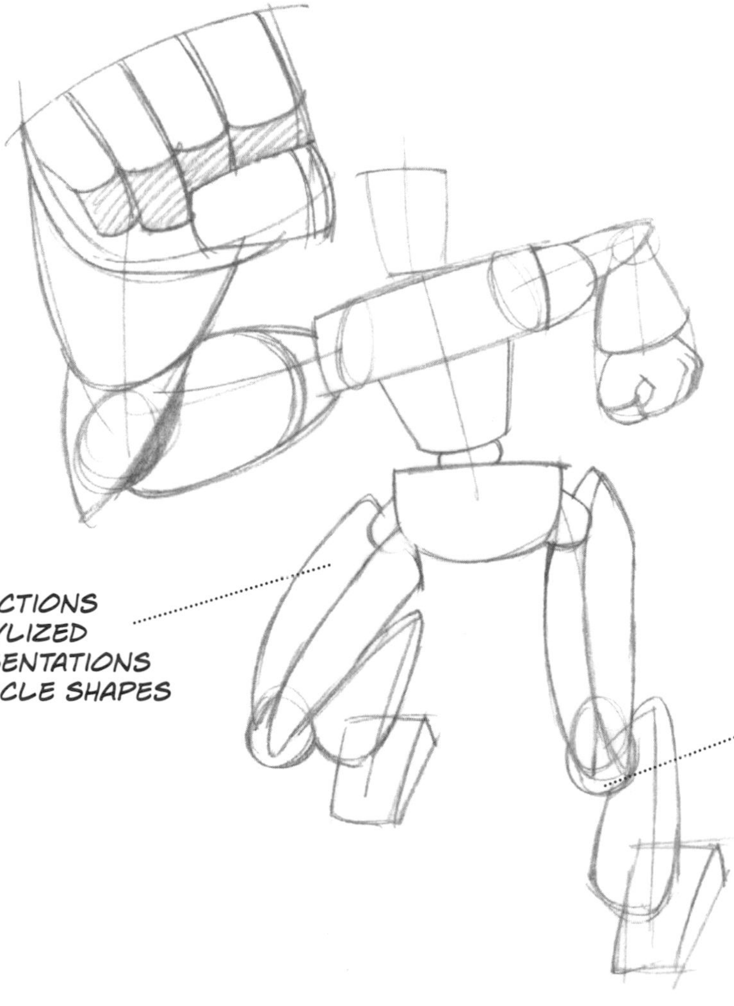
LEG SECTIONS ARE STYLIZED REPRESENTATIONS OF MUSCLE SHAPES
USE CIRCULAR JOINTS TO CONNECT THE SECTIONS

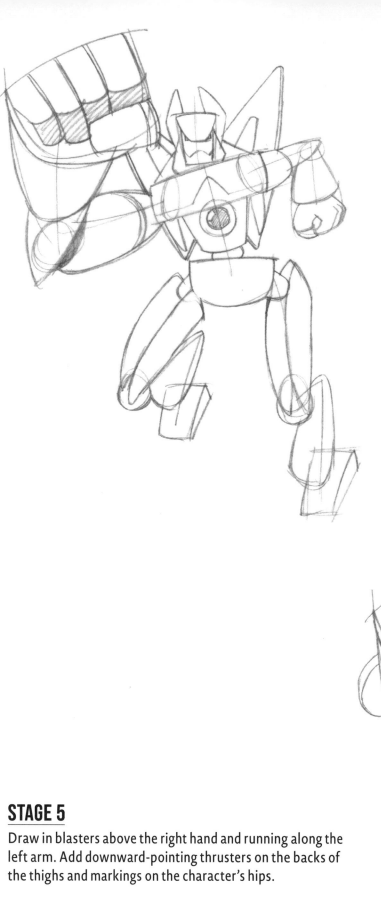

STAGE 4

Draw in a head with robotic mouth and eye shapes, and add fins to the back of it. Add wing shapes to the back and a large circular light source in the mid-section.

STAGE 5

Draw in blasters above the right hand and running along the left arm. Add downward-pointing thrusters on the backs of the thighs and markings on the character's hips.

STAGE 6

Draw an explosive blast beneath the feet and speed lines pushing the figure upwards.

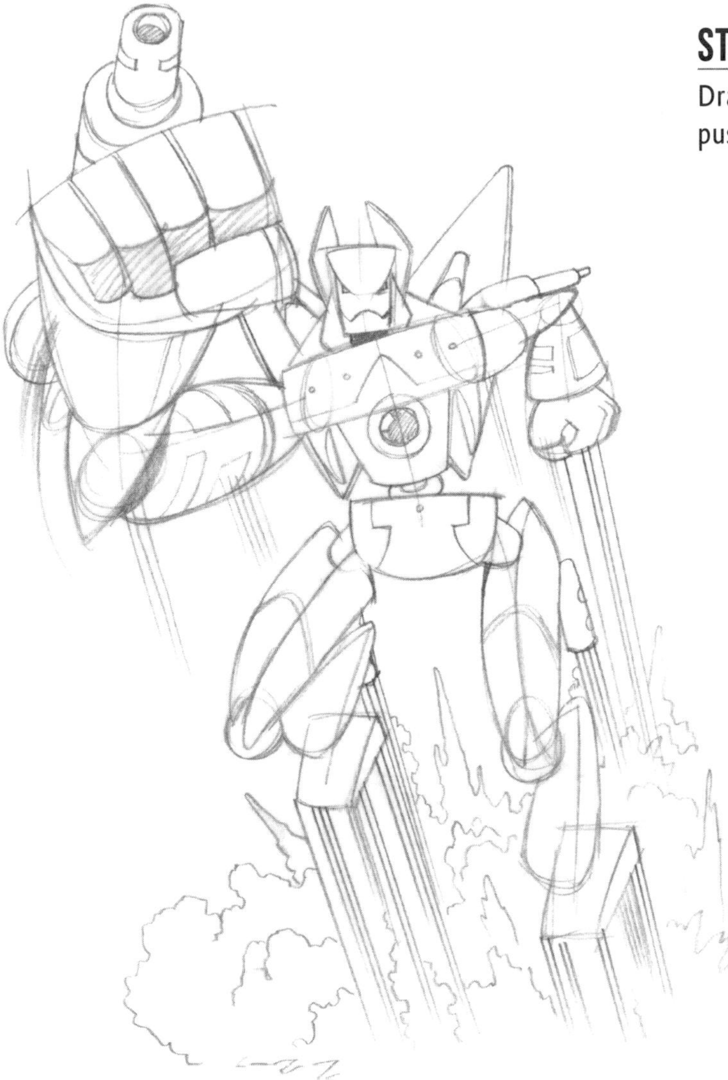

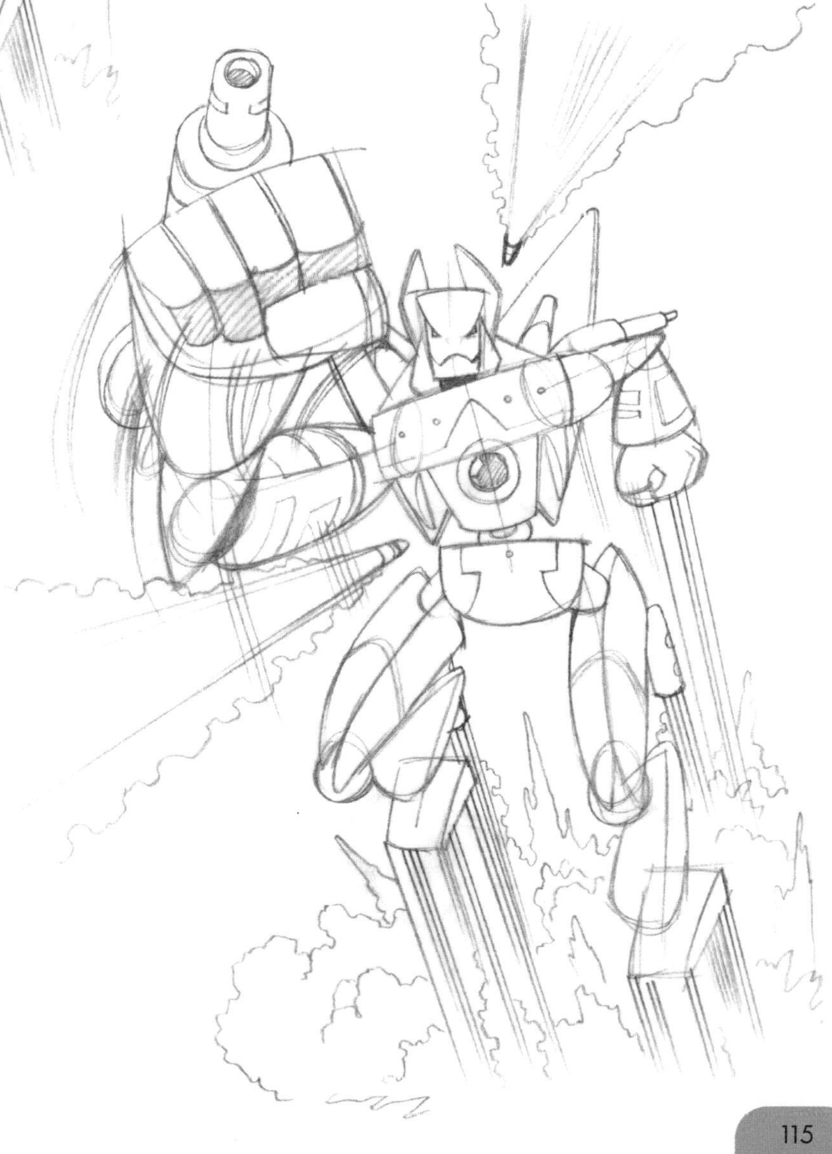

STAGE 7

Draw two projectiles blasting towards the figure. Note how the blast trails widen as they reach the edges of the page.

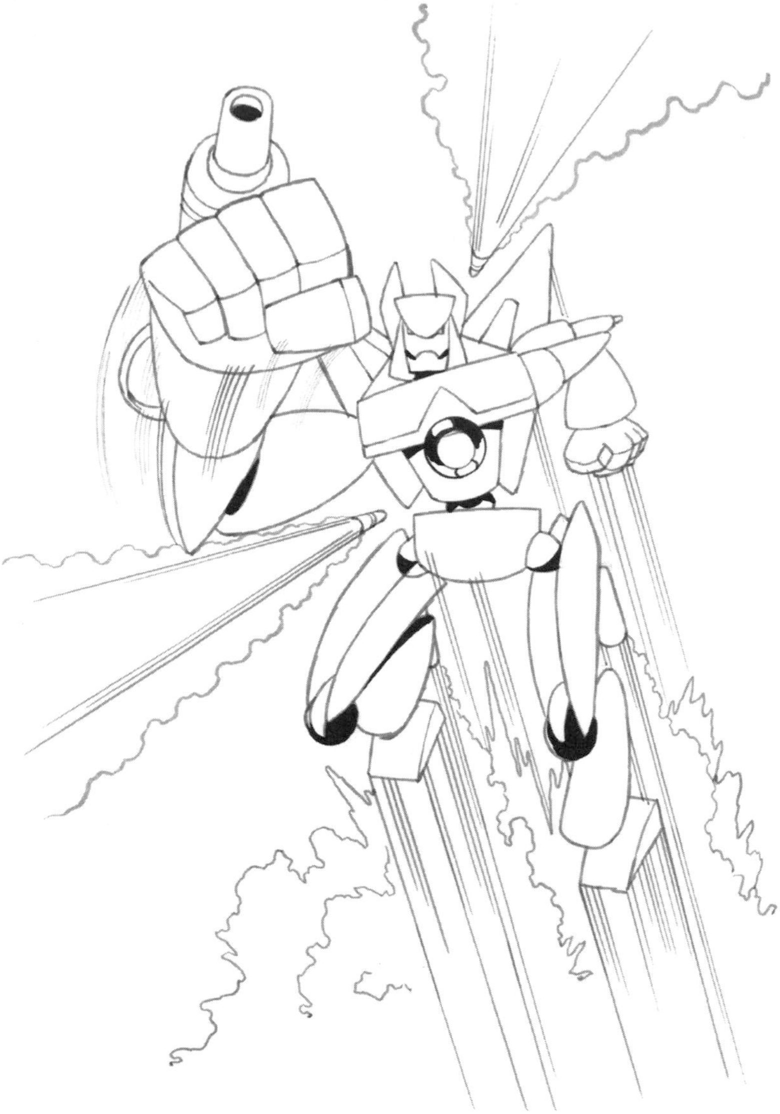

STAGE 8

Ink the drawing. I've used a grey pen for the outline to give a softer edge and to make the object look as though it is far in the distance. Fill in solid areas of black shadow.

STAGE 9

Draw in the fine detail on the body.

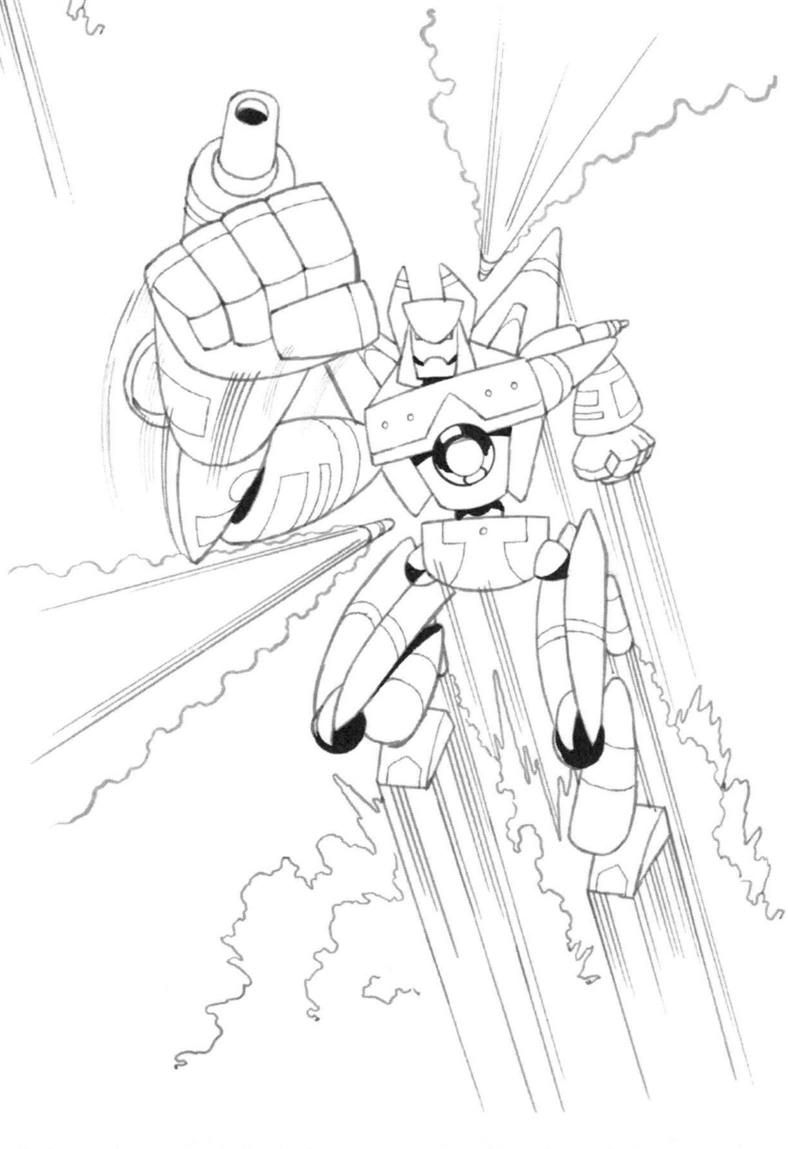

STAGE 10

Colour the character's body with green and yellow, leaving white highlights on the limbs to show gleams of light.

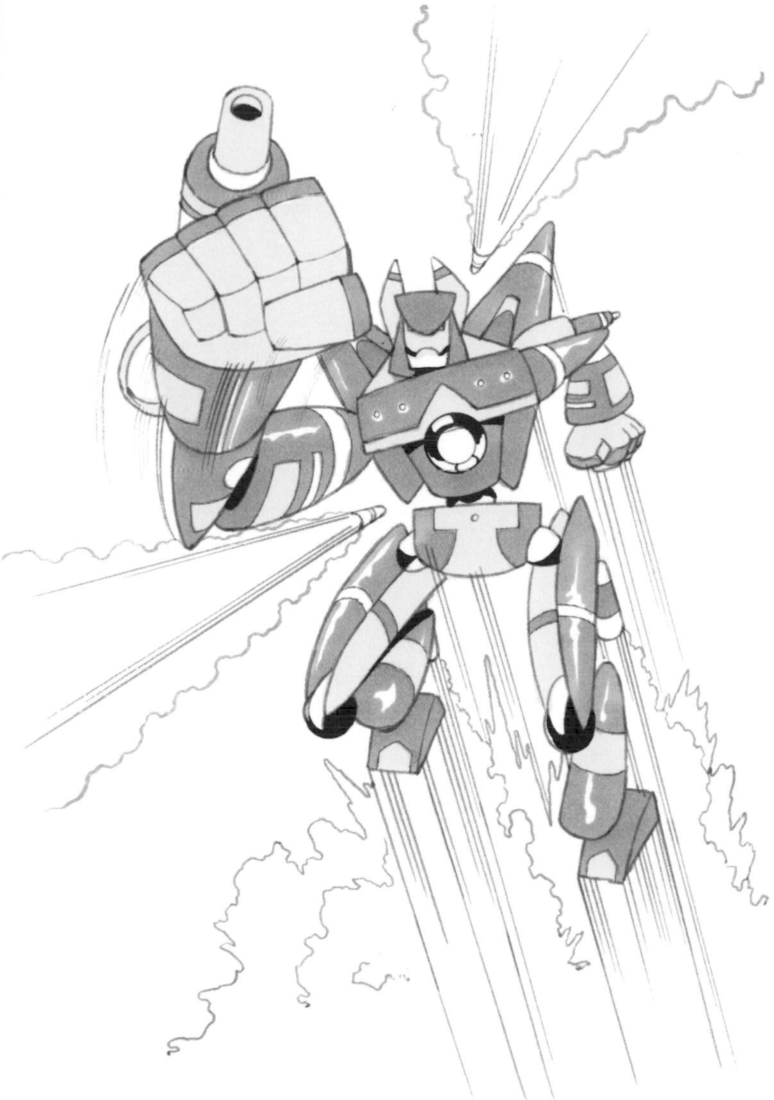

STAGE 11

Use dark green and golden yellow markers to add some shadows to the character and give it more shape.

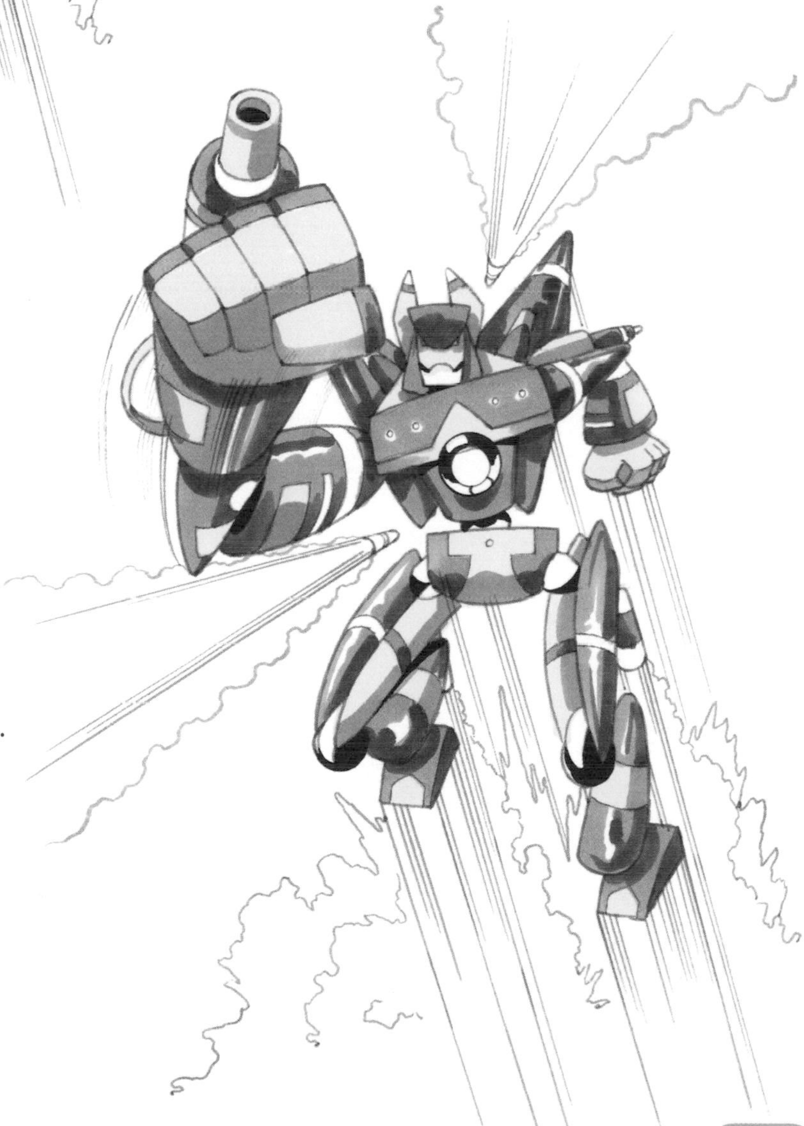

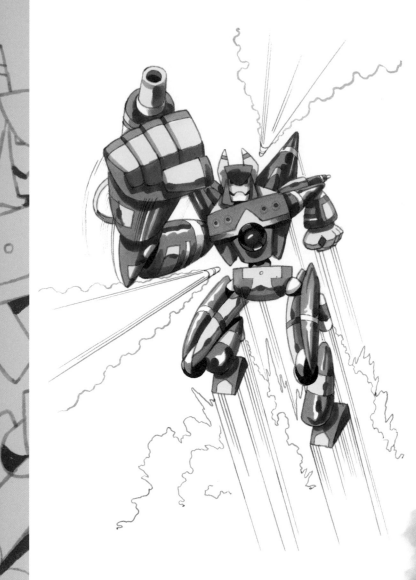

STAGE 12

Darken the shadows by reapplying the same colours, or using darker shades. Colour in the chest light with red and orange.

STAGE 13

Colour in the sky with a few shades of pale blue, using small, quick marks to give a varying tone.

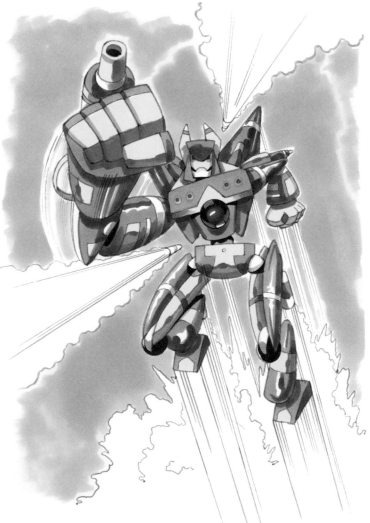

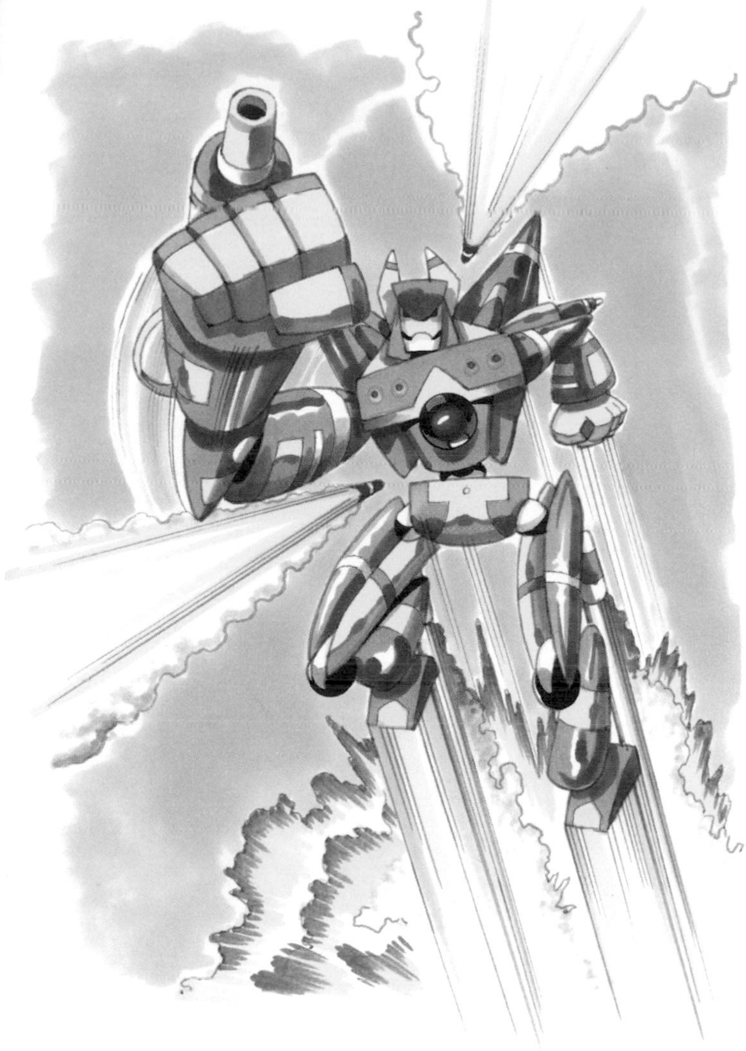

STAGE 14

Use yellow and orange to edge the blast streams and explosion. Edge the smoke with greys.

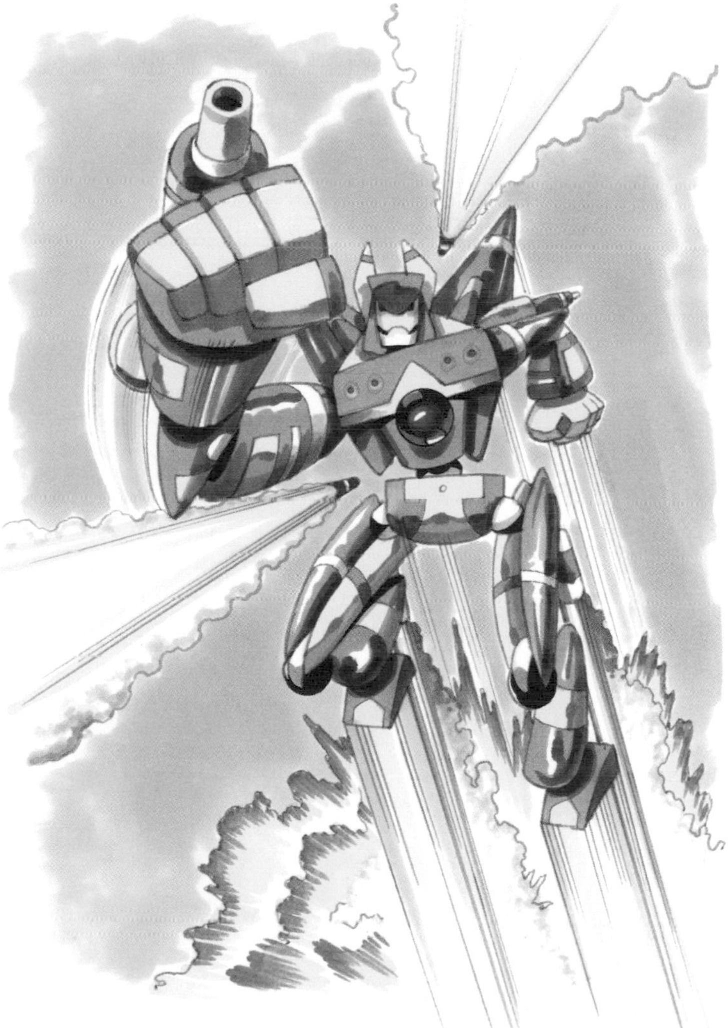

STAGE 15

Finish by adding a final shade of dark green to the body work!

FULL SPEED!

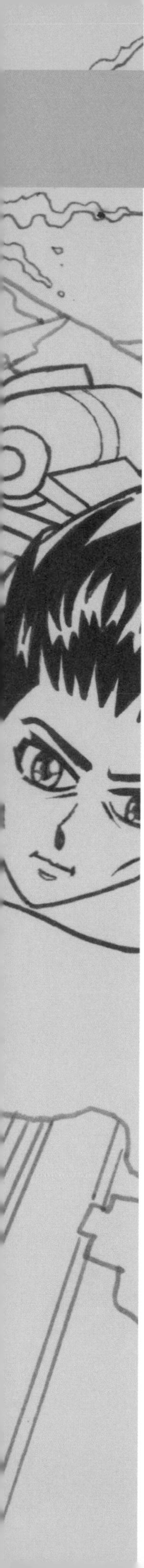

EXPLODING AT SPEED ACROSS AN ALIEN PLANET!

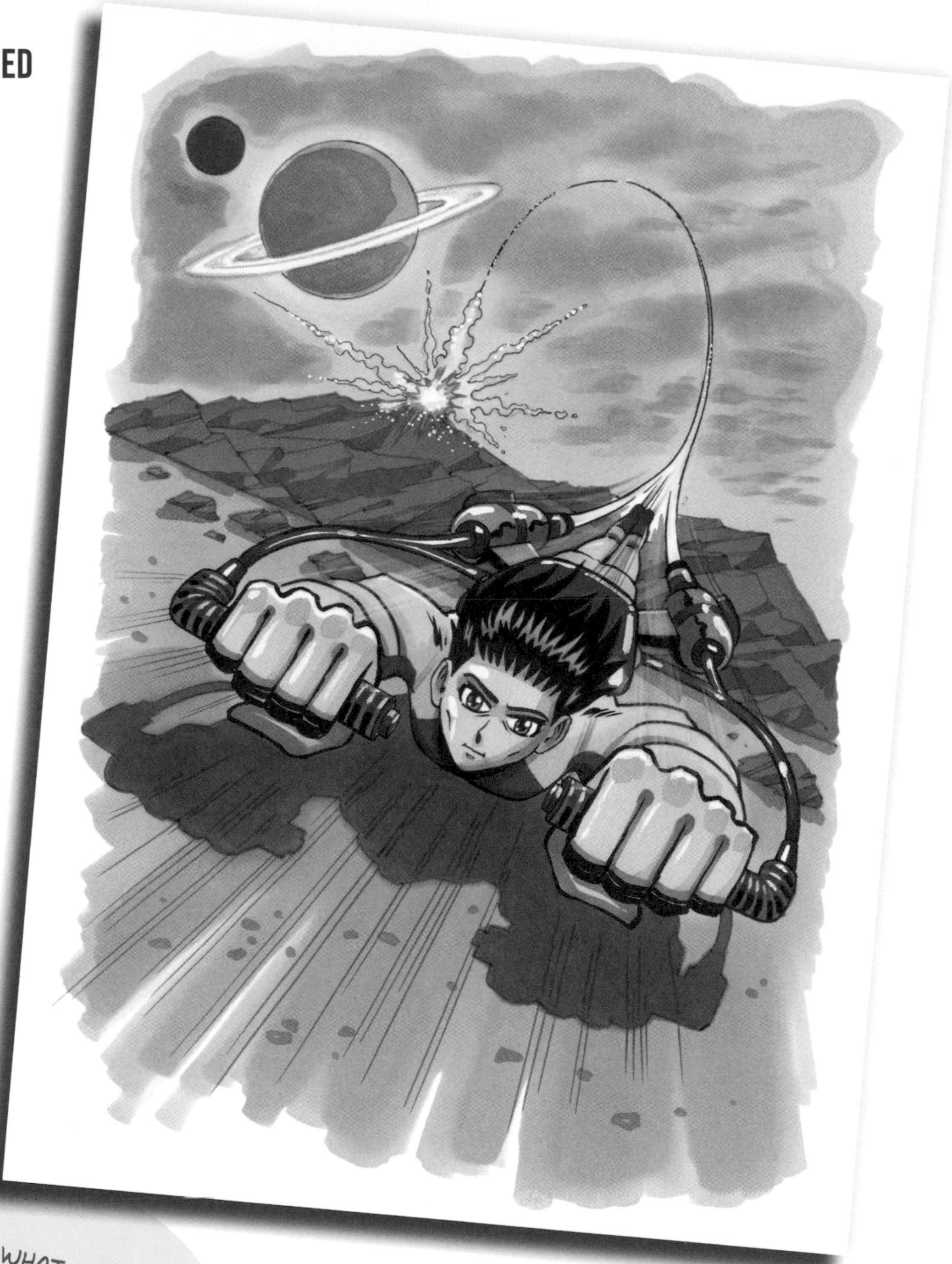

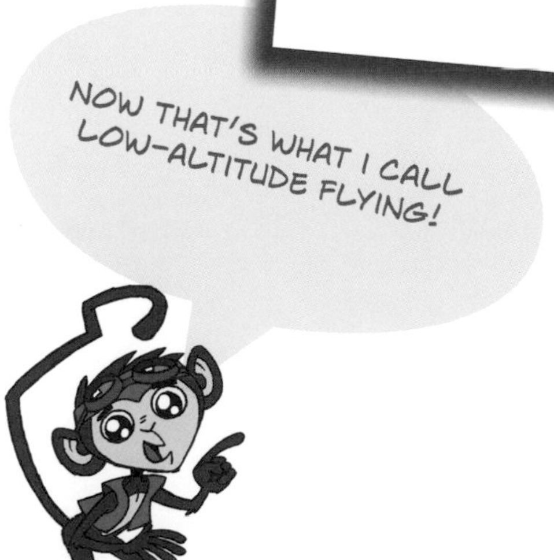
NOW THAT'S WHAT I CALL LOW-ALTITUDE FLYING!

STAGE 1

Begin by drawing a wireframe head and shoulders in the lower half of the page, with two large shapes for fists.

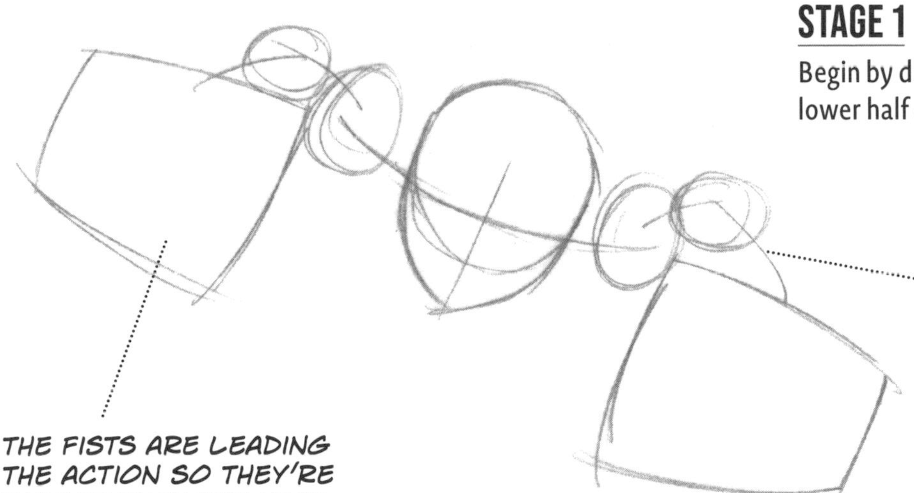
THE ARMS ARE STRETCHED OUT IN FRONT, MAKING THE SHOULDERS AND ELBOWS APPEAR VERY CLOSE TOGETHER
THE FISTS ARE LEADING THE ACTION SO THEY'RE BIGGER THAN THE HEAD

STAGE 2

Extend the figure back along a diagonal line, leading to a vanishing point – the body is extremely foreshortened, making the feet and legs appear very small.

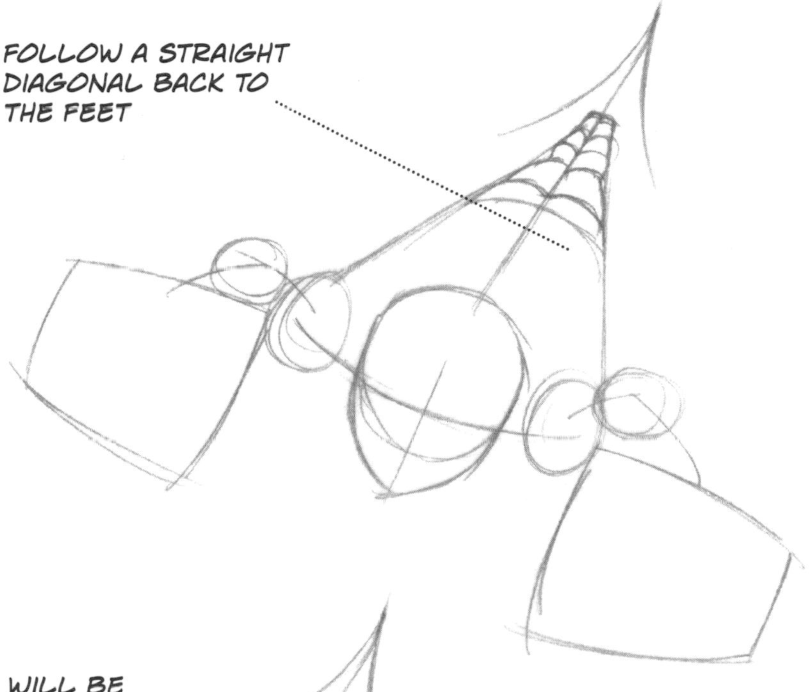
VANISHING POINT
FOLLOW A STRAIGHT DIAGONAL BACK TO THE FEET

STAGE 3

Draw in the facial features and add some spiky hair that is being blown backwards. Flesh out the torso and fist shapes.

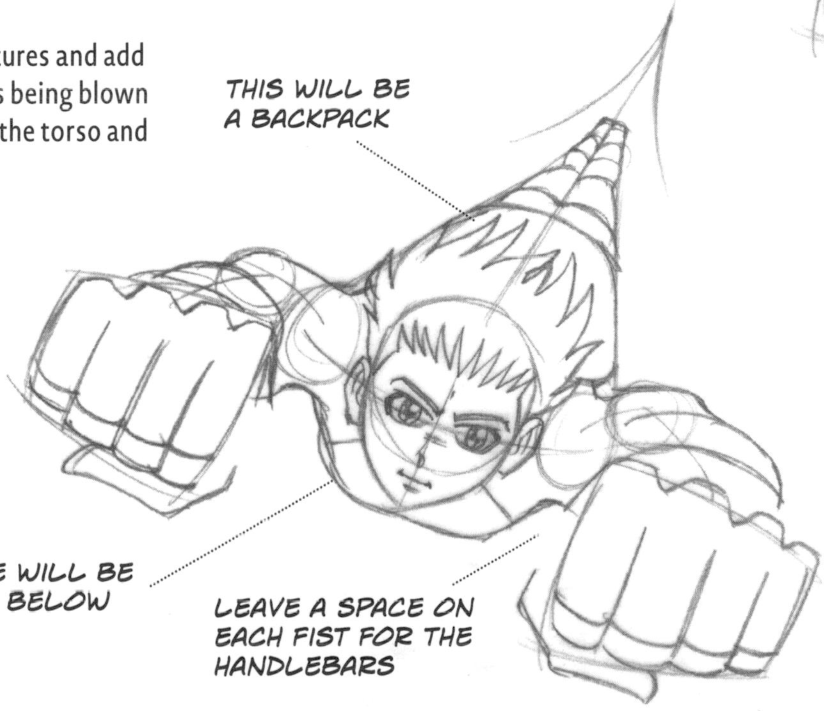
THIS WILL BE A BACKPACK
THE RIB CAGE WILL BE JUST VISIBLE BELOW THE FACE
LEAVE A SPACE ON EACH FIST FOR THE HANDLEBARS

STAGE 4

Construct the flying harness: draw handlebar attachments connected to the backpack by tubes, with rocket boosters on either side.

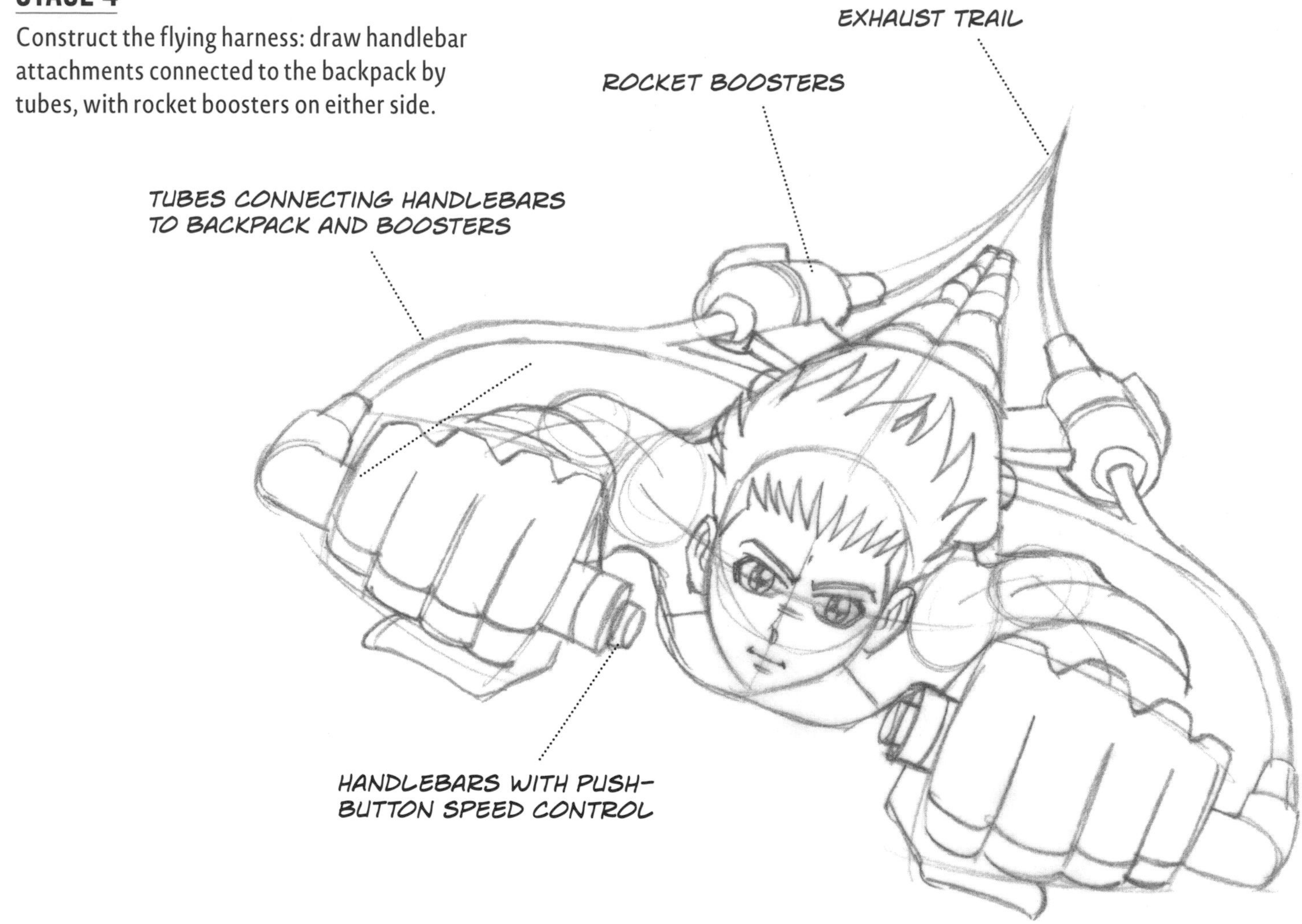
EXHAUST TRAIL
ROCKET BOOSTERS
TUBES CONNECTING HANDLEBARS TO BACKPACK AND BOOSTERS
HANDLEBARS WITH PUSH-BUTTON SPEED CONTROL

STAGE 5

Sketch a diagonal horizon line with a rocky mountain range in the distance.

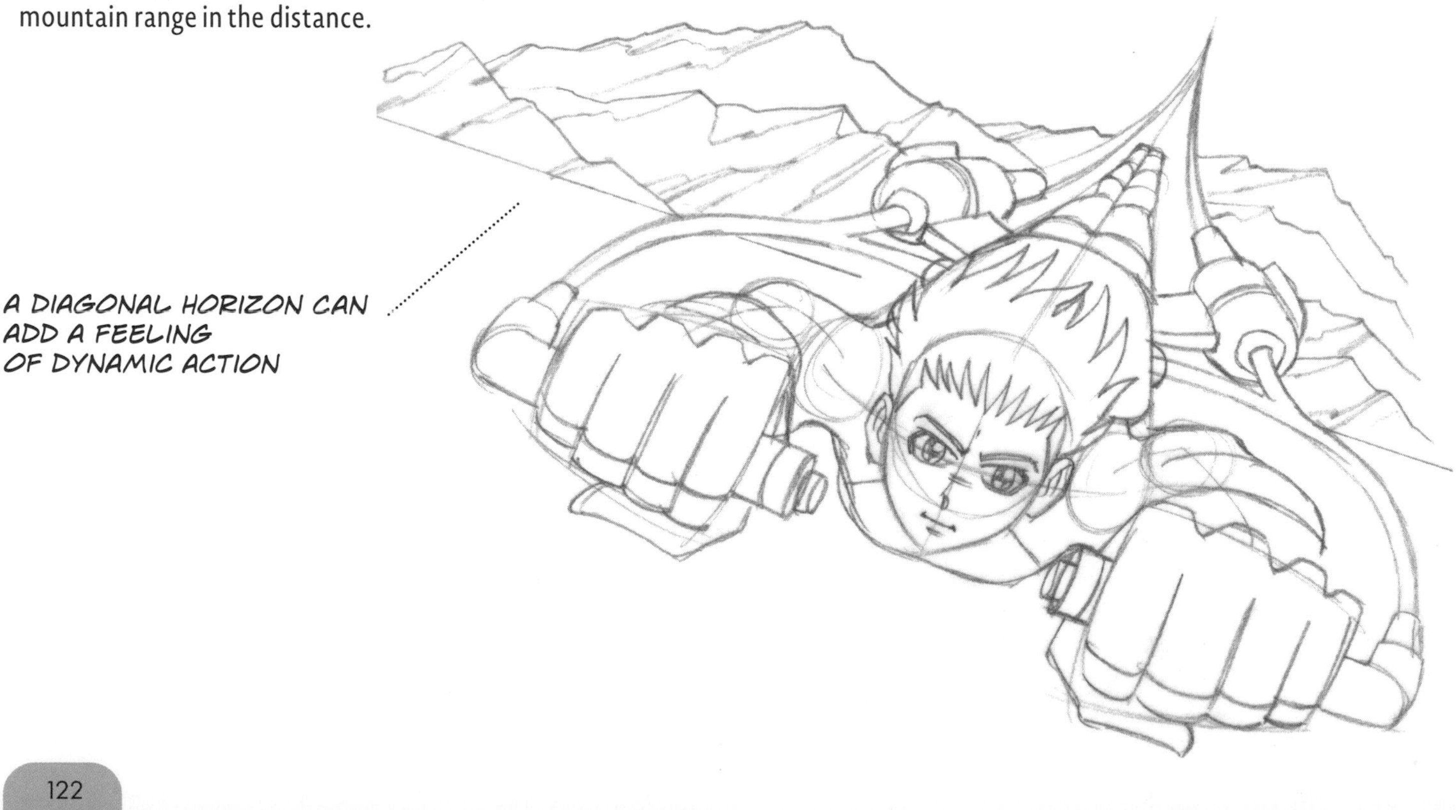
A DIAGONAL HORIZON CAN ADD A FEELING OF DYNAMIC ACTION

SMALL BITS OF DEBRIS STREAKING AWAY FROM THE EXPLOSION
VAPOUR TRAIL

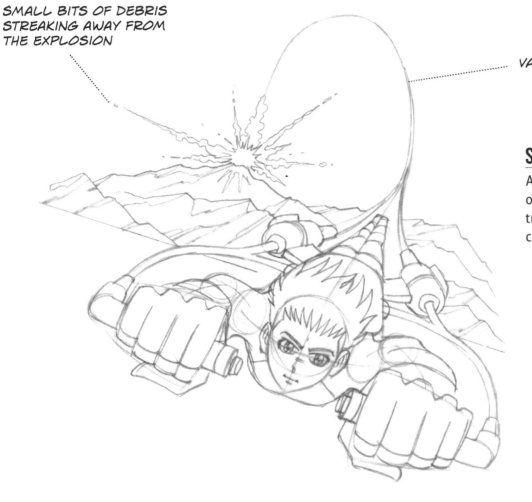

STAGE 6

Add an exploding departure point on the tallest peak, with a vapour trail leading up and down, before connecting to the boosters.

STAGE 7

To give an impression of an alien landscape, draw a ringed planet and a small moon in the sky. Sketch some scattered rocks on the surface, and add speed lines and a shadow underneath the figure.

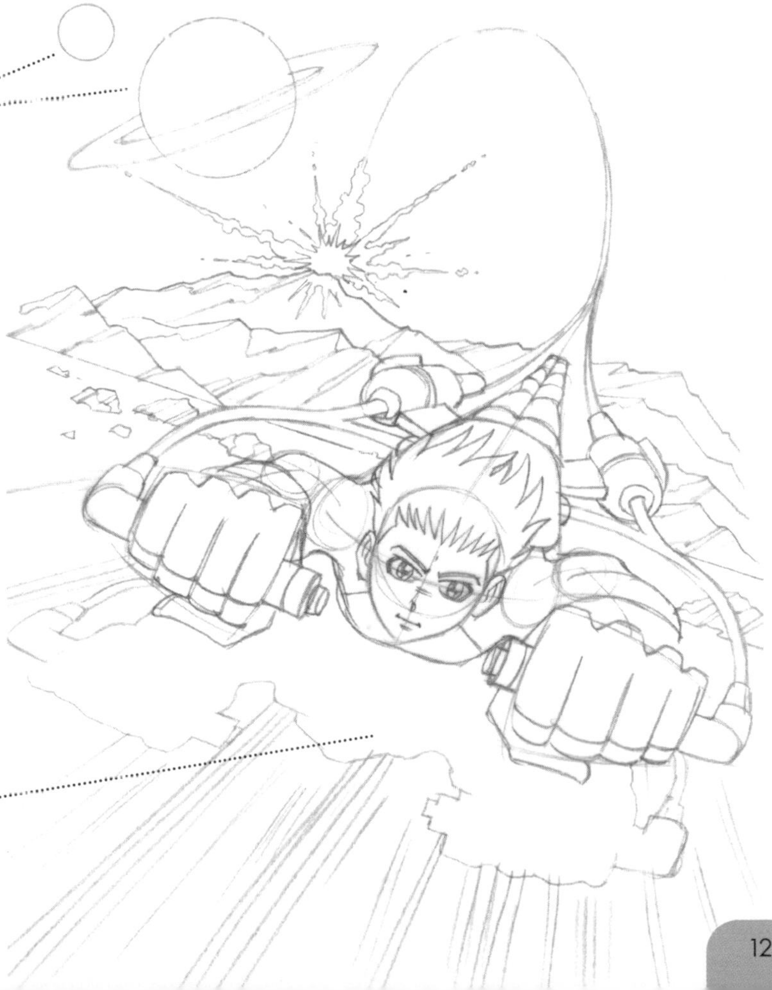

USE A PAIR OF COMPASSES OR A CIRCLE GUIDE FOR THESE SHAPES
THE SHADOW SHOULD ROUGHLY REPLICATE THE FIGURE

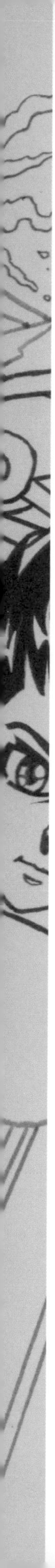

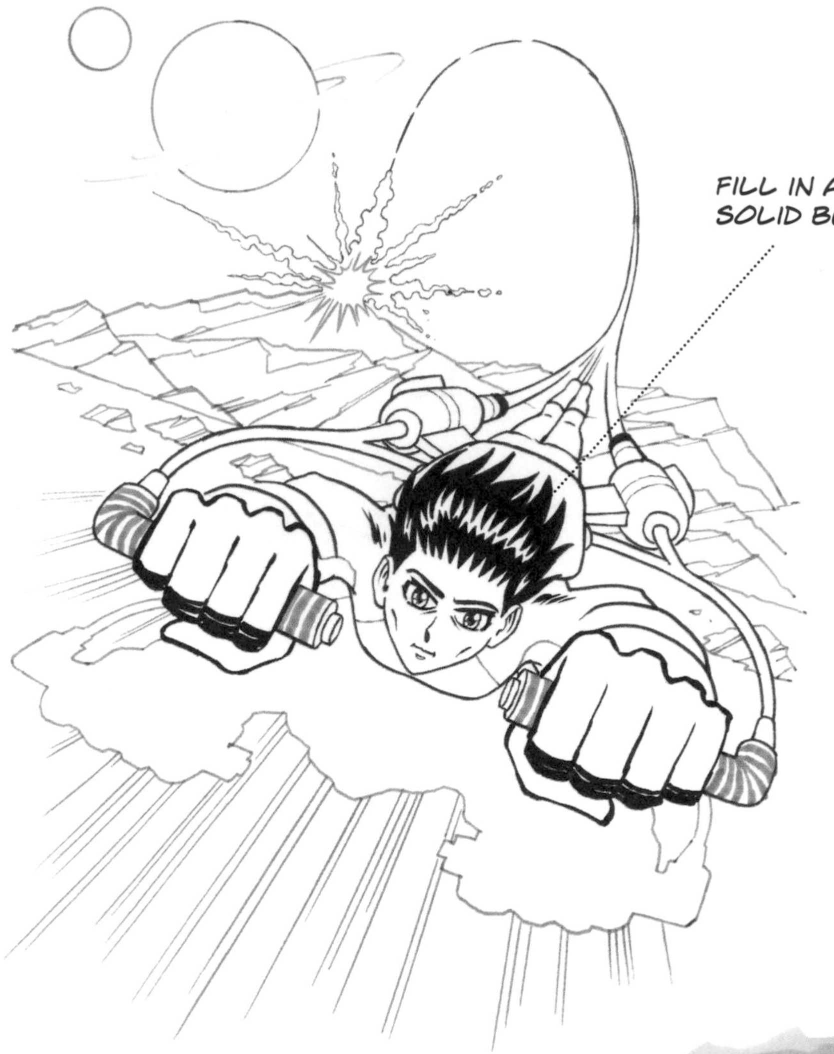
FILL IN ANY AREAS OF
SOLID BLACK

STAGE 8

Ink your figure with black and the background with grey – this will make the figure jump out of the picture.

STAGE 9

Colour your alien sky with mauve and pale grey clouds. Use pink tones on the large planet and red tones on the small one.

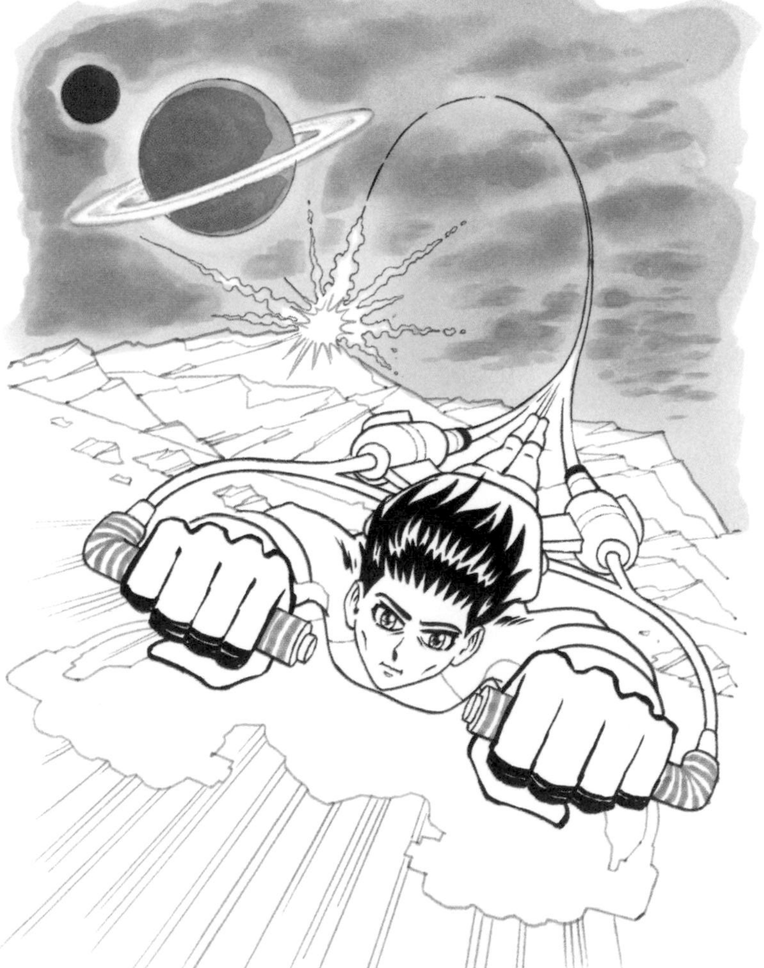

STAGE 10

Use a dark blueberry colour on the mountains and mauve on the ground.

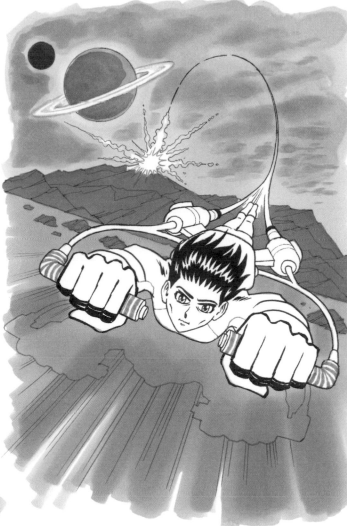

STAGE 11

Use a dark grey to create shadows on the mountains and underneath the figure.

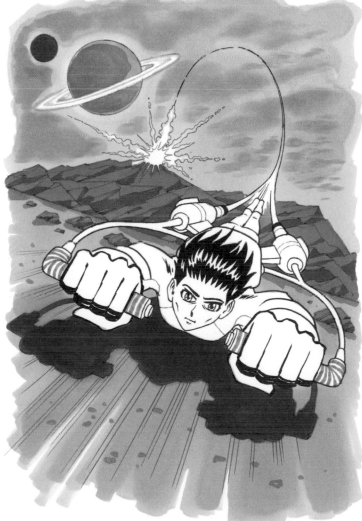

STAGE 12

Colour the figure's face and hands with flesh tones and the suit in red and yellow. Add shading using darker tones.

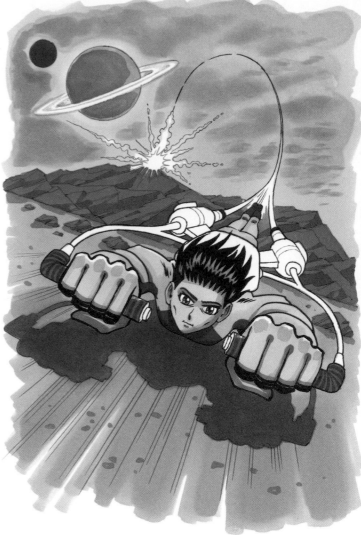

STAGE 13

Colour the tubes and booster details red and grey, and add yellow and orange to the mountain blast.

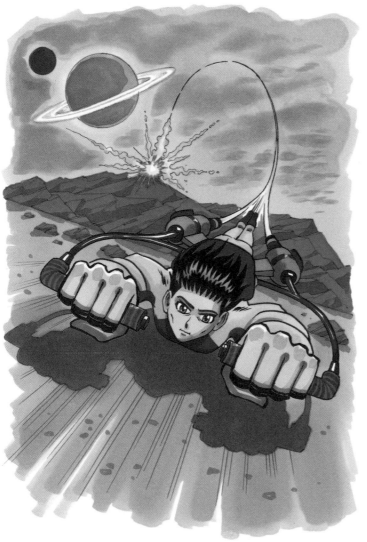

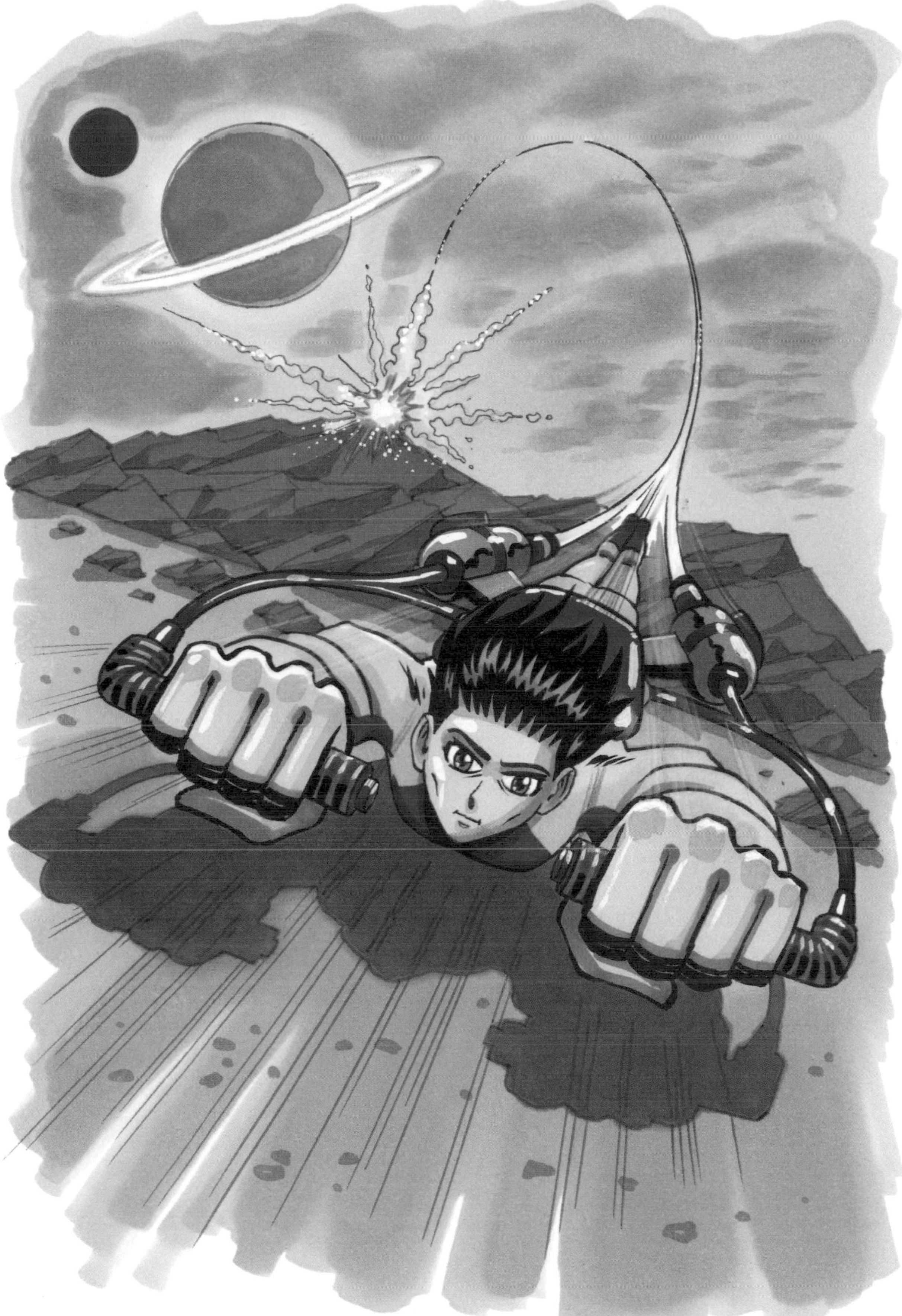

STAGE 14

Finish by adding some black shadows and white highlights, then add some faint speed lines behind the figure using coloured pencils.

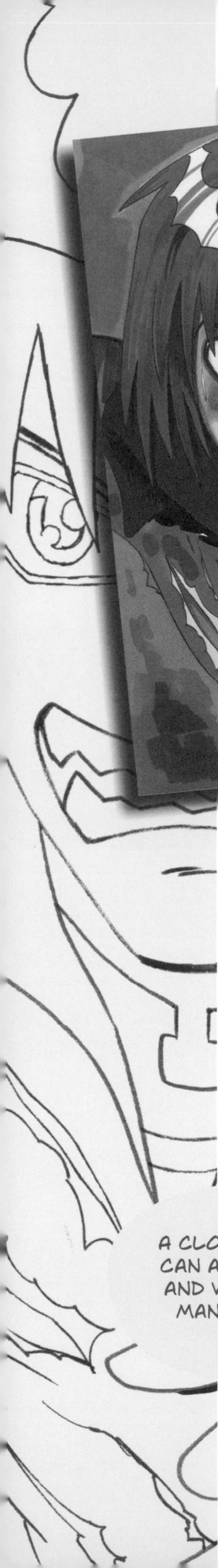

HEAT OF BATTLE

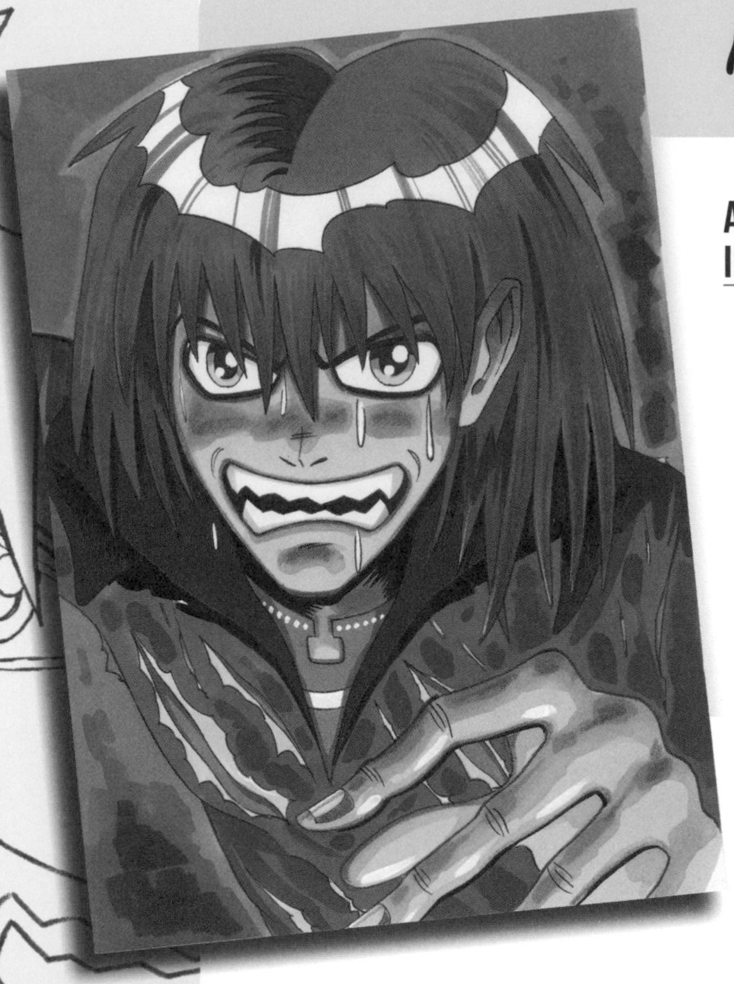

A CLOSE-UP ENCOUNTER WITH A STEELY-EYED HERO IN THE FIGHT OF HIS LIFE!

STAGE 1

Draw a wireframe for your figure, creating the head, sloping shoulders and spine.

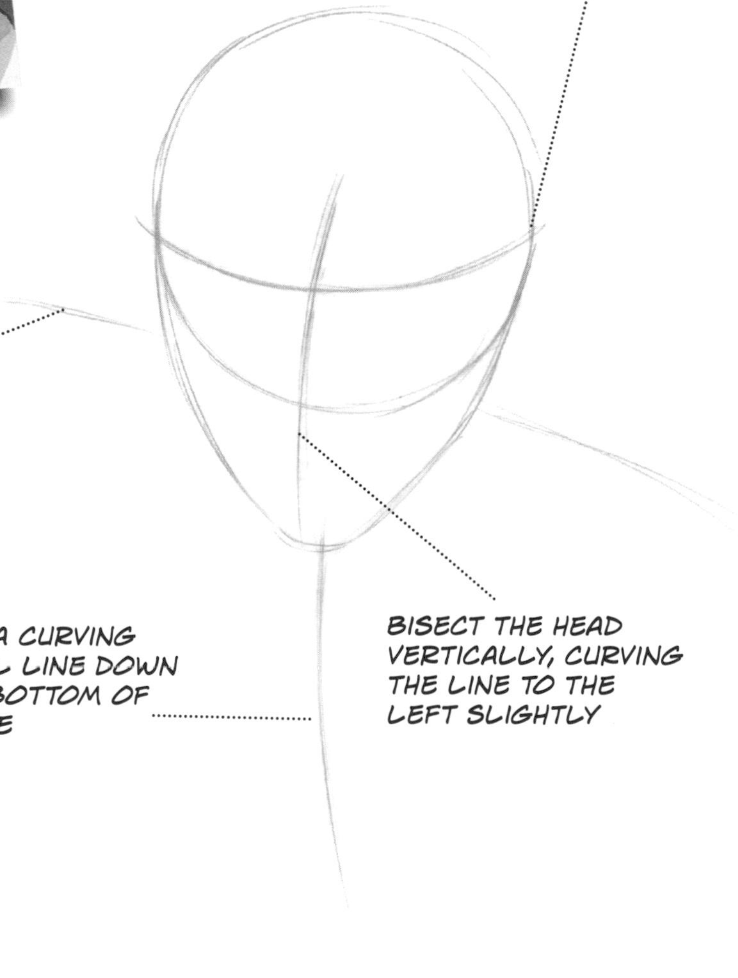
BISECT THE CIRCLE HORIZONTALLY, JUST BELOW THE MIDDLE, TO MARK THE EYE POSITION
THE RIGHT SHOULDER SHOULD BE HIGHER THAN THE LEFT
SKETCH A CURVING VERTICAL LINE DOWN TO THE BOTTOM OF THE PAGE
BISECT THE HEAD VERTICALLY, CURVING THE LINE TO THE LEFT SLIGHTLY

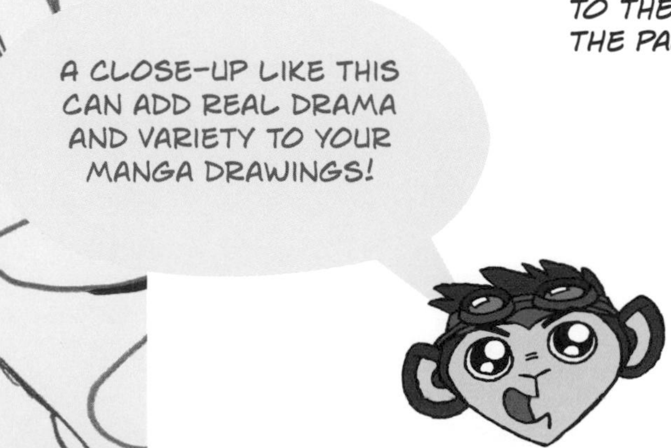
A CLOSE-UP LIKE THIS CAN ADD REAL DRAMA AND VARIETY TO YOUR MANGA DRAWINGS!

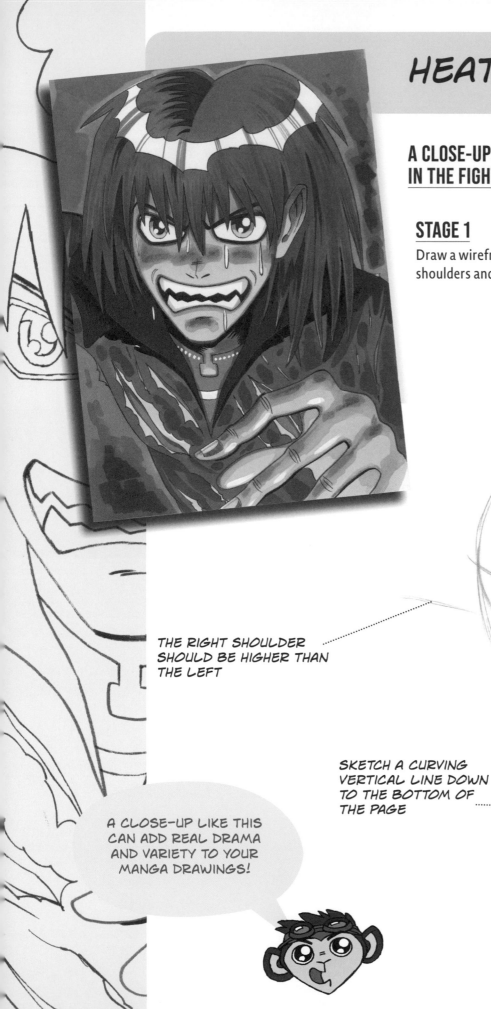

STAGE 2

Sketch in the facial features, including some angry-looking eyes and an open mouth.

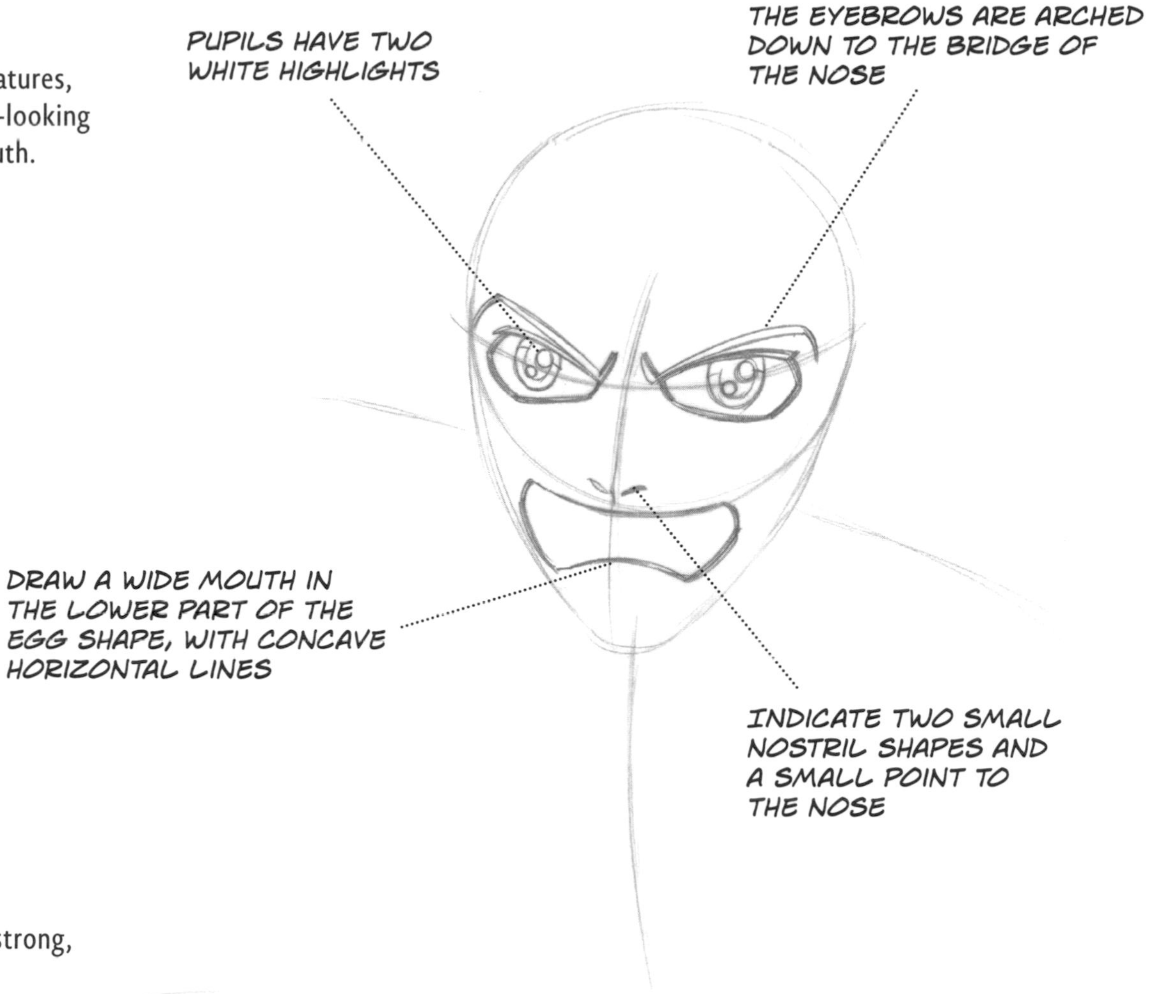
PUPILS HAVE TWO WHITE HIGHLIGHTS
THE EYEBROWS ARE ARCHED DOWN TO THE BRIDGE OF THE NOSE
DRAW A WIDE MOUTH IN THE LOWER PART OF THE EGG SHAPE, WITH CONCAVE HORIZONTAL LINES
INDICATE TWO SMALL NOSTRIL SHAPES AND A SMALL POINT TO THE NOSE

STAGE 3

Add some ears and a strong, angular jawline.

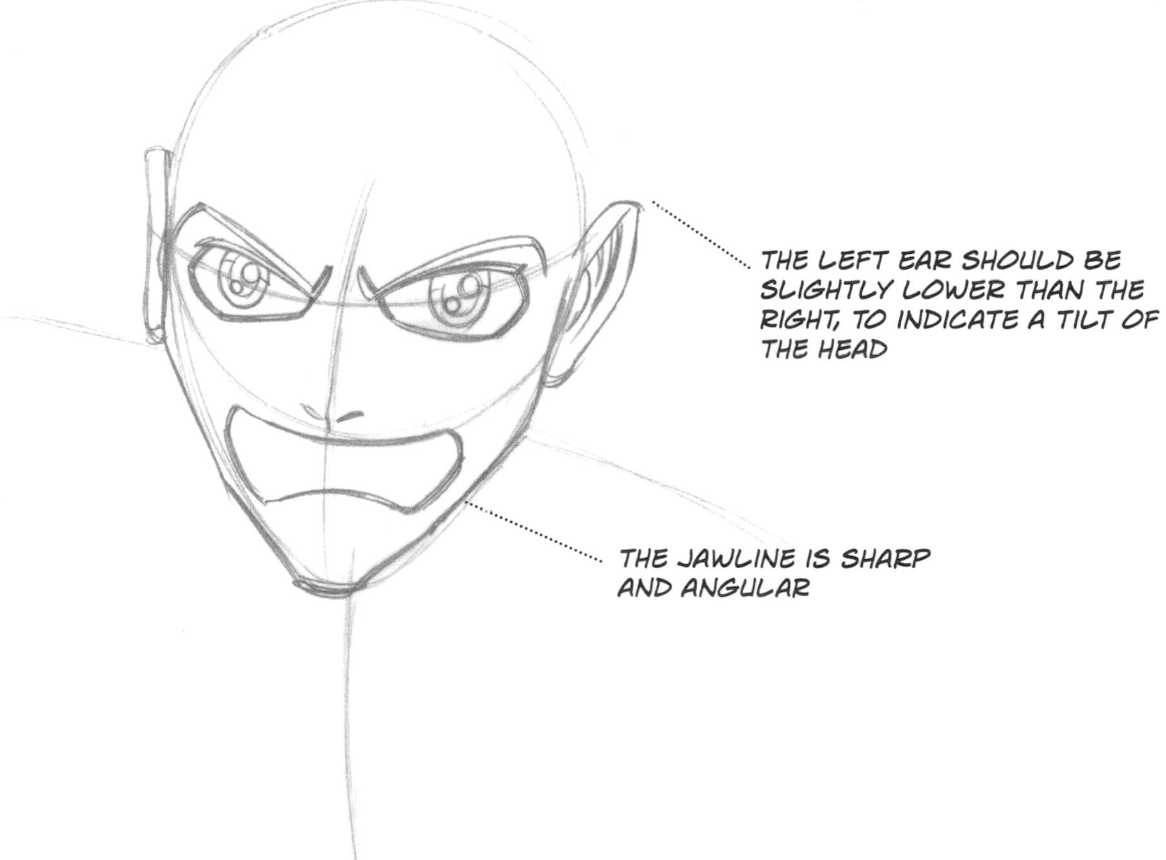
THE LEFT EAR SHOULD BE SLIGHTLY LOWER THAN THE RIGHT, TO INDICATE A TILT OF THE HEAD
THE JAWLINE IS SHARP AND ANGULAR

STAGE 4

Draw long, spiky hair falling down around the face on either side and add in some teeth.

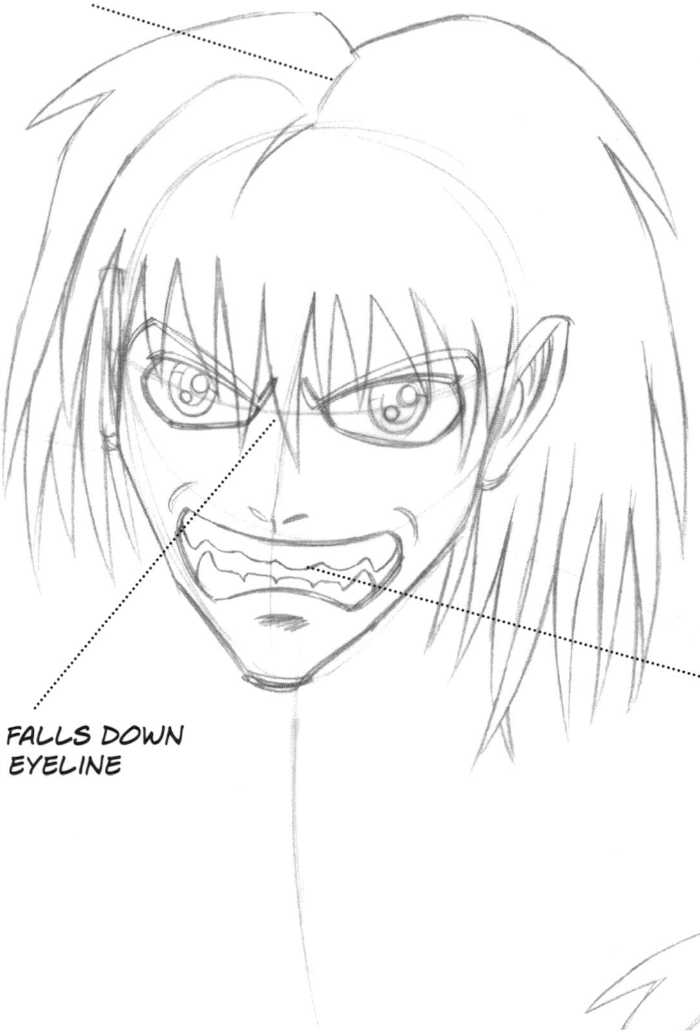
THE HAIR GROWS OUT FROM A CENTRE PARTING
THE FRINGE FALLS DOWN BELOW THE EYELINE
THE FARTHEST-LEFT AND RIGHT TEETH ARE POINTED, INDICATING ANGER OR DETERMINATION

STAGE 5

Draw in the hero's tunic, creating a wide, open collar.

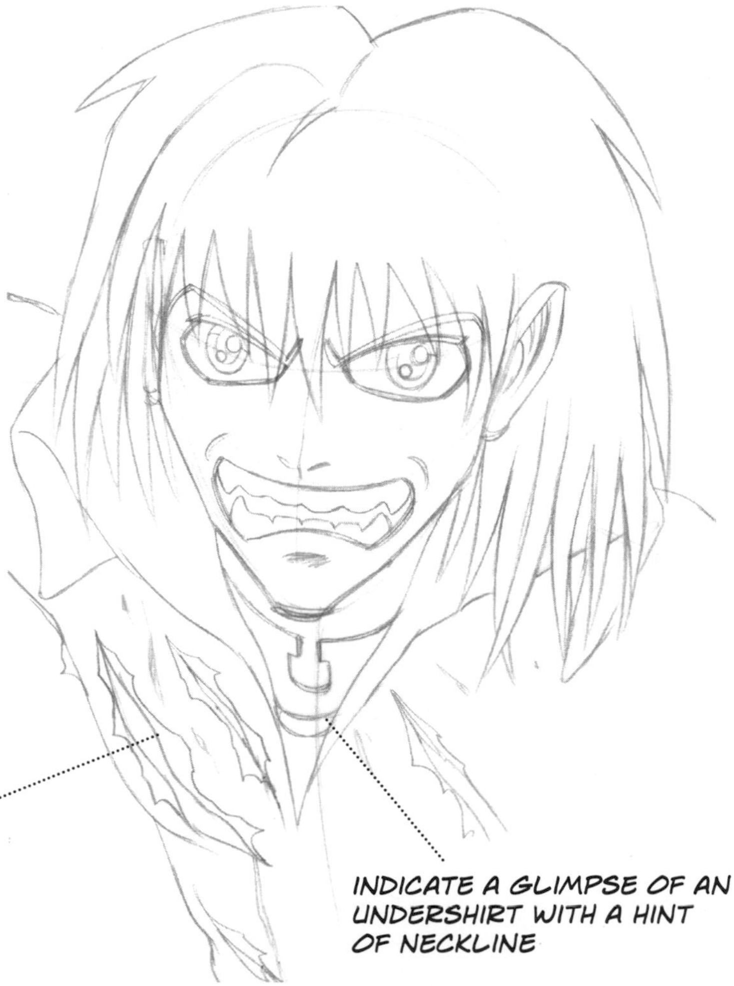
ADD SOME TEARS IN THE FABRIC TO SHOW HE'S IN A FIGHT SITUATION
INDICATE A GLIMPSE OF AN UNDERSHIRT WITH A HINT OF NECKLINE

STAGE 6

Sketch in a wireframe shape for an outstretched hand in the bottom right of the page, then flesh it out.

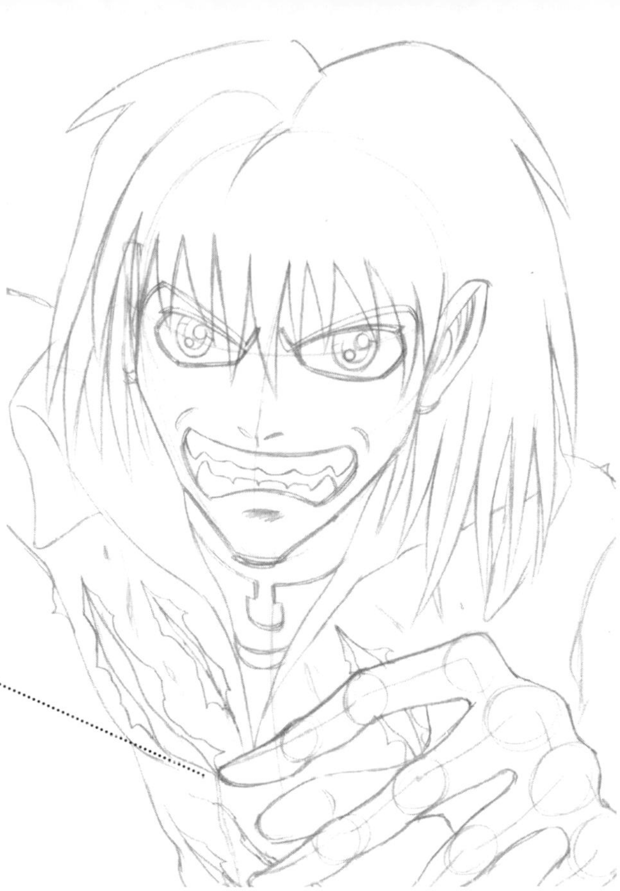
SHOW THUMB PARTLY CONCEALED BY FINGERS

STAGE 7

Ink your drawing in black and add a jagged shape across the hair for a highlight.

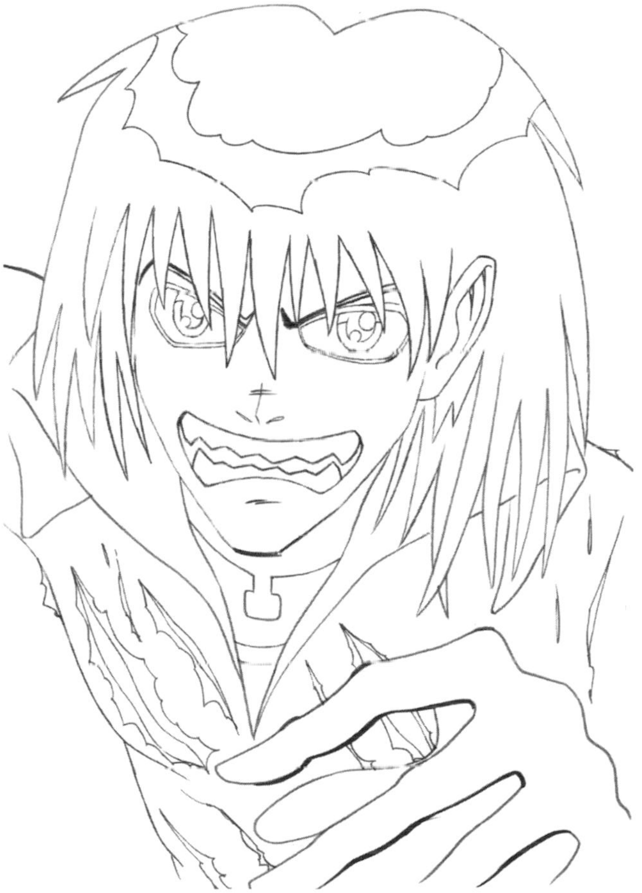

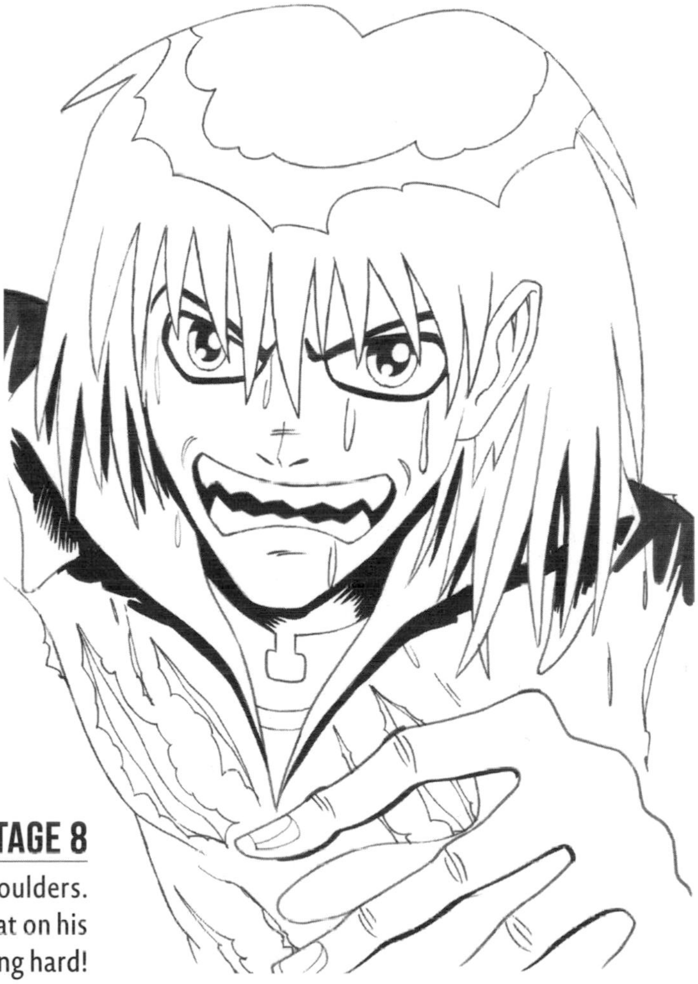

STAGE 8

Add solid black to the eyes, mouth, and on the shoulders. Draw in details on his hand and create drops of sweat on his face to show he's fighting hard!

STAGE 9

Colour in the flat areas of colour on the face and tunic.

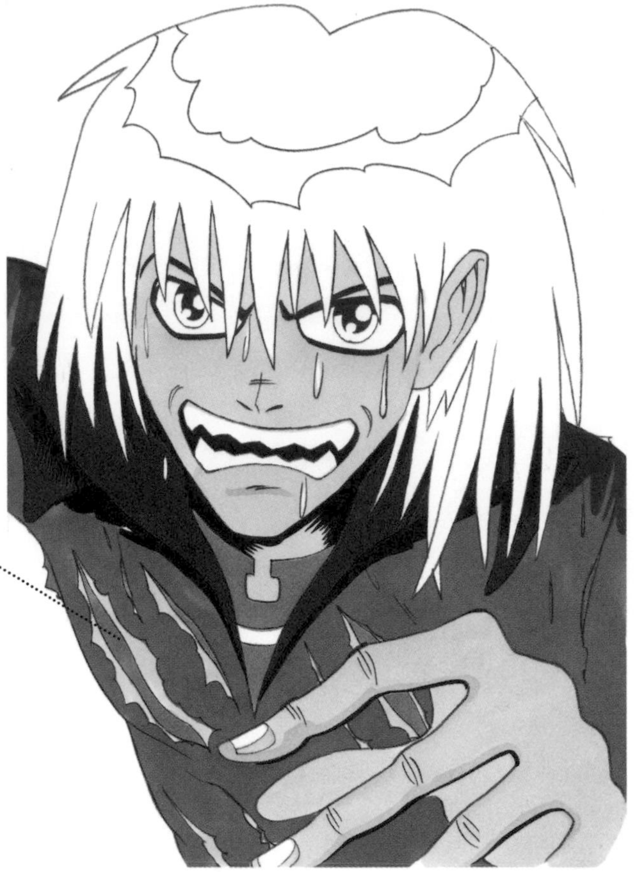
UNDERSHIRT IS VISIBLE THROUGH THE TORN FABRIC

STAGE 10

Colour the hair a dark grey and eyes a bright green.

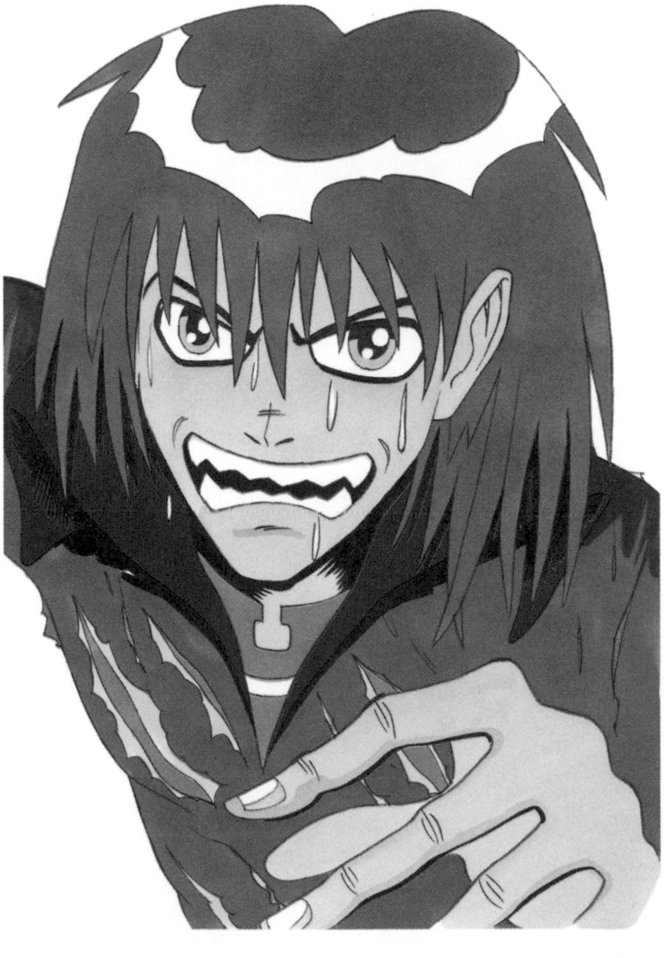

STAGE 11

Use darker flesh tones on the face and hands, to give an 'uplight' effect.

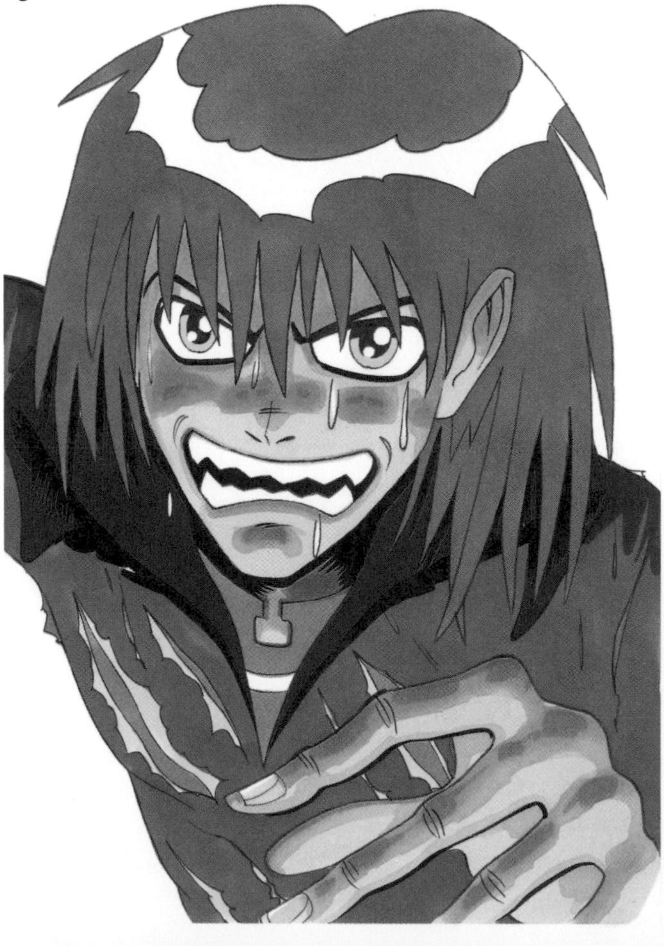

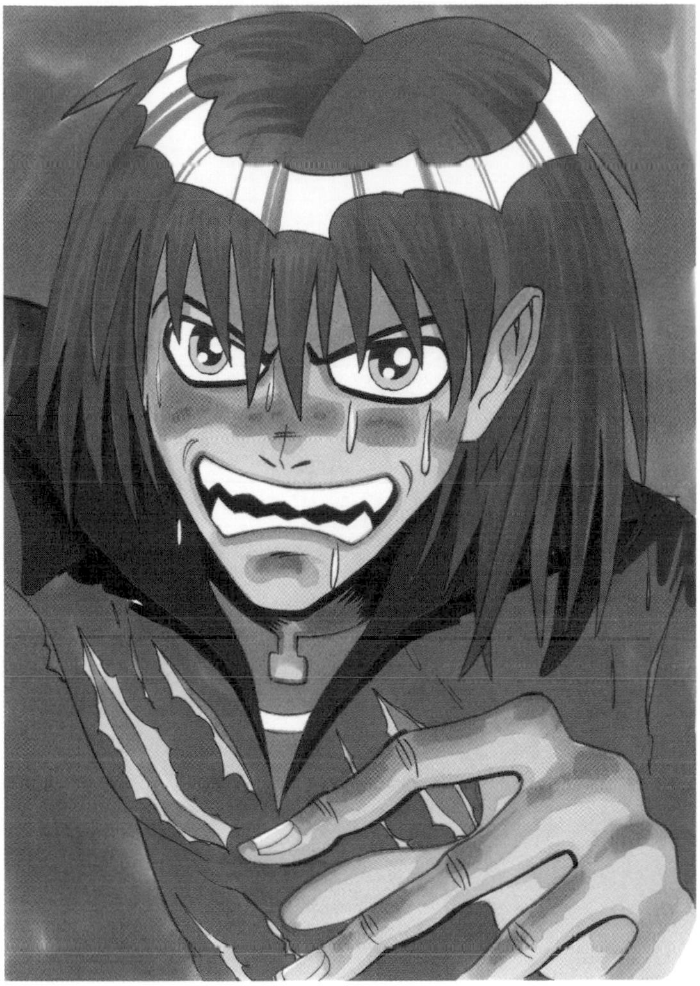

STAGE 12

Colour in the background with a strong orange to bring heat to the drawing. Add some grey texture lines to the hair.

STAGE 13

Finish with some textural shading in the large areas of colour, using darker shades. Use a purple pencil to add detail and colour to the hair.

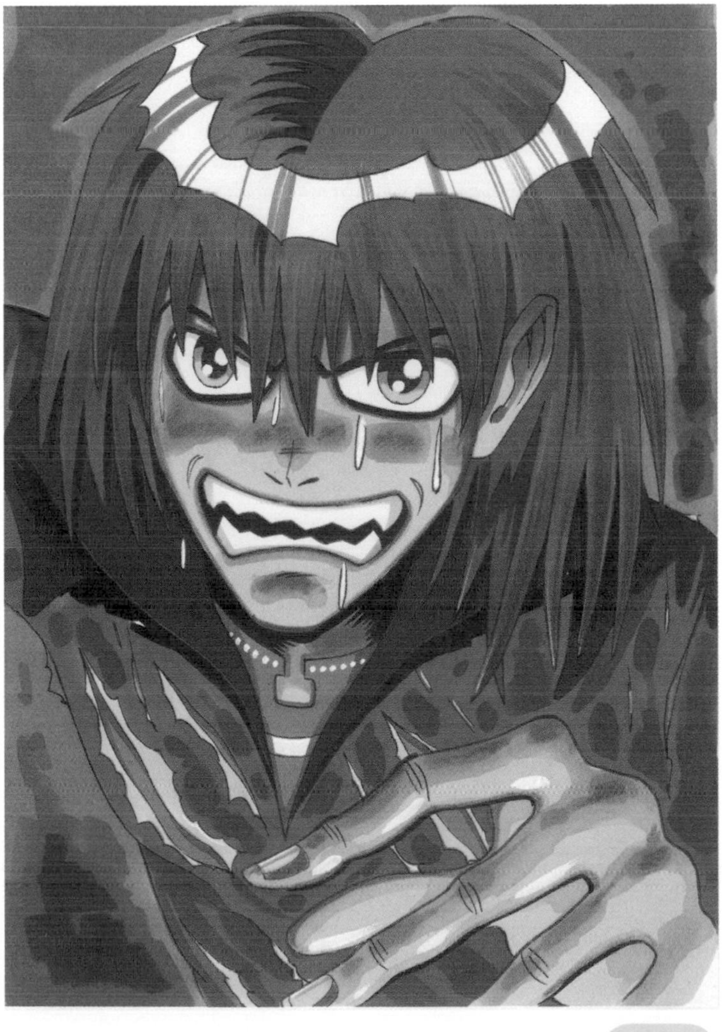

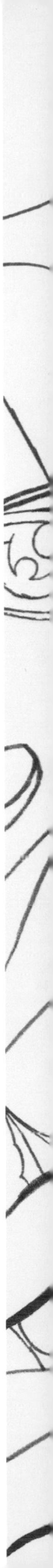

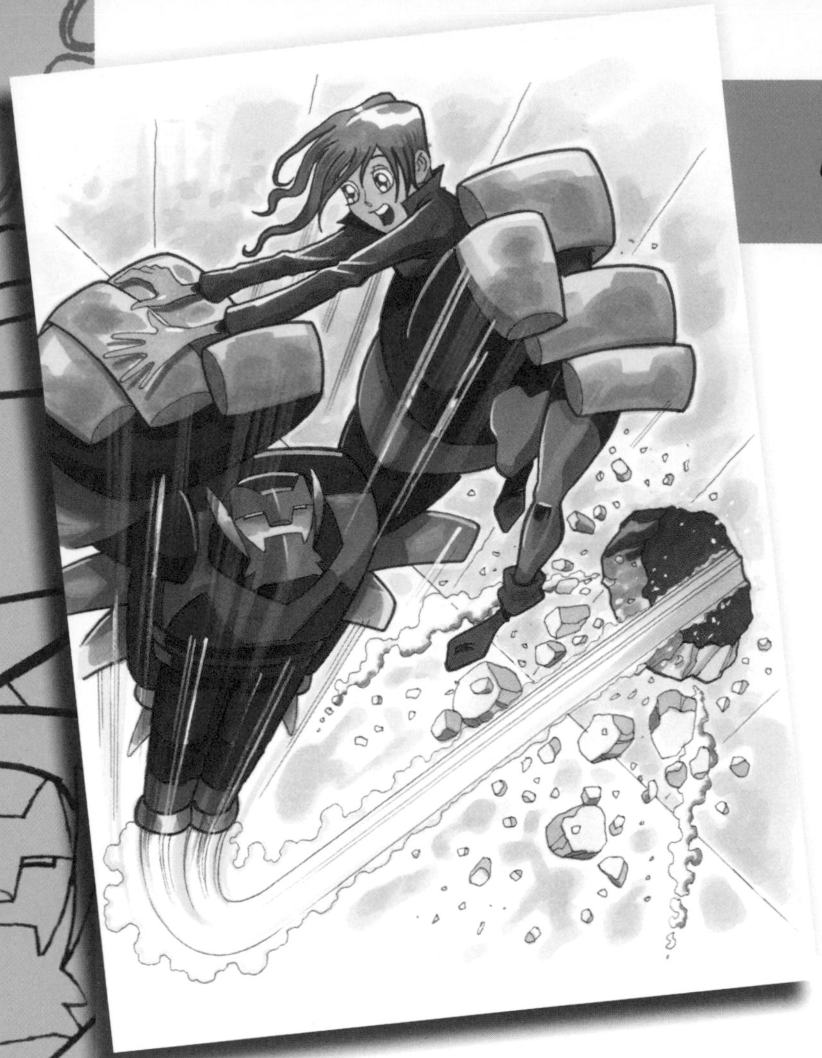

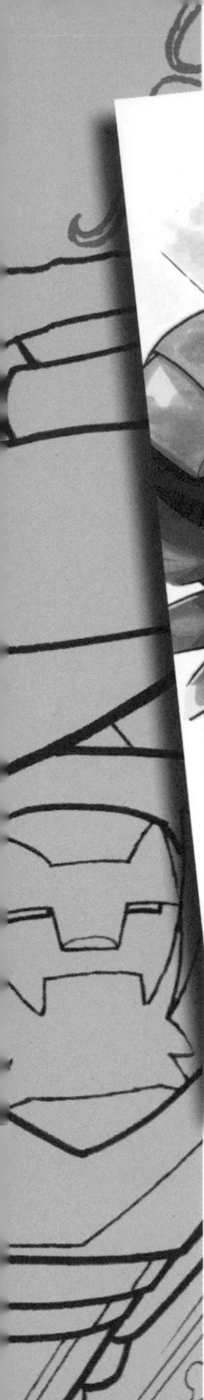

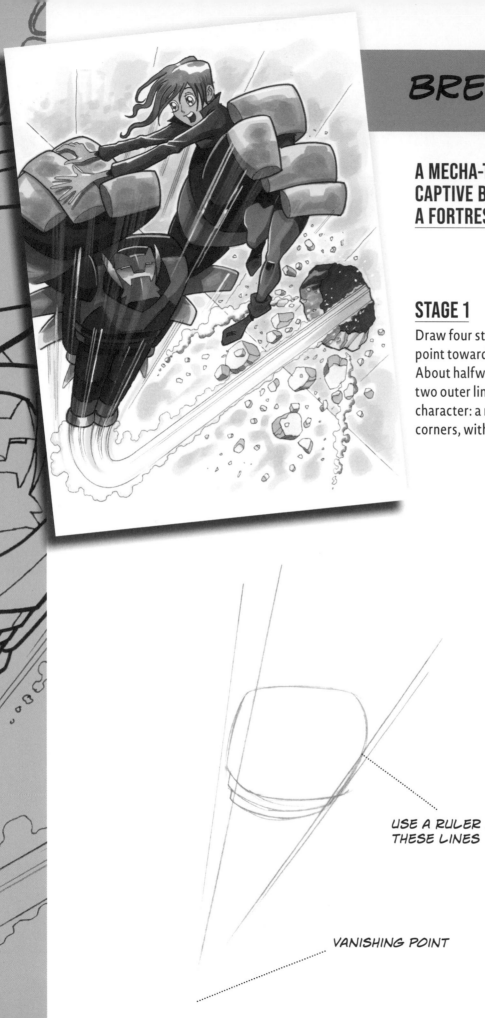

BREAK OUT!

A MECHA-TYPE FIGURE RESCUES A CAPTIVE BY BREAKING THROUGH A FORTRESS WALL!

STAGE 1

Draw four straight lines coming from a vanishing point towards the bottom left of the page. About halfway up the page and between the two outer lines, draw the torso of your mecha character: a rough square shape with rounded corners, with two lines below, as shown.

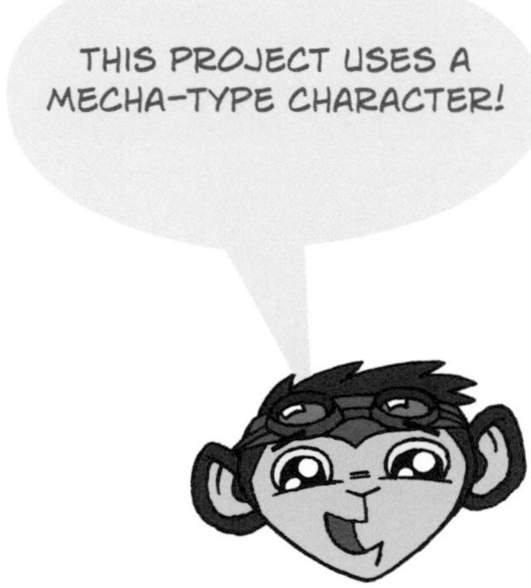
THIS PROJECT USES A MECHA-TYPE CHARACTER!

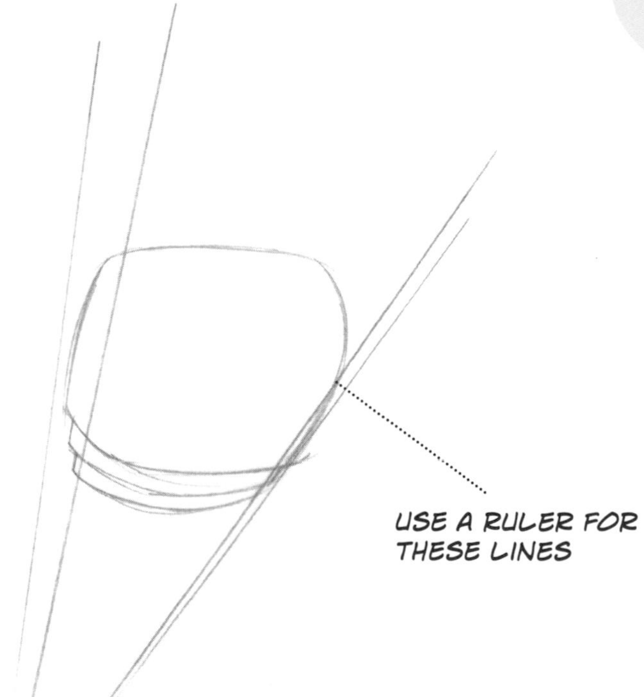
USE A RULER FOR THESE LINES
VANISHING POINT

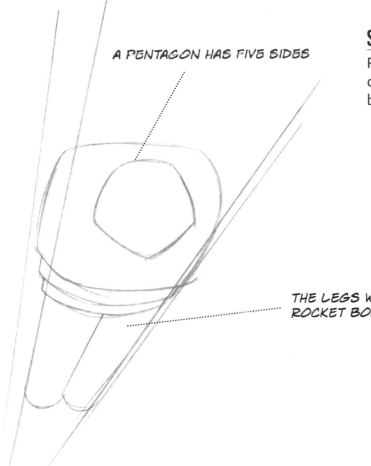

A PENTAGON HAS FIVE SIDES
THE LEGS WILL ACT AS ROCKET BOOSTERS

STAGE 2

For the head, add a pentagon shape with curved points towards the top right of the main body shape. Draw in tubular legs below.

STAGE 3

Add some back boosters and fins, and rims on the bottom of the legs, all following the perspective lines.

THE TWO FINS SHOULD NOT BE QUITE LEVEL, AS THE BODY IS TWISTED AT A SLIGHT ANGLE

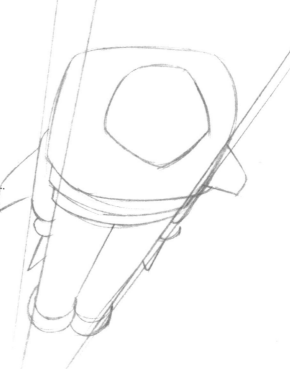

STAGE 4

Draw some large, gripping hands that fill the top part of the page, and some stabilizing fins coming from the back. Draw in some robotic facial features.

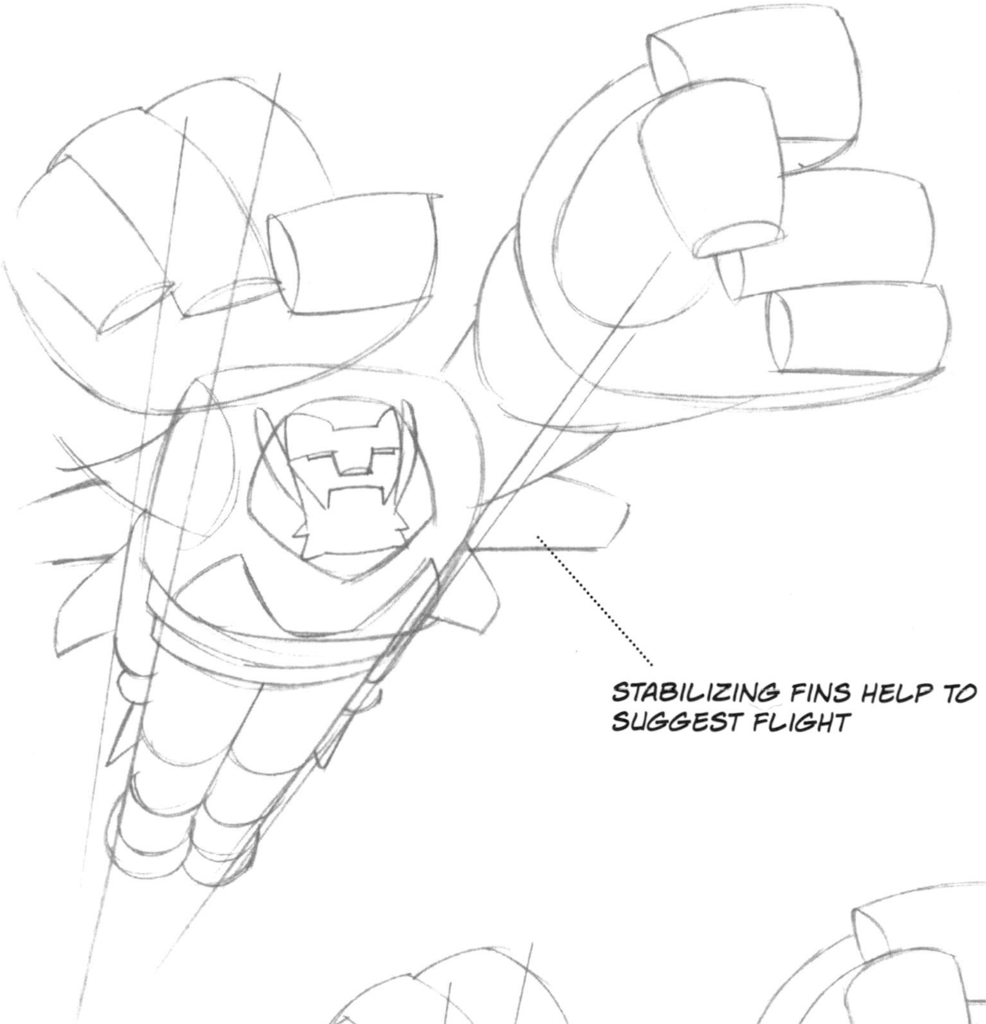
STABILIZING FINS HELP TO SUGGEST FLIGHT

STAGE 5

Draw speed lines coming down out of the leg boosters and making a sharp turn across the bottom-right of the page.

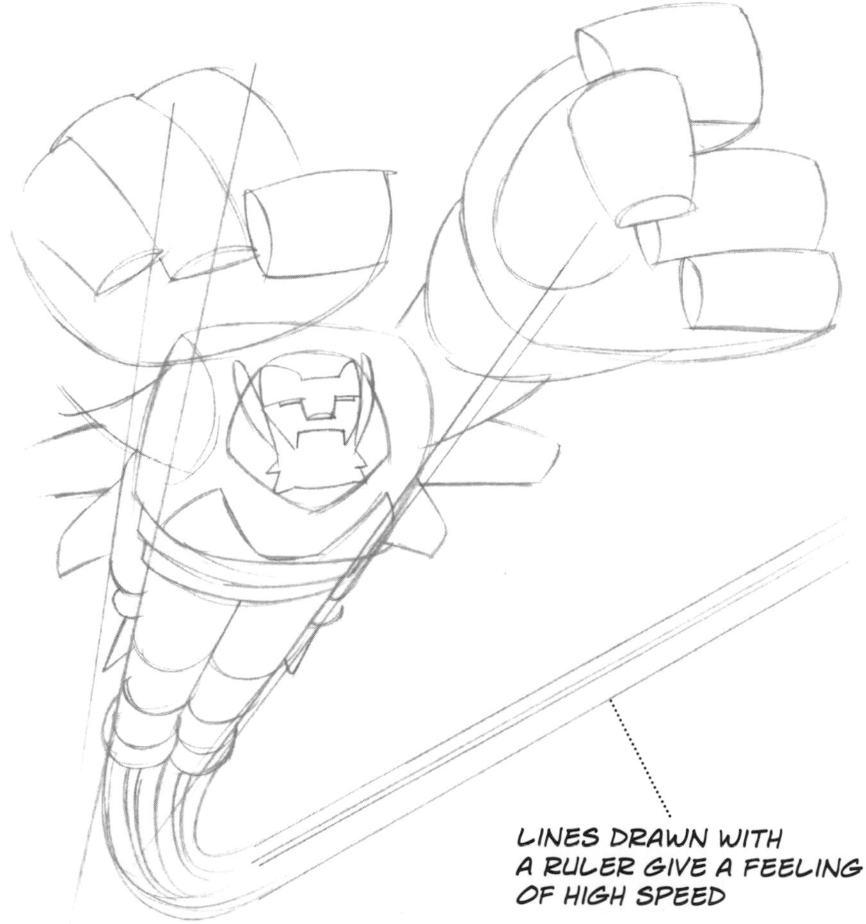
LINES DRAWN WITH A RULER GIVE A FEELING OF HIGH SPEED

STAGE 6

Draw a diagonal line to show where the wall meets the ground, then a hole in the wall around the speed lines.

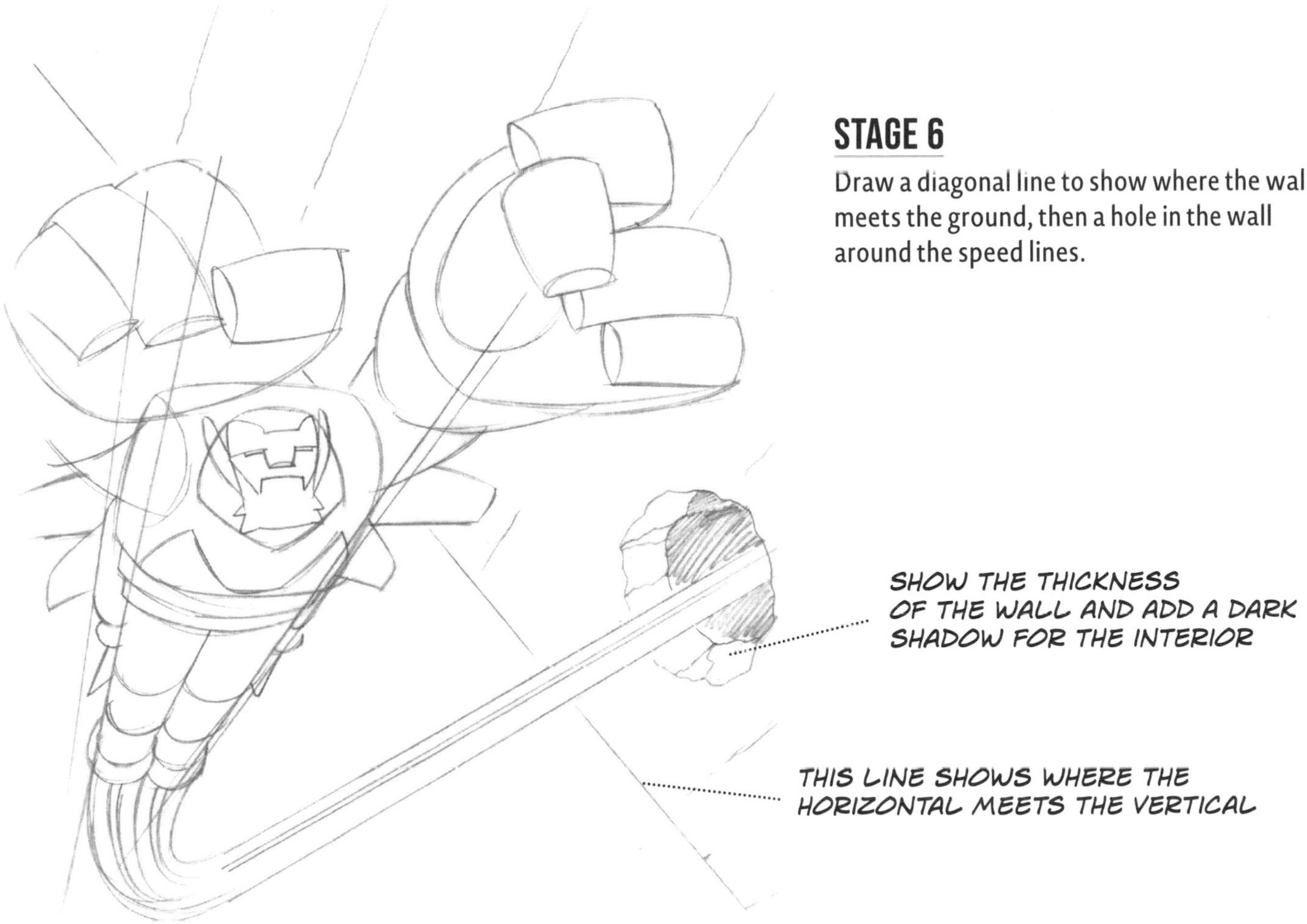
SHOW THE THICKNESS OF THE WALL AND ADD A DARK SHADOW FOR THE INTERIOR
THIS LINE SHOWS WHERE THE HORIZONTAL MEETS THE VERTICAL

STAGE 7

The mecha character is rescuing a girl from captivity – draw a wireframe for the top and bottom of her body, which is held in the figure's left hand.

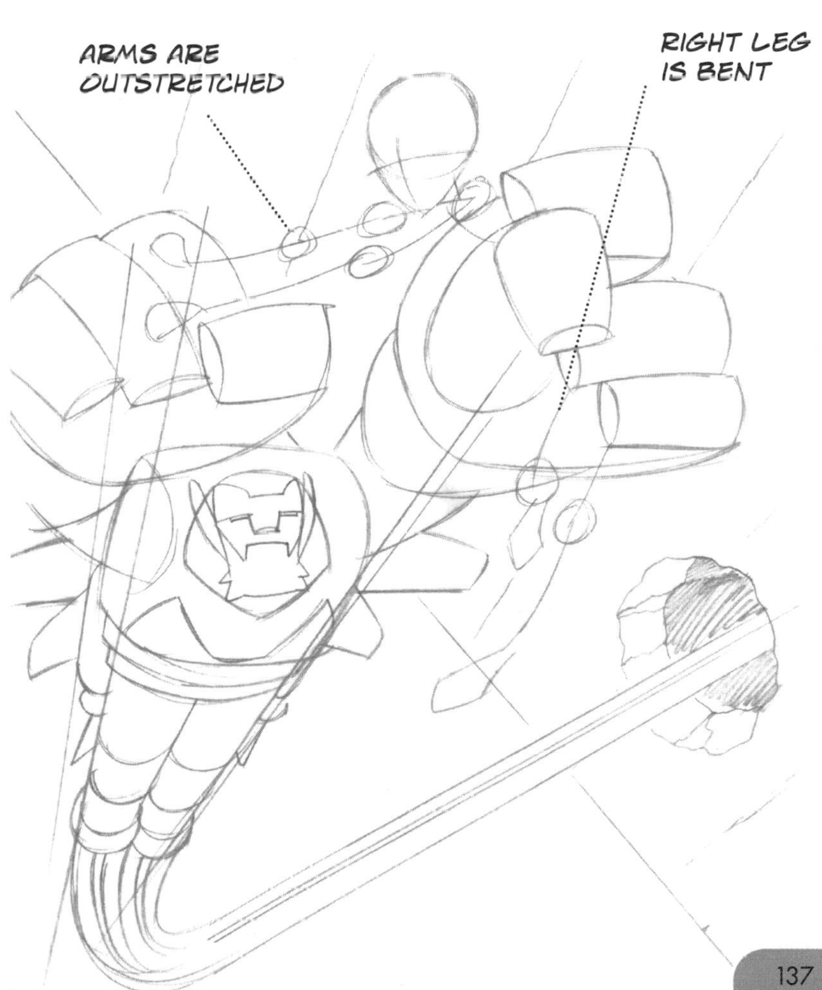
ARMS ARE OUTSTRETCHED
RIGHT LEG IS BENT

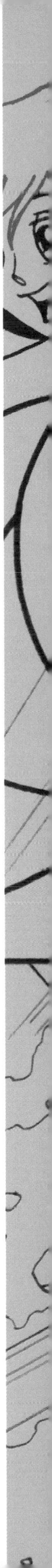

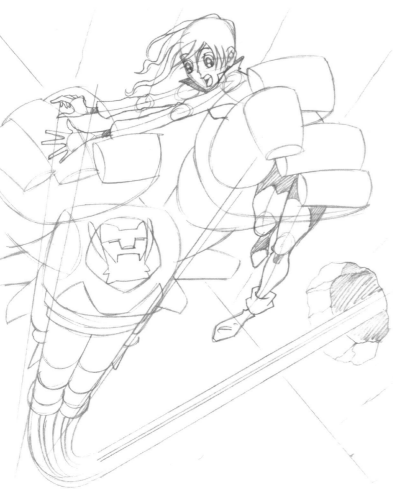

STAGE 8

Flesh out the girl with long, straggly hair, a jacket, leggings and ankle boots. Give her an excited facial expression and outstretched fingers.

STAGE 9

Add lots of rubble and broken rock bursting from the hole – the more the better!

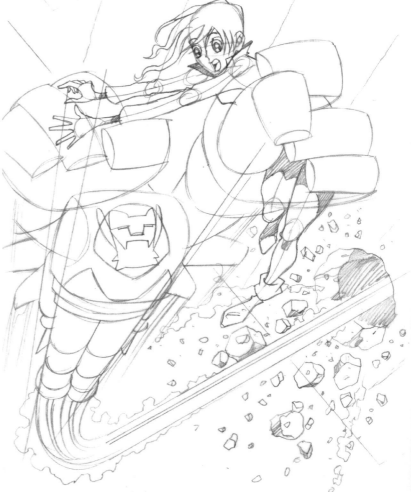

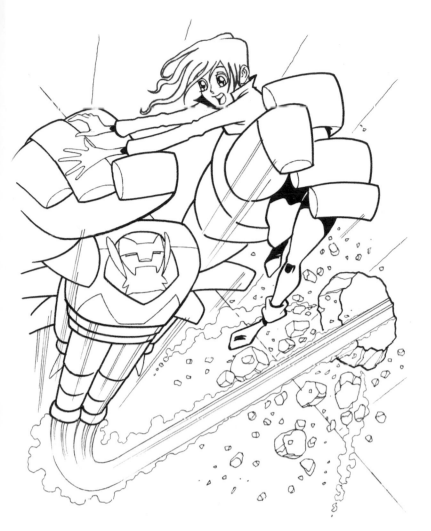

STAGE 10

Ink the whole drawing with black except the girl's hair, which should be outlined in red. Use a thick line on the mecha character and a fine line on the rubble and speed lines.

STAGE 11

Start colouring the wall with a warm beige, and build up several layers of colour. Fill in the hole with black and grey.

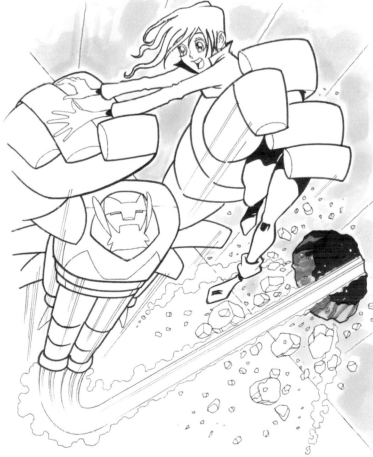

STAGE 12

Colour your mecha figure with bold primary colours and give it a dark grey face.

LEAVE AN AREA WHITE AS A HIGHLIGHT

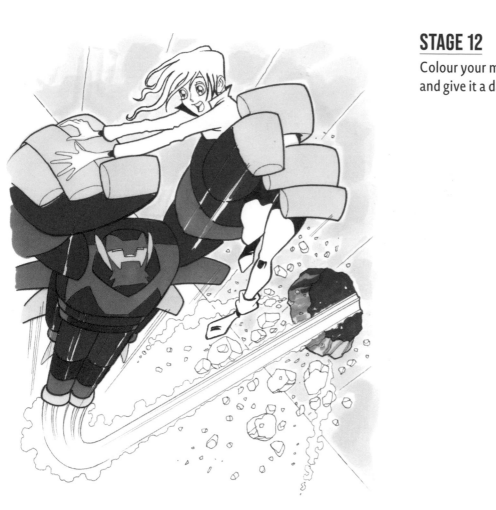

STAGE 13

Colour the girl's jacket and boots brown and her leggings grey. Colour in her hair bright pink and add flesh tone to her face and hands.

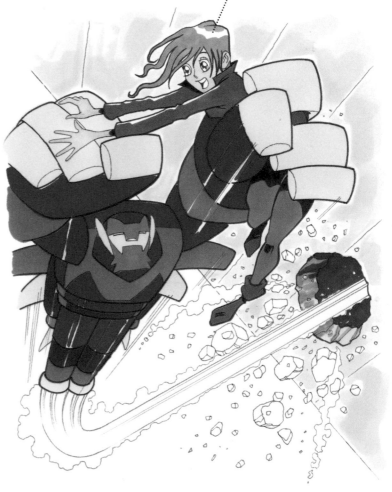

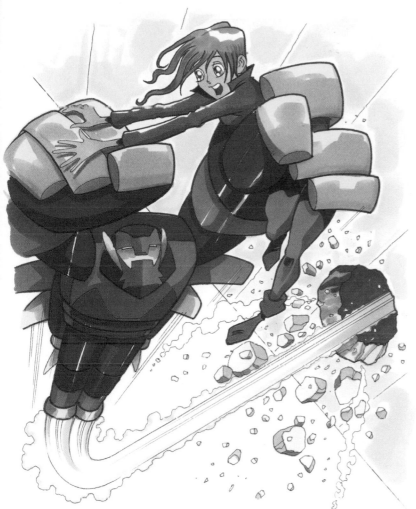

STAGE 14

Build up depth by adding darker tones and shading. Adding more than one layer of the same colour builds a rich warmth.

STAGE 15

Finish by applying even more layers of colour and use white paint to pick out speed lines. Add speed lines on top of the figure with coloured pencils.

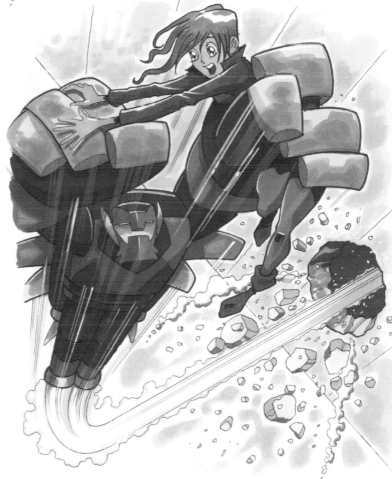

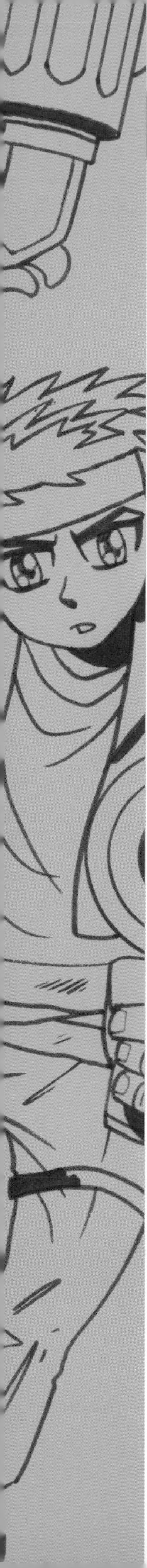

INCOMING!

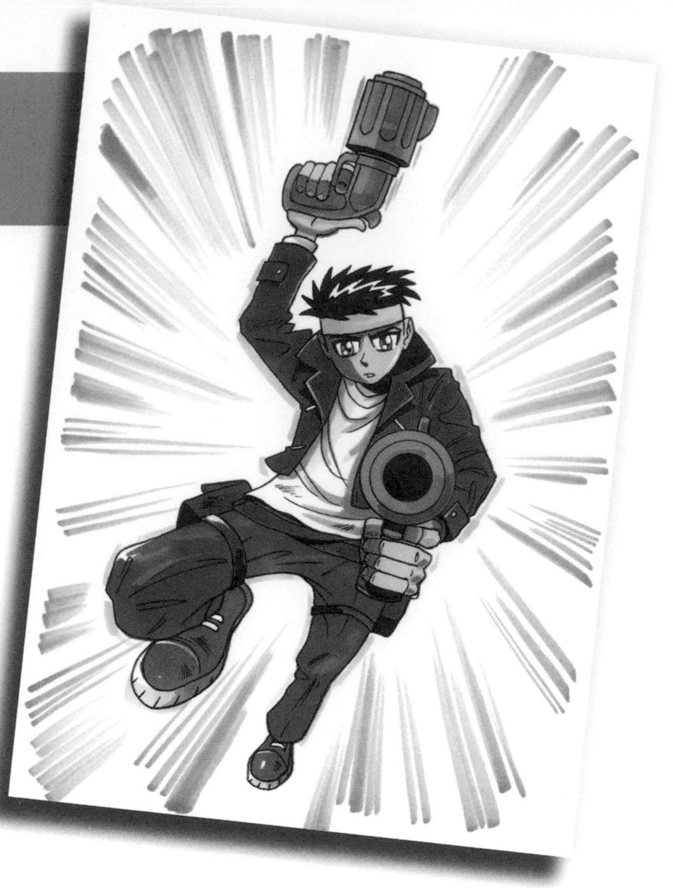

A TWO-GUN SALUTE COMING STRAIGHT AT YOU!

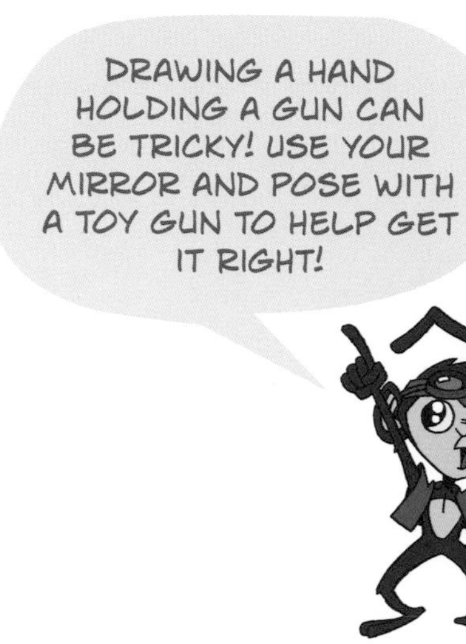
DRAWING A HAND HOLDING A GUN CAN BE TRICKY! USE YOUR MIRROR AND POSE WITH A TOY GUN TO HELP GET IT RIGHT!

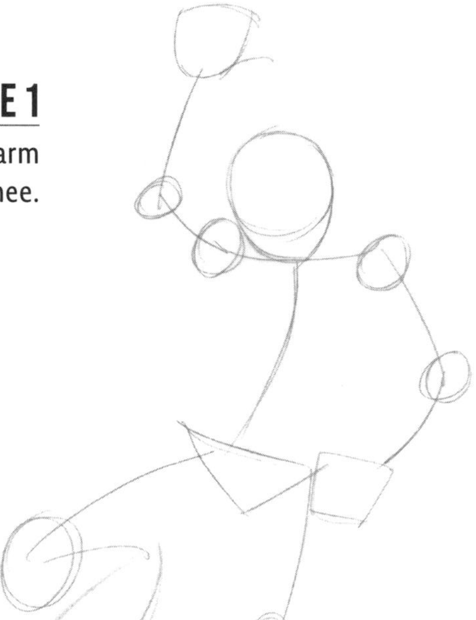

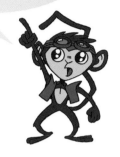

STAGE 1

Start with a leaping wireframe figure with right arm raised and right leg bent at the knee.

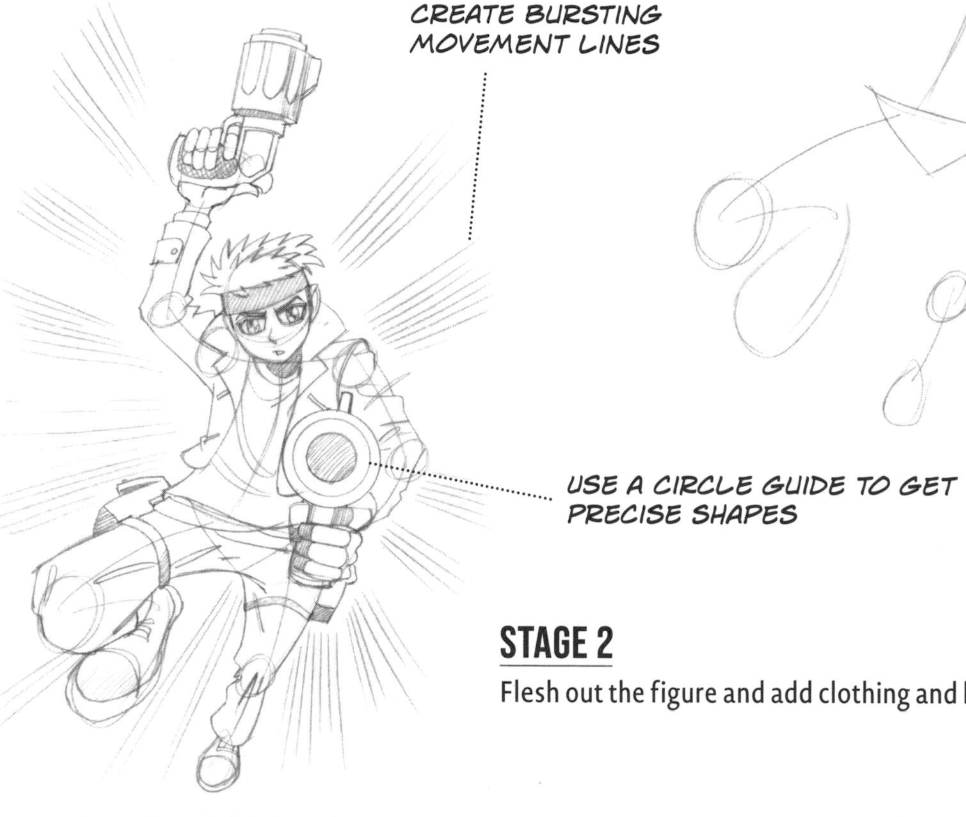
CREATE BURSTING MOVEMENT LINES
USE A CIRCLE GUIDE TO GET PRECISE SHAPES

STAGE 2

Flesh out the figure and add clothing and handguns.

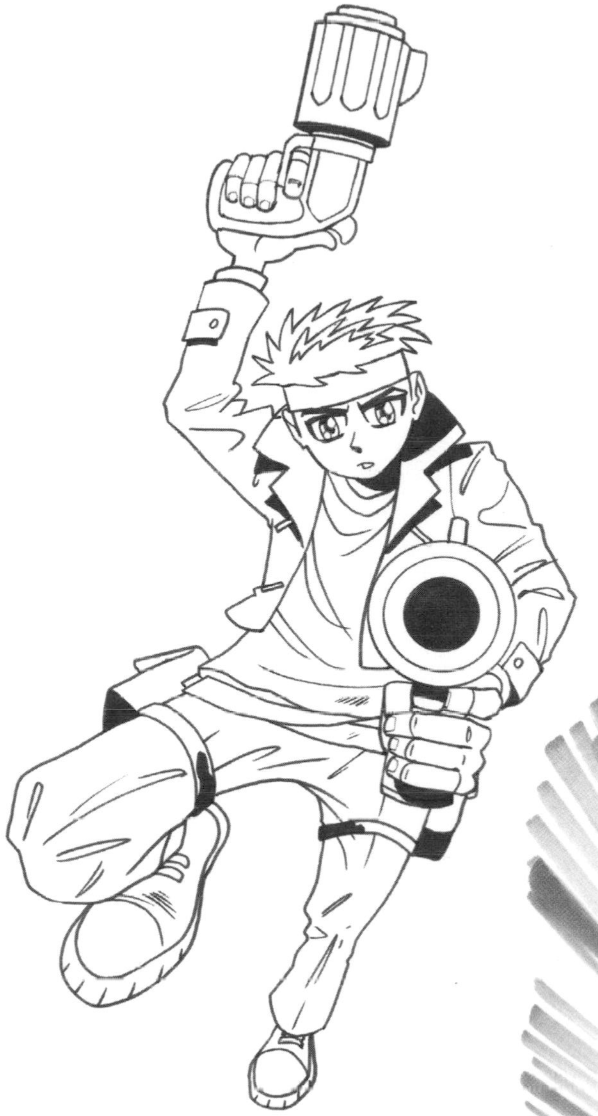

STAGE 3

Ink the drawing with black pen, filling in areas of shadow with solid black.

STAGE 4

Add colour and shading to the character – draw in a few lines outside the character's arms and legs using paler tones to give a sense of movement.

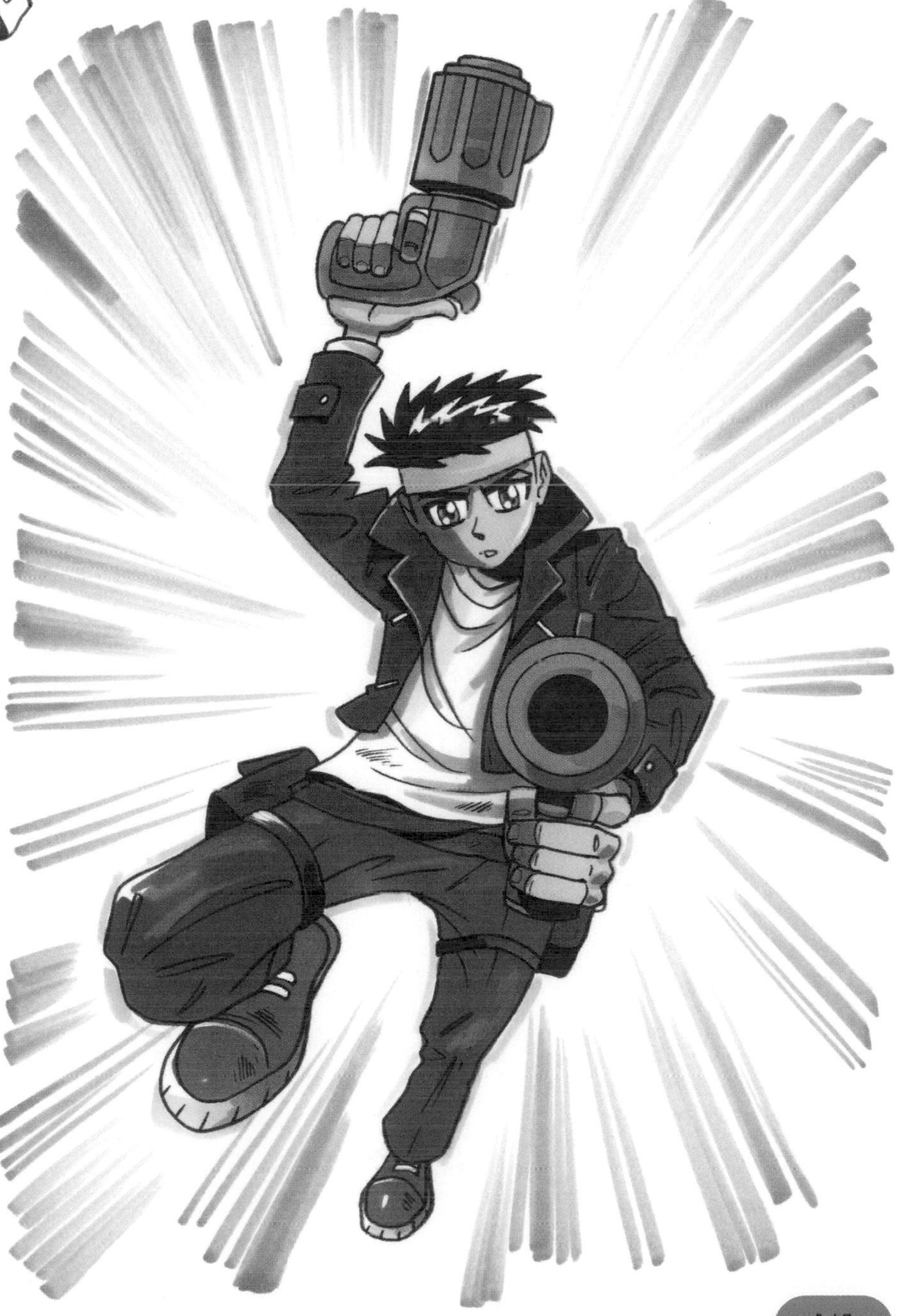

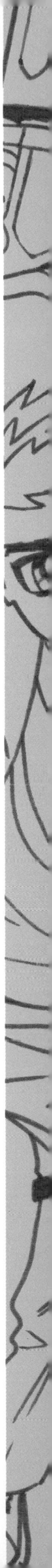

INDEX

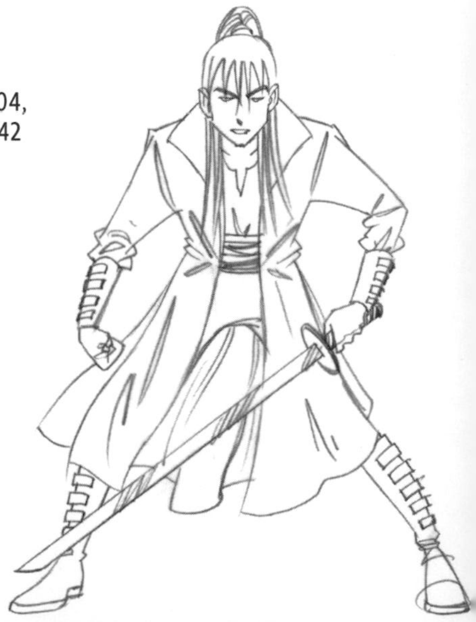